Accessibility for Everyone: Understanding the Section 508 Accessibility Requirements

JOHN MUELLER

Accessibility for Everyone: Understanding the Section 508 Accessibility
Requirements
Copyright © 2003 by John Mueller

Library of Congress Cataloging-in-Publication Data

Mueller, John, 1958-

Accessibility for everyone : understanding the Section 508 accessibility requirements / John Mueller.

p. cm.

ISBN 1-59059-086-4

1. Human-computer interaction. 2. Computers and people with disabilities. I. Title.

QA76.9.H85M82 2003

004'.087--dc21

2003005559

Printed and bound in the United States of America 12345678910

Trademarked names may appear in this book. Rather than use a trademark symbol with every occurrence of a trademarked name, we use the names only in an editorial fashion and to the benefit of the trademark owner, with no intention of infringement of the trademark.

Technical Reviewers: Mary Romero Sweeney, Eric Mashlan

Editorial Directors: Dan Appleman, Gary Cornell, Simon Hayes, Karen Watterson, John Zukowski

Managing Editor: Grace Wong

Project Manager: Tracy Brown Collins

Copy Editor: Rebecca Rider

Compositor: Susan Glinert

Artist and Cover Designer: Kurt Krames

Indexer: Nancy Guenther

Production Manager: Kari Brooks

Manufacturing Manager: Tom Debolski

Distributed to the book trade in the United States by Springer-Verlag New York, Inc., 175 Fifth Avenue, New York, NY, 10010 and outside the United States by Springer-Verlag GmbH & Co. KG, Tiergartenstr. 17, 69112 Heidelberg, Germany.

In the United States, phone 1-800-SPRINGER, email orders@springer-ny.com, or visit http://www.springer-ny.com.

Outside the United States, fax +49 6221 345229, email orders@springer.de, or visit http://www.springer.de.

For information on translations, please contact Apress directly at 2560 9th Street, Suite 219, Berkeley, CA 94710. Phone 510-549-5930, fax: 510-549-5939, email info@apress.com, or visit http://www.apress.com.

The source code for this book is available to readers at http://www.apress.com in the Downloads section.

This book is dedicated to Joyce Norton—only those who have experienced a special need can truly appreciate its impact.

Contents at a Glance

Contents

Chapter 6   Using Microsoft
Active Accessibility *183*

Chapter 7   Adding Usage Cues to
Desktop Applications *237*

Chapter 8   Developing Special Desktop
Application Capabilities *273*

Foreword

I KNOW THAT "foreword" is the title of this part of a book and that it should not be confused with "forward," but because they are so close in sound, when I see one, I can't help but be reminded of the other. "Forward" reflects a direction, a movement that is ahead, on the horizon, or at the brink of something new and wonderful. We talk of "forward thinkers" and hold them in esteem for their ability to see with clarity a path or direction that would move all the rest of us forward.

I believe that in this book, John Mueller presents himself as a forward thinker. He helps bridge a gap between law and technology to meet the real needs of real people. He presents information in this book that tries to go beyond the legal requirements and he challenges those in the technology field to see beyond the circuits, boards, screens, and everything else computer, into the human operators, the real people, on the other side.

I am an occupational therapist. I usually deal with the people aspect of my job, which involves assisting people to live as independently as possible with their special needs. My profession is about adapting to meet needs. I have worked with individuals with a variety of medical diagnoses including head injury, cerebral palsy, mental retardation, mental illness, arthritis, multiple sclerosis, and many other debilitating diseases. The individuals I meet have so much to offer, but because of circumstances related to their special needs, they are unable to fully express themselves as they would truly like. In many instances, judging them by their appearance alone, the world wonders why they would even want to try. But I am often awed by the resourcefulness and resilience of the human spirit. I have had to investigate and attempt to connect both these individuals and myself into the world of technology because they see the potential benefits such technology could bring to their lives.

Advocacy is the passion of one of my clients with cerebral palsy. The problem is that she can't use a computer because none of her body parts other than her eyes has adequate mobility. She has an augmentative communication device that we tried to hook up to her computer. After 15 plus hours of checking manuals, calling technical support, changing settings on the augmentative communication device and the computer, and hooking and unhooking cables in order to connect the two systems together when neither recognized the other, the two pieces were communicating. Unfortunately, the screen my client had to work with presented information too small for her to be able to read. When I increased the size of the picture, it distorted her document and she could not locate where she was on the page. Unfortunately, this is as far as we were able to get—her resources and mine had both run out. She has so much to say. It is important that she is heard. But until I learn more about the technology and until the technology becomes more applicable on her system, this is where we will remain—stuck.

I am just beginning to learn how much the field of technology could provide for my clients. Things like the following, for instance:

- A computer could help someone with a traumatic brain injury or mild mental retardation run an organizational program to sequence, organize, and complete routine tasks so that they could live on their own successfully.

- A computer and computer program linked to electrodes placed on several muscle group areas for a leg or an arm could stimulate more than one joint or muscle at a time, as occurs in normal movement. (Currently only one muscle group for one joint can be stimulated.) If more movement could be stimulated, the brain would have a better chance of speeding up the process of repairing a neural pathway and retuning that leg or arm to normal function.

- A software program or adaptation could be developed to allow an individual to create a document on an augmentative communication device. The device would then automatically type the document on the computer and then display it back on the augmentative device so that the person would be able to read and print the item for themselves.

Up to this point, my own experience of connecting technology to those with special needs has been frustrating. But I see so much potential for ways that such technology can be applied that I am willing to keep trying.

The people I work with are real people, who just happen to have special needs. When I tell them about this book, they respond with delight that someone is able and willing to communicate for them about just how ordinary they are. They do not see their special needs as a handicap; instead, as one of my clients put it, they see themselves as *handicapable*. Many have learned that their special need challenges them to learn other ways of doing things, and that often, there isn't just one way. Most of these special-needs people are looking for support, respect, interest, and care from others; they do not want to have things done for them—they want to be empowered to be the best that they can be on their own. I believe that the challenge of this book is to show developers that people with special needs can be and desire to be ordinary and that it should be the developer's goal to give them this chance. In other words, developers should start taking down the technological barriers, not because they are obligated to comply, but because they want to give those with special needs more opportunity. As one of my clients indicated, the only disability that really exists in the world is the state of being "normal." His thinking implies that being normal stunts forward thinking and causes those with this "disability" to lack the vision necessary to see possibilities and solutions beyond the one "accepted" method.

The current atmosphere for those with special needs in the social community at large is inclusion. This is a shift away from the institutions of old that encouraged individuals with special needs to be dependent. Inclusion fosters independence, self-responsibility, and self-advocacy. Technology offers the link. The advent and use of such improved technology, while it may not diminish a particular condition, can, in many ways, help support an individual in their access to and general use of the social community. Barriers are removed through the use of many devices such as augmentative communication devices that allow an individual to speak and state their needs, interests, passions, and problems. When the voices of all people can be heard and accepted, then the world community will be truly enriched.

New ideas can be difficult to embrace. As you read this book, I hope that the many insights John Mueller provides will encourage you to make a paradigm shift. Technology needs to include everyone. This book is a call to follow the spirit of the law by "seeing" those that might use such technology products as ordinary and "just like" the rest of us. This is bold—it involves seeing others as able and as consumers that are taking charge of their own lives.

John Mueller understands and can interpret technology, but he also has a genuine interest in and concern for others. He sees these others as able, ready, and willing to be responsible for their own lives. He is leading us forward.

Claudia Meyer, OTR
Occupational Therapist, registered

About the Author

John Mueller is a freelance author and technical editor. He has writing in his blood, having produced 58 books and over 200 articles to date. The topics range from networking to artificial intelligence, and from database management to heads-down programming. Some of his current books include a Web Matrix developer guide, a small business and home office networking guide, and several Windows XP user guides. His technical editing skills have helped over 31 authors refine the content of their manuscripts. John has

provided technical editing services to both *Data Based Advisor* and *Coast Compute* magazines. He's also contributed articles to magazines like *SQL Server Professional, Visual C++ Developer,* and *Visual Basic Developer.* He's currently the editor of the .NET electronic newsletter for Pinnacle Publishing. (Subscribe at http://www.freeenewsletters.com/.)

When John isn't working at the computer, you can find him in his workshop. He's an avid woodworker and candle maker. On any given afternoon, you can find him working at a lathe or putting the finishing touches on a bookcase. One of his newest craft projects is glycerin soap making, which comes in handy for gift baskets. You can reach John on the Internet at JMueller@mwt.net. John is also setting up a Web site at: http://www.mwt.net/~jmueller/. Feel free to look and make suggestions on how he can improve it. One of his current projects is creating book FAQ sheets that should help you find the book information you need much faster.

About the Technical Reviewers

David Clark has been a web developer and involved in technical accessibility for over ten years. While working at CAST (1994–2000) he was a member of the original team that designed, developed, and supported Bobby. He has also been a participant in W3C's Web Accessibility Initiative and has also served as chairman of Microsoft's Accessibility Advisory Council. Currently Clark is a consultant to corporations and nonprofits on accessibility and Web development, focusing on open-source technologies because of cost and customizability.

As a power wheelchair user with severe cerebral palsy, Clark is a fervent advocate of universal design. He knows firsthand its power and the benefits that accessibility modifications can have for all users. Clark graduated from University of California, Berkeley with a degree in Cognitive Science and Rhetoric. He now lives in Boston, Massachusetts and can be contacted at david@davidsaccess.com.

Russ Mullen has been involved in the computer field since the early days of MS-DOS. He has technically edited or coauthored more than 40 titles. He has been a Web developer for a large international company and the IT manager for an insurance adjusting company. Russ has a consulting/application development firm that does Web site design and application development (see http://www.whoyouare.com for more information). He enjoys getting up very early in the morning and coding with coffee in hand long before the sun

rises, and then retiring early to prepare for the next day's activities. You can reach Russ by e-mail rmullen@bellsouth.net.

Acknowledgments

THANKS TO MY WIFE, Rebecca, for working with me to get this book completed. This was an exceptionally difficult and emotion-filled book for both of us. I don't know what I would have done without her help in researching and compiling the information that appears in this book (especially the Glossary). She also did a fine job of proofreading my rough draft and page proofing the final result.

David Clark deserves thanks for his technical edit of this book. He greatly added to the accuracy and depth of the material you see here. Besides checking some of the source code in the book, David also supplied some of the URLs as well as other helpful tips and hints. It would be difficult to estimate the amount of help David provided.

Russ Mullen checked the source code in this book for accuracy. I greatly appreciate his unwavering support of my books over the years. Russ also supplied some of the URLs you'll find in this book.

This is a special book and I wanted to obtain the help and support of specialists in creating it. Claudia Meyer provided a wealth of comments that helped shape the content of this book—especially on my use of terminology. Some of the real world examples you see in the book come from her personal experiences. Chris Goodale provided me with insights on how to better organize and present some of the material. This book wouldn't contain checklists and other organizational aids if it weren't for his input.

Every book begins with a vision. I've wanted to produce this book for more years than I can remember. Karen Watterson saw the same vision I did, and I feel a special debt to her in helping me bring this book to print.

A number of other people also contributed to the book. They requested that I not use their names for personal, professional, and ethical reasons. I still want to thank them for their efforts because they helped shaped this book. A lawyer contributed his time to interpret some of the legal requirements in the various chapters. A physical therapist contributed her time to check my use of terminology. She also provided several of the real world experiences found in the book. Several people with special needs tested my code, ideas, and concepts to ensure that they actually work.

You'll find a large list of specialized equipment and software in this book. The vendors who produce this assistive technology have been especially helpful in providing me with evaluation products. The book contains mentions of every vendor that helped and that list would be too long to present here. All of these vendors deserve thanks for their efforts in helping me understand some of the hurdles that people with special needs must overcome.

Finally, I would like to thank Tracy Brown Collins, Rebecca Rider, Kari Brooks, and the rest of the editorial and production staff at Apress for their assistance in bringing this book to print. It's always nice to work with such a great group of professionals.

Introduction

ACCESSIBILITY—some people associate this term with physical accommodations such as parking places and ramps. Many developers are surprised to find that they need to make their applications accessible as well. A few developers are determined not to make their applications accessible until they learn about the U.S. government's Section 508 laws. However, these legal requirements shouldn't be the only reason you make your applications accessible. This book will show you how accessible applications help everyone and can even improve your development efforts.

The *Accessibility for Everybody: Understanding the Section 508 Accessibility Requirements* book helps you understand the legal requirements at the outset so that you can plan your new application or application upgrade. Together we'll discuss the requirements for both desktop and Web applications—a feature not found in any other book available today. However, once you get past the legal requirements, you'll learn how easy it is to comply with them and to get something of value for your users, the developers you work with, your company, and even yourself.

Accessibility is the art of making applications easy-to-use. As you read the book, you'll find that ease-of-use has many benefits that some developers don't consider. We'll also discuss usability and performance throughout the book. You may be surprised at how much you can improve the user experience and reduce your workload by employing a little careful planning.

One of the most important features of *Accessibility for Everybody: Understanding the Section 508 Accessibility Requirements* is that it acts as a resource guide. Just about every page will tell you about another way to obtain help, learn new facts, download free tools, or ease your development efforts. In fact, you'll find that a large part of making an application accessible is learning about the proper resources and then using those resources as part of your application. In short, accessibility really is for everyone.

What's in This Book

What will you get from this book? The following descriptions tell you how *Accessibility for Everybody: Understanding the Section 508 Accessibility Requirements* will help you create accessible applications quickly and in a way that enhances the application experience for everyone. More importantly, you'll learn a few tantalizing details about the U.S. government's Section 508 requirements that you might not have known about in the past.

Chapter 1: What Is Section 508 Accessibility?

Many developers haven't ever heard of Section 508 and don't know what it means. This chapter begins by introducing you to accessibility in general, and then to the Section 508 requirements in specific. You'll learn why making your application accessible is so important to everyone, including yourself.

The second part of this chapter is an overview of the law. Sometimes it's very hard for someone to understand what the government requires of them. The government writes laws in a form of legalese that gives lawyers gray hairs and often defies any attempt by the average person to decipher. This first chapter will help you understand what the law requires and why these laws are in place. More importantly, we'll begin to build a picture of what you need to do to bring your applications in compliance with the law.

Chapter 2: Understanding the Section 508 Requirements

Chapter 2 begins to break the law down into manageable pieces. This is the first chapter that makes a distinction between accessibility, performance, and usability. You'll learn about the law from the user perspective by delving into the needs that many users have. We'll also discuss some developer issues. For example, many developers are concerned that accessible equates to ugly, and that simply isn't true. You'll learn that accessible applications have every bit as much appeal as non-accessible applications. However, the big plus for developers is that application users will actually enjoy your work.

Chapter 3: Hardware, Resources, and Training

Chapter 3 looks at developer needs. You'll begin by looking at some hardware issues you need to know about in order to develop accessible applications. Generally, you'll find that writing accessible applications means not writing any special hardware-related code. The accessible devices work fine as equivalents of the generic devices you've also used. We'll also discuss some developer-specific needs, such as specialized coding tools, and learn about places that you can obtain training. Finally, the chapter shows you how to detect any Human Interface Devices (HIDs) installed on the user machine, and you'll learn why this type of detection is important.

Chapter 4: Developer Guidelines That Make Sense

Chapter 4 provides guidelines on how to create accessible applications in general. You learn what types of development you'll need to perform. This chapter helps you understand the requirements for accessible development in general. The final section of the chapter provides you with the first tool in the book—a color blindness simulator. Using this tool enables you to determine if the user can actually see the displays that you create. That's right, in some cases you might choose colors that make it impossible for someone to see the display; this application helps you avoid that problem.

Chapter 5: Desktop Application Essentials

Chapter 5 is our first entry into the realm of accessible desktop application development. In this chapter, you'll learn how to automate testing for accessibility requirements. In addition, you'll learn when applications require manual testing to ensure that they work as anticipated for the user with special needs. You'll also learn about a problem that most developers have never considered—the effect of the file format they choose for an application on accessibility. The examples in this chapter help you understand the user interface better. We'll discuss issues such as obtaining the current screen settings so that you can modify your application's setup to match the display. You'll also learn techniques for working with color and fonts in desktop applications.

Chapter 6: Using Microsoft Active Accessibility

Microsoft Windows actually provides a lot in the way of accessibility features. The problem is that these features are the best-kept secret of Windows. Many developers don't even know these features exist because no one ever discusses them in trade press articles or magazines. This chapter will not only show you how to use the Windows Accessibility features to test the performance of your applications, but it will show you how to turn these features on and off as needed within an application. You'll also learn how to create applications that show sound descriptions for users who have special hearing needs and how to work with the Windows Accessibility features in other ways.

Chapter 7: Adding Usage Cues to Desktop Applications

Chapter 7 is about the subtle art of adding cues to your application. When two people communicate, they normally pass as much information back and forth using cues as they do using spoken language. For example, body language can tell someone a lot about how you feel a conversation is going. Likewise, applications require cues to communicate well with the user. The examples in this chapter will help you understand the subtle and often forgotten art of adding application usage cues.

Chapter 8: Developing Special Desktop Application Capabilities

Many developers have heard about the special functionality that vendors have scheduled to arrive any day now for applications. Speech input is one of the major special application capabilities, but easy-to-use animation and other forms of special functionality are also high on developer's lists. This chapter shows you how to obtain many of these special capabilities today, and it makes you aware of the limitations of using them. You'll also learn some new ways to use existing application features. It's amazing to learn that you can use existing features to perform tasks that users have requested without adding a single line of code to your application. Sometimes, the way you look at an existing feature is more important than adding a new feature.

Chapter 9: Web Site Essentials

Chapter 9 is the first Web application–specific chapter. One of the first issues we'll discuss is how you can ensure that your Web application is accessible. You'll find that Web applications are simultaneously easier to make accessible and harder to check for accessibility. Fortunately, a number of tools on the market make your job a lot easier.

This chapter also delves into the theory of making a Web site accessible. We'll discuss common Web site design problems and you'll learn how to avoid them. You'll also begin learning about tags that can ease the accessibility development burden and make your Web site more fun to use as a bonus. Finally, this chapter includes a number of examples designed to demonstrate good Web site development principles.

Chapter 10: Designing Easily Maintained Web Sites

Chapter 10 will help you learn about the easiest way to create a Web site that is so flexible that it works with everything. That's right, the example in this chapter works equally well with a desktop machine, a Personal Digital Assistant (PDA), and a cellular telephone. Using the information in this chapter will help you understand that accessible Web sites have no functional limitations—you can make them work well with any device and that will make them accessible. This is the chapter to read if you want to present information on your Web site in a form that the maximum number of people can see and still preserve the accessibility required to make the information available to everyone.

Chapter 11: Adding Usage Cues to Web Applications

Chapter 11 contains a wealth of tips and techniques for adding usage cues to your Web application. Often, the user has to determine how to interact with a Web application based exclusively on these cues because they don't have a user's manual to use. Including the right usage cues can reduce user input time and the number of errors that your Web site code must overcome.

Adding usage cues to your Web application also means modifying the content in some cases. For example, if you include animation on your Web site, the animation must include captioning so that everyone can enjoy the content. This chapter discusses how this requirement affects all of the major media sources including QuickTime, RealAudio, Macromedia Flash, and Media Access Generator (MAGpie).

Chapter 12: Developing Special Web Application Capabilities

Chapter 12 helps you develop special capabilities, such as voice input and output, for your Web applications. You'll learn about the pitfalls of using speech and other special features on a Web site. This chapter also contains a number of examples showing how to use this functionality.

Chapter 13: Accessible Scripting Solutions

Chapter 13 discusses scripting, an issue that causes problems for many users. In many cases, the user's browser doesn't support scripting, so the Web page becomes unusable. In other cases, the script works, but it doesn't work in a way that the user can understand. Using scripts can improve the accessibility of a Web site; but, all too often, they simply make the Web site unusable. This chapter shows how to create accessible scripts that actually help the user have a better online experience.

Appendix A: 52 Tips for Creating Accessible Applications

This appendix shows you 52 unique ways to make your accessible application development experience better. Each tip is an essential nugget of information that you can use to change the way you view accessibility and learn more about what it can do for you. There's one tip for each week of the year so that you can enhance your accessible application development experience over time.

Appendix B: Six Best Web Sites for Accessibility Ideas

Sometimes the best way to learn about a new programming technique is to see an example. This appendix contains examples of some of the best Web sites out there from an accessibility perspective. The most important idea you can get from this appendix is that accessible Web sites vary greatly and that each one has some unique idea or feature that you can use on your own Web site.

Appendix C: Helpful Organizations and Agencies

Accessibility can become a complex topic because you're learning to work with users who have special needs as well as learning new programming techniques. Human issues are something that many developers have a hard time understanding and learning to work with. Developing truly accessible applications means learning to work with users who have many special requirements. This appendix provides you with a list of organizations and agencies that can help make the accessible application experience easier.

Who Is the Audience for This Book?

The main audience for this book is developers who need to create accessible applications of any type. The book discusses accessible applications in general, on the Windows desktop, and on the Web. In short, this book contains an application development environment for just about any developer who needs to write accessible applications, with an emphasis on the U.S. government's Section 508 requirements.

A second audience for this book is anyone who needs to learn about accessible application resources. This second group could include a wide range of people—including a number of non-developers. For example, two of the people who read this book while I was writing it (a Registered Occupational Therapist and a Physical Therapist) lack any programming skills. Even so, both said they were able to garner a lot of accessibility information that they didn't know previously simply by reading this book.

Finally, this book is about understanding the legal requirements for Section 508 compliance. It's my hope that you get a lot more out of the book than a simple understanding of these requirements, but the book does serve the need to help you learn about the law too. Understanding what you need to do in order to fulfill not only the letter but the spirit of the law is important. Consequently, this book provides an interpretation of the law in an easy-to-understand format.

What You Need

If you're reading this book simply to learn what the Section 508 law requires, you don't need anything more than a place to read. The examples in this book demonstrate accessibility principles, but you don't necessarily have to run the examples to understand what point the code is trying to make. I wrote this book with the idea that anyone could read it anywhere and still get something from it.

If you do decide to work with the coding examples (and I sincerely hope that you do), all you need is a machine running a version of Windows with the .NET Framework installed for the desktop applications. Modifying the desktop examples will require a copy of Visual Studio .NET. However, the source code folders all contain a compiled version of the code, so you can skip this requirement if necessary.

Most of the Web applications will run fine so long as you have a Web server and a browser installed. Some of the examples require that you use Internet Information Server (IIS), but I've tried to avoid this requirement wherever possible. The source code files are all standard HTML. In fact, you'll learn about some free tools that you can use to work with the examples in this book starting in Chapter 10.

Equipment Used

This section tells you about the equipment that I used to create the examples. As discussed in the "What You Need" section, you don't have to have any of this equipment to use the book. However, if you want to test and modify the examples, you'll need a machine capable of doing it. Consequently, the purpose of this section is to tell you what I used during development so that you know what you will likely need to modify the code.

I tested all of the desktop applications using a single machine. If you want to work only with the desktop examples, all you need is a machine that has the same features as the machine in the "Workstation Setup" section (or better).

Testing a Web application on a single machine doesn't really tell you very much, so I used a two-machine setup in this case. Using a single machine setup does work for testing theories or for learning. However, you should consider the fact that such applications are temporary and never leave them laying around for others to use. I've actually had vendor examples fail when I attempted to try them on a two-machine setup because the vendor never anticipated that anyone would test the application in this way. The problem is that many developers rely on the vendor applications to test their setup—it's supposedly a "known good" application designed to demonstrate the vendor's wares. In short, if you want to get the most out of the Web examples in this book, you should use a two-machine setup consisting of the machines in the "Workstation Setup" and "Server Setup" section.

Workstation Setup

The development workstation is where you'll install Windows 2000 or Windows XP, write your code, and perform any desktop-level testing. I tested the desktop applications using two workstations, one with Windows 2000 installed and a second with Windows XP installed. The version of Windows you install depends on personal taste and the number of machines you plan to use.

For a development workstation that you're going to use exclusively for development and not for testing purposes, make sure you get a reasonably fast processor, a lot of RAM, and even more hard drive space. My low-end test workstation includes 512 MB of RAM, dual 450 MHz Pentium II processors, and a 9 GB hard drive. This setup worked very well for my needs in creating code for this book—you'll obviously need to increase your hard drive space as you add more features and create applications that are more complex. Most developers will want a faster processor as well, but this addition isn't a requirement.

My development workstation also includes a full installation of Visual Studio .NET 2003 Enterprise Architect Edition, some business applications (such as Microsoft Office), and a few graphics products (such as Paint Shop Pro). You won't need all of these other additions on your system, but you do need a browser of some type. I tested all of the applications using Internet Explorer 6.0. If you use a different browser, you might notice some differences between my screenshots and what you see on your display.

TIP You may not think about the font you use to work on your machine very often, but working with monospaced fonts all day can lead to eye strain, bugs (like when you confuse an l and a 1), and other problems. Microsoft's choice of Courier for a monospaced font hasn't been well received by many developers because it doesn't do the job very well. Fortunately, there are alternatives, some of which are free. Paul Neubauer's Web site at: `http://home.bsu.edu/prn/monofont/` talks about how monospaced fonts are used on a typical Windows system and what replacement fonts are available should you decide you really don't like Courier. This Web site even includes reviews of the various fonts so that you can make a good choice the first time around.

Server Setup

As previously mentioned, I used a minimal setup for testing my applications because I didn't know what hardware you'd have in advance. You should have a Windows 2000 Server (or you can use a .NET Server when it becomes available) setup to work with the Web examples in this book. (At a minimum, you must have a machine that has a Web server installed.) I wrote all of the examples using the standard server product on a dual processor 450 MHz Pentium processor machine with 512 MB of RAM. However, you could probably get by with a single 450 MHz processor machine with 256 MB of RAM installed. I'd recommend a minimum of 9 GB of hard drive space, although more is certainly better considering how much space you'll use for the various programming language additions.

You don't actually need much more than access to a Web server. However, it's often helpful to have access to other server functionality. The following list summarizes the components that I installed while writing this book:

- Internet Information Server (Complete)

- Microsoft .NET Framework

- Management and Monitoring Tools (All)

- Networking Services (All)

- SQL Server (Version 7.0 or better)

- Microsoft Front Page Server Extensions

- Microsoft Posting Acceptor 2.0

NOTE   The name of my server is WinServer. Yes, I know it's not a very imaginative name, but it's easy to find in the code and short enough to see well on screen. Throughout the book, you'll see references to my server in the code. You must change these references to the name you've given your server in order to make the test applications run correctly. I'll provide additional information as needed as part of the coding example explanations.

My test server also has a complete copy of Visual Studio .NET Enterprise Architect Edition installed. I installed this product as part of my normal test server setup, but you don't need it to use this book.

Conventions Used in This Book

It always helps to know what the special text means in a book. In this section, we'll cover usage conventions. This book uses the following conventions:

Convention	Description
Inline Code	Some code will appear in the text of the book to help explain application functionality. The code appears in a special font that makes it easy to see. This monospaced font also makes the code easier to read.
User Input	Sometimes you'll need to type input precisely to obtain a certain effect. The user input for this book uses a special font so that it stands out and you know that you need to type the text precisely as shown.
[Filename]	When you see square brackets around a value, switch, or command, it means that this is an optional component. You don't have to include it as part of the command line or dialog field unless you want the additional functionality that the value, switch, or command provides.

Convention	Description
<Filename>	A variable name is a value that you need to replace with something else. For example, you might need to provide the name of your server as part of a command line argument. Because I don't know the name of your server, I'll provide a variable name instead. The variable name you'll see usually provides a clue as to what kind of information you need to supply. In this case, you'll need to provide a filename.
File ➤ Open	Menus and the selections on them appear with a right-facing arrow symbol. "File ~TRA Open" means "Access the File menu and choose Open."
URLs	URLs will normally appear in a different font so that you can see them with greater ease. The URLs in this book provide sources of additional information designed to make your development experience better. URLs often provide sources of interesting information as well.

Icons

This book contains many icons that help you identify certain types of information. The following paragraphs describe the purpose of each icon.

NOTE   Notes tell you about interesting facts that don't necessarily affect your ability to use the other information in the book. I use notes to give you bits of information that I've picked up while using Web Matrix, ASP.NET, C#, Visual Basic .NET, Windows 9*x*, Windows 2000, or Windows XP.

TIP   Everyone likes tips because they tell you new ways of doing things that you might not have thought about before. Tips also provide an alternative way of doing something that you might like better than the first approach I provided. In most cases, you'll find newsgroup and Web site URLs in tips as well. These URLs are especially important because they usually lead to products or information that helps you perform tasks faster.

 CAUTION   The Caution icon means watch out! Cautions almost always tell you about some kind of system or data damage that'll occur if you perform a certain action (or fail to perform others). Make sure you understand a caution thoroughly before you follow any instructions that come after it.

 ON THE WEB   The Internet has a vast store of information. The only problem is finding the information that you need, when you need it. Although this book can't provide leads to every potential source of information on the Internet, it does provide a wealth of links that you can use to learn more information than a single book could ever contain. This book uses URLs to various resources as an extension of the unique content the book provides.

Part One

An Overview of
Section 508 Accessibility

CHAPTER 1

What Is Section 508 Accessibility?

In This Chapter:

How Does Section 508 Address Accessibility Concerns?

How Do Accessibility Concerns Affect Everyone?

What Is a Special Need?

Why Should You Develop with Universal Access in Mind?

Will You Need to Implement All of the Section 508 Requirements?

How Should You Interpret the Section 508 Standards?

Where Can You Find the 508 Standard Information?

What Does the Phrase "Undue Burden" Mean?

How Do You Find Section 508 Specific in This Book?

WELCOME TO THE first chapter on Section 508 accessibility for application developers—the best move your company could ever make! Some of you might be taking that statement with a grain of salt; others might be laughing right now. The fact is many developers don't appreciate the true benefits of making an application accessible. By the time this chapter ends, you'll either decide that I've been in the sun too long or you'll feel as I do—that accessible applications are a huge benefit to everyone concerned. Your perspective at the end of this chapter will determine whether the changes we discuss throughout the rest of the book are something forced upon you by the legal system or something you want to do because it's beneficial.

As you can tell from the preceding list, this first chapter introduces you to the Section 508 requirements, tells you which of those requirements this book discusses, and discusses why you should implement those requirements. Of course, the big reason that many people will implement these accessibility requirements (at least at the beginning) is that anyone working with the government must do so by law—we'll also discuss this aspect of implementation. However, you need to know which of the requirements to implement because Section 508 is relatively large and developers aren't responsible for implementing every element.

This chapter will also begin deciphering the legalese the U.S. government uses to write Section 508. We'll begin with an actual quote from the law (in the heading of each section) and an interpretation of that law. When you complete the legal interpretation portion of the chapter, you'll know about all of the developer-oriented portions of the Section 508 requirements, which also include issues such as physical access to kiosks. Sometimes half the burden of implementing a requirement is figuring out what the requirement is. This portion of the chapter will begin taking the guesswork out of the process for you. With this in mind, let's begin to look at the Section 508 requirements.

What Is Section 508?

The first piece of information that most developers want to know is, "What is Section 508?" Most people haven't even heard of this law and those that have don't know what it entails.

In essence, Section 508 is a law that the U.S. Congress enacted in 1998 as an amendment to the Rehabilitation Act. The purpose of this amendment is to ensure that all Americans have access to information technology. The law applies specifically to all U.S. government agencies, but it also affects anyone who works with the U.S. government. The law details requirements to make information technology of all types accessible.

 ON THE WEB   Don't get the idea that accessible application development is something that is exclusive to the U.S. government or is only used within the United States. Many other countries are also getting into the act. For example, you'll find a wealth of accessibility information at the Ability Web site (http://www.ability.org.uk/design.html) located in the United Kingdom.

Developers will have an interest in the application development issues associated with Section 508. We'll discuss those topics in detail throughout the book. As part of the application development information, you'll also learn about documentation and support issues because documentation and support work hand-in-hand with accessible application development. Application developers should also know about hardware requirements so that their applications can meet those needs. These topics also appear in the book but with less frequency than software issues. Finally, Section 508 includes requirements for physical access to information technology devices, such as including instructions in Braille for a kiosk. We'll discuss those issues in this chapter, but only to the extent that they might affect application development or your interaction with other vendors. For example, as part of developing an application, you might need to consider how someone accesses a teletypewriter (TTY) device. Although the developer doesn't have to implement the functionality required by the law, the developer may have to interact with the vendor who does implement the TTY functionality.

What Is Accessibility for Everyone?

Many developers are under the misconception that accessibility refers to code that they add to an application in order to make it usable by people with special needs. While this is certainly one definition of accessibility, it's also the least productive and narrow-minded interpretation. Unfortunately, it's the most prevalent view of accessibility used by government and industry today because it's the viewpoint that enjoys legal status.

Accessibility is for everyone—not just those with special needs. A business that pursues accessibility as a cost center (something they must pay that won't return a profit) for a few individuals (those with special needs) as mandated by the government is certainly on the losing end of the proposition. Such an implementation will cost your company money because few people will use it. On the other hand, a business that pursues accessibility as a way to attract and keep new clients is certainly going to see a profit from their efforts. In addition, the employees of such a company benefit from better health, which in turn pays dividends in reduced sick time for the company. An application, whether desktop or Web-based, that's accessible is easier to use than one that lacks accessibility features.

The whole concept of accessibility is an important one that the developer needs to make part of the design process. The earlier the developer considers accessibility requirements in the development process, the less effort the developer will need to expend to implement accessible programming requirements. Unfortunately, most developers ignore the accessibility requirements until the last second and only pay attention to them as part of a legal requirement. Yet they should be aware that something as simple as making an application or Web site screen reader accessible can net large gains for anyone who chooses to use a screen reader. Some developers would say that this statement proves their point because only those with vision deficiencies would rely on a screen reader.

However, this is not always the case. For instance, although I have good vision, I use a text reader on any Web site with a lot of content (if the Web site will allow such use). The reason is simple. Using a text reader helps me concentrate on the content offered by the Web site. I get more out of the information I hear because I'm not constantly distracted by other Web site features, ads, or other embellishments. In addition, if the content is easy enough to understand, I can perform other tasks while my computer reads to me. Many people choose to multitask today in order to get their work completed and using a text reader allows them to do this. To employ this technique, the user listens to the Web site content while performing some other task.

NOTE   When working with on-screen text, it's important to know that there are two classes of applications. Text reading software is designed to read long pieces of on-screen text. This type of application helps someone understand the content without needing to visualize how that content is arranged, or it helps the person work with that content. A screen reader is designed to work with shorter pieces of text. It helps the user understand the layout and organization of the text in order to perform tasks such as word processing or application development. The two types of applications read text, but they have different purposes. Someone with special visual needs may have both application types on their system.

Including <ALT> tags and bubble help in an application may seem like something that no one would use—especially with graphics—because the developer assumes that the user can see the image on screen. But some applications and Web sites present many images in such a way that deciphering them is difficult. In these cases, it is the <ALT> tags and bubble help that provide clues for those with good vision, as well as those who might require a little additional help. The popup explanation becomes a source of additional information that everyone can use. In fact, the <ALT> tag information often provides usable data to search engines; so, as you can see, an <ALT> tag can have broader implications than you might think.

ON THE WEB   Lest you get the idea that accessibility affects only application use and that developers are only engaged in creating applications, there are many other areas of involvement, such as training. On `http://www.cdlr.tamu.edu/dec_2002/Proceedings/david_peter.pdf`, you can find an excellent piece written by David M. Peter entitled, "Usability and Accessibility—Everyone Learning," which presents the affects of accessibility on training. This white paper helps you understand how accessibility can affect training goals and requirements. It also shines a light on the issue of accessibility as a methodology that affects everyone.

Carpal tunnel syndrome is the scourge of our society. The main causes of carpal tunnel syndrome for office workers are the keyboard and mouse. The accessibility requirements designed to ease access for those who lack good coordination also help those who have normal use of their arms by reducing the effort required to input information. A business could easily write off the cost of improving the accessibility of their software by reducing the number of cases of carpal tunnel syndrome. In fact, because of the high cost of medical assistance (insurance), even one case of carpal tunnel syndrome prevented could pay for the required upgrades; anything after that would be money saved.

ON THE WEB   Carpal tunnel syndrome is a lot more serious and widespread than most people think. You can obtain a good overview of the topic at the National Institute of Neurological Disorders and Stroke (NINDS) Carpal Tunnel Syndrome Information Page (http://www.ninds.nih.gov/health_and_medical/disorders/carpal_doc.htm). In addition, there's a lot of good information for computer users at MSU's Computer Science and Engineering Web site (http://web.cps.msu.edu/facility/avoid-ct.php).

Even the colors used to present information on screen can affect the productivity of those who use the application. For example, many of the same color combinations that cause problems for those with color blindness also cause eyestrain for those with normal vision. Meeting accessibility requirements for color composition can also net surprising results in reduce headaches and time off spent recovering from symptoms such as dry eyes.

ON THE WEB   We'll discuss the issue of color blindness in several places in the book. If you want to obtain a quick overview of the topic, check out the article entitled, "Can Color-Blind Users See Your Site?" at http://msdn.microsoft.com/library/en-us/dnhess/html/hess10092000.asp. You might also want to visit the Color Perception Issues Web site at http://www.firelily.com/opinions/color.html.

The benefits from programming with accessibility in mind are more numerous than I've already listed in this section and we'll explore them as the book progresses. Accessible programming helps everyone by making the computer easier to use. To be more specific, businesses benefit with increased employee productivity, reduced costs, and improved customer relations. In short, you should embrace this technology with open arms because it has something for everyone.

Ranges of Abilities

There are two important concepts that developers should learn about when creating accessible applications. The first concept is that there are few (if any) people in the world with perfect bodies. I wear eyeglasses and need a hearing aid for a hearing problem. The eye problem is disabling if I don't wear my glasses because I can see at most a few feet in front of me. Likewise, my hearing denies me the pleasure of conversation in noisy environments such as restaurants. However, both disabilities are non-issues for me because someone cared enough to find solutions for my special needs. I have never met someone who lacked some type of physical problem that required some type of assistance—people just accept many disabilities as a part of life.

The second concept is one of enablement. You may notice that nowhere in the book will I mention the word "disabled" except in this section of the chapter. It's not because I have a problem with that word, it's a perfectly good word, but it doesn't apply to the topic at hand. If you take the word apart, it means literally, "not able." A therapist that I worked with while writing this book says that when someone initially comes to see her, they're disabled—not able to do something. However, by the time they leave, they are "enabled" (made able). The person is just as able as anyone else to perform a given task, but they have a "special need" that must be met in order for them to perform the task. (Just as my eyeglasses meet my special need for seeing.) Consequently, I have referred to special needs throughout the book because that's what we're discussing—the special needs that must be met in order to enable someone to interact with the computer.

I first ran into this use of terminology when I wrote an article entitled, "Hearing in a Different Sense" for *Coast Compute* magazine. At the time, the tactile vocoder was news. Just in case you don't know what this is, the person wears a computer around their waist in a belt that converts audible sound into vibrations. The person literally learns to hear through their skin. I was quite surprised to find out that young people without any sense of hearing at all (their bones are usually damaged or missing) can build up to a 95% comprehension rate using this technique. I made the mistake of referring to these people as disabled when talking with the researcher at the University of Miami who was developing the device. He kindly informed me that they simply had a special need and they were no longer disabled. I have since used the term special need.

The term special need is also more encompassing than disability. As previously mentioned, all of us have special needs that developers should meet, but many of us limp along using whatever the developer decides to give us. In part, the purpose of this book is to dispel the myth that accessible programming only affects those with a particular requirement. Many of the devices that we take for granted today, such as the remote control, were at one time equivalents of what accessible programming is today. Such devices meet special needs, so everyone is using them.

The next time you change the channel on your television, consider the fact that the device you just used meets a special need.

The Concept of "Universal Design"

In a perfect world, all software and hardware is compatible. You can use any piece of software with any piece of hardware. Developers always create applications that work with anything and hardware designers never try to improvise in ways that break application software. Vendors are all good guys who recognize the need for compatible software and never try to gain a marketing advantage by introducing compatibility issues into their products. Everyone looks to the needs of the user rather than the bottom line. In this world, creating an accessible application is never a problem because no one writes to a specific device. It isn't necessary to write to a specific device because properly written software can work with any device.

Welcome to reality. Vendors are in a cutthroat struggle to differentiate their product in some way. Each one looks at differentiation as a way to say that their product is better and that's why you should buy it. Application developers and hardware designers don't know the standards, so they create applications and hardware with compatibility problems. The real world is a mess and it's especially tough on those who can least understand the insane problems of getting a given application to work with a specific piece of hardware. In the real world, it's hard getting an accessible application to work, even when the vendor does consider the hardware.

However, I can't say that the vendors, developers, and designers are completely to blame. Sometimes the government steps in with requirements that aren't easy to implement using existing technology, so these parties must find a new approach. In addition, as technology advances and our knowledge about problem solutions increases, it becomes obvious that old solutions aren't as good as they could be. In a few cases, I've heard of vendors who try to placate user demands for functionality by implementing it using any technique they can. The vendor can choose between waiting to create a great product based on standards (and losing customers) or creating a nightmarish assemblage of parts and satisfying customer demand— at least for a while.

Therefore, on the one hand, you have the perfect world environment and on the other, you have reality. However, the world of hardware and software isn't as clear-cut as I have just presented it. Sometimes the developer can use a middle-ground approach to create an application or a piece of hardware that will come close to providing a universal solution.

You may notice that there is an overabundance of Web-based accessibility solutions on the market right now (including books). The reason that these solutions are popular is that it's possible to create an accessible application by ensuring that it runs on every browser around; but this usually means the application runs slowly, is buggy, and lacks functionality. (Applications that target a large number of browsers don't have to be slow, buggy, or lack functionality, but in my experience, they usually are because the developer is usually unwilling to test them fully or optimize the application in any way.) However, such applications do address the need for a universal solution as long as the user is willing to do everything on the Internet. Unfortunately, most of us don't work that way.

The Simple Object Access Protocol (SOAP) initially filled me with hope that there would be a universal method that a client could use to make a request of a server no matter what platforms were involved. *SOAP* is an XML-based technology that defines a means of packaging requests and data. The advantage of SOAP is that it works well with both browsers and desktop applications. The problem with it is that the vendors creating the SOAP specification jumped in with all kinds of neat additions to the specification and these cause compatibility problems. In short, SOAP has the potential to become a universal data exchange method between any client and any server (certainly a step in the right direction for a universal application), but it will take quite some time for vendors to work out their differences. Still, you can theoretically use SOAP to create applications that are almost, but not quite, universal in nature.

Is the concept of *universal design*—creating an application that works with any piece of hardware and hardware that works with all applications—a pipe dream? (This definition includes software that currently offers some level of flexibility in meeting the special needs of a variety of users—in the long run, meeting these special needs means creating a hardware and software combination that will work for that user.) It is today, but this problem might not always be with us. In the mean time, you can do a lot to make your application work with the broadest range of hardware possible. We'll discuss these techniques as the book progresses.

Does Section 508 Apply to You?

The question of whether Section 508 regulations apply to you is an important one—they don't apply to everyone directly, but there are situations in which you might want to implement them anyway. The following sections contain the three compliance scenarios: U.S. government agencies, federal contractors, and private industry. You'll find that even companies in the private sector must comply with Section 508 requirements in a few cases.

Government Agency

It goes without saying that Section 508 requirements affect U.S. government agencies and their employees the most. Anyone working for the U.S. government will have to consider Section 508 requirements for everything from software development to the purchase of their next piece of office equipment. (The government has made concessions for some areas of the government such as the military.) In fact, most government agencies will have a separate Section 508 Coordinator that other employees can contact for additional information. The Section 508 Coordinator ensures that government employees have sufficient information and ensures that their agency fully conforms to the requirements. The Section 508 Web site (http://www.section508.gov/index.cfm?FuseAction=Content&ID=53) also lists other job titles that are involved in making the Section 508 decisions for a given agency. The bottom line is that everyone in a government agency needs to consider Section 508 requirements, but these people also get the most help in following them.

Theoretically, all government applications and Web sites became Section 508 compliant by the 21 June 2001 deadline. The reality is that many of these Web sites won't pass the test today. All government Web sites have improved their accessibility features, but many have done it to avoid lawsuits, rather than as a means of making people more productive. Currently, the government is using a complaint process for each application and Web site that doesn't meet Section 508 requirements. See the story on *Government Computer News (GCN)* (http://www.gcn.com/21_16/s508/19076-1.html) for details. In short, eventually all government applications (both desktop and Web-based) must comply. If you're a developer for the government, then it's likely that you've already been involved in some of the fixes required to bring applications up to par with the requirements.

 ON THE WEB Government Computer News (GCN) is a good place to keep up with current Section 508 requirements. This online newspaper has a specific area for Section 508 updates at http://www.gcn.com/sect508/. You'll find that the GCN staff write most of the stories and seem familiar with every aspect of government-related Section 508 news. Because this site contains information that the public can use as well, it pays to subscribe to this newspaper electronically.

It's important to note that a few government activities don't require Section 508 compliance. For example, most of the military is exempt from this requirement because it's unlikely that an actual member of the military will have the kind of physical impairments covered by Section 508. You'll also find that Section 508 doesn't apply to the intelligence community—at least in some areas. A complete list of exceptions appears in the topic entitled, "Section 508 Subpart A 1194.3 General exceptions." This topic is available online at http://www.section508.gov/index.cfm?FuseAction=Content&ID=12#General.

Federal Contractor

The people who have the hardest time trying to decide about Section 508 requirements are federal contractors. The law clearly states that any portion of a vendor product created for government use must meet Section 508 requirements. However, nothing used strictly for private needs has to meet the same requirements. Of course, this places the federal contractor who also works with the private sector in a bit of a quandary. The federal contractor must ask four basic questions to determine their Section 508 compliance.

1. Will dual application support cost more than adding accessibility support for all applications?

2. Will a private sector–only application currently in use eventually see use in the federal government?

3. Do all of my subcontractors also provide Section 508 accessibility support?

4. How much will Section 508 accessibility requirements increase the price of my product?

There's no doubt that federal contractors will have to provide some level of Section 508 support, but the question is how to implement that support. Some federal contractors will undoubtedly decide to make a government version of their product and use the added support as a reason to charge more. The government contractor could also lay the implementation burden on the subcontractors used for the product. Of course, some vendors will add the support to all products and then use the support as another sales point in brochures. No matter what course your company chooses, you need to make a choice before you begin the design or upgrade process.

Private Industry

Generally, the larger your company, the more important it is that you provide some type of Section 508 policy. Because of the way that the government has worded the Section 508 requirements, you might find that you need to implement them even if your company has no direct contact with the government. The problem is that the government holds subcontractors responsible for implementing the Section 508 requirements no matter what the source of an application. This means that your noncompliant application will require added Section 508 support or the government won't be able to use it in any capacity. A small company is less likely to produce an application that will see general use and is consequently less likely to require Section 508 support.

Private industry is taking the Section 508 requirements quite seriously. Many large companies now include a statement about Section 508 on their Web sites if they feel they'll need to meet the Section 508 requirements. For example, Microsoft provides a Section 508 statement at `http://www.microsoft.com/enable/microsoft/section508.htm`. This statement is typical in that it assumes that the only Section 508 requirements that anyone is interested in are those that relate to people with special needs. It reflects the idea that accessibility is a single use item, when in reality it serves many needs. Negative connotations aside, you can learn a few things from the Microsoft Web site.

- The first section of the Web page introduces the topic of Section 508 support.

- The Web site clearly states a Section 508 policy for a large company.

- You'll find that a section of the Web site explains the company reason for implementing Section 508—support of the 54 million people who suffer from disabilities, in this case.

- The Web site includes documentation of continuing support for Section 508 requirements.

- There's a list of applicable resources near the bottom of the Web page so that users know where to look for additional information.

Of course, the question is whether your company should implement Section 508 if you see no reason to do so today. Perhaps your company is a small consulting firm that only writes custom code and never releases applications for public use. Your clients may not express an interest in spending money on Section 508 implementation and may even be hostile to the idea of doing so. Even if you find yourself in this situation, there are still good reasons to provide Section 508 support in your applications. The following list provides a few of the reasons why even a small company should pursue this goal.

- Adding Section 508 support to applications today builds skills in your company that will help you add support quickly tomorrow.

- Hopefully your company will grow—making it likely that you'll need to eventually add Section 508 support to your applications.

- Even users without any disabilities can benefit from accessible applications—pointing out these benefits to a client can help ease tensions.

An Overview of the Section 508 Standard

The developers of the government regulations we're discussing in this chapter wrote them in the usual legalese, making them a little difficult for the average person to understand. I'm sure that using legalese makes the regulations more precise in some respects, but it also makes them a lot more difficult for the average developer to understand. After all, I don't talk in legalese every day and I'm sure you don't use it either. Perhaps the accessibility regulations require some added accessibility themselves.

This section of the chapter will discuss the Section 508 regulations using terms that most developers will understand. It will also shed some light on the application details that the regulations describe. For example, when a rule says that you must use consistent bitmaps throughout an application, what precisely does that mean? (See the description of Section 1194.21(e) for details.) The headings in this section are direct quotes from the government regulations so you know exactly what the law says. The descriptive text that follows is an interpretation of the law. In sum, the following sections contain both the law and an interpretation of it so that you can see the full impact of Section 508 requirements on your development efforts.

ON THE WEB   This section of the chapter discusses the Section 508 requirements from a developer perspective. Although the section does include the actual Section 508 wording for developer issues, it doesn't include the full Section 508 text. To obtain the complete Section 508 text, go to http://www.section508.gov/index.cfm?FuseAction=Content&ID=12. You'll find a Section 508 summary written by the same folks who brought you the rules at http://www.section508.gov/index.cfm?FuseAction=Content&ID=11. If you'd like to see the Federal Register summary of the Section 508 requirements, check out http://www.access-board.gov/sec508/508standards.htm. Finally, if you want a very quick summary of Section 508 requirements that you can present to your boss or a nontechnical person, check out the CNN article at http://www.cnn.com/2001/TECH/industry/06/15/web.site.accessibility.idg/.

The Section 508 regulations are also quite large and the regulations contain sections that you'll never worry about—at least as part of your job. A heading for these regulations will still appear in the sections that follow for the sake of completeness; however, the description will tell you that the rule doesn't apply to application development.

> **NOTE** This chapter describes the Section 508 requirements in force at the time of this writing. There's a small chance that the government will relax some of the Section 508 requirements by the time that you read this book. Always check the current government regulations at the Section 508 Web sites described earlier in this section.

The final concept to remember is that this section of the chapter focuses on the rules that you need to follow. We'll discuss implementation details as the book progresses. What you should obtain out of the sections that follow is a clearer idea of that the regulations mean.

Software Applications and Operating Systems (1194.21)

All developers should know the contents of this section. The term *software application* refers to the applications you use on the desktop. The Section 508 regulations also provide special rules for Web-based applications in the "Web-based Intranet and Internet Information and Applications (1194.22)" section discussed later in the chapter. In short, you should use the rules in this section when writing your desktop applications. Of course, the separation of the two application types makes sense from the perspective of the environments in which they operate, but it does make it more difficult to write the applications.

Don't get the idea that you only have to concern yourself with the software application portion of the rules. If you're writing an application for the government, you also need to know that the operating system that the application will use meets the government criteria. For example, Microsoft provides several summaries of the support that its products provide for accessibility concerns. The best place to look for Section 508 information is their site at http://www.microsoft.com/enable/microsoft/section508.htm. Figure 1-1 shows what you can expect to see at this site.

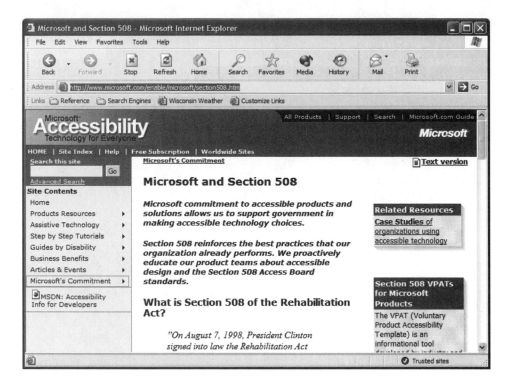

Figure 1-1. Microsoft includes several summaries of Section 508 support for their applications such as this one.

(a) When software is designed to run on a system that has a keyboard, product functions shall be executable from a keyboard where the function itself or the result of performing a function can be discerned textually.

The easiest way to read this rule is "mouse not allowed." In some respects, Windows comes very close to failing this test. You can move around Windows if you really want to without using the mouse, but it's a painful experience. The MouseKeys feature of Windows does help with this problem, but it's not a foolproof method of working with the product either. (Learn more about accessibility features that Windows does provide in Chapter 6 of this book.) The problem with MouseKeys is that it still relies on a visual method for moving the mouse cursor, which doesn't help people with special visual needs. MouseKeys will help someone with movement difficulties, however, so it does provide a partial solution. The bottom line is that Windows developers are already starting with a disadvantage before they put one line of code down.

Generally, to meet the requirements of this rule, your application must support a keyboard interface for all input. In addition, it must provide some type of text reaction. For example, when the user selects File ➤ Print, the application must output some text notification that the data actually went to the printer. We'll discuss methods for adding cues to applications in Chapter 7 of the book.

(b) Applications shall not disrupt or disable activated features of other products that are identified as accessibility features, where those features are developed and documented according to industry standards. Applications also shall not disrupt or disable activated features of any operating system that are identified as accessibility features where the application programming interface for those accessibility features has been documented by the manufacturer of the operating system and is available to the product developer.

This particular rule uses a lot of text to express a simple idea—one that developers should follow no matter who their audience is. In essence, don't change the user's environment unless you ask the user first or the change is impossible to avoid. I'm often surprised to find applications making changes to the environment on my machine. It's inconvenient and definitely not welcome. I can only imagine how irritated someone with special needs would be if an application suddenly decided to turn a special appliance or application support feature off. This type of behavior is actually worse than not supporting accessibility features in the first place.

You should note something special about the first requirement. It says that an application shouldn't tamper with other applications that provide accessibility options developed according to industry standards such as this one. There are actually a number of accessibility standards, so it's usually better not to tamper with other applications at all unless you know precisely how they work. The only exception that this rule leaves open to the developer is if a non-standard application is causing some type of problem with the system as a whole. Perhaps its non-standard use of accessibility features actually prevents you from implementing industry standard accessibility support. You can learn how to implement Windows-specific accessibility features correctly in Chapter 6 of the book.

(c) A well-defined on-screen indication of the current focus shall be provided that moves among interactive interface elements as the input focus changes. The focus shall be programmatically exposed so that assistive technology can track focus and focus changes.

There are two requirements in this rule. First, an application must provide some type of on-screen presentation of the selected component. Windows already provides this functionality; however, there's nothing that says you can't enhance the presentation should the need arise. We discuss this portion of the rule in Chapter 5 of this book.

Second, the application has to provide some means of detecting which control is selected for external applications—most notably, those used for accessibility purposes. The book contains several examples of how to perform this task—most of the examples appear in Chapter 7. This chapter also contains descriptions of the tools required to test your application for compliance.

(d) Sufficient information about a user interface element including the identity, operation and state of the element shall be available to assistive technology. When an image represents a program element, the information conveyed by the image must also be available in text.

Some developers confuse this rule with the bubble help that they add to the application. The bubble help does identify user interface elements and, if the developer does the job correctly, will tell the user what task the user interface element performs. The problem is that bubble help isn't necessarily available to the accessibility technology. However, you can ensure this information is available using the techniques discussed in Chapter 7.

Bubble help does answer the section requirement. If you use an image to represent any interface element, adding bubble help to it normally displays a text message that a screen reader will read with the correct coding. A user can also hover the mouse over the element to see what task the element performs.

In general, the law also requires equal treatment of bubble help and the information presented by the image. For example, if you have a button that tells the user they have eight email messages, the bubble help must also provide this information. So, simply labeling the button might not be enough—if the image provides dynamic information, the bubble help must provide this information as well.

NOTE Interestingly enough, many of the utility applications supplied with Windows don't include bubble help. For example, you won't find any bubble help with Notepad or Calculator. Consequently, you should avoid accessing these applications from your accessibility-enabled application. Doing so would create problems in adhering to the Section 508 requirements.

(e) When bitmap images are used to identify controls, status indicators, or other programmatic elements, the meaning assigned to those images shall be consistent throughout an application's performance.

Most developers who've written Windows code for a while already know to use consistent bitmaps. Unfortunately, some know to use the consistent bitmaps and then use something else just to be obstinate. The best rule of thumb is to create a set of bitmaps before you begin coding and then assign specific meanings to them.

Using the same bitmaps used by other Windows applications also reduces the learning curve for everyone and reduces the time required to write the application. We discuss this issue in the "Using Consistent Controls, Status Indicators, and Other Elements" section of Chapter 5.

(f) Textual information shall be provided through operating system functions for displaying text. The minimum information that shall be made available is text content, text input caret location, and text attributes.

Windows automatically provides all of these features. In fact, you'd have to go out of your way to circumvent them. This rule essentially says that the operation system has to be aware of the text you present on screen. The only way to circumvent this support is to write directly to the screen buffer—a problematic way to program in any circumstance.

(g) Applications shall not override user selected contrast and color selections and other individual display attributes.

This requirement is similar to rule (b). Generally, it's a bad idea to change the user's environment for any reason. It's especially wrong to change environment settings for accessibility users because you can remove the effects of the high contrast display, among other things. You can learn more about environmental settings and working with them correctly in the "Obtaining and Using the Current Display Settings Example" section of Chapter 5.

(h) When animation is displayed, the information shall be displayable in at least one non-animated presentation mode at the option of the user.

This rule is relatively straightforward. If you create animation for any purpose other than decoration, you need to provide a text or other version of the animation that will work with accessibility software. However, you also need to consider all of the other rules we've discussed so far and rule (k) that follows. Animation presents a major obstacle for users with special needs, so you need to use animation wisely and provide alternatives. You can learn more about effective use of animation in the "Animation and Animation Alternative Example" section of Chapter 5.

In the "Understanding User Needs" section of Chapter 2, we'll discuss what I call the *gadget factor* for applications. All too often, animation is simply a gadget that the user can do without in an application. If you do use animation, make sure that it accomplishes a specific task. If you have a hard time conceptualizing a non-animated version of the animation, you should ask if the animation is decorative. Although animation does provide eye appeal to an application, it's generally better to do without the decoration.

ON THE WEB   There are exceptions to every rule. Normally, animation does add to the gadget factor of an application. However, in some cases, animation is an integral part of an application that actually makes using the application easier for someone with special needs. London's Tate Modern gallery uses such an application to help those with vision difficulties "see" the art they have been missing. You can find out more about this application at http://www.wired.com/news/culture/ 0,1284,54256,00.html.

(i) Color coding shall not be used as the only means of conveying information, indicating an action, prompting a response, or distinguishing a visual element.

More than a few people have problems with color. Color blindness is one obvious problem area. However, those with low vision also have problems, as well as those who use screen readers. Aesthetic irritations aside, using color as your sole source of information to the reader doesn't make sense for cultural reasons either. A color that you associate with stop might mean something completely different in another country. You can learn more about the effects of color and color blindness in the "Building the Color Blindness Simulator Example" section of Chapter 4.

Does this mean that you can't use color in your applications? Color is an important application feature, but you need to add prompts or other text as well. A red button doesn't mean much—it could do anything. However, a red octagon with the word "Stop" in it does have meaning. To give the user even more help, you could add bubble help that says, "This buttons stops the application from sending information." The idea of this rule is that you provide the user with adequate input to use the application, no matter how the user has to interact with it. You can learn more about effective color use in the "Working with Colors in Controls and UI Elements Example" section of Chapter 5.

(j) When a product permits a user to adjust color and contrast settings, a variety of color selections capable of producing a range of contrast levels shall be provided.

This is another rule that's almost too easy to implement when using Windows. All you need to do is add the Color common dialog box to your application and then present it whenever the user has an opportunity to change the color. Of course, some developers will insist on creating a custom dialog box. The biggest requirement is that you not only provide a relatively large number of color selections, but you also allow the user to create custom colors as needed. You can learn more about effective color use in the "Working with Colors in Controls and UI Elements Example" section of Chapter 5.

(k) Software shall not use flashing or blinking text, objects, or other elements having a flash or blink frequency greater than 2 Hz and lower than 55 Hz.

There's an unspoken medical concern in this rule—one that you need to know about. A small percentage of the population reacts to flashing light. The frequency varies by person, as do the effects. However, many of these people suffer seizures and other physical problems when they see the flashing image or other light source. In rare cases, the seizure could result in death.

If anything in your application blinks, you need to provide some means to ensure that the blinking is outside the frequency range mentioned in this rule. Windows already provides support for changing the blink rate of some display items such as cursors. However, anything your application blinks due to an internal timer could cause problems. Not only do you need to ensure the blink rate is outside the specified range, but you should include some means for the user to change the blink rate—a relatively simple task requiring a dialog box entry. You can learn more about this issue in the "Understanding the Reconfigured System" section of Chapter 4.

(l) When electronic forms are used, the form shall allow people using assistive technology to access the information, field elements, and functionality required for completion and submission of the form, including all directions and cues.

This rule embodies some of the information we've already discussed for individual controls, but it speaks about the form as a whole. Any form you create must be accessible with a screen reader as well as any other output device the reader might choose. The form must provide complete information about every control, which includes the purpose of every field entry on the form. The form should provide safeguards that check for incorrect entries and ensure that the reader understands how to correct the input. Any submission buttons require clear labeling, including a full description of their purpose.

All of the form-based examples in this book follow this guideline. We'll discuss various techniques you can try as the book progresses. Generally, you need to provide accessibility output, button help, full prompts, and other information to ensure the user can fill out the forms you create. You'll find a data entry specific example in the "Data Entry Example" section of Chapter 5.

Web-Based Intranet and Internet Information and Applications (1194.22)

As mentioned earlier, Web-based applications use a special set of accessibility rules, which makes sense given the differences in this media. However, the use of special rules also makes development more difficult because you now have two sets of rules to consider. In addition, Microsoft products (among others) enable you to mix application environments; this mixing blurs the development picture. For example, you can place a browser window within a desktop application—making it harder to define which set of rules to use for the application.

The following sections discuss each of the rules for Web-based applications. Notice that most of these rules will affect the server end of the application rather than the browser (client) portion. However, make sure you consider both client and server needs when writing an application; they are both are essential.

(a) A text equivalent for every non-text element shall be provided (e.g., via "alt", "longdesc", or in element content).

Any element that isn't text—including graphic text—requires an <ALT> tag entry as a minimum. If the graphic or other non-text element is purely decorative, provide an empty <ALT=""> tag—don't use an entry that says the element is decorative. When you create a graphic or other non-text element that conveys information, you should also include the <LONGDESC> tag. This tag allows you to add a complete description of the non-text element. We'll discuss these tags further in the "<ALT> and <LONGDESC> Tags—the Low Tech Solution" section of Chapter 11.

This rule also applies to graphic sequences such as Macromedia Flash presentations. However, it's not enough to provide the tags in this case. If you look at the requirements for section 1194.24, you'll find that online movies or television presentations require open or closed captioning. You have to make every element of the presentation fully accessible to those with special needs. Anyone can make use of captioning when sound isn't an option (as in a crowded office). Having a transcript of the presentation is also handy for anyone who wants to see the presentation in detail.

Deciding Between Closed and Open Captioning

It's important to understand the difference between closed and open captioning. Closed captioning requires use of a special box for display purposes and the user must turn this feature on. Most television sets today come with closed caption circuitry, so the user can easily turn the feature on using the remote control. However, older televisions lack this circuitry, so the user can't see the captioning. Open captioning is always available.

The law offers the developer a choice between closed and open captioning, but most legal challenges have resulted in required conformance using closed captioning. Consequently, from a legal perspective, adding closed captioning is often the most defensible choice should you go to court.

However, you must also consider the preferences of those that the captioning choice will affect. Those with special hearing needs tend to prefer open captioning so that the feature is always available with the least possible effort. Designers seem to waiver between the two choices. The best choice is the one that meets your target audience's needs. If your application will be used mainly by those with this special need or in an environment, such as a noisy tavern, where such a feature will be useful, it's best to use open captioning.

(b) Equivalent alternatives for any multimedia presentation shall be synchronized with the presentation.

This particular rule is confusing because it actually refers to two requirements. First, it stipulates that the alternative presentation must contain the same material as the multimedia presentation. I've already seen a few Web sites where the transcript doesn't quite match up with the multimedia presentation, making the transcript a little misleading. We'll discuss this issue in the "Captioning Movies and Other Video Presentations" section of Chapter 11.

Second, the rule stipulates that the user should be able to view the alternative and multimedia presentations at the same time. For example, if you create a movie with sound, you also need to provide closed captioning that follows the sound portion of the movie. Otherwise, the user won't know which pictures go with what part of the movie.

(c) Web pages shall be designed so that all information conveyed with color is also available without color, for example, from context or markup.

The key word for this rule is "information." The rule doesn't indicate that color used for decoration is bad—it indicates that if the color conveys information, you must also make that information available using some other means.

 TIP One thing to keep in mind is that most applications that provide automated Web site testing for accessibility compliance don't know the intent of color on the Web page, so they automatically mark any use of color as suspect. When you receive the report from the testing application, you'll see every instance of color use on your Web site. It's up to the developer to determine if that color conveys information.

There's a potential for problems with this rule because many people don't think about the ways in which color can convey information. For example, many Web sites will place special text (such as notes) in an alternate color. The color is conveying information in this case, although the developer might not think so. Using color in this way requires a special tag because the color is setting off a special section. Unfortunately, most application development software will simply indent the text and not add the special tag. We'll discuss this issue in detail in Chapter 11.

(d) Documents shall be organized so they are readable without requiring an associated style sheet.

The cascading style sheet (CSS) has become a staple for organizing and displaying information for many Web sites. Unfortunately, many developers go too far in using CSS and make the associated HTML page almost useless without it. (For example, a developer could theoretically create a page that consists of <SPAN> tags with no HTML structural elements.) This rule says that your Web page must provide the same organizational characteristics with or without CSS (or other style sheet technologies).

Notice that I didn't say that the regulations limit you to ugly Web pages that lack pizzazz. Screen readers and other aids for those with special needs ignore CSS because the user often has no use for such formatting information. By placing the formatting information in a CSS document, you can create a beautiful presentation for those who can use it, yet organize and present the information in plain text for those who don't.

The effect of this rule is that you must place all information and organizational data within the HTML document. The formatting can appear in the CSS document, but you must not place any of the information there. In sum, this rule specifies how to sort the information contained within the two documents but doesn't limit your use of CSS technology. You'll see a demonstration of this rule in the "Using CSS Example" section of Chapter 11.

(e) Redundant text links shall be provided for each active region of a server-side image map.

Image maps are those large images that you see on some Web sites. If you click on one area of the image map, you go to one location—click on another area, and you go to an entirely different location. Developers use image maps as an artistic method for moving from one location on a Web site to another.

The problem with image maps is that they assume the viewer can see them. Actually, they assume you can figure out what the various regions mean—something that users with good vision have a hard time doing on some Web sites. This rule says that you must provide text links to navigate the Web site in addition to the image map. Given the difficulty of using image maps, it might just be better to stick with the text links. We'll look at an image map example in the "Working with Image Maps Example" section of Chapter 11.

(f) Client-side image maps shall be provided instead of server-side image maps except where the regions cannot be defined with an available geometric shape.

Essentially, this rule says that if you must use an image map, then the image map must appear as part of the HTML page sent to the client, rather than reside on the server. In most cases, Web sites already use this technique to reduce bandwidth requirements. You'll find additional information about this topic at `http://www.ihip.com/cside.html`. A corresponding article on server-side image maps appears at `http://hotwired.lycos.com/webmonkey/html/96/39/index2a.html`.

(g) Row and column headers shall be identified for data tables.

This is a common sense rule. It states that you must provide row and column headers for data tables and that those headers must include appropriate identification by using the correct tags. In this case, you must use the `<TH>` tag and not the `<TD>` tag. Using the correct tag ensures that a screen reader can interpret the header as a header and not as standard table text. We'll discuss this and other common tag issues in Chapter 10. Make sure you also look at the example found in the "Creating Accessibility Friendly Tables Example" section of Chapter 9.

(h) Markup shall be used to associate data cells and header cells for data tables that have two or more logical levels of row or column headers.

This rule applies to complex tables. Normally, it's best to follow the rule that simple is better. Using multiple single-level tables is generally better than using a single complex table with multiple row and column header levels. However, sometimes you can't avoid creating a complex table because the interactions you need to represent in a limited space won't work with a simple table that uses a single level of row and column headers.

In this case, what you need to do is ensure that every data cell has a specific place in the table hierarchy. You can't place a single data cell out in limbo because it seems like a good idea at the time. In short, this rule says that you must provide tables that follow a definite organizational hierarchy. We discuss this issue in detail in the "Creating Accessibility Friendly Tables Example" section of Chapter 9.

(i) Frames shall be titled with text that facilitates frame identification and navigation.

Most of the Web sites that I visited in the past used frames to organize information, but I've noticed recently that many developers are shying away from this technology because many browsers can't use it. Frames also cause problems for screen readers and other accessibility programs. In general, it's a good idea to avoid frames unless you have a specific reason for using them that you can't meet in any other way. We'll discuss frames and other problem Web page constructions in the "Avoiding Web Site Problems" section of Chapter 9.

If you must use frames, then every frame must include a title using the `<TITLE>` tag. The title ensures that screen readers and other accessibility applications at least have a slim chance of making sense out of your Web page. The screen reader will include the title as it reads the Web page to ensure that the user can associate content with a particular frameset and create an overall mental image of the page.

(j) Pages shall be designed to avoid causing the screen to flicker with a frequency greater than 2 Hz and lower than 55 Hz.

This rule has the same meaning and explanation as 1194.21(k). Please refer to the explanation for that rule.

(k) A text-only page, with equivalent information or functionality, shall be provided to make a web site comply with the provisions of this part, when compliance cannot be accomplished in any other way. The content of the text-only page shall be updated whenever the primary page changes.

This is the "developer has failed" rule. It says that if you can't comply with the accessibility rules in any other way, you must provide a text-only Web page. In general, this rule says that the developer values presentation more highly than content. We discuss the problems with this approach in the "Understanding User Needs" section of Chapter 2. Except in certain cases, if you have to implement a separate text-only version of your Web page, then it's probably filled with too many gadgets for the average user anyway and you should reconsider your position. We discuss how to create text-only Web pages in Chapter 10.

(l) When pages utilize scripting languages to display content, or to create interface elements, the information provided by the script shall be identified with functional text that can be read by assistive technology.

Some Web sites end up being one huge script. You can use the View ➤ Source Code command in Internet Explorer (or an equivalent in most other browsers) to view the Web page. All you'll see for code is a call to a script, which calls another script, and so on. (In most cases, these pages also include a mix of applets and objects, making the whole thing a big mess that's difficult to understand.) A Web page designed using this technique must be a nightmare for the developer to maintain. One thing is certain—it's impossible for screen readers and other accessibility applications to navigate. The bottom line is that if you want to make your Web site accessibility friendly, you must include all of the content within the HTML document. You can learn more about this issue in the "Creating Accessibility Friendly Scripts Example" section of Chapter 13.

(m) When a web page requires that an applet, plug-in or other application be present on the client system to interpret page content, the page must provide a link to a plug-in or applet that complies with §1194.21(a) through (l).

This rule states that if you use any type of application such as Macromedia Flash on your Web page, you must include a link for downloading the application on your Web site. Note that the rule doesn't say that you can make the download automatic—the rule specifically says that you must include a link. A user might decide that they don't want to use your application. The automatic downloads used by some Web sites force the user into a situation they might not want. We discuss this issue in detail in the "Avoiding Web Site Problems" section of Chapter 9.

(n) When electronic forms are designed to be completed on-line, the form shall allow people using assistive technology to access the information, field elements, and functionality required for completion and submission of the form, including all directions and cues.

This rule has the same meaning and explanation as 1194.21(l). Please refer to the explanation for that rule.

(o) A method shall be provided that permits users to skip repetitive navigation links.

This rule actually goes along with several other rules we've discussed in this section such as the need to provide text links for image maps and the rules regarding the use of frames. Abiding by all of the accessibility rules we've discussed so far can mean that your Web page has multiple versions of each navigation link. To comply with this rule, you have to provide some method for skipping past the repetitive links. We discuss this issue in detail in the "Avoiding Web Site Problems" section of Chapter 9.

(p) When a timed response is required, the user shall be alerted and given sufficient time to indicate more time is required.

Except for educational purposes such as taking an exam online, I can't think of a good reason to use timed responses on a Web site. Certainly, they aren't a comment element. However, if you do need to provide a timed response, then this rule states that you must provide some measure of time to the user that a screen reader or other accessibility application/device can read.

There's one potential time when you could end up breaking this rule inadvertently because most developers won't think of this issue. Some Web sites will use a timed page when a link has moved. A user goes to the page. Because the page has moved, the Web page owner provides a timed interval in which the user can click on a link. After that interval, the new Web page should automatically display. Because it does involve a timed interval, you must provide an alert and give the user sufficient time to react. You must also provide some means to stop the action or let the user indicate they need more time. We discuss this, and other timed issues, in the "Avoiding Web Site Problems" section of Chapter 9.

Telecommunications Products (1194.23)

Most developers won't need to worry about this part of the Section 508 requirements. These rules cover the use of physical aids such as hearing devices, Telecommunication Device for the Deaf (TDD), and the teletypewriter (TTY) used by those with hearing difficulties. It also includes the inclusion of volume controls and other functionality that will help someone communicate using the telephone system.

In some cases, the developer might need to work with someone else to implement this requirement properly. For example, someone with cerebral palsy might need a special telephone interface to order to get onto the Internet or perform other telecommunications tasks that your application helps them perform. In this case, you might not need to do anything special with your application, but you may need to test it to ensure it works properly with the solutions provided by other vendors. Because your application interacts with other facets of the accessibility environment, you need to be prepared to provide any required assistance, even if a requirement doesn't affect you directly. For example, this could be an issue with voicemail systems or tele-info portals.

Video or Multimedia Products (1194.24)

Because computer systems now include television tuners and other multimedia devices, and developers are using these features for a number of application needs including training, it's important to consider the requirements of this portion of the Section 508 requirements. Not all of the rules are applicable to computer systems. In some cases, even if the rule is applicable, application developers won't be the ones to implement the law.

The following sections contain the laws that do apply to developers. Some subsections are missing because they simply don't apply. If you're curious about these other subsections, you can view the Section 508 Web site mentioned earlier. For the most part, you'll find that you only need to implement these requirements when you create special application types and only when those applications rely on some type of media transmission, such as a television signal or video playback.

 NOTE The Section 508 requirements gave vendors until July 1, 2002 to add caption decoder circuitry to widescreen digital television displays, including those incorporated into computer systems. This means that even if your application and associated media follow all of the Section 508 requirements, the computer used to present the information might not perform the task correctly. Make sure that any media device you purchase includes the closed caption circuitry. Generally, you can assume that any device installed before the deadline date doesn't include the required circuitry.

(c) All training and informational video and multimedia productions which support the agency's mission, regardless of format, that contain speech or other audio information necessary for the comprehension of the content, shall be open or closed captioned.

This rule essentially says that if you provide any type of content-oriented multimedia on your Web site, you must also provide captioning for it. Some developers might be tempted to read some additional criteria into this rule that probably doesn't apply. For example, the rule states that these presentations support the agency's mission, so some developers might be tempted to avoid making the required changes because the presentation is "just for fun." The safe approach is to view all multimedia as requiring captioning. We'll discuss this issue in detail in the "Captioning Movies and Other Video Presentations" section of Chapter 11.

(d) All training and informational video and multimedia productions which support the agency's mission, regardless of format, that contain visual information necessary for the comprehension of the content, shall be audio described.

Some developers will have no clue as to what "audio described" means. It means that the presentation must literally describe in words (using audio) what the images in the presentation are trying to convey. This requirement is in addition to the text captioning that the law requires. (See the "Captioning Movies and Other Video Presentations" section of Chapter 11 for details.)

Complex graphics are more problematic. In this case, you'll likely need a professional studio to help with the presentation. Such presentations are outside the scope of this book, so I won't discuss them.

(e) Display or presentation of alternate text presentation or audio descriptions shall be user-selectable unless permanent.

This rule states that you must make use of captioning and make use of audio description user selectable unless you choose to make both features a permanent part of the presentation. I've never seen a presentation where captioning or audio descriptions are on all the time, so most developers make the information optional. We'll discuss this issue in detail in the "Captioning Movies and Other Video Presentations" section of Chapter 11.

Self Contained, Closed Products (1194.25)

A small group of developers will need to consider these Section 508 requirements, but we won't discuss them in this book. This section applies to devices that contain embedded systems and associated code but don't run external applications. For example, transaction machines, copiers, printers, calculators, and fax machines all fall within this category, but because these devices won't run anything other than the application they're designed to run, we won't discuss them in this book.

The rules in this section discuss the need to add physical accessibility features to these devices. For example, a fax machine will require Braille key identifiers. Other requirements define the need for a touchscreen, such as the one used for a kiosk display. In addition, most devices will require some type of auditory output as well as a means for privately listening to that output.

Unfortunately, the government also groups the kiosk in this category. There are actually several classifications of kiosk, and the one referenced for this category is the type used for a single purpose. For example, a kiosk that shows the layout of your local mall is unlikely to run any other application and usually doesn't provide an external programming capability. Such a kiosk is essentially a large embedded device. Consequently, it falls within this category of device. However, an interactive kiosk that includes the capacity to accept external programming more likely falls into the desktop application category as well as this category. We'll discuss the programming requirements for such a kiosk as part of the desktop application programming requirements, but we won't discuss special needs such as the inclusion of a touchscreen.

Desktop and Portable Computers (1194.26)

As a developer, you're responsible for knowing the hardware limitations of your target system, as well as the software limits. The reason is simple. Although you won't actually implement the hardware requirements, the application you create must provide access to the hardware. Consequently, when the rules say that a computer that uses biometric authentication must also include a secondary authentication method, you must write your application in such a way that it can accept both forms of authentication from the user.

Some of the requirements in this section don't apply directly to developers and we won't cover them in the book, so I didn't include them here. If you're curious about these other subsections, you can view the on the Section 508 Web site mentioned earlier. Generally, the missing rules refer to the method used to input the character—the physical element of the input—rather than something monitored or maintained by the application.

 NOTE   Two requirements that you do need to consider appear in the 1194.23(k)(3) and 1194.23(k)(4) portions of the rules. These rules say that if the input device supports a key repeat feature, then the developer is responsible for making the repeat feature adjustable. In addition, the repeat feature should wait as long as 2 seconds before it displays the next character. The second rule states that the locked status of a key should be visually visible as well as provide some type of sound. Windows already includes features that handle both of these requirements. However, both features are also programmable, which means that you have a responsibility as a developer. Generally, you shouldn't change any setting that might affect these usability requirements. However, if you want, you can provide the means within your application to help the user adjust this feature—making the application a lot more convenient to use.

(c) When biometric forms of user identification or control are used, an alternative form of identification or activation, which does not require the user to possess particular biological characteristics, shall also be provided.

Biometric authentication is becoming more popular because it's very hard to fool some biometric devices. In addition, users commonly lose or compromise both identification cards and passwords. However, not everyone has a fingerprint or an iris to check using biometric means. This rule states that you must provide an alternative method of identification when needed. The key word for this phrase is "alternative form of identification or activation." The alternate form of identification is in addition to the standard biometric method.

Most experts take this rule to mean that a system must provide support for passwords or other alternative identification methods, but that the alternative doesn't have to be active unless someone with a special need requires it. In addition, you could easily make the option available only to the person and continue requiring biometric authentication from everyone else. We'll discuss this issue in detail in the "Biometric Device Issues" section of Chapter 3.

Functional Performance Criteria (Subpart C)

Most developers associate the term "performance" with speed, and lots of it. However, in the world of accessibility, performance takes on a whole new meaning. In some cases, the word performance means, "How slow does it go?" because many applications don't go slow enough. In other cases, performance actually means functionality. For example, the accessibility requirements address the need for an application to provide both visual and audio clues for operation. Applications today address the visual requirements, in most cases, and, in some cases, leave even that cue to the imagination of the user. Performance also means, "How many steps does a task require?" It's not sufficient to provide accessibility—you must do it in a way that doesn't require an inordinate number of steps on the part of the user.

While a developer can create a checklist to ensure an application meets the requirements we've discussed in several other sections, performance is a subjective measure of application usefulness. In some cases, the Section 508 rules state specific levels of performance, but often the performance levels are based on the subjective viewpoint of the user. After talking with several developers who've worked through this particular issue, it's apparent that this is the most difficult portion of the Section 508 rules to implement.

The following sections describe the performance criteria for accessible applications. In some cases, you'll find that the description doesn't provide hard and fast rules you can use to implement the requirement. We'll discuss how you can determine the performance of your application from an accessibility perspective as the book progresses. This is one case where an example describes the implementation of the rule better than any thing I could say.

(a) At least one mode of operation and information retrieval that does not require user vision shall be provided, or support for assistive technology used by people who are blind or visually impaired shall be provided.

Some developers are so certain that no one will ever use the accessibility features of their application that they go out of their way to make it a separate mode of operation. This rule states that the developer can take this course of action and still comply with the rules. However, this book takes the approach that it's less expensive to create applications with a single mode of operation that includes accessibility features as a built-in function. In general, all of the examples take the approach that accessibility features are helpful to everyone given the right conditions. You can learn more about the Windows functionality provided to address this need in the "Using the Display Features Example" section of Chapter 6.

(b) At least one mode of operation and information retrieval that does not require visual acuity greater than 20/70 shall be provided in audio and enlarged print output working together or independently, or support for assistive technology used by people who are visually impaired shall be provided.

This is a different issue from working with someone who's blind. Someone with low vision can use a high contrast display with large lettering and still read it without using a screen reader. Windows provides this functionality by default—the user can choose a large text, high contrast display. However, your application also requires special coding to ensure the placement of user interface elements will work with a high contract, large text display. We discuss this issue in detail in the "Understanding the Reconfigured System" section of Chapter 4. Of course, the application must also detect the user setup before it can make the required changes. We discuss this issue in the "Obtaining and Using the Current Display Settings Example" section of Chapter 5. You can also learn more about the Windows functionality provided to address this need in the "Using the Display Features Example" section of Chapter 6.

(c) At least one mode of operation and information retrieval that does not require user hearing shall be provided, or support for assistive technology used by people who are deaf or hard of hearing shall be provided.

This rule addresses the needs of those with poor hearing. However, this rule also addresses the needs of those who simply want a quiet work environment. Windows provides the features to make applications silent, yet interactive. We discuss this issue in the "Using the Sound Features Example" section of Chapter 6.

(d) Where audio information is important for the use of a product, at least one mode of operation and information retrieval shall be provided in an enhanced auditory fashion, or support for assistive hearing devices shall be provided.

This rule discusses the needs of those with reduced hearing. It essentially says that if your application requires sound for proper use, then you have to provide a non-sound alternative of some type. You can meet this requirement in several ways. First, you can use the Windows features to provide a text version of the sound that you're presenting to the user. This is the approach I recommend whenever possible. We discuss it in the "Using the Sound Features Example" section of Chapter 6.

Unfortunately, some sounds aren't easy to represent as text, so you have to use the second method of supporting special accessibility devices for those with hearing problems. For example, most developers would find it impossible to create a wildlife presentation using text cues. Because each of these devices has a different programming interface, this book won't discuss them in depth. However, you'll find a discussion of the issues involved in the "Special Devices for Those with Special Needs" section of Chapter 4.

(e) At least one mode of operation and information retrieval that does not require user speech shall be provided, or support for assistive technology used by people with disabilities shall be provided.

Most computer applications don't use sound input because sound technology is notoriously unreliable. However, as vendors that market sound input devices solve the problems of the past, applications that use sound input become more of a reality. This rule says that you must provide some alternative to sound input if you write a sound enabled application. We discuss this issue in Chapters 8 (desktop application) and 12 (Web-based applications).

(f) At least one mode of operation and information retrieval that does not require fine motor control or simultaneous actions and that is operable with limited reach and strength shall be provided.

This rule requires that the developer provide a means for helping those who don't have good motor control. For example, the user might not be able to press the Alt and the X keys simultaneously to exit your application. Adding this support would be impossible without some level of operating system cooperation. Windows provides separate support for the mouse and the keyboard. We'll discuss both issues in Chapter 6.

Interestingly enough, this is one requirement that may also require the use of specialized hardware. For example, someone without fine motor control might need to use an infrared pointer (usually mounted on a headband) to point to objects, text, or a keyboard on screen. Specialized software interacts with the infrared point to provide input to your application. However, if your application isn't tolerant of long delays in data entry input, it might frustrate the user's attempts to input information. In sum, accessibility programming often mean anticipating the unexpected.

Information, Documentation, and Support (Subpart D)

Most developers would rather not consider documentation and few have to deal with support issues, but these requirements are still part of the application. The requirements in this section would be relatively easy to implement if applications provided detailed help files in an organized format. However, the first problem that many applications will have to overcome is creating good help files in the first place.

The requirements of this section go beyond good help and support, however. You'll find that most of the rules encourage help in alternate formats. Many developers will feel that this means providing more than one help file with each application. However, I think that Microsoft has an optimal answer in this case. You'll notice that most of their help files are now in HTML format. Using HTML means that any application that can read Web sites in more than one format can also read HTML formatted help files in more than one format. We'll discuss this issue more as the book progresses, but it's an interesting concept to keep in mind.

The following sections describe the three innocent looking rules that will keep many developers awake at night. As you read the rules and explanations, remember that the government is assuming that you've already created a comprehensive help file or support system for users with average needs. If you don't have these elements in place, you'll need to create them before you can do anything with the Section 508 requirements.

(a) Product support documentation provided to end-users shall be made available in alternate formats upon request, at no additional charge.

Despite your best effort, some users might need to have their help files presented in a format other than the one used by most users of your application. Most developers today find that using HTML-based help overcomes most of these issues because a user can read it with a screen reader and view it even with a large text display. The browser comes with most of the functionality required by anyone with a special need. Some users might require help in a PDF or other format to meet a special requirement. We discuss this issue in the "Application Help and Support Issues" section of Chapter 4.

(b) End-users shall have access to a description of the accessibility and compatibility features of products in alternate formats or alternate methods upon request, at no additional charge.

You have to tell users about the accessibility features of your application so that they know if the product will meet their needs. Generally, you can tell the user about the features of your application by adding a separate section to the help file and to any printed documentation for your application. It's a good idea to provide this information on your Web site. We discuss this issue in the "Application Help and Support Issues" section of Chapter 4.

(c) Support services for products shall accommodate the communication needs of end-users with disabilities.

Developers only need to worry about some aspects of this rule. For example, you do need to tell the support staff how your application meets a specific accessibility need and how to troubleshoot that feature. However, you don't have to worry about how the company supports TTY access. The "Application Help and Support Issues" section of Chapter 4 discusses the issues that are pertinent to the developer; however, you shouldn't consider this section complete coverage for a company as a whole.

Understanding the Concept of Undue Burden

One of the confusion factors for Section 508 compliance is the use of the phrase "undue burden" throughout the government documents. You'll find this phrase used in a number of places and in a number of ways, but usually without any definition. In fact, the only definition for the term appears in Subpart A 1194.4 Definitions (http://www.section508.gov/index.cfm?FuseAction=Content&ID=12#Definitions).

Most of the requirements discussed in this chapter have this phrase attached to them. It's a loophole of sorts because the term is ambiguous and offers a vendor or government agency a way out of the Section 508 requirements. In general, the rules state that you must comply with the regulations unless doing so would cause an undue burden.

Sometimes the concept of undue burden is relatively easy to demonstrate. For example, the government doesn't expect a small company to implement Section 508 changes as quickly as a large company because the small company has fewer resources. The economic burden placed on a company by the Section 508 requirements are quantifiable and relatively easy to ascertain. The government does expect the small company to continue making progress toward Section 508 compliance, so this isn't a situation where a company could completely ignore the requirements. Undue burden, in this case, means getting more time to comply with the rules.

Another situation in which undue burden might occur is if the technology to implement a Section 508 requirement doesn't yet exist. Given the speed at which computers change, you should probably consider this form of undue burden temporary as well. The government requires that an agency or vendor exhaust every possible avenue for fixing a problem before saying that it's not possible. You can also be sure that the government will give such a claim close scrutiny.

You might find situations where undue burden is a little more difficult to prove. For example, consider the issue of security. An application that talks might help someone with a sight problem, but could cause security problems in sensitive applications. The application might not fall within the exceptions list that we discussed earlier, so proving that a Section 508 change poses a security risk is difficult. The Section 508 document at http://www.access-board.gov/sec508/508standards.htm contains additional text that helps in this case. The Access Board extends the undue burden definition to include security issues, but be aware that this addition isn't part of the actual criteria and is therefore subject to change.

It's easy to see that the term undue burden can mean a number of things depending on the situation and the people involved. This makes it hard to provide rules that say that an undue burden always exists with one set of conditions and doesn't exist under another set. Whenever you have a question about the viability of an undue burden claim, it's a good idea to contact the Access Board (http://www.access-board.gov/).

Section 508 Quick Reference for This Book

In the "An Overview of the Section 508 Standards" section of the chapter, you learned what each section of the law means—at least as an overview. We'll discuss every important issue presented by those sections somewhere in this book. Table 1-1 provides a quick reference you can use to find the correct section of the book quickly. This table will help you find just what you need to make your next application accessible. Note that some requirements have two or more entries because more than one section of the book applies.

Table 1-1. A Quick Reference for Section 508 Developer Requirements

Requirement	Chapter	Section Name
1194.21(a)	6	Entire chapter.
1194.21(a)	7	Entire chapter.
1194.21(b)	6	"Using the Keyboard Features Example," "Using the Sound Features Example," "Using the Display Features Example," and "Using the Mouse Features Example."
1194.21(c)	5	"Tracking the Screen Focus."

Table 1-1. A Quick Reference for Section 508 Developer Requirements (Continued)

Requirement	Chapter	Section Name
1194.21(c)	7	"Exposing the Screen Focus," Obtaining and Using Microsoft Active Accessibility," and "Using the .NET Accessibility Features."
1194.21(d)	7	"Implementing Consistent Controls, Status Indicators, and Other Elements," "Considering Balloon Help Issues," and "Adding Context Sensitive Help."
1194.21(e)	5	"Using Consistent Controls, Status Indicators, and Other Elements."
1194.21(f)	N/A	This feature is normally implemented by the operating system.
1194.21(g)	5	"Obtaining and Using the Current Display Settings Example."
1194.21(h)	2	"Understanding User Needs."
1194.21(h)	8	"Addressing Animation and Animation Alternatives."
1194.21(i)	4	"Building the Color Blindness Simulator Example."
1194.21(i)	5	"Working with Colors in Controls and UI Elements Example."
1194.21(j)	5	"Working with Colors in Controls and UI Elements Example."
1194.21(k)	4	"Understanding the Reconfigured System."
1194.21(l)	5	"Tracking the Screen Focus."
1194.22(a)	11	"<ALT> and <LONGDESC> Tags—the Low Tech Solution."
1194.22(b)	11	"Captioning Movies and Other Video Presentations."
1194.22(c)	4	"Building the Color Blindness Simulator Example."
1194.22(c)	9	"Avoiding Web Site Problems."
1194.22(c)	11	"Alternatives to Using Color for Information Example."
1194.22(d)	11	"Using CSS Example."
1194.22(e)	11	"Working with Image Maps Example."
1194.22(f)	11	"Working with Image Maps Example."
1194.22(g)	9	"Creating Accessibility Friendly Tables Example."

Table 1-1. A Quick Reference for Section 508 Developer Requirements (Continued)

Requirement	Chapter	Section Name
1194.22(h)	9	"Creating Accessibility Friendly Tables Example."
1194.22(i)	9	"Avoiding Web Site Problems."
1194.22(j)	4	"Understanding the Reconfigured System."
1194.22(k)	2	"Understanding User Needs."
1194.22(k)	10	Entire chapter.
1194.22(l)	13	"Creating Accessibility Friendly Scripts Example."
1194.22(m)	9	"Avoiding Web Site Problems."
1194.22(n)	5	"Data Entry Example."
1194.22(n)	9	"Schema Additions for the Database Developer."
1194.22(o)	9	"Avoiding Web Site Problems."
1194.22(p)	9	"Avoiding Web Site Problems."
1194.23	N/A	The developer might need to provide support to a third party vendor but won't implement this requirement personally.
1194.24(a)	N/A	N/A
1194.24(b)	N/A	N/A
1194.24(c)	11	"Captioning Movies and Other Video Presentations."
1194.24(d)	11	"Captioning Movies and Other Video Presentations."
1194.24(e)	11	"Captioning Movies and Other Video Presentations."
1194.25	N/A	The developer might need to provide support to a third party vendor but won't implement this requirement personally.
1194.26(a)	N/A	N/A
1194.26(b)	N/A	N/A
1194.26(c)	3	"Biometric Device Issues."
Subpart C (a)	6	"Using the Display Features Example."
Subpart C (b)	5	"Obtaining and Using the Current Display Settings Example."
Subpart C (b)	6	"Using the Display Features Example."

Table 1-1. A Quick Reference for Section 508 Developer Requirements (Continued)

Requirement	Chapter	Section Name
Subpart C (c)	6	"Using the Sound Features Example."
Subpart C (d)	4	"Special Devices for Those with Special Needs."
Subpart C (d)	6	"Using the Sound Features Example."
Subpart C (e)	8	"Relying On Speech as the Second Input Method."
Subpart C (e)	12	"Avoiding the Pitfalls of Speech-Only Input."
Subpart C (f)	6	"Ensuring Your Application Allows Multiple Input Methods."
Subpart C (f)	9	"Supporting Both the Mouse and Keyboard."
Subpart C (f)	13	"Include Both Mouse and Keyboard Support."
Subpart D (a)	4	"Application Help and Support Issues."
Subpart D (b)	4	"Application Help and Support Issues."
Subpart D (c)	4	"Application Help and Support Issues."

Summary

This chapter has presented Section 508 in several different ways. First, we discussed the reason why Section 508 is important to companies in general and the developer specifically. Second, we converted the legalese of the Section 508 requirements into something that the average human can understand. Finally, we discussed implementation—the details of what you need to know in order to add full Section 508 support to your application.

Now it's time to do something with the information you've learned. Reading a simplified version of the requirements doesn't necessarily mean you actually understand them. You need to begin applying the requirements to your applications—both desktop and Web-based. Make sure you check out the Web sites that I included in this chapter because they'll help you understand Section 508 better.

Chapter 2 will also help you begin to apply the Section 508 requirements to your application. No, we aren't going to begin writing code immediately—you need to create a design first. Applying the Section 508 requirements to your application in a logical order and creating an implementation plan will make your application update job easier. Of course, this chapter also applies to new application development. The best time to adhere to the Section 5.08 requirements is before you've added a single line of code to your application.

Understanding the Section 508 Requirements

In This Chapter:

What Are the Usability Requirements for Section 508 Compliance?

What Are the Performance Requirements for Section 508 Compliance?

Why Is Content More Important Than Presentation?

How Do I Learn What the User Needs?

Are There Special Issues to Consider?

What Are Typical Developer Questions about Section 508?

KNOWING THE RULES—the letter of the law—is only useful if you know what the rules actually mean. In Chapter 1, we discussed the letter of the law, and the various sections put the law into plain language that everyone speaks (versus the lawyer-speak of the government regulations). However, we still haven't answered the question of what these rules actually mean to the developer. This chapter will take the rules apart and help you understand what you'll actually need to implement as part of an application design or upgrade.

The chapter divides the rules into functional areas (you'll find there's some overlap) that include usability, performance, user needs, and special requirements. The usability section deciphers what you actually need to do in order to comply with the Section 508 requirements. The performance section points out the need to make the usability changes and still maintain a certain level of application throughput. The user needs section includes the concept of making changes that users will understand and use without a lot of developer intervention. Finally, there are some requirements that don't affect the application's usability, performance, or the user's ability to interact with it—these rules appear in the special issues section.

This chapter also has a question and answer section at the end. I based the questions on those found in newsgroups and on others sent to me personally.

None of the questions is a direct quote. I plan to keep adding to this question and answer list on my Web site at `http://www.mwt.net/~jmueller/` after this book is finished. If you have a question, send it to me at `JMueller@mwt.net` and let me know if I can publish both the question and answer on my Web site.

Usability Requirements

There's an important distinction between usability and accessibility. For instance, a developer can create an application that includes all of the required accessibility features and the application can still be unusable. *Accessibility* is a measure of a user's ability to interact with the application. *Usability* is a measure of the user's ability to understand the application's operation, purpose, and contents. Only when an application is both accessible and usable can a user use the application to perform a given task with little or no outside (human) help. The problem is that many applications today aren't usable, much less accessible.

Usability takes many forms. For example, you could measure the time required for a user to figure out how to type in a word processor. At one time (some of you might not have even experienced this problem), word processors weren't necessarily easy to type in because the user had to create a document first. Today, word processors normally present a blank document when you start them. When working with these older word processors, the process of creating a document was outside of the user's experience because writing a document by hand, or even typing it, didn't require this step. Word Perfect was the first word processor to get this part of the picture correct. A Word Perfect user could start the application and begin typing immediately. At one time, this simple advantage was all Word Perfect needed to dominate the marketplace.

Most users will try to use procedures they learned early in life to interact with the computer because they have no other way of interacting with it. Consider the fact that many users anthropomorphize their computers. They'll say that the computer hates them or that it went out of its way to make life miserable, when in reality, the computer has no feelings at all. Trying to explain that a behavior always has a logical origin is difficult when even the engineer can't replicate a given behavior all of the time. Computers are complex devices, but it's your responsibility as a developer to make them easy to use. The developer has to make the computer fit the user's perception of the world. To do this, it's important to consider what the real world looks like to most people.

TIP One of the most common errors that developers make when checking the usability or accessibility of an application is relying on input from users who are too familiar with the application. Not only is the user familiar with the interface, but the user is also aware of special terminology used with the application. Familiarity, even with users who do have special needs, gives a false indication when testing new functionality. The user has no learning curve to overcome and therefore provides a false input on the difficulty of using a feature or the usefulness of a new interface element. Always run usability and performance tests with inexperienced users. In fact, choose someone who's never seen the application before for the final set of application tests. Using this technique is the only way you'll get a good usability and accessibility reading.

Unfortunately, as many researchers have already found out the hard way, figuring out what's usable to a group of people is difficult. As soon as someone feels that the researcher is watching them, they alter their behavior. Surveys also have problems because many people view them as a test to pass, rather than as a chance to provide valuable input. In fact, the problem is so significant that many researchers have used bizarre lab setups to ensure the quality of the input they receive—unfortunately, the input is still suspect. So, how do you ensure your application is usable if you don't get good input using the direct approach? Here are a few tricks that *I've* tried that seem to work well because they approach the problem of usability from an entirely different perspective.

- Look at the number of complaints about application content.

- Track how often people actually use an application feature by discretely recording its use in a log.

- Assume the user doesn't know about the feature and tell them about it during a training session—body language will often tell you all you need to know.

- Obtain copies of files created with the application to see how users are putting documents together.

- Add an item to the application Help menu that lets the user quickly access a support person or at least a support request form.

- Create a suggestion box–type application where users can input suggestions anonymously.

All of these suggestions require some tact. Remember that the focus is the application and the user's needs for it—not your coding ability or design skills. You'll also want to gain approval from management before you implement any of the suggestions. For example, many users will consider tracking use of an application an invasion of privacy unless you obtain the proper permissions first. Consider making at least some of the input Web-based. Many companies now have online suggestion boxes such as the one shown in Figure 2-1. Note that you'll find this example at `http://www.schaffnerelectrotest.com/suggestion.html`.

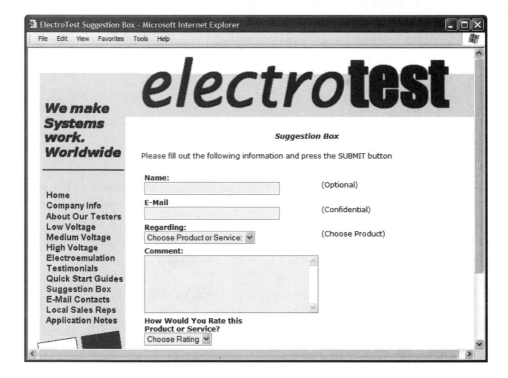

Figure 2-1. Web-based suggestion box applications help employees make suggestions from wherever they might be.

This suggestion box application is typical of most applications of this type. It contains blanks for a name, email address, the main topic or product, the suggestion text, and a rating. Notice that the name and the email address are optional. You want to encourage the user to provide the information, even if they have to provide it anonymously. In some cases, this is the only way that you'll receive usability information of any kind.

Performance Requirements

Many developers make the mistake of equating performance with speed. This is a skewed vision of the term endorsed by the media and supported by vendors with a desire to sell (and upgrade) products. Speed is exciting, so equating speed (excitement) with performance (a desirable trait) can help drive both application and hardware sales. However, if you look at the dictionary definition, you'll discover that performance has nothing to do with speed—how fast someone can accomplish a task. The best way to view performance is as a measure of how the application helps someone perform a task, with an emphasis on performing the task *well*. It doesn't matter how fast someone can perform a task if they perform the task incorrectly or incompletely. In addition, performance is often a measure of the ease or efficiency with which the user can work with the application.

So bear in mind that when the Section 508 requirements speak of performance—they aren't considering the speed at which someone performs a task. The fact that the user can perform the task at all is somewhat amazing in many cases. In addition, the focus isn't on the user—it's on the application. The application provides features that enable a user to perform a given task well—not necessarily fast. In short, performing the task completely and correctly with the least amount of effort is the true measure of performance—speed is the result of an application that performs well in many cases, but it isn't a required result.

Here's an example of how performance differs from speed. An application that automatically changes resolution with an increase in display pixel count so that the viewer sees a clearer display but doesn't observe a change in display elements performs well. (We'll discuss the issue of resolution versus display pixel count in the "Helping Users with Visual Needs" section of the chapter.) The application isn't any faster, but it does help the user perform a task well by getting the most our of the display's capabilities. The following sections describe the Section 508 performance requirements.

 TIP The many faces of performance we discuss in this section don't include speed for one reason—speed is often the end result of everything else that you do to bring a site into compliance. An interesting article, "The State of Web Accessibility," that discusses some of the side effects of following the accessibility guidelines appears at http://www.extremetech.com/article2/0,3973,11774,00.asp. There are a couple of concepts that this article brings out. The first is that a good Web page is like a good restaurant—it provides comfort that keeps customers coming back again and again. The second is that a Web page that follows the accessibility guidelines will also load fast and be highly efficient.

Developing with Consistency in Mind

Consistency is one of the big performance indicators for Section 508. An application that performs well has an interface where the meaning of user interface (UI) elements remains the same from one screen to the next. However, consistency goes beyond interface element functionality. It also means that the effect of an action is always the same, no matter how the user arrived at the decision point in question. Finally, consistency means that the user will obtain the same results every time they use the application to perform a given task.

 TIP   If you want to learn all the ins and outs of user interface development, look at *User Interface Design For Programmers* by Joel Spolsky (Apress, 2001). You can find the book at `http://www.apress.com/book/bookDisplay.html?bID=10`. Joel makes user interface design seem simple and fun. You can also learn more about Joe by checking out his Web site at `http://www.joelonsoftware.com`.

Unfortunately, most applications today *aren't* consistent. Let's consider the issue of UI elements first. The following list tells you what you need to consider as you judge the consistency of an application you create from a user interface perspective.

Buttons and Other Controls: Some applications will give two buttons the same name, yet assign the buttons different purposes. Click OK on one screen and the application cancels the action because you agree that it's not a good action to take. Yet, on another screen, clicking the same OK button will tell the application to take a selection action. Even more confusing is when clicking OK simply closes the dialog box and you don't see any action at all. The same holds true for all other controls. If you want maximum application performance, the application must provide consistent control action.

Error Messages: Providing the user with an error response can prove difficult because of the various ways in which the user will interact with the application. However, it's essential to provide consistent error messaging because otherwise the user is likely to get confused and/or frustrated. I've seen some applications that will display some error messages directly on the form, some in a message box, and still others on the status bar. Some applications simply beep at you and hope that you'll notice. Strive to make the error message content as well. A good error message box provides simple input to the user. It should state, in the simplest terms possible, what went wrong, tell what the potential results are, and say how to fix the problem. The message box should also provide a pushbutton for displaying diagnostic information that the user can easily copy and send to the developer.

Prompts: I'm often amazed at the prompts that applications provide because they confuse, rather than help, the user. One custom database application included the same prompt for every field, "Type some text." Many people have laughed about the user who searches for the "any" key after seeing the "Press any key" prompt. These are examples of just two prompts that don't quite do the job. Make sure the prompts in your application are specific. For example, you can tell the user to "Press Enter" because every keyboard in the world contains such a key. The prompts should tell where to obtain required information—direct them to a manager if nothing else. Finally, a prompt should provide examples if necessary. For example, in a first name field of an employee data entry form, you could provide this prompt, "Type the first name of the employee, such as John or Mary, as it appears on the job application."

Labeling: Make sure that any labeling you provide for an application is consistent. If you identify a dialog box as the Widget Selector in one place, make sure you use the term consistently throughout for the same dialog box. This concept applies to the language used for prompts, capitalization, and all other labeling elements as well. For example, if one data entry field label ends with a colon, make sure they all end with a colon. In fact, it often helps to set up a style guide for labels as part of the specification for your application.

Organization: An application should use a consistent organization of user interface elements. For example, if your application starts with a menu system, it should always use a menu system. If prompts appear on the status bar of one screen, they should appear on the status bar of all screens. The menus should always use the same format. For example, the Exit command should always appear as an item on the File menu. If you include a Window menu on one screen, then include it on every other screen unless the menu item has no purpose. Also, place fields and prompts in the same locations on forms. Don't fall into the trap of organizing only the visual elements of your application—make sure that the application structure (the user interface elements that make the application operational) is organized as well. For example, the tab order of a form isn't apparent when you look at it, but it becomes apparent when you use the form.

Speed Keys and Shortcuts: People with special needs rely heavily on the speed keys and shortcuts that applications provide. A speed key can reduce the number of keystrokes the user has to make to perform a task (or determine whether they can perform the task at all). Of course, if the speed key appears on one screen and not another, it serves as a source of confusion, rather than as a navigational aid. The same holds true for shortcuts. Large forms are hard for someone with special needs to navigate, but a shortcut can help the user access the field quickly. Make sure you always underline the trigger character and always use a consistent key access technique (Alt+<letter> is the most common). Fortunately for Windows desktop application developers, all you need to add is an ampersand (&) in front of the character you want to use for the trigger and the Windows API takes care of the rest.

On-Screen Text: This is probably one of the worst problems that applications have and the most confusing for users. The problem is made worse because Windows seldom uses consistent screen text, so any access of common features leaves your application open to consistency problems. You should decide how to create the screen text during the design phase. For example, make sure the application uses a single term, phrases, or sentences throughout. The single term form of "User Name," might appear as "Enter User Name" in phrase form, and "Type the user's first name." in sentence form. Generally, most users find the single or the phrase form easier to navigate so long as the application provides good prompts.

Developing with Reliability in Mind

This is one of those categories that some developers place in the "impossible to achieve" category. However, it's possible to create reliable applications—I've even seen a few. Unfortunately, they're a rare and endangered species. We won't delve into the intricacies of creating reliable applications because that's a topic for another book, but we will discuss some reliability issues as part of the examples later. It's important to consider reliability as the topmost priority for any application. Reliable applications save time, money, and effort.

Of course, there are a few things you should consider when creating reliable, accessibility-friendly applications. For example, many developers assume too much about the keying ability of the user. However, this is the first check an application should make because it can cause the most trouble. Make sure the input is the right type and the right length for starters. Try to validate the input to ensure that it's correct. Offer specific choices whenever possible. Always add error checking to handle unanticipated input, because it will happen.

As part of the reliability considerations, you also need to create applications with as much input and output device independence as possible. You do need to consider several problems in this area. For instance, taking the common device approach does tend to make your application more accessible by helping it work with more devices. Broader device support usually translates into better reliability.

However, there is also the reality of vendor differentiation to consider. At some point you need to consider whether your application is going to accomplish a given task using the feature set common to all devices. In most cases the answer is yes, but in some cases you might find that the common feature set is too small. It's an imperfect world where the developer must consider how the feature set of the input and output devices will affect the reliability, friendliness, and performance of the application as a whole.

An application should also monitor the operating system, the hardware, the network, and the user environment. Flexible applications detect changes and try to accommodate them. The loss of a printer shouldn't mean that the application curls up and dies somewhere in the corner. Make sure the error handling you provide is specific—this might mean providing more than one layer of error handling so that your application can detect specific causes of problems and tell the user about them.

When a reliable application finally exhausts every potential means for resolving a problem, it should degrade gracefully and not fail. The application should tell the user that a specific feature is inaccessible and make sure the user understands why (if it's possible to determine the specific cause). Remember, for a reliable application, failure is not an option.

Developing Thrifty Applications

An application should use resources efficiently. The common thread for today's developer is that time is money and everyone has a powerful system with infinite resources. Both of these fallacies can cause problems when developing an application. More importantly, making these assumptions will reduce the appeal of your application to those with special needs because they characteristically own older machines with limited resources.

Let's look at the first fallacy—time is money. Actually, it should say that the inefficient use of time wastes money. The use of time to create a reliable application that provides both good performance and is easy-to-use actually saves time. The shortsighted approach of getting an application out the door as quickly as possible usually results in applications that require an infinite number of patches and a large support staff. In addition, users waste time learning how to use the application and contending with its poor design. A commercial vendor also spends money trying to repair the damage to the marketability of the application. When a company considers developer time more important than any other factor, everyone loses.

Some companies have also stopped optimizing their code because they consider it too expensive. After all, it's much easier to force the user to obtain a larger hard drive or more memory. The problem is that many users are happy with the performance of their hardware and have no desire to update it. Most trade press magazines have run one or more stories recently that sales of hardware have decreased. As user hardware continues to age, the users will demand that applications use resources more efficiently, and there isn't any reason to disappoint them. In addition, you must consider the fact that accessible technology tends to run 12 to 18 months behind the current technology curve because the companies that produce this technology have smaller research and development budgets.

Developing Applications with Added Functionality

We discussed a number of performance criteria in the "Functional Performance Criteria (Subpart C)" section of Chapter 1. If you want to know precisely what the law requires, this is the section to check. However, these rules stop short of making performance the type of feature that everyone will want. The previous sections provide the added features that you need in order to make the functionality appealing to everyone.

The law does discuss specific modes of operation. When you design your application, you need to include these special requirements as part of the application, not as an attachment or afterthought. For example, attempting to add screen reader support after the fact is very difficult. It's nearly impossible (not to mention more costly) to write an application that automatically adjusts itself to the user environment. Such adjustments might mean moving controls around so that they display correctly when the user selects a large text or high contrast mode. Figure 2-2 shows the results of a failure to plan when a user decides to use a large text font in high contrast mode in a common application.

If you're wondering if this is the Accessibility Options dialog box, you're correct. I placed my system in high contrast mode. Unfortunately, there are several problems with just this simple dialog box. Notice that the title bar didn't expand to include the additional text—it's cut off so that you can no longer read the title of the dialog box. The text within the dialog box didn't change. Therefore, the user of this application can see that they can no longer read anything in the Accessibility Options dialog box, but they might not be able to do anything about it. The dialog box doesn't expand either. In addition, Windows doesn't provide the user with any instructions for correcting the display—not that they could read them even if the dialog box included them.

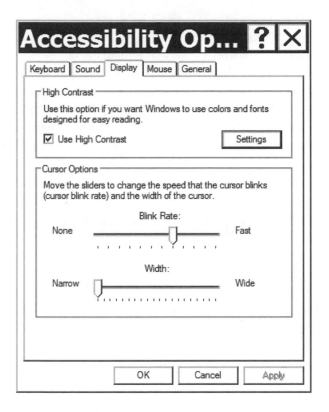

Figure 2-2. Failure to plan for user needs often results in applications that don't work in accessibilty modes.

NOTE Even when accessible technology is operative and usable, it doesn't always help as intended. Consider the complaint of a therapist who said that someone she helped had problems even when the assistive technology worked. This person needed to magnify the text on the computer screen to be able to read it, but the text became distorted and consequently, it was difficult for the therapist to assist her. It turns out the problem was physical, rather than software related. The user had to work very hard to shift the screen around to see everything. Because of spatial difficulties and the user's limited head coordination, an assistant still had to move the screen, which defeated the purpose of the assistive technology. A combination of additional hardware and software would have resolved the situation, but they weren't available to this user.

This situation is correctable—at least a little. Figure 2-3 shows another view of the same dialog box after I changed the various font settings manually. I also had to change the DPI setting for the monitor (located on the General tab of the monitor and display adapter Properties dialog box). Notice that the results are still disappointing, but more usable for the person with special needs. Unfortunately, these changes force everyone who uses the computer to see everything in large type, even if they don't want this feature. Of course, everyone could change the system and reboot it every time they log on—not the most convenient way to work with the computer.

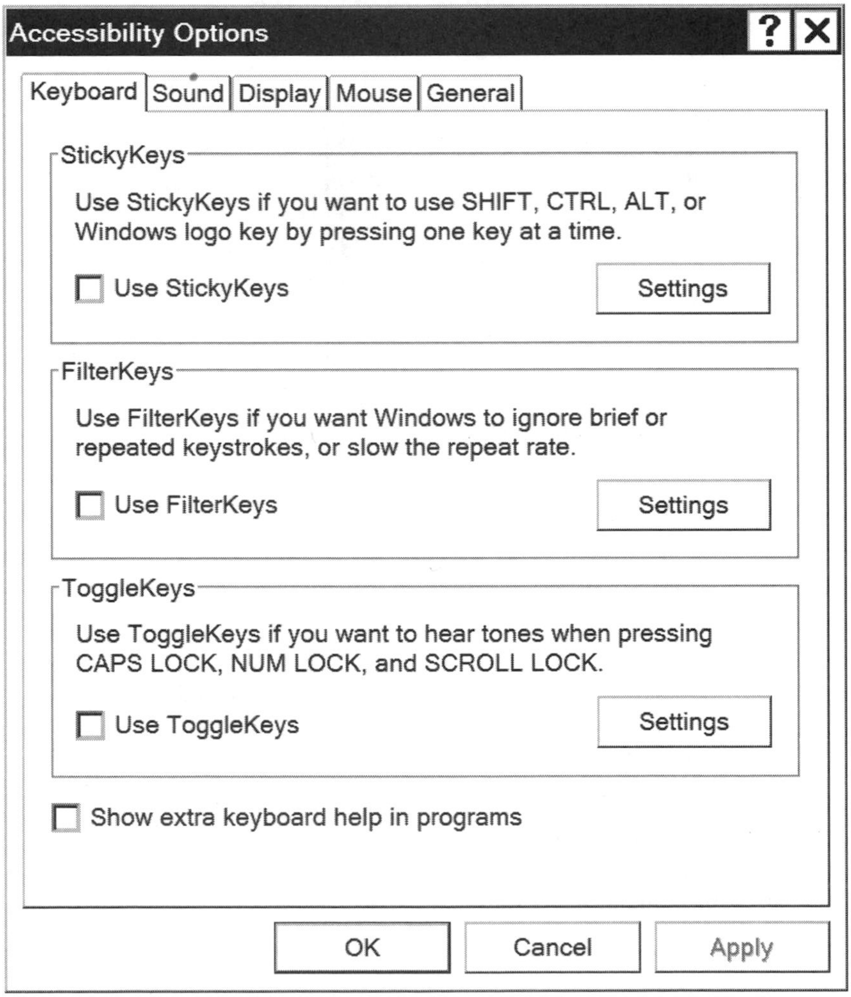

Figure 2-3. Attempting to compensate for poor planning by changing the environment normally doesn't work.

In short, no matter what the user does, the Accessibility Options dialog box is going to remain somewhat unusable. Now consider the fact that Figure 2-2 is what the people who actually use the accessibility features regularly see and you'll understand why most of them consider accessibility support less than thrilling. Getting to Figure 2-3 requires an intermediate to advanced knowledge of Windows, and even this solution is problematic.

Some developers might find the functionality requirements difficult to meet and might ask why they should implement them at all. Let's look at some other functionality requirements that everyone takes for granted today. Consider the television remote control. This device originally came as an option for those with restricted movement. As you know, all televisions come with remote controls today. A person with full mobility can get up and adjust the television, but most of them use the remote control because it's easier.

In the not too distant future, most computers will come with a speech and text reader interface as a part of the standard feature set. Using large text mode might become more common as people with tired eyes begin to realize that there's relief available at the touch of a button. High contrast displays are already quite useful when working with a computer at the beach or other area where the sun is a problem. In short, the features that developers consider extra today will become common tomorrow.

Understanding User Needs

A developer friend of mine stated that he never understood what users needed so well as he did after spending several months training them. Application operations that he thought were clear and easy to understand turned out to be counterintuitive for many users. He learned important lessons by interacting with the people who would eventually use the application he had built. Many developers could benefit from the same experience—learning new user-oriented development skills by interacting with users. After all, if a user can't understand an application, then all the creative programming that you used to create it doesn't accomplish anything.

ON THE WEB It's truly essential to get the "user eye" view of usage problems when creating accessible applications. The Bridge School (http://www.bridgeschool.org/main.html) Web site is important because it discusses current strategies for using assistive technology (AT), and augmentative and alternative means of communication (AAC) applications. Visiting this site can help you understand the user eye view of how accessible applications can help everyone become more productive.

In fact, the technique of developers studying user behavior to see if there's a better way to do things has been at the heart of many computer evolutions in the past. Consider the story of the Xerox Palo Alto Research Center (PARC) research. The reason that the Macintosh and Windows user interfaces behave the way they do today is, in part, due to this research. Unfortunately, it seems this research didn't go quite far enough. Yes, both Windows and the Macintosh feature user interface elements that make them easier to use than the text-based interfaces of the past, but there are still a lot of problems with the current system. For example, working with the interfaces isn't always as easy and straightforward as it could be. Consider the experience of a therapist who wanted to connect an accessibility device to a Windows machine. A technical assistant, unfamiliar with the interface device, spent upwards of 5 hours matching up the keyboard interface between the Vanguard talker and the Windows computer. A more intuitive interface would have greatly reduced the time and frustration of installing this device.

TIP Studying some of the successes and failures of PARC can prove enlightening. The main PARC Web site is at `http://www.parc.xerox.com/`. You can find some interesting historical information in many places on the Web. One such place is the Xerox PARC—History of the GUI Web site at `http://www.cs.stir.ac.uk/~sjr/xerox.html`. Another good site is TechTV—History of Xerox PARC, which you can find at `http://www.techtv.com/screensavers/supergeek/story/0,24330,3325561,00.html`. There are many other good places to look; this is just a very small sampling.

The biggest problem in creating interfaces is one of communication. For many developers, the idea that someone can't figure out how to use their application is absurd. The developer can simply look at most applications and figure out how to use them in a matter of minutes. However, most users aren't developers and some are hostile to the entire concept of computers. In many cases, the user doesn't understand the computer and doesn't want to understand it. Section 508 requirements can even help in this area by helping make applications almost light switch simple to run.

Sometimes a real world example is the best way to understand a problem. A recent Baseline case study of the Detroit Resource Management System (DRMS) pronounced "dreams," shows that the system quickly became a labyrinthine maze of old and new procedures. (See the article at `http://www.nyq.baselinemag.com/article2/0,3959,655936,00.asp` for details.)

The article contains a number of lessons for the astute developer. One piece of information to note in the article is that training costs for the project quickly reached five times the amount that the project leaders originally budgeted. Users required training in such basics as mouse usage—something the project developers never anticipated because the very thought that someone might not know how to use a mouse never entered their minds.

One of the case study conclusions is that the new system might have worked better if it had considered worker abilities and provided a means of changing some archaic work processes. Given that the employees were used to using a keyboard-only system from the 70s, it might have been easier for them to learn a keyboard-only system with the new application. Now consider the fact that keyboard-only accessibility is a Section 508 requirement and you'll understand how complete compliance with the requirements could have helped this situation.

With these problems in mind, let's look at some of the areas where current application development can improve. The following sections discuss the issues that the Section 508 requirements described in Chapter 1 help solve. Each section looks at a different area of accessibility including visual, audio, physical, and cognitive. As you go through these sections, remember that I'm trying to present the conflict that's taking placing in application development today with the user's needs and the Section 508 requirements as the focal point. The advice provided might run counter to what most developers actually provide in a given situation.

Avoiding Gadgetitis

One of the essential problems in creating usable and accessible Web sites and applications today is what I call the "gadget factor." There's a basic conflict between the issues of presentation and content on most Web sites today caused by the gadget factor. Although desktop applications aren't quite as bad as Web-based applications when it comes to overt signs of too many gadgets, desktop applications often suffer from feature bloat created by supposedly useful features that no one actually uses.

Most developers truly want people to use their Web site or application, so they dress it up with gadgets in an effort to make it more appealing. Presentation becomes the vehicle by which the developer hopes to obtain a level of recognition. The developer becomes a showman who hawks wares using the tired tactics of the carny. Unfortunately, the Web site or application might not be the greatest show on earth precisely, because it does contain too many gadgets.

The problems for Web-based application developers aren't limited to presentation. Developers also need to consider compatibility issues. The gadgets used by one browser don't necessarily work with other browsers. Consequently, developers constantly fiddle with the HTML on their Web sites in an effort to enhance compatibility. However, as the developer adds more gadgets and fiddles with the HTML, the Web site may actually become less usable and definitely less accessible. You can read the details about this problem at http://builder.cnet.com/webbuilding/pages/Authoring/Accessibility/.

The user, on the other hand, doesn't care about the presentation nearly as much as the content provided by the Web site or application. Accessing information quickly and without much thought is at the center of the user's universe. In short, the very gadgets that are supposed to make the application more appealing, end up distracting the users that can navigate them and making the application inaccessible to those who can't.

Section 508 rules tend to side with the needs of the user. Whenever a Web site or application contains a feature that doesn't serve any useful purpose (other than gaudy decoration), you should consider whether the feature is even useful. For example, do you really need an animation showing a rotating "New" sign that also flashes the name of your company in Morse code? Sometimes a simple icon is all you need. The point is that you need to think about the usefulness of a gadget before you add it to a Web site or application.

Helping Users with Visual Needs

Most people take their vision for granted—they assume that they'll continue to see the world every day. However, vision isn't a given and many people have special needs in this area. Of course, the most extreme vision problem is not being able to see at all, but visual acuity problems vary from slight to a need for thick glasses. Users with moderate vision loss often require larger fonts and dialog boxes in order to see these screen elements. Sometimes visual acuity isn't the question— the person may not see color or may not understand what they see. In sum, the visual perception that most people take for granted is less reliable than most people think.

Many computer systems are visual in nature. In fact, until recently, there was no other aspect to some computer systems. Sound cards are a relatively recent innovation given the time that computers have been in use. The problem with having a visual-only source of information is that it doesn't work well when you can't see. Until the last few years, computers were completely unusable by those who can't see. The presence of a GUI doesn't always mean easy access. Originally, people developed screen readers for DOS. These readers worked well, so Windows 3.1 was actually a step backward for those who used screen readers until new software became available. The use of screen readers helps make computers accessible today, but only when applications cooperate.

The problem with the visual aspects of computers isn't limited to those without vision; the visual problems also affect those with other eye ailments. For example, some beautifully colored Web sites are almost invisible to those with color blindness. The same is true for some types of desktop applications, but to a lesser degree, because the Windows environment tends to enforce some color constraints. Of course, the problem isn't just limited to those with color blindness—color also causes problems for those using black and white displays or those with displays that have other limitations. In general, you want to avoid using similar colors and use the color blindness checker that we'll build in Chapter 4 to ensure that your application is readable.

 TIP Some people think there's only one type of color blindness, but there are several. In addition, the term "blindness" isn't precisely correct—the person has a perception problem. The color still registers—it just doesn't register correctly. In other words, they still see something, but it isn't the right color as the majority of the population sees it. You can learn more about the physical problems of color blindness at `http://www.firelily.com/opinions/color.html`. Another good place to learn how color blindness can affect a user's perception of your Web site is at `http://msdn.microsoft.com/voices/hess10092000.asp`. This particular site has some actual color output you can use to better understand the problems some people have with color. Notice how some of the text is nearly invisible, even when the colors are different.

The color issue is a sticky one because teachers and parents teach most children to use color for expression from an early age. Some of you might wonder just how many people use black and white displays today. After all, for some developers the black and white display went out with the green screens of ages past. However, high contrast displays used by those with low vision are essentially black and white. In addition, many small devices such as personal digital assistants (PDAs) rely on black and white screens. In some cases, kiosks also use black and white displays because they work better in public environments. In other words, black and white displays appear in many places that you wouldn't expect. We'll discuss the color issues in detail in the "Developing with Color in Mind" section of the chapter. For now, consider color one of the more problematic issues for those with vision problems.

Another problem has crept into the computer environment almost unnoticed, but it's getting progressively worse. At one time, everyone had a small display, so most vendors designed applications around a 640×480-pixel display. Technology improved, so vendors moved to an 800×600-pixel display. At this point, many developers assume the user has a minimum of a 1024×768-pixel display and that number is increasing.

Now, consider what the number of pixels does to the display. Say you have a 17-inch diagonal display. That number actually reflects the size of the cathode ray tube (CRT) or other display device inside the monitor. The bezel—the outer covering that holds the CRT in place—reduces the display size of the monitor to about

16-inches in most cases. Given the 16-inch actual diagonal display area, the horizontal display width is 12.75 inches and the vertical display height is 9.5 inches. At the 640×480-pixel display size, there are 50 dots (pixels) per inch (dpi). Using an 800×600-pixel display increases that number to 62.5, and at a 1024×768-pixel display size the user is looking at 80 dpi. As you can see, each increase in display size increases the dpi, which means that display elements appear smaller unless you increase their size to make use of the additional resolution.

How much smaller do display elements appear to the user? Let's consider a 17-inch monitor again. On a 640×480 display, a 640×480-pixel dialog box would consume the entire 12.75×9.5 inches of the display. Move to an 800×600-pixel display and the same 640×480-pixel dialog box is only 10.2×7.6 inches. The 1024×768-pixel display in common use today makes the dialog box shrink to 8×6 inches. A user that can see a dialog box well using 640×480-pixel display may not see it at all using a 1024×768-pixel display given the same monitor size. Of course, if the number of pixels used by the dialog box increases in proportion is the display resolution, the dialog box physical size won't change and the user gains a clearer display due to the increased resolution (dpi). Unfortunately, few, if any applications on the market actually consider the display resolution, so the user simply sees a smaller dialog box.

Vendors are using the increased number of pixels on the display to present more information to the viewer. The size of the display elements hasn't increased, but the number of elements on a given screen has. The problem is that using such large dialog box sizes makes it impossible for those with low vision to navigate the display. Some people with low vision use a 640×480-pixel display so that they can see the various screen elements. Using a lower resolution display means that dialog boxes that would fit on the display for anyone else don't fit for the person with special needs (a dialog box sized to 800×600 pixels doesn't fit well on a 640×480-pixel display). The fact that the dialog box isn't sizeable makes the problem worse. Microsoft attempted to get rid of this particular issue in Windows XP by removing the source of the conflict—you can now use the system only in 800×600-pixel display mode and above. The 640×480-pixel display mode that many people with vision problems relied on is gone.

The visual problems also extend to the user interface. A lack of cues, disorganized displays, and faulty descriptions all conspire to make an application unusable. We'll discuss many of these issues as the book progresses. In fact, we'll discuss some of these problems in the "Adding Visual and Audio Cues" section of this chapter.

Helping Users with Audio Needs

Very few Web sites and desktop applications use audio in any significant way today. The main reason is that most businesses wouldn't function well if every cubicle in the building had some type of audio playing. The resulting cacophony would derail any benefits of using sound. Consequently, most developers will have fewer audio problems to consider in their applications than the visual problems we just discussed.

The main problem of using audio occurs when you need it to convey information of some type. The Section 508 requirements state that you must include some non-aural method of obtaining the same information. Unlike visual information, it's not always easy to describe a sound. For example, how would you describe the sound a jet makes and describe how it differs from a similar sound, such as a tornado, to someone who is and always has been deaf? In short, it would be tough. However, I don't think the Section 508 requirements are asking you to perform this task—information is construed as something you can describe.

Generally, if you have someone speaking on your Web site, such as part of an online presentation, then you also need to provide a transcript of what they say along with closed or open captioning of the actual words. The closed or open captioning must remain in synch with the presentation so the person with a hearing difficulty can follow along just as easily as someone with normal hearing. Finally, you need to provide some means to make the presentation flow smoothly with the closed captioning in place. For example, you wouldn't want the words to appear over an important drawing—that error would leave the user without any clues as to how the text applies to the presentation.

You also have to ensure that sound doesn't interfere with the use of assistive technology. For example, you wouldn't want music used to enhance the atmosphere of your application to interfere with the use of a screen reader. The user should have some means of turning the application specific sound off (or at least down) to hear the screen reader voice better. In Chapter 1, we discussed that your application can't interfere with the operation of assistive technology, and unwanted sound would definitely interfere.

Helping Users with Physical Needs

Most people associate computer use with couch potato syndrome. After all, you're just sitting in front of a screen all day. Some developers are apparently trying to correct this perception by engaging the user in finger gymnastics. At least no one using a computer will have fat fingers. The other day I had to get my fingers to work around a Ctrl+Shift+S combination to invoke the Search dialog box of an application. Now, imagine that you only have one arm or perhaps no arms, or that you need to use a head control interface device and are trying to perform this combination—impossible! What if you have full use of your limbs, but arthritis or carpal tunnel syndrome prevents full mobility. The finger gymnastics go from fun to undoable in one easy step.

Finger gymnastics aren't the only problem facing those with physical problems. Have you tried to get around Windows lately without using a mouse? It's possible, but hardly easy or straightforward. In fact, using the keyboard alone is nearly impossible with Windows and is impossible with some applications. The lack of usable keyboard shortcuts and speed keys makes using either Windows or the application an incredibly painful experience. The originators of the graphical interface never meant the mouse to replace the keyboard, but in some cases, it has.

Add to these problems that fact that many people suffer from perceptual and cognitive problems. Imagine trying to figure out that you need to press Ctrl+Shift+S to display a search screen if you already have difficulty learning to use the Start menu or repeating a search by pressing F3. Some people can't remember that Ctrl+Alt+F3 displays a menu in one application and erases a file in another. If your application requires odd keyboard or mouse movements to accomplish the simplest task, you'll find that many people can't use it at all.

Understanding Shortcuts and Speed Keys

For those developers who don't know what shortcuts and speed keys are, a *shortcut* is a quick method to execute an application command, while a *speed key* is a quick method to access a field on the display. (Some developers also call shortcuts *accelerators* because that's the term used in some development packages such as Visual C++.) Shortcuts normally appear on the menu to the right of the menu action. For example, most applications list Ctrl+P as the shortcut for printing the document. Here is an example of a shortcut used on an application menu.

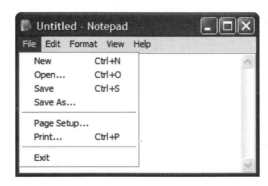

Microsoft has never defined a standard for shortcuts, which is problematic because different applications use different shortcuts. However, developers who want to make life easy for the user will normally choose the same shortcuts that standard applications, such as Notepad, use. For example, most users associate Ctrl+P with printing, so a developer who wants to improve accessibility will use that combination consistently. Likewise, Ctrl+N is normally used for a new file. Shortcuts can use any combination of control characters and function keys. For example, as already mentioned, F3 repeats the last search in many applications.

Speed keys appear as underlines beneath the field names or prompts. For example, look at the underlined "P" in Properties or the underlined "N" in Name. A speed key helps the user access the field quickly. All the user needs to do is press Alt+<Key Letter> to access the field. Here is an example of a Print dialog containing some speed keys.

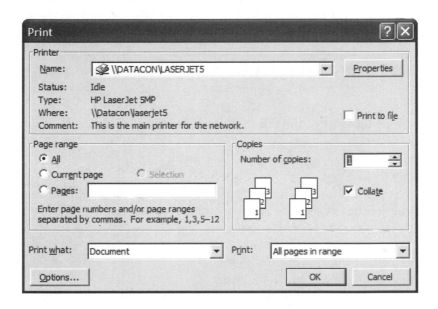

Note that there may be several alternative terms for essentially the same technology. The speed keys and shortcuts found in desktop applications often use the name "access keys" in Web-based applications. Consequently, you might find your discussions with another developer thwarted when the two of you use different terms to refer to essentially the same technology. See the Web Accessibility Guidelines topic at `http://www.w3.org/TR/WCAG10-HTML-TECHS/#link-accesskey` for details.

In this example, pressing Alt+A tells the application to print all of the pages in a document, while pressing Alt+e will print only the current page. The author of this dialog box made a mistake in creating the speed keys, however. Notice that all of the buttons except OK and Cancel have speed keys associated with them. The OK button is the default action, so you could activate it by pressing Enter. The user will know that this is the default action because there's a dark square around OK. However, there's no obvious quick method of accessing Cancel. You can activate it by pressing Escape, but this is hardly common knowledge and leads to usage problems. In short, all of the buttons should have speed keys associated with them. (Some developers will say that the user has access to the controls on a form using the Tab and Shift+Tab keys, but this option can prove cumbersome when there are more than a few controls on the form.)

The Section 508 requirements address all of these problems. In fact, the rules contain elements for both desktop and Web-based applications because the problem is of such an extreme nature. Any application you build must support the keyboard completely. It should also support the mouse and as many assistive devices as possible. In general, the assistive devices mimic either the mouse or keyboard, so providing complete support for both is a good first step. Here are a few things to consider for your implementation.

- Always implement every application control action for both the mouse and the keyboard.

- Provide shortcuts and speed keys whenever possible.

- Use consistent shortcut and speed key implementations, along with all other controls such as buttons and menus.

- Use the same buttons, controls, shortcuts, and speed keys as standard Windows applications whenever possible.

- Key the buttons, controls, shortcuts, and speed keys simple to avoid finger gymnastics.

- Focus on common functions that every user will need, such as printing and document saving, when creating shortcuts.

- Add a speed key for every field, button, and control on every form or dialog box that you create.

Making your application easy to use also means that you need to spend some time in the other person's shoes. Try using your application in keyboard-only mode to determine whether you can access every feature using just the keyboard. After you give the keyboard a workout, try using just the mouse to access every application command and feature. It helps to use features such as the on-screen keyboard we'll use for testing later in the book so that you can see what it would be like to type using just the mouse. Likewise, look for odd key combinations that create finger gymnastic scenarios. Attempt to use your application with just one hand—preferably, not your dominant hand (use just your left hand if you're right-handed). Try simulating use with a head or mouth pointer (unless you have one at your disposal) by typing with a clean stick (a sturdy straw can work, but try finding something a little more substantial than that—some developers use the eraser end of a pencil for this purpose). All of these steps will help make your application more usable to those with special needs.

Helping Users with Cognitive Needs

Have you ever looked at a display and had a blank because you didn't know what to do? I doubt that many developers have had this problem. Most developers pick up application functionality without thinking about it much. The screen is an open book—every feature is obvious, every function simple. After many years of answering reader questions, I'm convinced that developers are an extreme minority. Most people have problems figuring out some or all of an application—for them, it's neither simple nor easy-to-understand.

Some developers equate cognitive ability with intelligence. I've even heard developers tell users that they're stupid because they don't understand the simple dialog box that appears to plague everyone that uses the application. In fact, these same developers often confuse intelligence and knowledge—the two are different.

Cognitive ability has nothing to do with intelligence or knowledge—it has everything to do with awareness, perception, reasoning, and judgment. Very few of the users that will access your application are aware of the intricacies of computer development and most don't care. Some users can perceive the smallest sound, but don't have the ability to process some of the information they see. A user can be quite intelligent, but lack the abstract reasoning required to navigate a computer display. In a few cases, a user will understand the choices presented, but will lack the understanding required to make a decision—to judge between the available options.

The Section 508 requirements address the cognitive requirements of the user, not their intelligence or knowledge. As a developer, you're responsible for helping the user understand their choices, make sense of what they see or hear, and make good choices. This requirement means your application must provide prompts (balloon help) for every control and field on the display. The help should be specific, easy-to-understand, and complete. You need to make additional context-sensitive help available using Shift+F1. The help should provide the same information using different techniques to provide input to the user in different ways. Finally, the application must include checks that attempt to determine that the user understood the input you provided. For example, you should include range and value checks to ensure that the user doesn't input an incorrect value. If the user does make a mistake, don't beat them over the head and call them stupid—offer to help them provide a correct value. In short, do everything possible to ensure that the user has a good computing experience and you'll find that the user responds by enjoying your work.

Other User Needs to Consider

So far, the chapter has discussed basic user needs and discussed how they relate to the Section 508 requirements. We looked at the usability and performance requirements for the applications that you create. However, we haven't discussed some special issues that will affect your application development. Users have special needs that you might not consider unless you also have the same needs. For example, few developers are even aware that the flashing lights they add to an application can actually cause bodily harm.

TIP Developers will become involved with accessibility requirements in a number of ways over the next few years. Some of these avenues of opportunity might not even be apparent today. Consider the case of a high school senior named Ryan Patterson who designed a glove that interprets sign language and displays it as text on a computer screen. The use of this glove could potentially free those who lack the ability to speak from using interpreters all the time. This is an example of an application that didn't exist previously and could also have a big impact on the hearing impaired. You can read more about this new technology at http://www.wired.com/news/technology/0,1282,49716,00.html. The point of this story is that accessibility represents a new application horizon for computer developers—one that we should begin exploring as soon as possible.

The following sections discuss three special issues associated with the Section 508 requirements that might not affect most users, but will have a definite impact on those with special needs. In order to provide full compliance, you must address these needs in some way, even if you don't think the typical user will require the functionality they provide. You might be surprised—a feature you add to your application for those with special needs today could become the remote control of tomorrow.

Developing with Color in Mind

We've discussed the issue of color in regard to color blindness, those with color perception problems, and equipment that doesn't display color at all. However, you need to consider other color issues that might not affect the average user. The use of color in applications can become an emotional issue—some uses of color just don't work very well because they have a negative effect on the users of the application.

Consider an experience by some law enforcement officials. The officers were having considerable behavioral problems with some of the drunks that came in and often resorted to physical restraints to control the drunks. The officer in charge noticed that the color of the room was a sort of orange. However, the problems decreased significantly when the officers painted the room pink. The drunks hadn't changed—only the color of the room had changed.

 TIP You'll find a number of studies, both scientific and experiential, on the effect of color on humans on the Internet. For example, there's an interesting psychology article on the effects of color at `http://psychology.about.com/library/weekly/aa031501a.htm`. In addition, a historical account of the significance of color in human history appears at `http://www.innerself.com/Magazine/Health/Color_Therapy_part_1.htm`. You can find a bulletin board for discussing color issues and effects at `http://www.colormatters.com/bubdarc9a-physio.html`. If you really want to learn some interesting information about color, check out the latest color studies at `http://www.shibuya.com/garden/colorpsycho.html`.

Color plays an important role in other ways. For instance, many people consider green a restful color—one that's easy on the eyes. In some cases, people consider some tones of amber restful as well. On the other hand, red often evokes a response because it signifies alarm; in fact, psychologists say that red can actually increase blood pressure. Developers often use it to grab the user's attention.

In previous sections, we discussed color as an entity. For example, you learned that some people can't differentiate between some colors because they can't perceive them. The user sees a color, but it isn't the same as the one most other people see. Therefore, the improper use of color can make elements of the Web site invisible. The Section 508 requirements discuss this issue as part of the required support for people with color blindness.

The Section 508 requirements also discuss the use of color to convey meaning or evoke a specific response. If a user is blind, has a color deficiency, requires a high contrast display, or simply uses a black and white screen, the meaning intended by the use of color is lost. Consequently, you must convey this meaning in some other way. The Section 508 requirements specify text as one alternative—you can describe the color and its meaning. For example, if a field ends with a red asterisk, you can say that the field is required and that the user must provide the information to complete the form. If you are trying to evoke a particular response, then the description provided with the color can also help evoke the desired response. Sometimes, all it takes is the right punctuation mark to evoke a response. For example, ending a sentence with an exclamation mark instead of a period tends to evoke excitement!

Adding Visual and Audio Cues

Adding visual and audio cues to your application is a good way to draw attention to specific application features, needs, and events. When an error occurs on a system, a dialog pops up, providing a visual cue that an event (an error) occurred. In addition, the system makes a distinct sound to tell the user that the event occurred. Finally, the application forces the user to look at the message by preventing the user from doing anything else until they clear the error message dialog box. In short, the application provides a wealth of feedback to tell you that something has happened and you need to do something about it.

The problem for users with special needs is that one or more of these cues are missing or not presented correctly. For example, someone with a hearing problem won't hear the special sound that an error dialog box makes. If another application hides the dialog box, the user might not see it at all. In addition, because the user can't hear the special sound, it's easy to confuse an error dialog box with an informational (or other) dialog box. The user might not realize that the dialog box presents critical, rather than helpful information.

Section 508 requires application developers to provide alternatives for informational cues. For example, if a dialog box makes a sound but the user can't hear the sound, then the applications requires some other presentation for that sound so that the user knows that an event of a specific type occurred. The best way to accomplish this task in Windows is to ensure that your application works with the various accessibility features. For example, the Windows SoundSentry accessibility feature will present a visual alternative to a sound if your application provides the correct information. Chapter 6 provides complete examples of how to create alternatives for visual and audio cues in your application by relying on Windows accessibility features.

Understanding the Effects of Flash Rate

We've all seen flashing screen elements in one form or another. In general, developers use flashing screen elements to draw attention to a particular area of the screen. Here are some common examples of flashing screen elements.

Operating System or Application Function: Windows uses this technique to show when an application has completed a task or experienced some other event.

Accidental Effect: A developer might attempt to create smooth animation on a machine that doesn't have the required resources, resulting in a display that flashes.

Environmental Factor: The flashing effect can also occur when certain environmental factors are present. For example, using a computer monitor with florescent lighting can cause flashing if the monitor's refresh rate is set too low.

Flashing images or screen elements can cause more than a few problems for users. In many cases, the flashing will cause eyestrain. The flashing could also cause hallucinatory effects—the user could see something that simply isn't present on the screen. In some users, the flashing effect can cause an undesirable side effect such as increased blood pressure or even anger. However, the most severe effect of a flashing screen is one in which the user experiences a seizure. Such epileptic seizures could result in decreased physical capacity or even death. In short, avoid using flashing screens or screen elements—they simply aren't worth the risk.

 TIP Photosensitive epilepsy is a significant problem for about 1 in 10,000 people. You can read more about this condition at http://dspace.dial.pipex.com/town/park/sk98/factsheet_04.htm. Another good article appears at http://www.epilepsy.org.uk/info/photofrm.html.

Typical Developer Questions About Section 508

Most developers have at least a few misconceptions about Section 508 requirements and many others are simply apprehensive about anything the government endorses. In many cases, the problems the developer sees on the horizon aren't really problems at all—they become non-issues as the developer resolves application accessibility problems. A few of the problems actually are real, but they could take a form other than the one that the developer initial thought they would take. Finally, some issues are the result of misinformation by some developers who appear to know something about accessibility, but really don't know much at all.

The following sections might not answer every question you have, but they do answer the questions that most developers seem to ask before they start creating their first accessibility friendly application. In general, you'll find that the answers tell you what to expect and how to resolve issues that the question points out. The answers will also help you separate hype from the reality of accessible development. Many developers actually find that following the Section 508 requirements nets returns that they had never anticipated. Some of these developers become true evangelists of the accessibility doctrine, but I'm not expecting anything quite so grand from these answers. What you should gain is a better appreciation of why accessibility is important and what it can do for your personally.

Does Compliance Require a Lot of Time?

Contrary to common belief, accessibility friendly Web pages should actually require less time to maintain because the code is correct from the outset and the simplified design means you won't spend as much time tending to the gadgets. Some accessibility advocates say the only way to obtain a truly accessible Web site is to hand code every page. This notion is the source of the perception that these pages will require a lot of time to create. The truth is that you can use applications such as FrontPage to create your Web page and then tune the resulting code as needed. By combining automation and good design techniques, you'll reap the benefits of a usable and accessible design that requires less time to code and maintain than anything you might have created in the past. The bottom line is whether you fully understand the code generated by your preferred tool, rather than how the code is generated.

TIP   The question of how long it takes to add accessibility to a Web site varies by developer. Most developers who have actually developed Web sites that include accessibility features agree that the time required isn't much. However, the technique recommendations vary. For example Marti McCuller, a developer who became involved with accessible Web site design after the loss of her own vision, states that it's actually easier and less expensive to design the accessible Web site from scratch. To learn more about this developer's perspective, read the article at http://www.masshightech.com/displayarticledetail.asp?art_id=58468. Given that many of you already have extensive Web sites to maintain, this book assumes you'll want to update, rather than start from scratch. However, it's important to consider the issue from all perspectives before you begin.

It's important to consider some of the time investments you'll make as part of your decision to create an accessible Web site. One of most important considerations is the time you'll spend testing the Web site. This time will actually increase because you must ensure that the page is actually meeting all of the requirements. The use of automated testing techniques can help keep the testing time to a minimum, but at least some of the time you save in other areas will be spent in additional testing. You'll find discussions of automated testing techniques for desktop applications in the "Using Automated Testing Techniques" section of Chapter 5 and for Web-based applications in the "Using an HTML Checker" section of Chapter 9.

Will Section 508 Requirements Destroy My Application's Appearance?

Some developers fear that Section 508 compliance equates to bland applications that rely on text alone to provide content. The display will be devoid of color or artistic expression—it will use only white and black to interact with the user. In short, the world will become a boring place where even shades of gray will provide a welcome change to the monotony. Consequently, these developers view Section 508 as the government's way of enforcing some type of mundane existence on the developer community in general, and the user in particular. If Section 508 actually meant such an extreme change in the appearance of applications, you wouldn't be reading this book right now because I like to add pizzazz to my applications.

It's important to remember that the Section 508 rules discuss augmentation for the most part—making your application more accessible by adding new features, rather than removing existing features. It's true that you might have to change the color scheme of your application or provide some additional prompts, but you would want to change these items in order to interact with all users anyway. Providing better descriptions, ensuring that users can see your application properly, and adding accessibility features in general will improve the user experience and keep them coming back for more. For example, Figure 2-4 shows a Web site that has lots of color and interest, yet it meets the Section 508 requirements.

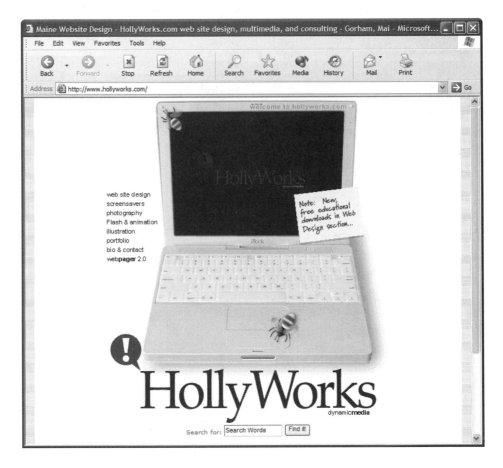

Figure 2-4. Section 508–compliant Web sites don't have to be dull.

The best way to look at an application is as an information restaurant. It doesn't matter how good the food in a restaurant is if the entrance is mounted 50 feet above the sidewalk so that only rock and mountain climbers can enter. The best decorations in the world won't attract customers if your information restaurant lacks basic amenities, such as a place to sit. The point of Section 508 compatibility is not to make your restaurant into a drab hole in the wall that no one wants to see, but to make it a comfortable place that the user will enjoy visiting.

In sum, the answer to this question is that Section 508 requirements will only have a slight affect on the appearance of your application, but they will have a big impact on the comfort level of your application. Consequently, your application will attract more users because everyone will want to go to a place that's comfortable and serves good information.

When Have I Done Enough?

For some developers, Section 508 compliance is a nuisance and will always be a nuisance—it's something they would rather avoid. In fact, there's a booming business for entrepreneurs who can show a company how to comply with the letter of the law, rather than consider the spirit of the law. Compliance becomes a matter of checking off items on a list and hoping that no one will notice if some of the checks are less than perfect. In most cases, these developers are spending more time dotting i's and crossing t's than if they had simply considered the users' needs.

Even some of the large vendors are getting into the act. For example, IBM recently released a version of DB2 that theoretically meets the Section 508 requirements. (You can read more about this product at `http://www.ibmlink.ibm.com/` `cgi-bin/master?xh=AEx1iZHEDTs8zz1USenGnN9332&request=announcements` `&parms=H%5f202%2d085&xhi=usa%2emain%7cusa%2einfolink&xfr=N.`) However, if you read the Section 508 material from this Web site (shown in Figure 2-5), you'll notice that the wording places the burden of compliance on the assistive technology—not on DB2 where it belongs. It essentially says that DB2 Section 508 compliance will work so long as you adapt your assistive technology to meet IBM's requirements. The only problem with this approach is that Section 508 compliance is supposed to make technology accessible to those who need it with fewer restrictions.

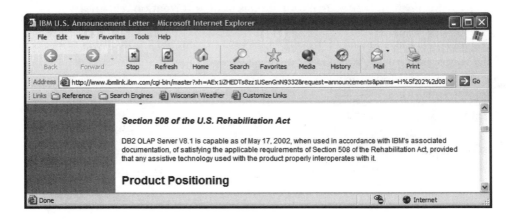

Figure 2-5. Some techniques for adapting a product for Section 508 compliance work better than others do.

Obviously, the IBM Web site demonstrates adherence with the letter of the law, rather than the spirit of the law. Unfortunately, the letter of the law seems to be the rule of the day. A recent *Washington Post* article (`http://www.washingtonpost.com/wp-dyn/articles/A37741-2001Aug20.html`) makes it clear that many companies are providing help for those who must implement Section 508 as a purely economic move. Therefore, the question of how much you must do remains.

The answer to this question is actually easier than you might expect. You have done enough when the people who want to access your site can do so without experiencing problems. When you meet this goal, you have achieved the spirit of the law. As a developer, you'll find that achieving this goal provides many rewards—not the least of which is a blessedly quiet telephone free of user questions and complaints. However, beyond the personal issues, knowing that you've helped a fellow human being get more out of life should count for a lot.

The Thin Edge of Sensitivity

Over the years, I've witnessed a broad range of reactions to just about any situation. Sometimes the reactions are unexpected—in other cases, they're unwarranted, but understandable. The concept of doing enough means different things to different people and I can almost guarantee you won't satisfy everyone. At some point, no matter how hard you try, someone is going to become dissatisfied with your efforts. They'll misinterpret your efforts as a personal affront, decide that there's no hope because you're hopelessly inadequate, and generally question your integrity in creating a particular application.

I've noticed that the whole issue of Section 508 compliance can stir up a storm of controversy, arguments, finger pointing, and sometimes screaming. The accusations fly so thick that you could walk on them from one end of the room to the other. Generally, I find that these arguments are counterproductive because no one comes away convinced of anything. The edge of sensitivity is extremely thin when it comes to issues of this sort. As a developer, you will find that users constantly force you to consider every side of an issue that you honestly want to resolve but may not fully understand. Even when you do understand the issues, there are situations where poor graphics design or content can sabotage your efforts to create a Section 508–compliant application.

So where does it all end? It often helps if you can put the other person in your shoes for a moment. Ask them how they would resolve the issue at hand. In some cases, you'll walk away with a new idea, or at least the other person will better understand that what they're asking might not be possible. Unfortunately, in other cases, you'll end up in a stalemate because the other person has no idea of what they want or perhaps lacks the ability to articulate it. At some point, you have to decide that you've satisfied both the letter and the spirit of the law. The important issue is to keep an open mind and to try to resolve issues to the best of your ability.

Where Can I Find Additional Information?

As mentioned previously, most large computer product vendors have a personal stake in government contracts, and therefore they support Section 508 requirements. We discussed Microsoft's main Section 508 Web page in Chapter 1. However, this company also has a general accessibility Web page at http://www.microsoft.com/enable/. This Web site discusses general accessibility requirements and shows how Microsoft is working to meet them. In addition, you'll find resources. For example, at the time of writing, Microsoft was promoting their new general accessibility book and demonstrating the Windows XP features that help developers meet accessibility requirements.

Vendor Web sites tell you about implementation—usually their vision of how to meet specific accessibility requirements. In the "Input Devices of the Future?" sidebar in Chapter 3, you'll learn about new technologies that universities are developing. University Web sites are often the best place to learn about upcoming technologies that will help you solve accessibility requirements. Finally, standards and government Web sites are the best places to learn about the accessibility goals you have to meet with existing or upcoming technologies. We'll continue to discuss these three types of Web sites as the book progresses.

Summary

This chapter has helped you understand what the Section 508 requirements will mean to your application development efforts. In some cases, the changes are small, but in many cases, you'll need to make changes to the way you write code or add more features to your applications. The user needs sections of the chapter also pointed out that you might have to remove features from an application to make it more accessible—some applications are simply too gadget bound for their own good. It's my hope that you also found the question and answer section useful.

To make maximum use of the information you've learned in this chapter, you'll need to start looking at your applications. Create a hit list of features that you'll either add or remove to make the application comply with the Section 508 requirements. Make sure you look at all of the areas of compliance. One of the major problems with accessible applications today is that they offer the developer view of accessibility or they don't perform well. The requirements spell out that you need to achieve all of the Section 508 goals in order to create a compliant application.

Make sure you save up your questions for me as well. I really do like to hear from you and I consider the questions and associated answers a good learning tool for everyone. In short, I'm trying to make this book more accessible to you. Be sure to check my Web site from time-to-time for new questions and answers.

Chapter 3 recognizes the developer's need for help in accomplishing the accessibility goals for any application and the relative lack of any tools to perform the work. If you've created your application hit list at this point, you know that some of the goals are going to be difficult to achieve without help. This chapter tells you were you can get help outside of this book. Starting in Part II of the book, we'll look at actual application code and see how you can update it, but there are other tools and resources that the typical developer needs to get started. The goal of Chapter 3 is to provide you with these additional resources.

Hardware, Resources, and Training

In This Chapter:

What Types of Alternative Input Devices Are There?

How Should You Resolve Biometric Device Issues?

Where Can You Find Section 508 Information?

Where Can You Find Section 508–Specific Training?

How Can You Determine the Capabilities of a Human Input Device (HID)?

As WE LEARNED in Chapter 1, Section 508 requirements encompass everything from application data presentation, to the physical design of devices, to workstation furniture measurements. The rules tell you about the accessibility goals for your applications—they signify a desired result. In this case, the requirement is a law issued and implemented by the U.S. government and cooperatively followed by others, but the principle is that you have to accomplish application accessibility goals whether or not compliance is mandatory.

The problem is that you know where your application is today and where it needs to go tomorrow, but you don't know how to get there. Developers lack training in a broad range of accessibility issues. This chapter discusses some of those issues and then tells you how to obtain help overcoming them. I've divided the issue into three areas:

Hardware: Most developers take a common feature approach to working with hardware. This chapter shows that such an approach often causes problems for users and definitely adds to the cost of making an application Section 508 compliant.

Resources: The Integrated Development Environments (IDEs) used to develop most software today lack any form of accessibility aid. Without this development aid, companies task the developer with implementing all accessibility features manually—a time consuming and error prone task.

Training: None of the college programs I contacted provides any sort of accessibility training as part of the bachelor's degree curriculum. Consequently, the developer must seek this training as a separate educational goal; few choose to do this.

As part of the resources portion of this chapter, we'll look at a development need that most computer books ignore—the Human Interface Device (HID). The example program in this chapter helps you understand what a HID is and how you can access it. In many cases, HIDs take common forms such as the mouse and the keyboard. In other cases, a HID is a special device designed to meet a special need. Although Microsoft has provided some HID support as part of Windows, most people ignore it completely. The sample application shows that while HID support is incomplete in Windows, it does provide you with valuable information you can use to make accessibility decisions.

An Overview of Development Issues

Many developers will wonder why they need to search high and low to find any resources for accessibility development. It's extremely easy to find lists of rules and pretentious advice about the issues, but nearly impossible to find any help in resolving accessibility issues. The problem is one of original design—including everything from the lowest part of the OS to the user interface of applications. The originators of most application environments never considered accessibility requirements in the design of any part of the computer, including the tools used to create computer applications. Consequently, the tools that developers use today offer little in the way of help in creating an accessible application or Web site.

The issues faced by the developer are many—that's why this chapter is so important. To create an application that runs well, is usable, and is accessible all at the same time, the developer has to provide the required support during the design phase. Adding this support means having the training, the resources, and the hardware required to perform the task—the three pieces of information you'll find in this chapter.

The following sections consider two main issues confronting developers. The first is a lack of development tools. A developer needs tools that help create accessible applications. The second is a lack of knowledge about hardware issues. For example, when a developer creates an application of a cellular telephone, an emulator helps the developer model the application before testing it on the real device. The developer can't say the same of accessibility aids—accessible device emulators are extremely rare (if you can find them).

Considering the Tool Issues

The GUI tools used today make it easy for anyone to design a Web site or write an application. However, this design doesn't include the concept of accessibility functionality, so while the application does perform the specified task, it often does so using inconvenient methods. In addition, the code that the IDE automatically generates on behalf of the developer often fails to meet accessibility coding guidelines, which constitutes a hidden accessibility flaw for the developer. The application works, but the design is flawed by usability and accessibility issues. Consequently, the user must spend an inordinate amount of time trying to figure out how to perform a given task, rather than focussing on the work at hand.

Coding isn't the only area where developers are at a disadvantage in producing usable and accessible applications. Consider the issue of graphics development. None of the graphics tools that I've used includes features that would tend to make the image more accessible to those with special needs. For example, none of the applications I've seen shows what an image will look like to someone with color blindness. (See the "Building the Color Blindness Simulator Example" section of Chapter 4 for a way to overcome this problem.) This is a big disadvantage to the developer because there's no way to know if the image will work for everyone. Likewise, few graphics applications provide the features to add captioning and other accessibility support. For that matter, few programming tools provide accessibility support, making it difficult for the developer with special needs to use them.

A lack of tools that help developers create accessible applications automatically means that developers must perform this design task manually. Unfortunately, schools generally don't provide developers with the training they need. My college experience didn't prepare me to create either usable or accessible applications. Generally, my professors were happy to see a working application. However, with the current government regulations (in almost every country), I hope that schools begin to take a serious look at adding accessibility to their list of things to teach.

In general, the developer lacks the tools required to interface with most accessibility devices. For example, individuals with cerebral palsy (or other types of traumatic brain injury) often have augmentative communication devices that can interface with a computer. However, there are perceptual problems in matching these systems to communicate together. Often the user must make the computer screen information significantly larger than the developer originally anticipated, thus distorting the information, and making it senseless without the assistance of a secondary person who helps interpret the display. If the developer had the tools required to develop applications that could truly interact with these devices, the user would gain a better interface and more independence.

NOTE Many of the terms in this book will seem strange to developers because they are part of the word list used by Physical Therapists (PTs) and Occupational Therapists (OTs). I chose these terms with the assistance of experts in this field—the words convey a specific meaning. The Glossary contains descriptions of accessibility terminology and provides links to places on the Internet where you can learn more about these terms. Whenever possible, I'll provide a definition for difficult terms inline or as part of a separate Note for the first usage of the term. For example, an augmentative communication device is a piece of specialized hardware such as a stylus that a person with special needs uses to perform tasks such as typing. Vendors constantly introduce new devices, so providing a precise definition in this book is impossible. For the developer, an augmentative communication device provides a means for the user to interact with the computer in a way that doesn't require any special programming on your part. Likewise, a perceptual problem is any difficulty the user might experience in using the five senses to interact with the computer. For example, a lack of the sense of touch will inhibit the user's ability to interact with devices such as the mouse.

Even when a developer gains access to tools that permit development for accessibility needs, the tool is often difficult to use. Consider Visual Studio .NET— many of the components include special properties to add accessibility support. Unfortunately, adding this support isn't as straightforward as adding values to the properties. We'll discuss these properties in the "Using the .NET Accessibility Features Example" section of Chapter 7. You might be surprised at just how useful these features are once you figure out how to use them. Unfortunately, learning how to use these features is a major hurdle that many developers don't have time to overcome.

Considering the Hardware Issues

Another issue is even harder to overcome—that of hardware support. Section 508 contains some distinctive hardware requirements that many developers can't meet today because they're unfamiliar with the devices involved. It's very hard to write software for a device that you've never seen. There are also problems obtaining the required documentation and driver support so that a developer can write the code and test it. In short, a developer could find that the hardware really is the problem in accessibility development.

NOTE Something the developer must consider is that the hardware alone won't determine the hardware support problems for a particular application. The user response to and interaction with the hardware also affects what the application will see as input. Many of these individuals have slower than usual response times. Input that would require less than a second from most people can take someone with special needs anywhere from 5 to 60 seconds to complete. The user can also have great difficulty holding a position in order for their response to register. It may take three or more tries to obtain the registration of the response that they want. In short, accessible application development isn't just about hardware or software—it's about the individual.

As a point of comparison, if you want to write an application that works on a PDA, you can find an emulator to test the software. The emulator even provides a screen that shows how the PDA will look so that you can adjust application appearance as needed, as shown in Figure 3-1. However, if you were to try to find emulators for most assistive technology devices, you'd have to look a long time and would probably not find anything of value. The lack of emulators causes a problem because it's very hard to determine performance without some gauge. How can you tell the usability of an application with a device that tracks eye movement if there's no emulator for such a device and you don't have access to the real thing? Training can help by showing you how the device will react and giving you source information to use in estimating application response.

Figure 3-1. PDA emulators add value by showing you how an application will look on screen.

The bottom line for hardware issues is that the developer is a partner with the user. In most cases, the user has to use an interactive device in order to connect to and communicate with the world. It's often their head (pointing), mouth (breathing), and voice (speaking) that performs the communication, rather than a pair of hands on the keyboard.

Alternative Input Devices

PCs can accommodate a wide range of alternative input devices. For example, you can choose to use a mouse, keyboard, joystick, or trackball as standard input devices. Scientific users choose from a wide range of RS-422 devices including data loggers and live inputs, such as thermometers. Consequently, a device that sends eye movement or a puff on a tube as input to the PC is not that different from standard input devices—unless you're the person who relies on such a device as your only means of input to the computer. People with special needs often require help from alternate input devices to create an interface with the PC.

Many alternative input devices mimic a standard PC input device or use an interface that mimics the input device. For example, a device that receives input from the user in the form of eye movement can mimic a keyboard. In fact, that's precisely how the device works. Users can rest their eyes on a particular key on a keyboard mock-up. The device (along with associated software such as drivers and a special application) registers the action as a key press. Needless to say, a user who's inputting words and actions one character at a time using such a device won't want to hear that the input was lost or the application suddenly decided not to work any longer.

Sometimes an alternative input device will use the Universal Serial Bus (USB) port on a system. It will still emulate a standard input device, but you might find that it causes some interesting problems with your application if it also polls the USB port. The alternative input device might appear as a separate USB device and your application could become confused if you don't interact with the USB port properly. Generally, the best idea is to use standard interfaces to interact with devices that you think the USB port might access and leave direct USB access to the operating system.

In some cases, the alternative input device could appear as a HID. I discuss this topic in more depth in the "Input Devices of the Future?" sidebar and show you an example of how to interact with a HID in the "Developing for the Human Input Device (HID) Example" section. In most cases, you'll find that working with a HID is the same as any other device. The main difference is that you'll work with a special driver—you might also require access to special objects. The vendor normally supplies the special support.

One of the more interesting places to learn about specialized hardware is AbilityHub (http://www.abilityhub.com/). This Web site helps you understand specialized hardware such as the eye gaze system shown in Figure 3-2. You can also see what the devices look like and obtain a few technical details about them.

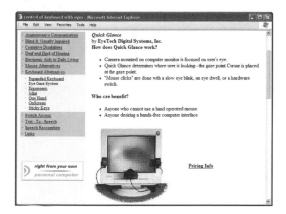

Figure 3-2. Eye gaze systems help a user who can't use a keyboard or a mouse to input information into the computer.

TIP   Sometimes a new application will come out on the market that doesn't change the output of a device, but does dramatically change the way the user interacts with the device. In many cases, these changes help someone make better use of accessible technology and can point the way to other innovations. Consider Dasher (http://www.inference.phy.cam.ac.uk/dasher/)—a text entry system that many users equate to a "video game" experience. Dasher uses a unique interface that developers of other application types could use as an example of how to improve their applications. The fact that Dasher is an open source product makes it a perfect example for developers who want to try something new and helpful. The feature that makes Dasher important is that it blurs the line between accessibility needs and those required for general input. For example, you could use Dasher with a small device such as a PDA. You can download a copy of the Dasher software at http://www.inference.phy.cam.ac.uk/dasher/Download.html.

One of the more interesting technical details is that most of these devices interact with more than just the PC. For example, the Quick Glance product shown in Figure 3-2 can control outside devices such as the lights. The device can also control a telephone and perform other tasks. In short, the user uses this product to interact with more than just your application, so direct access isn't a good idea. As you get into more of the details, you'll find that this system can interact with voice software—making it possible for the user to perform some input tasks by talking, rather than looking.

Whoever said that necessity is the mother of invention said a mouthful. The very people who have a special need created many of the accessible devices that you'll find on the market today. Consider a special device created for the blind that enables them to perform text messaging. This device takes the place of the standard text messaging system in common use today. The people who helped develop this device felt isolated from other people—they had a need that has been answered by a device they helped design. You can learn more about this project at http://news.bbc.co.uk/1/hi/technology/2403913.stm.

Input Devices of the Future?

Some developers view HIDs as any device that you can use to interact with a computer. Under Windows, this term has a special meaning because you can interact with HIDs programmatically (something you'll learn about in the "Developing for the Human Input Device (HID) Example" section of the chapter). Such devices have a few more constraints than standard devices, not the least of which is the required driver support. (Many vendors don't provide the required driver support, so you won't see the device listed as a HID, although it qualifies as a HID.) In general, these devices sport a USB interface, which allows the device to describe itself with a higher degree of accuracy than older busses and interfaces. Most mice today come with HID support. You'll find them in the Human Interface Devices folder of Device Manager as shown here.

Stanford University's Archimedes Project is a prototype of a HID for those with special needs. (The device has been in the planning stages for quite some time.) However, instead of having a separate device for each need, this HID is a single device designed to meet every need. In addition, the engineers designed the device to work with a single individual. Wherever the individual goes, the device goes with them. This means that the individual is free to visit any computer within the work place because they always have their special support devices with them. A computer becomes a common item, rather than a specially configured device. The name of this setup is the Total Access System (TAS) and it relies on an accessor—the device used to access the computer and a TAS port (the element that makes the connection between the computer and the accessor).

Each accessor contains all the required features for accessing the computer system. For example, it contains a speech recognition module, as well as a module for tracking head and eye movements. If this device sounds like something you'd like to know more about, you can check out these Web sites.

- The main Archimedes Project Web site: `http://archimedes.stanford.edu/`

- A case study on Project Archimedes: `http://hci.stanford.edu/pcd-archives/pcd-seminar/1996-/0020.html`

- An article from Stanford's Partner, Silicon Recognition: `http://www.silirec.com/cgi-bin/template.pl?ID=4`

- One of many Neil Scott articles: `http://domino.watson.ibm.com/arccs/csnotesx.nsf/8b47dcaf7f045773882568cb0079d647/fa73b5bd4e5928a18825693b00615620?OpenDocument`

- Some of the related Web Accessibility Initiative (WAI) projects: `http://www.w3.org/WAI/References/`

- A Wired News article on the topic: `http://www.wired.com/news/school/0,1383,53930,00.html`

Biometric Device Issues

Security is becoming the never-ending issue for companies. Not only do applications, operating systems, and even hardware present security risks, but there's also the problem of working with the weakest link in the chain—humans. I read new stories about security issues every day in the trade press magazines and I'm sure you do too. In fact, you might have noticed that the number of stories has increased and that the level of security threats has too.

By now, you've heard the many stories of problems with the human link in the chain. People often give out their password to a complete stranger just because the stranger asks them for it. You'll find passwords written down and placed in the most obvious public places, such as a note attached to a monitor. Some users choose short passwords such as dog or cat. In some cases, they'll choose a "devious" password such as "master" and think they'll actually thwart a cracker using it. In short, you might have problems with the vendors you use to obtain your computer equipment, but that problem is nothing when compared to the humans you have to deal with.

 NOTE For the purposes of this book, the term *cracker* will always refer to an individual who's breaking into a system on an unauthorized basis. This includes any form of illegal activity on the system. On the other hand, a *hacker* will refer to someone who performs authorized (legal) low-level system activities, including testing system security. In some cases, you need to employ the services of a good hacker to test the security measures you have in place, or you are apt to suffer the consequences of a break-in. This book will use the term *hacker* to refer to someone who performs these legal forms of service. The best way to think about the difference between these two types of people (at least if you like westerns) is that the hacker wears a white hat and the cracker wears a black hat.

Over the years, vendors have created numerous ways to circumvent the human problem. The solution begins at the operating system level—new features try to force the user to choose a better password. Unfortunately, humans are smarter than computers and the user normally finds a way to choose a ridiculously simple password anyway. Vendors have tried credit card sized password cards. A business normally combines the password card with the employee's identification card. Unfortunately, employees lose the cards and let other people use them—hardly secure. At least the user has to use a secure password in this situation.

Biometrics is the latest technology that's supposed to fix the human problem with security. A biometric solution relies on physical characteristics of the individual (such as their voice or fingerprints) to generate a password. It has many advantages over previous methods. For example, the password is complex and guaranteed to be unique. The user can't give their biometric data to someone else and there's little chance that they'll lose it either. It would appear that biometrics is the perfect solution for a sticky problem. As we'll see in this section, perfection requires another look.

TIP Developers interested in pursuing biometric security should learn about the Biometric Application Programming Interface (BAPI). A consortium of vendors including IBM, Compaq, IO Software, Microsoft, Sony, Toshiba, and Novell originated BAPI. Learn more about BAPI at the I/O Software Web site (`http://www.iosoftware.com/pages/ Products/SecureTec%20SDK/index.asp`). The I/O Software BAPI offering is now part of their SecureTec SDK. You can download an overview, general information, and technical information. Lest you think that all of these APIs are vendor specific, you can also find a biometrics standards Web site at the Biometrics Consortium Web site (`http:// www.biometrics.org/`). This site contains helpful information about seminars, standards progress, and public information such as periodicals. Another interesting place to look for information is the National Institute of Standards and Technology (`http://www.itl.nist.gov/ div895/isis/projects/biometricsproject.html`). The main interests at this site are the publications, conferences, products, and success stories.

From a Section 508 perspective, the main problem with biometric authentication is that the user may lack the required body part. (In some cases, the individual has the required body part, but isn't able to move it into a required position, or it could be a matter of the individual not being able to speak.) I'm sure that someone will eventually find a way to use DNA for authentication, but until that happens, a lack of the requisite body part would be a problem. The regulation seems to indicate that you must resort to passwords when biometrics won't work. However, you could at least consider more secure alternatives. The following list provides some solutions that you could try, but you need to be aware that passwords are still going to be the universal (and least secure) solution.

Multiple Biometric Validation: The problem that Section 508 is trying to address involves users who lack a particular body part, can't move the body part into a required position, or can't speak. If security is the most important consideration and cost isn't a factor, then you could use multiple biometric authentication techniques. The probability that the user can't speak, doesn't have any fingers, and doesn't possess eyes all at the same time is quite low. Theoretically, providing a choice of iris, fingerprint, and voice identification would satisfy the Section 508 requirement. However, this also means that every entry point and every computer in your company would require all of the requisite readers—expensive to say the least.

Password Cards: Although password cards are less secure than biometric technology, they're still more secure than passwords. At least only one person can have the password card at a time and using a password card means that the user must use a secure password. The only problem with this solution is that the user might not have the dexterity or resources to use a password card. For example, a quadriplegic user or an individual with cerebral palsy would have a problem with this solution unless someone assisted them. (In some cases, increasing the reception range and strategically mounting the key on the wheelchair could help this problem.)

Physical Security: Some companies rely on a combination of physical security and passwords. The user requires a key to unlock the keyboard or other essential element of the system. One company that produces physical security solutions is Interface (`http://www.crocodile.de/`). Unfortunately, this solution also assumes that the user has enough mobility to use the security feature and this isn't always the case.

Alternative Technologies: A few technologies fall outside the strict biometric realm, but they also present risks. For example, it's unlikely that your users will lack a face; so, facial characteristic recognition is a potential solution. The problem with this approach (and the reason that most security experts reject its use) is that facial recognition technology could see more than one person as having the same facial characteristics. Obviously, this is a non-unique solution to the problem. Other alternative technologies have the same problem—they often rely on some characteristic that someone could potentially copy.

Biometric authentication has other possible problems that a developer will need to consider. One of the most problematic is that some people fear it will make them too identifiable. A recent eWeek article (`http://www.eweek.com/article2/0,,361993,00.asp`) makes the problem relatively easy to understand—extreme personalization is a scary concept that many people aren't willing to deal with. These individuals already feel that everyone around them knows too much.

Some developers are also under the misconception that biometrics are completely foolproof and risk free. These developers assume that most people can't fool biometric authentication. However, even a casual cracker can fool the biometric authentication given the right tools. A cracker with enough time, resources, and tenacity, can outwit any security scheme. In fact, you'll already find Web sites that tell you how to circumvent biometric security. For example, the "Body Check" article at `http://www.heise.de/ct/english/02/11/114/` provides relatively complete instructions that include pictures. You'll find a good overview of the subject in The Register article at `http://www.theregister.co.uk/content/55/25300.html`. Finally, you'll find a slideshow presentation of the topic at `http://www.itu.int/itudoc/itu-t/workshop/security/present/s5p4.pdf`.

Eventually, vendors will fix the problems with biometrics and the price of biometric readers will come down. Expect biometric vendors to come up with Section 508 compatible solutions in the future as well. After all, the only constant about technology is that it changes. For today at least, you still need to consider all of the ramifications of using biometric security—not the least of which are the Section 508 problems of using biometric security.

Locating Section 508 Information

We've already discussed several Section 508 Web sites in the first part of this book and I assure you that we'll discuss more as the book progresses. Fortunately, there are other good sites that you should consider using. You'll also want to spend some time looking at what's available on newsgroups. Let's consider the Web sites first. The following list provides you with some general Web site information in addition to the Web sites that we've discussed so far in the book.

Accessibility Forum (`http://www.accessibilityforum.org/`): This Web site hosts a cooperative environment in which members discuss Section 508 accessibility issues. In some respects, this group is similar to many of the computer standards groups on the Internet. For example, one of the projects at the time of this writing is focusing on a set of objective measures that will help companies determine if they've met Section 508 requirements.

Center for IT Accommodation (CITA) (`http://www.gsa.gov/Portal/content/offerings_content.jsp?contentOID=22804&contentType=1004&PMKC=1&S=1`): You won't find a lot of information on this Web site, but there are some basics about selling products to the government. The best way to interpret this Web site is as a place to learn the government's point of view on Section 508 requirements concerning product purchases. In some ways, this information tells you a little about the difference between the rule of law and the realities of commerce for the government.

Department of Justice Workforce Investment Act of 1998 (`http://www.usdoj.gov/crt/508/508law.html`): In general, this Web site is important because it provides you with the law as it appears in the "books." The Web page offers the law in plain text without any embellishment or interpretation. Consequently, if you want to get the law as the government will see it when reviewing your site, this is the best place to look.

Government Computer News (GCN) Resource Section 508 (`http://www.gcn.com/Resource/section508/`)**:** This is a news Web site that helps you check current developments for Section 508. Most of the articles are general—they aren't developer specific, but you still need to know the information. One of the nicer features of this site is that GCN makes webcasts of breaking issues and for training purposes. GCN is also a good place to look for validation tools and expert opinions on implementation questions that you might have.

I haven't listed the wealth of government Web sites because they're already in an easy-to-use list at `http://www.section508.gov/index.cfm?FuseAction=Content&ID=80`. This list contains a few unusual entries, such as the Department of Agriculture. For the most part, the listing contains entries that you'd expect, most of which can provide you with additional information for your specific needs. For example, you might want to contact the Census Bureau (`http://www.census.gov/`) to learn if they provide any statistics that you can use to make an application better suited for the needs of people in your area.

Another good source of information is disability organizations. You'll find a list of them at `http://www.section508.gov/index.cfm?FuseAction=Content&ID=81`. In some cases, the organization provides information you can use to develop an application solution right on the Web. For example, ABLEDATA (`http://www.abledata.com/Site_2/Default.htm`) provides a list of about 18,000 products from approximately 2,000 companies. I was interested to see that this Web site includes a standard and a low-graphics version of their pages. The low graphics version (shown in Figure 3-3) has all of the features of the standard version, but it's easier to work with using a screen reader. (This version is also Bobby approved—see the "Using an HTML Checker" section of Chapter 9 for details.)

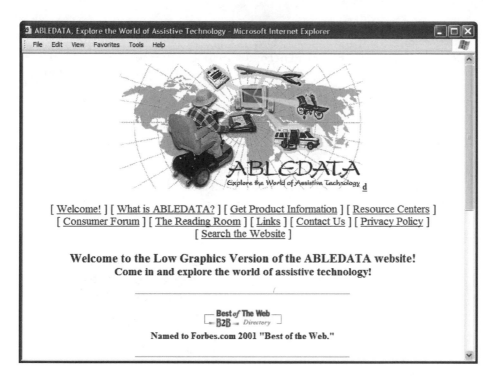

Figure 3-3. The ABLEDATA Web site is one of the few that provide both a standard and a low graphics version of their pages.

Web sites are helpful for obtaining static information about Section 508 requirements, but they don't help much if you have a question that you need answered. Newsgroups help fill in the gaps in this case. There are more newsgroups devoted to accessibility in general and to the Web Accessibility Initiative (WAI), than to Section 508 requirements, but all of these groups can prove helpful in learning more about accessibility needs and requirements. (You'll remember from previous chapters that WAI is an alternative accessibility specification—you can learn more about it at http://www.w3.org/WAI/.) The following list tells you more about each of these groups.

NOTE Some of these newsgroups will only appear on private servers. For example, you might need to subscribe to the `news.micorosoft.com` news server to access the Microsoft offerings. Likewise, if you want to access the Netscape newsgroup, you might have to subscribe to the `news.mozilla.org` news server.

`alt.comp.accessibility:` This newsgroup is the only non-Microsoft offering I found with any traffic. It seems to be the place to go if you have a non-Microsoft product question. For example, at the time of writing, there was a thread about training the NaturallySpeaking product from Dragon software (`http://www.scansoft.com/naturallyspeaking/`).

`comp.speech:` There are three newsgroups in this folder. Although all three newsgroups concentrate on computer speech issues, you'll also find more than the usual amount of discussion on accessibility issues. This newsgroup also supports a Web site at `http://www.speech.cs.cmu.edu/comp.speech/` that includes Frequently Asked Questions (FAQs) on speech technology in general, plus some good information on how speech works from a programmer's perspective.

`microsoft.public.accessibility:` There are nine newsgroups in this folder (as of this writing) that deal with everything from Internet Explorer (`microsoft.public.accessibility.ieaccess`) to developer issues (`microsoft.public.accessibility.developer`). The newsgroups tend to focus on Microsoft products, for the obvious reasons. In most of the groups, you'll find questions about how to perform tasks using the accessibility features. The Microsoft staff usually provides helpful tips, tells the person that there isn't any help for a particular need, or indicates that the Microsoft staff is working on the issue. In general, you'll find that these newsgroups are very responsive.

`microsoft.public.windowsxp.accessibility:` You'll use this newsgroup for general information on Windows XP accessibility features. Normally, you won't find any developer level information in this newsgroup. However, it does provide a good way to learn how people are using the Windows accessibility features and understand where they're having problems. You might also learn a few new usage tricks.

`netscape.public.mozilla.accessiblity:` This newsgroup deals specifically with the Mozilla browser issues. In general, you'll find a mix of user and developer questions with an emphasis on feature requests and Web site design. Peer help seems to be the order of the day on this newsgroup. Many of the questions on this newsgroup are generic, meaning that they apply equally well to all accessibility needs.

`wash.assistive-tech:` This is an example of a state-based newsgroup that could provide help on state issues, as well as provide a view on assistive technology at the local level. The Washington Assistive Technology Web site provides an archive of newsgroup messages at `http://www.wata.org/forum/` so that you can learn what has happened in the past.

It's interesting to note that Microsoft is the heaviest supporter of accessibility related newsgroups. Despite the Microsoft Web site failings that I've noted in this book (and will continue to note), they're at least trying to provide resources that other vendors haven't provided.

Obtaining Section 508 Developer Resources

The previous section provided links to some Section 508–specific Web sites and newsgroups that you need to know about. However, the Section 508 Web sites we've discussed so far have focussed on the rule of law and general information—they've discussed the question of which goals you have to achieve in order to satisfy the requirements. The remainder of the book will focus on specific solutions for some problems that you'll encounter as you upgrade your applications. This section contains some general references for developers that will help you make the required upgrades faster.

TIP Developer resources aren't necessarily limited to accessibility alone. For example, the Section 508 requirements specify limitations on the use of style sheets, so you might need to learn more about them. The `comp.infosystems.www.authoring.stylesheets` newsgroup is one place to gain more information about how to use style sheets correctly.

As a developer, you know that resources can encompass a broad range of products—everything from IDEs to graphics. We won't discuss the generic types of developer resources in this section. The following list contains some resources that could be useful in helping you implement accessibility in your next application. Consider this list a preview of some of the other products we'll discuss as the book progresses.

Accessible.net (`http://www.accessiblenet.com/developertools.html`): This company provides a variety of developer aids and utilities. The focus of this vendor is on a series of template programming tools that help you achieve the effects of hand coding in less time. In addition to a standard template, this vendor markets one that works well with Macromedia Flash. You'll also find a wealth of accessibility products, such as special browsers designed to meet specific needs. For example, BrailleSurf is a special browser designed to output Web site text to a Braille bar or output the text as speech.

AccVerify (`http://www.hisoftware.com/msacc/`): We'll discuss more than a few ways to verify the level of accessibility support your application provides as the book progresses. This particular product validates Web pages created with Microsoft FrontPage. The unique characteristic of this product is that it also checks for other accessibility requirements, such as those for the Web Content Accessibility Guidelines (WCAG). According to the vendor, the product can also check for the Canadian standards. The best part of this product is that you can download and try it free.

Estrada Web Technology (`http://www.estrada-onstage.com/`): Template programming is a popular way to speed development tasks. According to this Web site, Estrada has found a way to improve on generic template programming by adding Section 508 features to its templates. In short, the approach taken by the tools on this site is to prevent Section 508 problems by developing the site using Section 508–compliant templates.

Macromedia (`http://www.macromedia.com/macromedia/accessibility/`): One of the most prominent plug-ins on the Internet today is Macromedia Flash. In many cases, developers will use Macromedia products for all of their gadget additions to a Web site. Unfortunately, although Macromedia does make accessibility features available, the developer hasn't implemented them in many cases. This is the Web page to visit if you want to know more about using the accessibility features in Macromedia products. You might also want to visit this Web site to learn Macromedia's interpretation of the law and understand how you can create better Web sites even if you don't use Macromedia products.

Site Valet Developer Tools (http://valet.htmlhelp.com/tools.html)**:** As
you might expect, this site concentrates on Web site development tools. In
most cases, these tools perform some type of code or content validation.
For example, the site includes a special tool for validating the use of the
Web Accessories feature in Internet Explorer versions 5.5 and above.
The tools work with an amazing number of file formats including
HyperText Markup Language (HTML), eXtensible HTML (XHTML),
Mathematical Markup Language (MathML), Synchronized Multimedia
Integration Language (SMIL), Wireless Markup Language (WML) and
other WapForum types, and eXtensible Markup Language (XML).

Visible Systems (http://www.visible.com/AboutUs/section508.html)**:**
I included this last company because they actually have a section that
provides a point-by-point comparison of how their products satisfy the
Section 508 requirements. The site contains tools that any Web site
developer might use, but the fact that you know their level of Section 508
requirement compliance at the outset is extremely helpful. Figure 3-4
shows an example of the Web site so that you can see how this validation
system works.

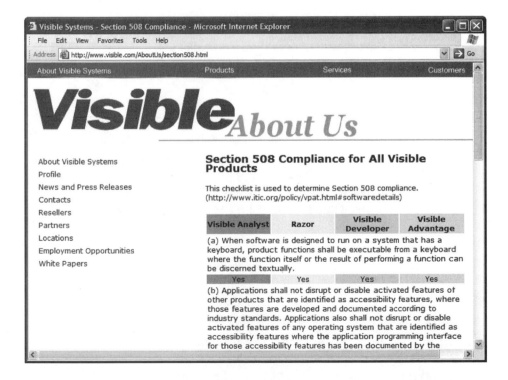

*Figure 3-4. Visible makes their product's level of Section 508 compliance easy to see
and understand.*

Locating Section 508–Specific Training

Somewhere along the way, you'll probably want to get some training. There are many schools offering Section 508–specific training, along with generic accessibility and WAI training. Everyone I've talked with says that they wished they'd spent a little time working on accessibility issues before they went to the schools because the classes tend to be fast paced. The best advice is to try the government's free training at `http://www.section508.gov/index.cfm?FuseAction=Content&ID=5` first, work with your Web pages, and then go to the instructor led classes. With this in mind, the following list tells you about a few of the schools you might want to try.

NOTE   Most companies that offer training also offer consulting services. If you feel that you need additional help after you attend the courses, many of these companies can help. Make sure you check on consulting requirements before you attend the classes.

Accessibility Systems Inc. (`http://www.accessible-systems.com/training.htm`): This company offers a number of courses. Some courses focus on general accessibility, while others are Section 508–specific. Interestingly enough, Accessibility Systems Inc. is one of the few companies that offer client application design courses, as well as a course for disability awareness.

Criterion 508 Solutions (`http://www.criterion508.com/`): As the name implies, this company focuses on Section 508 training, consulting, and other needs. The training doesn't appear to focus on developer issues, but it does discuss issues such as ensuring that your applications and Web sites comply with legal requirements. You'll also find a unique course on Customer Resource Management (CRM) assistive technologies—something I haven't seen offered anywhere else.

Idyll Mountain Internet (`http://www.idyllmtn.com/services/training/`): This company customizes its services for the individual client's needs. The Web site doesn't list any information about content or tell what you can expect to receive. However, if you look at the remainder of the Web site you'll see some high quality offerings for a price.

Information Technology Technical Assistance and Training Center (ITTATC) (`http://www.tvworldwide.com/event_ittatc_061801.cfm` or `http://www.ittatc.org/training/index.cfm`): Unlike many other offerings so far, this company seems to offer all of its training online in the form of webcasts. At the time of writing, you could view the latest presentation online in slideshow or video format with full accessibility input, including closed captioning. The Web site also contains a complete list of presenters, with contact information. In short, this is a great place to go if you want to learn about Section 508 without leaving your office.

Web Accessibility Initiative (WAI) (`http://www.w3.org/WAI/wcag-curric/`): This Web site features a free course called "Curriculum for Web Content Accessibility Guidelines 1.0." What's especially nice about this course is that you can download it and take it as time permits. You can download the training course in slide, RealMovie, or QuickTime movie format. There's also an online format available that works well even with a dial-up connection.

Web Accessibility in Mind (WebAIM) (`http://www.webaim.org/ productsandservices/`): In general, you'll find that this Web site has a lot of information to offer, but the training opportunities are a little slim. At the time of writing, the company offered just one Section 508 course. However, that course includes a wealth of resources, so it's worth the effort to look at it. You can also obtain a DVD containing the training sessions if you can't attend in person.

Developing for the Human Input Device (HID) Example

The term Human Input Device (HID) is a bit nebulous in that it doesn't tell who, why, or how. A HID can include any type of input device from a joystick to a keyboard. The most common HID is the mouse. The reason the mouse is the most common HID is that it's the most flexible from an input connection perspective. The reason you would create a HID is to enable a device to work equally well no matter how you plug it into the system. For example, my current mouse can use a PS/2, 9-pin serial, and a USB connection, all without adding any additional software support (the mouse still requires the Windows driver). The device driver will recognize the mouse no matter which method I use to plug it into the system.

It's easy to get lost in the intricacies of what constitutes a HID and why the HID specification is so important. However, we need to consider one other important issue. In the world of HIDs, the standard that the developer is most interested in is the USB HID standard (see `http://www.usb.org/developers/hidpage/` for a wealth of HID related information). This is the same standard used by Macintosh and Linux developers—of course, each operating system has its own quirks. Part of the purpose of this standard is to ensure that HID and non-HID devices can work together transparently.

This book won't tell you how to develop your own HID drivers. That's a topic for another book. However, we'll discuss the two types of clients that Windows supports for HID information. The first relies on DirectInput. An application can instantiate a DirectInput object and use it to determine the characteristics of a

HID. The second technique is to call on the HID driver directly. This is the technique currently used by many applications because many developers are unaware of the benefits of using DirectInput. The following sections tell about both access techniques.

HIDs and DirectX

It may seem a little odd to see anything written about DirectX in a book on application accessibility—it seems more like the topic you would see in a graphics or game programming book. In some respects, DirectX is a hidden gem that many developers ignore because they think it's too hard to use, doesn't provide much of interest, or that it simply doesn't work well. The truth is that you can use DirectX for more than presentation needs—it also provides the means for detecting hardware and for determining the state of the system. In many cases, from an accessibility perspective, you can learn more about your hardware by using DirectX calls than you can using any other technique.

DirectX does provide support for using HIDs through the DirectInput device functionality. For example, if you want to determine the capabilities of a HID, you can use the `IDirectInputDevice8.GetDeviceInfo()` method. This method returns the HID information in a `DIDEVICEINSTANCE` data structure, which Visual Basic wraps in a `DirectInputDeviceInstance8` object. The `dwDevType` member (obtained using the `GetDevType()` method) will identify a HID as a `DIDEVTYPE_HID` device type. You won't see the `DIDEVTYPE_HID` device type used alone—DirectInput combines this value with the actual device type (such as a mouse) in the `dwDevType` member. However, the fact that you can detect a HID using this method makes DirectInput an interesting solution to the problem of working with a HID in your application.

Lest you think that you can only detect the HID, you can also gain detailed information about it using the `IDirectInputDevice8.GetCapabilities()` method. This function returns specific information about the HID in a `DIDEVCAPS` data structure. The `DIDC_EMULATED` tells you when a HID is emulating a core device such as a mouse or joystick. Using a HID can slow processing because a HID will normally rely on a ring 3 driver instead of the ring 1 kernel mode driver. Normally, this isn't a problem when you're developing a business solution. However, it could become a problem if you're developing an application that must work in real time.

It's time to see if the HID support provided by DirectInput actually works. The following sections provide you with a quick overview of the code to check for a HID using DirectInput. The application is quite simple—all you need is a form with a pushbutton on it to start. The name of the sample application is CheckHID, but you can use any name you like.

Performing the Application Setup

Visual Basic .NET isn't exactly on friendly terms with DirectX 8.1, the version of DirectX available at the time of this writing, so we'll need to perform a little extra work to get this example going. The first thing you'll need to do is add a DirectX DLL reference to your application. The following steps show you how to add the reference.

1. Right click the References folder in Solution Explorer and choose the Add Reference option. You'll see an Add Reference dialog box similar to the one shown in Figure 3-5.

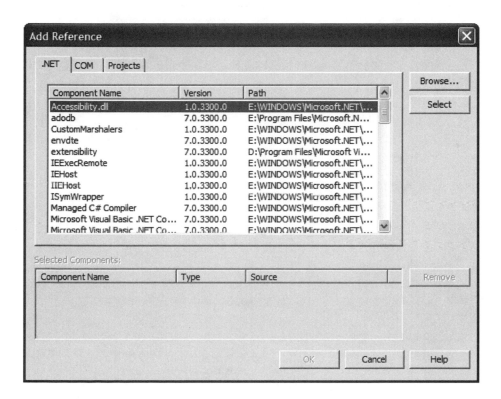

Figure 3-5. Use the Add Reference dialog box to add a reference to the DirectX DLL.

2. Select the COM tab. Wait a few seconds for Visual Studio to populate the list of available COM objects.

3. Highlight the DirectX 8 for Visual Basic Type Library entry, and then click Select. The library will appear in the Selected Components list, as shown in Figure 3-6.

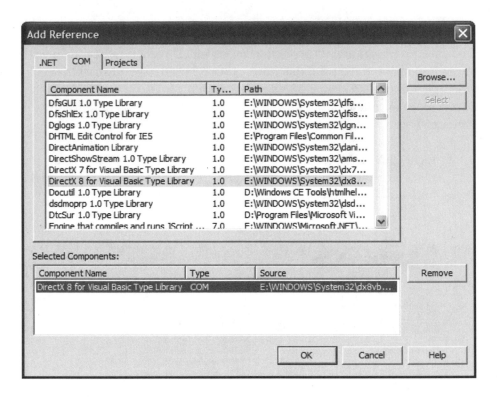

Figure 3-6. Select the DirectX 8 for Visual Basic Type Library to add it to your application.

4. Click OK. Visual Studio will add a reference to the DLL to your application. You'll see it as DxVBLibA in the References folder. However, adding the reference doesn't provide you with quick access to the object. We still need to add a bit of code to make the application work properly.

5. Add the following three lines of code at the very top of the code file for the form. These three lines provide you with quick access to the DirectX 8 DLL and some needed .NET Framework functionality.

```
Imports DxVBLibA
Imports System.IO
Imports System.Text
```

6. Use the Build ➤ Build Solution command to build the application. This step ensures that you added the external support correctly. If the setup or code is incorrect, the application will refuse to build.

Adding Some Code

Before we can do anything with the example, we need to initialize the DirectX objects used to detect the devices on the system. To perform this task, you'll need to override OnLoad(), as shown in Listing 3-1.

Listing 3-1. Creating the DirectX Objects

```
'DirectX objects.
Private DX8 As DirectX8                      'DirectX 8 Object
Private DI8 As DirectInput8                  'DirectInput 8 Object
Private DIDI8 As DirectInputDeviceInstance8  'DirectInput 8 Device

Protected Overrides Sub OnLoad(ByVal e As System.EventArgs)
   'Initialize the DirectX objects.
   DX8 = New DirectX8Class()
   DI8 = DX8.DirectInputCreate()
End Sub
```

As you can see, the initialization problem is simple. First, you create the DirectX 8 object, and then you use this object to create the DirectInput object. The reason you want to make this object global to the class is that constantly creating and destroying unmanaged objects in the managed environment can have some unwanted effects on both performance and memory. It's better to create the object once when you enter the form, and then destroy it when you leave.

The example is set up to check your mouse because that's the most common HID on a standard system. In an actual application, you'd need to check every device, or, at least, every device of interest. Consequently, it pays to separate the code checking a specific piece of hardware from the code that will do something with the information. Listing 3-2 shows CreateInputDeviceInstance(), which creates a device instance, and btnTest_Click(), which acts upon the device instance.

Listing 3-2. Determining if the Mouse Is a HID

```
Private Sub CreateInputDeviceInstance(ByVal DeviceName As String)
   Dim Devs As DirectInputEnumDevices8         'DirectInput device enumeration.
   Dim DevInst As DirectInputDeviceInstance8   'A single device instance.
   Dim Counter As Integer                      'Loop counter

   'Create a list of devices for this machine.
   Devs = DI8.GetDIDevices(CONST_DI8DEVICETYPE.DI8DEVCLASS_ALL, _
                   CONST_DIENUMDEVICESFLAGS.DIEDFL_ATTACHEDONLY)
```

```
    'Search for the correct GUID. Remember to start the
    'Counter at 1 for VB.
    For Counter = 1 To Devs.GetCount()
        'Get a device instance.
        DevInst = Devs.GetItem(Counter)

        If (DevInst.GetProductName().ToUpper() = DeviceName.ToUpper()) Then
            DIDI8 = DevInst
            Exit For
        End If
    Next
End Sub

Private Sub btnTest_Click(ByVal sender As System.Object, _
                        ByVal e As System.EventArgs) Handles btnTest.Click
    'Make sure the DirectInput 8 Device Instance is empty.
    If (DIDI8 Is Nothing) Then
        DIDI8 = Nothing
    End If

    'Get the device information.
    CreateInputDeviceInstance("Mouse")

    'Display the status information.
    If DIDI8.GetDevType() And CONST_DI8DEVICESUBTYPE.DIDEVTYPE_HID _
                            = CONST_DI8DEVICESUBTYPE.DIDEVTYPE_HID Then
        MessageBox.Show("Mouse is a HID")
    Else
        MessageBox.Show("Mouse is not a HID")
    End If
End Sub
```

The functional part of the code begins with the `CreateInputDeviceInstance()` method. This method accepts a string as input. This string specifies the DirectInput device that you're looking for. In this case, we're looking for a mouse, but I'll get to that later in the discussion.

The `Devs` variable contains a complete list of all of the DirectInput devices on the target system after a call to the `GetDIDevices()` method. We could have specified just the mouse devices, but getting all of the devices makes the function flexible. Notice the use of the `DIEDFL_ATTACHEDONLY` constant. Using this constant ensures that the code only obtains devices the user has attached to the machine. The default `GetDIDevices()` method behavior obtains all of the installed devices— attached or not. If you want to determine HID status for an executing application, you want only the attached devices—the ones that the user can actually use.

Now that the code has access to an enumeration of all the attached DirectInput devices, it can use a loop to find the device specified by DeviceName. To do this, the code creates a device instance using the Devs.GetItem() call. A device instance is a single device—one that you can interact with in this case. By comparing the product name of the device instance using the GetProductName() method to the DeviceName value, the code can determine if the requested device instance exists. If it does, the code places the device instance in the application global DIDI8 variable and exits.

 NOTE   The example in Listing 3-2 leaves out a lot of error checking code in the interest of simplicity. For example, I'm assuming you have a mouse attached to your system—any installed mouse will do. If you don't, the application will likely crash and burn.

The btnTest_Click() method begins by ensuring the DIDI8 variable doesn't contain anything. Failure to make this check will create a huge memory leak in your application because the Garbage Collector knows nothing about the COM objects you create. You must manually release the memory they use before the application loses contact with them. Otherwise, the object sits out in memory somewhere until the user restarts the system.

Once the code determines that the DIDI8 variable is usable, it fills it with a device instance using the CreateInputDeviceInstance() described earlier in this section. In this case, the code requests a mouse, but you could modify the code to work with any installed DirectInput device (such as the keyboard).

The code continues by checking the device type of the device instance contained in DIDI8 using the GetDevType() method. Notice the technique for checking for the existence of a specific flag value. You must And the flag value returned by the GetDevType() method with the CONST_DI8DEVICESUBTYPE.DIDEVTYPE_HID. If the returned flag contains the constant, then the result will equal CONST_DI8DEVICESUBTYPE.DIDEVTYPE_HID, as shown in the code. This technique works for checking any single flag value. In the end, the application outputs a message box saying whether the mouse is a HID.

At this point, you might think the application is complete, but it isn't. I can't emphasize this requirement enough—you must clean up your COM objects before the application exits. The best place to do this for applications of the type in this section is to override the OnClosing() method. Listing 3-3 shows the simple code that you'll need to clean up the objects.

Listing 3-3. Cleanup of the DirectX Objects

```
Protected Overrides Sub OnClosing( _
    ByVal e As System.ComponentModel.CancelEventArgs)
    'Clean up the objects.
    DIDI8 = Nothing
    DI8 = Nothing
    DX8 = Nothing
End Sub
```

Detecting the Presence of an HID Using a Driver

Some developers will balk at using DirectX simply to check the existence of a HID, despite the fact that this is a very simple technique. However, Microsoft does provide support for a second method of accessing HID information by working directly with the drivers. Some caveats to consider when using this technique are listed here.

- You will need to use PInvoke to use this method because the calls are part of the Win32 API—Microsoft hasn't (and probably never will) convert these calls so that they appear as part of the .NET Framework.

- Because Microsoft thinks DirectX is the greatest product on earth, Visual Studio .NET doesn't come with any documentation for working with the device drivers.

- Some developers will find the information they need hard to locate. The documentation you need does appear in the MSDN subscription under the Windows DDK Documentation ➤ Interactive Input Devices topic, or you can find the information online.

- Using this technique means learning low-level coding techniques.

There are some benefits to using this technique. For example, this method is faster and requires less memory than DirectInput. In addition, all Windows systems that support HIDs also support this method. When you use the DirectInput approach, you're assuming the target system has DirectX 8 or above installed. Because you can't be sure what the user will have installed, this method is actually better in some respects; it just isn't very easy to implement.

Locating the Online Sources of HID Information

Many developers don't have an MSDN subscription for a variety of reasons. If you want to use the HID calls, you must have a source of documentation for the calls. Consequently, you'll need to look for this information online. Fortunately, Microsoft does supply this information as part of the MSDN site and they grouped it together in one place. The following list tells you the most common HID information sources—topic and related URL.

- System-Supplied Components for HIDClass Devices (`http://msdn.microsoft.com/library/en-us/intinput/hh/intinput/iiarch_8gpz.asp`)

- Driver Stacks for HIDClass Devices (`http://msdn.microsoft.com/library/en-us/intinput/hh/intinput/iiarch_2b6v.asp`)

- HIDClass Devices (`http://msdn.microsoft.com/library/en-us/intinput/hh/intinput/hidclass_0ftz.asp`)

In general, you'll always implement the user-mode client for your application because there isn't a good reason for your application to run in kernel-mode. Microsoft provides a relatively complete procedure you can use for any user-mode client connection at `http://msdn.microsoft.com/library/en-us/intinput/hh/intinput/iiarch_4crr.asp`. Of course, that procedure is missing a little information and all of the function call descriptions assume you're using Visual C++ in unmanaged mode.

TIP This book won't teach you everything you need to know to use PInvoke. However, you can learn the complete facts about PInvoke in my book, *.NET Framework Solutions: In Search of the Lost Win32 API* (Sybex, 2002). You can find this book at `http://www.amazon.com/exec/obidos/ASIN/078214134X/`.

To use PInvoke, you need to know a little more about the functions than the procedure and the function descriptions tell you. The most important piece of information is which DLL contains the calls listed in the documentation. No matter how hard you look, you'll never find that information. However, if you look in the System32 folder, you'll notice a little file called HID.DLL. This DLL holds all of the calls you need. To verify this fact, open the DLL in Dependency Walker and you'll see all of the functions listed in the exports window, as shown in Figure 3-7.

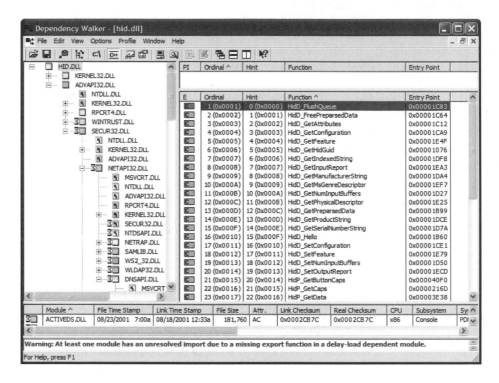

Figure 3-7. The HID documentation will leave you out in the cold unless you know where to look for the missing pieces.

Once you know the sequence of calls you need to make and where to find them in a DLL, you'll need to set up the required function declarations, data structures, and enumerations to use the HID calls in your application. Listing 3-4 shows an example of what type of code you'll need to create to exercise this option.

Listing 3-4. A PInvoke Example for HID Support

```
'This function obtains the GUID of the top level HID devices.
<DllImport("HID.DLL", CharSet:=CharSet.Auto, SetLastError:=True)> _
Public Shared Sub HidD_GetHidGuid(<Out()> ByRef HidGuid As Guid)
End Sub
```

```
Private Sub btnTest_Click(ByVal sender As System.Object, _
                          ByVal e As System.EventArgs) Handles btnTest.Click
   Dim HidGuid As Guid   'The top level GUID

   'Get the HID GUID and display it.
   HidD_GetHidGuid(HidGuid)
   MessageBox.Show("The HID GUID is: " + HidGuid.ToString(), _
                "Application Output", _
                MessageBoxButtons.OK, _
                MessageBoxIcon.Information)
End Sub
```

As you can see, this example demonstrates the first and easiest step of setting your application up for HID support using the device driver method. You must declare the function as `Public Shared` or `Private Shared` (with `Public Shared` being preferable in many cases). Notice the use of the `<DllImport>` attribute. The listing shows the three elements you should always include with this attribute: the name of the DLL, the character set, and support for retrieving error information. The `btnTest_Click()` method makes the call to `HidD_GetHidGuid()` and then displays the GUID in a message box. Figure 3-8 shows the output of this short example.

Figure 3-8. The first step in adding HID support using the device driver method is to obtain the HID GUID.

Summary

This chapter has helped you to make another step on the road to writing accessible applications. We've discussed some of the problems you'll face and you've learned how to overcome them through better resource access and training. In addition, this chapter contains the first programming example for the book. You've learned how to detect, list, and use HIDs.

There's still a lot to do based on the content of this chapter. The first thing you should consider it getting some Section 508–specific training. The contents of this book will help considerably, but some developers might find that they want structured classroom time as well. You'll also want to develop a hardware plan for your application so that it supports all of the required devices. If your company decides to use biometric security methods, you'll need to provide alternative password input methods for users without the required biological features. Finally, make sure you spend some time obtaining the resources you'll need for future development requirements.

Now that you know what the issues are and what problems you'll face in implementing the Section 508 requirements, it's time to look at how you achieve accessibility goals. Chapter 4 will begin looking at the paths that many developers take to upgrade their applications. We'll begin to discuss programming specifics, such as how color will affect your development. In fact, the example in this chapter shows how to build a color blindness simulator you can use to make your applications more accessibility friendly.

CHAPTER 4

Developer Guidelines That Make Sense

In This Chapter:

How Do You Evaluate the Audience Needs?

How Can You Organize the Required Changes?

Which Application Features Are Impossible to Implement?

Why Should You Include Accessibility as a Design Issue?

How Do You Learn About the Reconfigured System?

What Special System Configuration Features Does Windows Support?

When Should You Implement Usage Cue Options?

Which Special Capabilities Are Commonly Implemented?

What Are the Section 508 Application Help and Support Issues?

How Can You Simulate Color Blindness for Design Purposes?

MOST DEVELOPERS FIND that the Section 508 requirements spell out what they have to do for compliance, but not how to meet these requirements. So far, the book has looked at the rules, discussed the requirements the rules enforce, and explained how you can get training to meet the demands of the rules. However, nailing down a precise set of rules for actually updating an application, or creating a new one, is difficult because every application is unique and meets the needs of a different audience. In this chapter, you'll learn about general implementation guidelines—the techniques you'll use to actually upgrade an existing application or create a new one.

Accessible applications consider the needs of the user as the first design issue, so we'll discuss that topic first. You also need to prioritize and document any required changes to your design. This process ensures that you've met all of the requirements, considered every user need, and proven application compliance. Of course, you might run into requirements that fall into the "undue burden" category that we discussed in Chapter 1—it's important to document these issues too.

The chapter continues by providing guidance on the reconfigured system. It tells about the common configuration and helps you learn how to work with the user, instead of placing roadblocks on the path to learning. We'll discuss issues such as usage cues and special application features that you can include. In addition, we'll spend some time looking at the requirements for help files and support.

The final section of this chapter shows how to build a color blindness simulator. It's amazing to see how a display will look to someone who has this particular vision problem. Unfortunately, some people make assumptions about color blindness that simply aren't true. For example, most people have no idea that there's more than one kind of color blindness and that they have to consider them all when they are designing an application. More importantly, this section provides you with an important tool that you can use while creating all of your applications.

Evaluating Your Audience

It's important to evaluate the needs of your audience when you write any application. In some cases, this means performing some usability and performance testing at the outset to determine which features work best. For example, some software vendors use hidden cameras to record usage sessions as part of a strategy that determines how a user reacts to a given interface. A small change can sometimes net a large gain in user performance. (Remember that in the world of accessibility, performance indicates how well the application works—not how fast the application works.)

Consider the contact management database. For many years, developers provided a blank field on the form to hold the two-letter state identifier. In many cases, the user would enter the wrong identifier, which caused errors in the database or forced the application to reject the information. Most contact managers today use a drop-down list that contains all of the state identifiers. Using a drop-down list significantly reduces user think time for this field and eliminates data entry errors. The drop-down list is an example of how user evaluation led to a change in application design that provided gains for everyone. Predetermined values appear in most database applications today because they're so successful in preventing entry errors and increasing user performance.

 TIP Although this book concentrates on the accessibility features provided by the Windows platform, at least in the desktop application realm, it's important to develop your application with the right platform in mind. For example, you might find that many of the users in your target group already know how to use a Macintosh—forcing them to learn the Windows platform probably isn't a good idea. With this in mind, you'll want to know what level of accessibility support the Macintosh provides. The Apple site at http://www.apple.com/disability/ is a good place to start.

Unfortunately, evaluating the needs of those who have special needs often means thinking outside the design box that most developers create for themselves. I say "unfortunately" because many developers fall into design ruts that are difficult or perhaps impossible to overcome. For example, one consultant that I knew assumed that everyone used a mouse. Consequently, his training methods and application design techniques reflected a strong orientation toward mouse usage. In one case, all of the users of an application he created were touch typists. None of these users had any mouse usage experience. The user performance hit was so significant that the company required an application redesign that almost put the consultant out of business.

Another problem that developers must overcome is a lack of knowledge about the special devices used by many people. For example, many eye gaze systems require part of the display to show the keyboard used by the individual. If an application doesn't provide flexible screen space usage, it might present problems for those who use an eye gaze system. The user can't interact with the computer without the eye gaze system, yet the application requires the entire screen, which means that the eye gaze system and the application vie for the same screen real estate. As a result, the application becomes unusable because the screen constraints are too rigid. It's important to evaluate alternative display setups if the desired setup is unavailable. Note that this evaluation process will help your application development as a whole because very few people use just one application all day. Building flexibility into an application for accessibility purposes also nets gains for other uses.

TIP Sometimes the best way to gain an understanding of how these devices work is to obtain one and try it out. After all, many developers create their best applications in response to a need that they noticed while using another product. Accessibility works in the same way. Using the aids makes you aware of needs that programming can answer. Not only are you better attuned to the needs of the user, but you can also learn about the functionality that an application can provide that the user might not know to ask about. One of the most common accessibility aids is the screen reader. Every developer should try a few sessions using such an application while blindfolded. The results are often illuminating! (Don't forget to use common devices, such as the trackball, in an accessibility mode as well—it's important to stretch your imagination and try various tools to see how they work.)

Actually, it's at this point in learning how to address the Section 508 requirements that you need to start looking at the Accessibility features that Windows provides. We'll discuss these features in detail in the "An Overview of the Standard Accessibility

Options" section of Chapter 6. However, you need to know that Windows does provide the On-Screen Keyboard utility shown in Figure 4-1. (This utility is found on the Start ➤ Programs ➤ Accessories ➤ Accessibility menu.) You can place this utility on screen and then try to use your application. I was surprised at how hard some applications are to use with this little utility plastered somewhere on screen— I couldn't access some application features at all. Now, consider the fact that I use a relatively large monitor with a high-resolution display—where did all that screen real estate go? In many cases, it was simply wasted. The developer could have easily created a more economical display that would have accommodated the On-Screen Keyboard. Note that this keyboard is fully functional—you can control it with a mouse or any number of other input devices.

Figure 4-1. Use the On-Screen Keyboard to experiment with the functionality provided by devices such as an eye gaze system.

 TIP It's interesting to note that you can use the On-Screen Keyboard with a joystick. This might not seem like much of a challenge, until you actually try it for a while. Even simple data entry tasks quickly become quite tiring when you have to do it using a joystick. Add the arcane key combinations that some developers use and you'll find that using this alternative input device isn't nearly as easy as it might first appear. Make sure you configure the On-Screen Keyboard to work properly with a joystick using the options on the Typing Mode dialog box (accessible using the Settings ➤ Typing Mode menu option). You'll also want to use the options on the Keyboard menu to configure the On-Screen Keyboard to match your needs. For example, I found the block layout (accessed using the Keyboard ➤ Block Layout command) much easier to use than the regular layout.

The developer must also consider presentation as part of the evaluation process. An experienced user will balk if every prompt on the screen consists of several explanatory sentences. On the other hand, novice users have a hard time understanding one word prompts. In many cases, using balloon help doesn't provide an answer because the novice user probably lacks the knowledge to use it and the experienced user won't need it. The problem is worse when you consider accessibility requirements because you must also support those with cognitive needs. Part of the evaluation process must consider presentation issues to ensure that everyone can understand the application without becoming completely frustrated by having too much help.

Sometimes it's the small things that count most. For example, providing a quick access key for every field in a form is easily accomplished, yet provides an alternative means of access that might be critical to someone with special needs. This particular change to programming practice is important because it can double the number of methods used to access a spot on the form, yet costs the developer at most a few seconds adding another property value to a control. This is the likely type of change that a little evaluation will turn up.

Categorizing the Required Changes

At some point, you'll finish the evaluation process and have part of the application designed. You then need to categorize the accessibility feature additions to an application, especially if the additions are part of an upgrade to an existing application. In at least one case, a company included a full list of accessibility features as part of an update and ended up not implementing any of them in the final application. Let's discuss this problem first because you need to understand why categorization is an important part of designing applications with accessibility in mind. (Actually, it's important for any application, but especially so for the applications that are the focus of this book.)

 ON THE WEB   You're going to learn a lot of new terms as you read this book. The world of accessible programming has its own special terms, just as application development does. The TechDis Accessibility Database Web site at http://www.niad.sussex.ac.uk/glossary.cfm includes a wealth of terms that you need to know. I found this glossary unusually easy to understand. Of course, you'll also find a complete list of terms for this book in the included glossary.

More than a few companies make the mistake of creating an impressive features list that they can't possibly add to an application within the development time allotted. The lead developer may honestly feel that the entire list is doable, but experience shows that the list will get trimmed somewhere along the way in the interest of saving time. The problem is that none of us can see the significant development problem that will cost several weeks to fix in advance. Every delay costs the developer time, which means that every delay eventually translates into lost features. Time is an enemy that anyone who writes code has met.

I've also seen politics take their toll on an application's feature set. Just about every complex application in existence today has one or more features that no one uses. In a few cases, no one actually knows why the feature is present and, in other cases, no one even knows the feature exists. The application has the feature because it was someone's favorite and they had the political clout required to keep the change intact. No one wants to admit that the feature set of many applications is the result of political battling, but the reality is that politics have a lot to do with the resultant features. Politics often bend the feature set of an application in directions that none of the originators had in mind.

Some developers are also slaves to the whims of marketing. Someone in marketing does a little research that says a particular feature is going to become "hot" this season, so your application must have it. The role of marketing is evident in the feature bloat found in many applications. The application ends up with every feature because no one in marketing wants to admit that another application could potentially do a job better.

Time, politics, and marketing are just three of the many reasons that you should categorize the feature set of an application at the outset. The problem is that many developers view accessibility features as time consuming to implement. Accessibility features aren't a political hot button either, unless your company is one of the few that have an enlightened sense of how important they are. With the exception of a very few products (DB2 from IBM is one of them), I've never seen accessibility features touted as a marketing bullet either. In short, accessibility features are the ones most likely to get left out of an application unless you make a conscious effort to make them a priority.

Of course, not every application needs every accessibility feature as part of the first release. It's important to balance all of the requirements of an application. As mentioned in Chapter 1, you must eventually implement all of the Section 508 requirements in your application; however, the government also provides you with time to implement the features as your company resources dictate. The "Understanding the Concept of Undue Burden" section of Chapter 1 speaks of the need to implement accessibility features in a way that shows progress, yet doesn't make accessibility the sole point of focus for your organization.

Consider this example. You're building a data entry application for a company that sells standard items from a catalog. The company has already hired several people with special visual needs, but you don't have anyone else with a special need on staff. In fact, because of the requirement for conversation, it's likely that the company will never hire someone with some special needs, such as a speech difficulty, for this position. Categorizing the accessibility features of the application so that you meet the needs of those who have visual problems first, other problems (such as impaired movement) second, and a speech difficulty third is reasonable in this case. It would be nice if you could implement the full set of accessibility features in the first pass, but categorizing the needs in this way provides alternative paths you can consider.

 CAUTION This book isn't advising you of your legal or moral obligations concerning hiring practices. For example, it would be very hard to deny someone employment in a catalog center, even if they can't speak, because most catalog centers have positions that don't require speaking ability. I designed the examples in this section to help you think through the design and categorization process. You might not have someone with a specific special need working at your company today, so adding a particular feature to an application might not appear high on the list. However, you might have someone with that need working at the company tomorrow, so you eventually need to add the required feature.

Application Features You Can't Implement

A placard posted outside a development area once grabbed my attention, "We do the impossible with nothing." The tongue-in-cheek comment indicated that the workers had a significant humor problem. More importantly, it pointed out the lengths that this group was willing to go to solve a problem. However, reality is that you can't solve every problem unless you have a minimal number of resources and some creativity to go with them. For example, many developers are grappling with the need for better security on computers. Unfortunately, every software-only remedy to date has failed. Most security experts have determined that an acceptable level of security will require some type of hardware addition because the hardware can control the environment without leaving itself open to compromise. (No one would ever claim complete security for any environment.)

Most application developers today don't know how far they can go to meet the Section 508 requirements because they truly don't understand the resources they have at their disposal. Accessibility support begins with the hardware. However, it only begins there and you don't need special hardware support in every case. The operating system is actually the key to accessibility support in most cases. Unlike most operating systems in use today, Windows actually provides a wealth of accessibility resources that most developers don't even know about. (Both the latest version of Linux and MAC OS 10.2 do have improved accessibility functionality—

see http://www.apple.com/disability/, http://www.sun.com/access/, and http://developer.gnome.org/projects/gap/ for details.) You can answer the needs of many people who have vision, hearing, and movement problems without any additional support.

ON THE WEB Sometimes it's helpful to get advice from someone who's already worked out the problems of making an application accessible. One organization that provides a forum for obtaining this type of help is the Alliance for Technology Access (ATA). You can learn more about them at http://www.ataccess.org/. This group will actually get you in contact with someone who will test your application to ensure that it meets the accessibility requirements. ATA is actually a network of about 45 independently operating centers. Each center has resource days where the public can try various types of hardware and software. Learn more about the various centers at http://ataccess.org/community/centers.lasso. Needless to say, getting this type of input is worth its weight in gold when you have a deadline to meet and need to get everything right the first time around.

It's important to realize, however, that you won't know about some resources at the user's disposal at application design time. For example, you have no way of knowing if the user will have an eye gaze system. You can make the application display flexible, but you can't add extra support for an eye gaze system unless someone tells you that the user will have such a device. Even if you know about the device, you still need to have access to drivers and documentation for the device in order to develop an application that uses it. In short, you can prepare the application to make special device use feasible, but you can't ordinarily add support for specific devices.

NOTE In the chapters that follow, we'll see that using APIs can help reduce the work required to provide accessibility device support. For example, many accessibility devices now rely on the Universal Serial Bus (USB), which means you can poll the system for their existence and provide standardized support in many cases. Your application might not use special features of an accessibility device, but it could use the device in a generic way.

Another scenario to consider is one in which the technology isn't available. For example, it would be nice to add full speech capability to applications for those with visual or mobility aid requirements. However, the reality is that the best applications today provide minimal speech assistance. The problem is that the computer can't understand the speaker. Yes, it can input the words and parse them, but the words have no context, and therefore no meaning. The best you can hope to achieve, in many cases, is a means to input commands without using the keyboard. Even so, adding this feature can mean a great deal to someone who needs it.

 TIP The lack of speech capability in applications might not always exist. Vendors and universities have spent a lot of time, effort, and money trying to resolve this issue. Past efforts have always assumed the computer would need to parse the language in the same way that a compiler does. Recent efforts have shown that the parsing is far more intense—the computer needs to break the sentence into parts of speech before it parses the words. This two-step process gives meaning to the words so the computer can understand them in context. Even so, the effort is still in the design phase. Read more about this exciting technology at http://www.pcmag.com/article2/0,4149,580771,00.asp.

A last implementation concern is the environment. You have to consider the environment in which the application is used. For example, what happens if you design an assembly line control application for use by someone with movement difficulties? The application can work and the user can perform the task. There's no doubt that you can achieve success from a purely functional level. However, you need to consider whether the user will have the reaction time required to perform the task. We don't have the technology to make brain-to-device transfers instantaneous yet, so reaction time is a factor. In short, this situation points out that even if we have the interface technology, the application provides full support for it, and the user is willing, adding the feature is still impractical. In fact, this is one situation in which you can't add the feature because it might involve the safety of others using the assembly line. If the person monitoring the assembly line doesn't have the reaction time required to perform the work safely, then it's usually not a good idea to add the feature to the software.

Including Accessibility as a Design Issue

Everything that we've discussed so far in the chapter won't make any difference if you don't look at accessibility as a design issue. Bolting accessibility support onto your application at the end of development won't work very well. Good accessibility support is integrated into the application starting with the design phase.

Most developers know that they need to include certain interface elements as part of a good design. For example, most developers realize the importance of context sensitive help—it's something they design into the application rather than add as an afterthought. The same principle holds true for adding accessibility features. You need to add them as part of the design process—the same process that determines the other requirements for the user interface work for accessibility features too. Accessibility features are an item that you should add to your design checklist to ensure that the features actually appear as part of the design.

So, how do you design for accessibility needs? Chapters 5 through 8 will fill you in on the specifics for desktop applications. Chapters 9 through 12 will tell you how to create accessible Web-based applications. However, there are some criteria you can use for any application, no matter where you might use it eventually. The following list is an overview of these criteria.

- Always provide more than one input method of accessing any given application feature.

- Use short descriptive prompts that tell the reader what they should type or what task a control performs.

- Avoid prompts that form complete sentences or, worse still, entire paragraphs.

- Provide balloon help that offers additional details about a field or control without overwhelming the reader with too much information.

- Ensure that your balloon help tells what the control or field will do, why the user should use it, and when they should use it in no more than three sentences.

- Include context sensitive help.

- Make all controls and fields accessible using both the keyboard and the mouse.

- Determine which features to implement as part of a designer and which to implement programmatically.

- Create and test a color scheme, including art such as icons, before you build the rest of the application.

- Add non-audio prompts in addition to audio prompts for application events, help, input, and other needs.

- Test all proposed keyboard inputs to ensure that they support single-handed operation.

- Add flexibility to the display to support large text or high contrast presentations.

- Research any special devices before you begin the application design process.

- Provide dialog boxes or other configuration methods that adjust every aspect of your application.

- Include a reset option for every configuration feature so that the user can quickly return an option to its default state.

As you can see, the design phase is important for accessibility support because it forces you to consider a number of elements that you might not have considered in the past. For example, I know many developers who add context sensitive help after the application is complete. The help design process should begin with the application design. Creating the help for your application forces you to consider how someone will access a feature and shows how many steps that use of a feature requires. The user interface is more than graphical elements—it's also the methods the user must employ to interact with the application.

Another design consideration is the effect of the full Section 508 requirements on your application as a whole. Even if you decide that your company lacks the resources to create an application that embraces the full set of Section 508 requirements during the first release, you should still design your application to meet the full set of requirements. Designing support into the application now means that the application will have room to grow later. The design can also act as a checklist of Section 508 requirements that you have and haven't implemented for your particular application.

Considering the Odd Implications of Design

Application design is difficult because you never know where your application will end up. As a real world example, consider a consultant friend of mine who developed a contact management database for a small company of 5 people about 10 years ago. The company then grew to about 25 people, so he had to move the application from a small database manager to SQL Server. At one time, this type of move would have completed the application and the consultant would have moved on.

However, the real world has a tendency to break the mold of what worked yesterday. This company soon grew to about 50 people and started employing sales representatives to visit important customers. Eventually the company decided that their sales people on the road would need access to the contact management database, so the consultant added a Web interface. The road warriors were happy with the application until they discovered the usefulness of PDAs. Unfortunately, the Web interface didn't handle PDAs, so the consultant had to modify the application to work in this environment. Of course, as soon as that happened, people also wanted the information on their cellular telephones. Needless to say, the prolific standards generation of the computer industry dictated yet another application change to support cellular telephones.

The company has grown enough that it now works with the government through the Small Business Administration (SBA). Now the consultant is modifying the same application, yet again, to include Section 508 accessibility. I can only imagine that he will eventually have to make some other change. This project has turned into the never-ending story.

Now consider your data storage application. Where could it end up? The problem with most designs is that they work well for one problem, but aren't flexible enough to handle future problems. For example, I don't image that most banks thought that they'd eventually display customer information on a kiosk, yet that's precisely what happened. Like the consultant in my example, they originally designed the kiosks without any accessibility support. However, this soon changed because of the laws in effect for kiosks. This article points out some of the thorny issues for kiosk design: `http://www.kioskbusiness.com/NovDec01/articles/article3.html`. If you paused at the fine for not including accessibility features at a kiosk when you read this article, as I did, you might want to consider that application design again.

The point of all this information is that you don't know where your design is going to end up, so it's important to plan for change. However, sometimes it's just better to include the feature as part of your design today and save money by not having to make a change tomorrow.

Understanding the Reconfigured System

At some point, you'll have finished the design of your application and built it. We'll discuss the actual building process in the chapters that follow. However, before you start distribution, there's a step that follows the development of your application. Sure, you can test it on your local machine, but that type of testing only checks the application's functionality—you still need to verify that the application will work in a real world environment. Generally, this second level of testing requires that you set up some standard user machines and have users pound away at the application looking for flaws. (You'll see in the sections that follow that you can perform a limited amount of testing on your local machine—all you need is the right setup.)

Adding accessibility support to your application doesn't mean that you'll suddenly have to adopt new and truly weird testing procedures. You'll still beta test the application, just as you always have. However, you'll want to use a mix of machine types—those with and without accessibility features added. Otherwise, you won't know if the application works for those with and without special needs. You'll also want to test the application with beta testers who have a range of needs and requirements, just as you always have.

One of the most common problems that developers face when testing applications is configuration. In fact, anyone who performs beta tests on products knows that one of the first questions the vendor's application support staff asks is about the user's configuration. The vendor wants to know every detail about the hardware because the system configuration affects the operation of the software. In sum, knowing the configuration of the beta test system is essential to the software developer.

Now consider the topics in this book. We've discussed a number of issues related to alternative software and hardware support. In some cases, you might not even know what hardware and software the user will have installed on their system. Configuration takes on greater significance because so much rides on the user's setup. The following sections can't provide every answer, but they can help you understand the issues. You'll learn how accessible hardware configurations affect post development testing.

 ON THE WEB The reconfigured system can rely on software alone, but, in many cases, it relies on a combination of hardware and software. The hardware must provide the physical interface that the user requires to interact with the software. For example, when working with a user who has limited mobility, you need to consider issues such as the force needed to push a button. IBM has provided an accessibility checklist that every developer should consult as part of the process of creating an accessibility application. You can find it at http://www-3.ibm.com/able/accesshardware.html. Hewlett-Packard also provides a wealth of accessibility information you should consider at http://www.hp.com/hpinfo/community/accessibility/. Even if you don't need to actually recommend or purchase hardware, the application you create must be capable of interacting with accessible hardware. Knowing the requirements is a good first step to creating such software.

Common Configuration Issues

It's important that you take advantage of as many testing scenarios as you can using standard hardware and software that's configured for accessibility use. Of course, the easiest place to find free software is in Windows. Newer versions of Windows provide better functionality, but some of the features we'll discuss in the "An Overview of the Standard Accessibility Options" section of Chapter 6 have been around since Windows 95. This book will show you the features provided by Windows XP, but these older versions of Windows work well too.

TIP   Microsoft has paved the way in the area of accessibility support. Most of their products include extensive accessibility support that you can use to augment the accessibility support for your application. You can also use these products as a baseline for creating your own applications and as a source of ideas. To learn more about the accessibility features found in various Microsoft products, check their Web site at http://www.microsoft.com/enable/products/microsoft.htm.

All of the actual Windows accessibility applications reside in Start ➤ Programs ➤ Accessories ➤ Accessibility (at least if you have them installed). If you don't have these options installed, you can add them using the Windows Components Wizard of the Add or Remove Programs applet located in the Control Panel. Use the Accessibility Options dialog box shown in Figure 4-2 to control the settings for individual accessibility features. We'll discuss each of the tabs shown in Figure 4-2 in detail in Chapter 6. The important thing to realize is that you can perform a great deal of accessibility testing without spending anything for special equipment. The issue of configuration becomes one of setting Windows up correctly for testing, rather than locating the correct equipment for the job.

NOTE   As unfortunate as it might seem, you won't find much accessibility support in Windows 3.*x*. Part of the problem is that Windows 3*x* presented a number of obstacles to accessibility development, which meant that many developers used DOS applications that avoided Windows completely. However, given the age of this product, you'll probably be better off getting something a little newer if accessibility is a primary goal of your application.

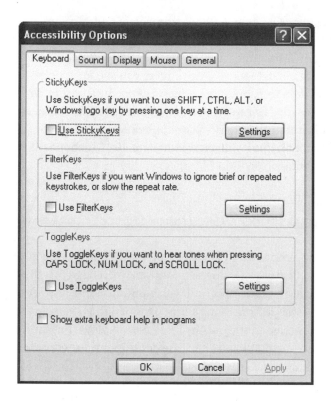

Figure 4-2. Create a specific accessibility setup using the settings found in the Accessibility Options applet.

At some point, the functionality provided by software alone will fail to meet the needs of your intended audience. You'll need to know about the hardware configuration options at your disposal and test your application to work with these options. One of the more interesting places to look for hardware solutions is Freedom Scientific (http://www.freedomscientific.com/). For example, this company produces a hardware augmentation device for the blind called the PAC Mate that will work as a Pocket PC. It provides a modified keyboard and screen reader interface. Using a PAC Mate helps someone with a special visual need use a Pocket PC—freeing the user from cumbersome desktop setups. The PAC Mate works well enough that Microsoft highlighted it on their Web site (http://www.microsoft.com/presspass/features/2002/Oct02/10-16NDEAM.asp). The part that I find interesting about the PAC Mate is that it enables blind users to download and use the same applications as sighted users in many cases.

Each user is different—especially when it comes to special needs. In some cases, that means your application will need to work with more than one special device. For example, your application might have to provide access for someone with both a visual and a hearing need. Most of the products you see for special needs on the market are very adaptable, but targeted toward use by a particular special need population. The reason is simple. Each of these devices has to meet a variety of needs—every user is unique. Likewise, your application will have to provide a level of adaptability that helps it meet individual needs, which means being aware of configuration issues.

Understanding the Large Text Display

One of the most obvious and common examples of an application designer who just didn't think ahead is an application that doesn't work well with large text displays. In many cases, an application that works well with standard fonts doesn't work well at all with large text. (I actually saw one situation when the reverse was true—the developer was so interested in supporting large text displays that the application didn't work well with normal sized text.) The developer must consider three issues when working with large text displays.

User Preferred Text Size: An application should always detect the user text size preference and use that size of text for display purposes. It also helps to detect the user's font face and style selection. For example, a user might want to use a sans serif font, rather than the traditional serif font for text on screen. The user might also want to use bold text to make it easier to see.

Automatic Element Adjustment: When an application resizes the text it uses to meet user requirements, some of the text can be hidden by screen elements such as pushbuttons and text boxes. Theoretically, you can detect the size and position of the text, and then accommodate the large text display by moving the screen elements precisely as needed to ensure optimal text viewing. In reality, most developers won't have time to test every possible combination of text to ensure that the display will work as anticipated. The best alternative is to test the application in a worst-case scenario (using the largest text that you expect the user to need) and provide an alternate large text display setup.

Reduced Element Count: Sometimes an application will automatically adjust the text it uses and reposition the elements—making the application almost impossible to use in the process. A display that's quite readable and usable using standard sized text becomes a scrolling nightmare for the large text user. In this case, you need to consider reducing the number of on-screen elements when using a large font. The interface should allow the user to remove elements that they don't absolutely have to have to use the applications. Toolbars are always a good first choice—most applications have too many toolbars and some applications won't even allow you to remove them. Use shorter prompts whenever possible and get rid of any extra widgets as well. The important thing is to make your display as flexible as possible and give the user full control over what appears on the display.

Flashing Text and Other Blinking Issues

Many developers feel that flashing text and other gaudy displays give their Web site some type of attention grabbing edge that other sites don't have. Unfortunately, such displays often act more as a deterrent to repeat visits than as an incentive to visit the site in the first place. I've seen some online ads that flash at such a frequency and in such colors that they give me a headache. I can only imagine how people who have problems with the blinking displays feel about them.

Flashing displays are more than just a little inconvenient for some members of the population. In some cases, the result can be far more severe than a simple headache. The viewer can experience seizures and other problems. In fact, in certain circumstances, such a display could conceivably result in death, which is a pretty high price to pay to attract attention. Let's just say that this is the one accessibility issue that no one should have a problem complying with because it actually addresses a need that shouldn't require attention in the first place.

Even with the problems of screen flashing, there are some situations in which using some form of flashing is necessary. For example, Windows uses flashing to indicate a change in application status while preventing the application from assuming the screen focus. The default Windows setup flashes the appropriate entry on the Taskbar three times to indicate a change in status. Unfortunately, this setting isn't accessible unless you install the Tweak UI utility (see http://www.microsoft.com/windowsxp/pro/downloads/powertoys.asp for details). Figure 4-3 shows the entry for changing Taskbar flashing in the Tweak UI dialog box. In general, Windows uses flashing correctly, but making the setting accessible without having to install a separate product would make the feature even better. This is an example of how a developer can get almost everything correct, but miss an important user interface element.

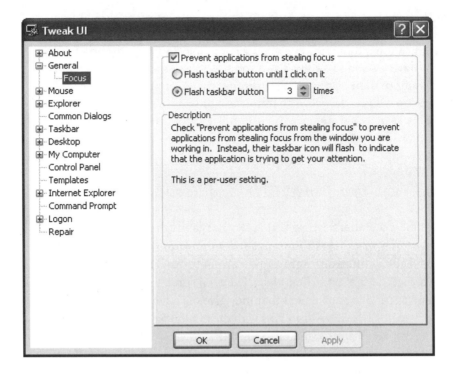

Figure 4-3. Windows uses flashing to provide minimal functionality but doesn't make the settings accessible.

Another place where Windows uses flashing is the cursor. Flashing the cursor makes it easier to find on screen. In this case, Microsoft does make it easy to change the setting through the Accessibility Options dialog box shown in Figure 4-4 (we'll discuss these features in detail in Chapter 6). Notice that you can change both the blink rate and the size of the cursor as needed.

The bottom line is that you should avoid flashing anything on the screen. If you must flash something to make the application work properly, make the element as small as possible and keep the number of flashes small. Always make any screen element that could prove distracting completely adjustable and ensure that the user can turn it off.

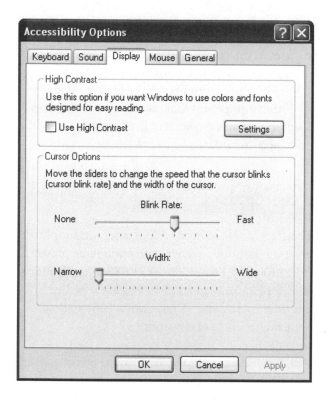

Figure 4-4. Always make features that could prove annoying, such as a flashing cursor, completely adjustable.

Considering Hardware Placement

Until I spent some time working with some of the equipment used by those with special needs, I never realized how awkward it could be to have a system that insists on displaying information in a certain location. Microsoft realized that this was a problem at some point, and now even allows the user to move the taskbar into a more logical place. However, some application elements remain the same. For example, the status bar always appears at the bottom of the application—I've never seen an application that uses the status bar in any other place. Unfortunately, this means that the status bar could become obscured if the user has a piece of physical hardware or an application such as the on-screen keyboard in the way.

Let's talk about some specifics. When you look at an eye gaze system, there are two cameras on either side of the monitor at a minimum. These cameras judge the position of the eye and provide input to the computer based on where the user is resting their eye on the screen. Experience shows that it's easier to view items in the center of the screen, but that the user gets better results with items that are slightly off center. The cameras or other equipment that the user must rely upon to provide input can obscure items at the edge of the screen. In short, make sure the user can move elements around to accommodate any hardware they must use.

An Overview of Usage Cue Options

We'll discuss usage cues throughout the book. Many developers rely on simple text and a little sound to provide every usage cue option when such options are provided. Most desktop applications today don't provide any usage cues. Web applications are only slightly better, but considering most Web applications are new, the support provided isn't all that impressive. In general, developers have to do a lot better job telling users about application usage and events.

This section considers two needs that don't appear elsewhere in the book. The first section deals with a problem that most developers have when working with special devices. In most cases, applications don't provide proper support for these devices, so the user doesn't get the type of feedback that they expect. The second section discusses a need for creative solutions. Sometimes, the solution that takes a different path is the one that works best.

Special Devices for Those with Special Needs

Sometimes it's very helpful to look online and see what types of special devices are available for use with applications. The vendors are good at providing pictures of the device both alone and in use. If you're lucky, you might be able to find a store locally that can provide a demonstration of these special devices. The point is that you didn't start developing applications that used the display, mouse, and keyboard before you experienced using them. Although vendors design special devices to emulate non-special hardware (so a developer doesn't theoretically need special knowledge to write an application that uses it), trying the device will help the developer learn about little things an application needs to do to work well in this environment.

Creating an application that uses a device you've never seen or experienced is difficult, perhaps verging on the impossible. Therefore, the best way to overcome the special device problem is to begin looking at special devices. Two of the better places to obtain this information online are the Apple site at http://www.apple.com/disability/ and the Hewlett-Packard site at http://www.hp.com/hpinfo/community/accessibility/. However, you'll also want to visit some of the accessibility device-specific Web sites such as DynaVox Systems (http://www.dynavoxsys.com/) and the Prentke Romich Company (http://www.prentrom.com/). The point is to spend time learning about these devices from both a usage and a programming perspective.

Once you've gained knowledge about special devices, you might find ways to incorporate them into your application. For example, how would you communicate animal sounds to someone who's deaf? Sometimes, all you need is a balloon on screen with the word roar for a lion, but, in other cases, a special device might provide a connection that you couldn't ordinarily provide. The goal is to provide more than one way to present application output, such as sound, to the user.

Creative Solutions for Difficult Problems

Sometimes you won't find a solution to a particular user need on the first try—sometimes you won't even find it on the fiftieth try. Often, a problem requires a creative solution. For example, I know of one developer who's currently experimenting with techniques for moving around all of the display elements on a form. The user selects a special menu option to allow the screen elements to move, and then deselects the option to enable them for normal use. So far, the developer hasn't created a commercial application with his technique, but I think we'll see it soon enough because it answers a lot of needs.

Many of the best problem solutions I've implemented have come from users, not from my own bag of tricks. The user might not know how to implement the idea, but they've used an application long enough to see deficiencies they'd like corrected. The standard answer to this source of input is to provide a form or a suggestion box where the user can provide static input. Unfortunately, these suggestion methods seldom work because there's no interaction between the developer and the user. Creating an application with a great interface is a communication process. You must be willing to spend time talking with someone about their ideas in order to make them work properly. After all, the user and you are speaking in two different languages—you have to combine the ideas of the user with the realities of development.

Creative solutions aren't limited to the cubicle either. Consider children's toys for a moment. Some of the world's best ideas have come from observing children play with toys such a Legos. Sure, the toy doesn't actually do anything practical, but it's a source of an idea—a concept that you could develop into a creative solution. The idea is to get out of the cubicle and into the real world for a while—look around and you might see an idea in something as mundane as a twig or as magnificent as a sculpture.

Application Help and Support Issues

The law requires certain minimal support requirements and we discussed those requirements to an extent in Chapter 1. Essentially, you must provide help in multiple formats, accommodate the requirements of users with special needs, and discuss issues such as compatibility and accessibility with the user at no additional cost. All of these issues are pretty straightforward and most people understand at a basic level that satisfying these requests is a requirement even if the law doesn't exist.

The following sections address a few help and support considerations for the developer. I'm not trying to tell you everything you ever wanted to know about product support, but were afraid to ask. However, these sections will help you understand how product support can be a helpful experience for both parties. In some respects, it's a shame that developers don't spend more time supporting their products because they'd learn more about the human side of the applications they create.

Meeting Special Help Requirements

Help files, when you can get them with the application, generally come in one or two formats. The most popular format today is a Web-based help file that obtains updates from a Web site as needed. This text appears on screen and hopefully tells the viewer what they need to know about your application. In some cases, you'll also receive a printed form of the documentation that's more portable than online help but is also subject to becoming out-of-date.

To provide full support for your application, you should also consider two other formats for the help file. The first is an audio version of help that provides the same accessibility as the text version. Eventually, companies will probably provide some form of interactive, speech-enabled help for all applications. Learning to work with this type of help now puts your company in a good position to cope with future needs and requirements (the need for paper or text documentation will never go away, however, because people with hearing difficulties will always use them).

A second format to consider is the PDF file. Many companies are using the PDF as the transportable replacement for paper. Not only do you obtain a document that looks like print, but also Adobe has worked hard to make the PDF fully accessible as well. If you do use this technique, make certain that you use the full functionality that a PDF can provide. For example, many of the PDFs that I download don't include bookmarks to make information easy to find. (Read more about making PDFs accessible at `http://partners.adobe.com/asn/developer/pdfs/tn/ReadPDF_MSAA.pdf`.)

There's a side benefit to all of this preparation for most companies. Few pieces of product documentation that I receive are error free. Working with the documentation in several formats can help your company produce better documentation.

For example, the process of creating the audio version of the documentation often helps point out errors in spelling and grammar that go unnoticed otherwise. In addition, the conversion process can help a company better organize the documentation.

Meeting Special Support Requirements

Can you hear me? This is the unspoken question that most users ask when they call for support. It signifies the vendor's need to acknowledge and fulfill a request for assistance. Seldom will anyone actually ask this, but the question of whether the company can actually hear the user is important. Most users feel that they're just a paycheck to the developer. They're someone the company welcomes during a purchase and tries to ignore afterward.

Earlier, I mentioned that users are often the best source of creative ideas for fixing application problems. This idea applies to all kinds of problems—not just those related to accessibility. Most users have great ideas that they'd like to share, even if they don't have any idea of how to implement them. Of course, to gain access to these ideas you have to actually listen to the user.

People with special needs often require a special level of listening. In some cases, they can't express an idea very quickly. In a world where response times are measured in seconds, it's important to slow down and take the time to listen to all of the users that require support. In some cases, the listening process involves asking questions and drawing the answers you need out of the user requesting support. Perhaps your product already meets a special need, but the user doesn't know how to phrase the request in such a way that you can recognize a product feature.

ON THE WEB   Often, advocacy groups are your best resource for information regarding special needs. In many cases, using a local group will help you learn about local needs, requirements, and biases better than a national group. For example, Independence First (`http://www.coperesources.net/iris/fx0ilyq7.htm`) is a group that helps people in Wisconsin. If you can't get enough help locally, try national groups such as the American Occupational Therapy Association (AOTA) (`http://www.aota.org/`), the American Physical Therapy Association (APTA) (`http://www.apta.org/`), and the American Speech-Language-Hearing Association (ASHA) (`http://www.asha.org/`). According to therapists, part of the problem of special needs is that the human services and the technological fields just don't communicate. Contacting and working with these groups can help you make your application more usable.

At this point, you might think I'm talking exclusively about people with special needs, but it isn't true. All users need to feel that they're important to your organization; this means you need to spend the time to talk with them and actually understand what they're trying to say. The additional 10 or 15 minutes you spend trying to understand one user will very likely reduce the time you will need to answer the same question from every other user that asks it.

Providing Helper Assistance

There's a point when many companies try to throw in the towel on user support—it's when they have to start discussing a support question through a third party. Often, the people who call you for help will need a helper (and I'm not just talking about those with special needs). My network room is small—it's packed with a lot of equipment. When I have a hardware question, I normally have my wife operate the telephone while I answer the questions of the support person. She has to help because I have my head stuck in the equipment—hardly the place to put a telephone. You wouldn't believe how many support people become quite rude in this situation.

Helper assistance is required for any type of application you build. In some cases, the person you're trying to help won't be able to hold the telephone, answer your questions, input some new settings, and still try to make sense of what they're doing. This problem doesn't always happen, but it does, so it's important to provide the help when needed.

Something that does help in this situation is to provide the user with a pre-printed list of every question that the support person is going to ask for every call as part of the documentation. Some companies provide a list of questions they're going to ask and it makes the process much smoother. Also, make sure your application provides the information the user will need in a convenient place, such as in the About dialog box.

Considering the Issues of Privacy and Security

This book has discussed accessible applications, training, user needs, and all kind of other accessibility issues. In some people's minds, accessibility equates to openness because that's what access normally denotes to them. Given the special needs of some of these individuals, openness does seem to be a key factor and consideration. However, accessibility development isn't a license to disregard either the security or the privacy of the individual. In fact, these concerns take on new meaning because individuals with special needs are often vulnerable.

I was reading an article the other day regarding privacy issues for applications (http://www.baselinemag.com/article2/0,3959,669669,00.asp). This article caused me to think about the privacy and security concerns that developers have to consider for those with special needs. In this article, companies are concerned that the appliances they're developing will open people up to an invasion of privacy because someone could break into their home network. However, in the grand scheme of things, let's face it—the amount of beer you consume might be embarrassing, but the fact that someone else knows about it isn't a life or death situation.

Privacy and security for someone with special needs could, in fact, be a matter of life and death. When you create these applications, you're responsible for ensuring that the application works as expected—all of the time (or at least that it fails gracefully when it can't). More importantly, the support you provide must remain confidential, and any information tracked to meet the needs of the user must remain secret. As a developer, you must resolve to help maintain the privacy and security of the individuals that you help with your application.

Building the Color Blindness Simulator Example

Color blindness is one of the more common problems faced by users of your applications, yet no accommodation is made for these users in most cases. The statistics vary, but most of the resources I read in preparation for this section say that between 8 and 9% of the male population and about 0.5% of the female population have some type of color blindness. Given the number of people with this problem, someone who uses your application will have color blindness—it's not one of those issues that you can avoid.

Some developers have the misconception that they can avoid developing accessible applications because they only work for the military or only work with specific subgroups of the population. Color blindness affects every walk of life. Even members of the military have color blindness. As a former member of the Navy, I know that the service tests members for color blindness and places affected personnel in rates (jobs) where color discernment isn't an issue. It doesn't matter who the application is for; someone using it is going to have color blindness. Consequently, every developer, no matter what kind of application they develop, needs to test their application for color blindness issues.

CAUTION It's never a good idea to view the output of the example application as an exact replica of what the user will see. An individual user's vision will vary, so the palettes used in building this application provide you with a good idea of what they'll see, but they can't show you precisely what they'll see. In addition, the adjustments of your monitor, your own color perception, and environmental factors such as the amount of ambient light will affect the output of this application. In general, this example is design to provide you with some basic input about your application or Web site, but you shouldn't rely on it for specifics for a given user.

There are a number of ways to test your application to ensure that it's friendly to those with color perception needs. This section of the chapter discusses two techniques. We'll look at a packaged application that you can easily access online first. This application has some limitations, but it works very well. The second application is one that we'll develop for desktop use. This application uses a palette to immediately change the color values of a bitmap. You could also change the individual pixel values, but this technique is faster and more consistent.

ON THE WEB The palettes used for the example in this chapter are based on the chart shown at `http://more.btexact.com/people/ rigdence/colours/colours1.htm`. These charts are based on mathematical characteristics and observation.

Using the Vischeck Alternative

Many developers are leery about writing a calibrated tool of the kind found in the example application for this section of the chapter. A calibrated tool is one in which the user anticipates a specific output given a specific input under all conditions. Writing a color blindness simulator that provides inconsistent output doesn't help anyone. If you decide that you'd rather use a prebuilt tool for this purpose and don't mind uploading screenshots of your application to a Web site, you can using the Vischeck site at `http://www.vischeck.com/vischeck/vischeckImage.php`.

ON THE WEB   The Vischeck Web site actually hosts several useful applications. One of these applications demonstrates the process of *Daltonization*—correcting color for someone with color blindness. Of course, you can't actually make someone see the full spectrum of color if their eyes are unable to detect it, but you can improve their ability to see an image despite the color blindness. You can read about this process at `http://www.vischeck.com/daltonize/`. Of course, it helps to see Daltonize at work, so you'll want to try out the online version at `http://www.vischeck.com/daltonize/runDaltonize.php`.

This Web site works similarly to many of the other testing sites we'll visit in this book. Figure 4-5 shows the initial page for this Web site. Click Browse to locate a GIF or JPG file on your local hard drive. You can't paste an image from the clipboard to the program online. Also, it appears as if you can't specify a Web URL—the image must appear on your local hard drive.

Figure 4-5. The Vischeck site accepts a file from your hard drive as input.

After you provide the name of a file on your hard drive, select a color blindness option (only the most common conditions are provided on this Web site) and click Run Vischeck! Figure 4-6 shows typical output from this application when the Protanope option is used. The left side of the screen shows the standard display, while the right side shows the modified display.

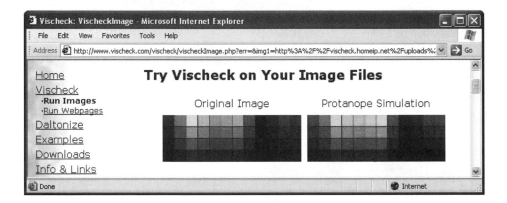

Figure 4-6. Use the output of the Vischeck site to validate your Web site pages.

As you can see, this Web site is especially useful if you only have a few images to check. To use Vischeck on a Web site, you'll need to obtain a screen capture of the target Web site, save it as a JPG or a GIF file on your local drive, and then provide it as input to the Vischeck site.

Vischeck is a good place to start, but it isn't a complete solution. Using Vischeck on more than a few sites or to check more than the three common forms of color blindness might prove difficult. That's the reason the sample application in this chapter is important—it accepts input that you copy and paste directly from the Web site with no intermediate steps. The sample application also checks all six forms of color blindness. In addition, you can use the sample application for a number of common file formats in addition to those supported by Vischeck. For example, the sample application will work with a BMP file.

Writing the Essential Code

Color manipulation can become relatively complex, even if your only purpose is to spruce up an existing picture with a little extra color. Simulating color blindness also involves complex equations that determine what someone with color blindness is actually seeing. The problem for the developer of such an application is that the person with color blindness has no point of reference on which to base input. They've never seen the color that you're trying to tell them about, and consequently, they can't tell the developer how to model an application that simulates the color blindness.

During my research for this application, I noted that developers use everything from logarithmic calculations, to neural networks, to model color blindness. In general, the output from these various calculations is similar, but not precisely the same. Even if the people modeling color blindness could agree on one way to calculate the effects of such a perception problem, individuals would vary, which means that your model would work precisely for at most one person. (A poorly designed model might not even work for one person.) In short, the application in this section provides a very good model, but it's only a model; you should consider it a guideline that will help you create color blindness–friendly applications.

This application relies on in-memory tables of color value replacements and a palette to modify the color of the individual graphics. Some images may not work well using this approach, but most images will work fine. There are a number of alternative paths I could have explored for this application, including calculating the individual pixel values on the fly and manipulating individual pixel values. The reason I chose the approach used in this example is that the conversion is fast, reproducible, and easy to understand. We won't discuss all (or even most) of the application code for this example. You'll find the complete application in the \Chapter 04\ColorCheck folder of the source code that you can obtain from the Downloads section of the Apress Web site (`http://www.apress.com`). This section describes just the essentials of the conversion process.

Developing the Palette

At one time, developers used a number of techniques to create palettes for their images. The result was a vast array of image types and styles that didn't work well with each other. Every image competed with every other image for use of the one system palette that Windows use to display its image content. Background images often suffered because they would appear in gruesome color combinations that no one could see very well. Consequently, most graphics use a standard 216 color palette consisting of 6 bits for each of the 3 colors: red, green, and blue. In general, you should always use a standardized palette to create Web applications, but a standardized palette is still optional for desktop applications. You can find these standardized palettes online at the BTexact Technologies site at `http://more.btexact.com/people/rigdence/colours/PalFiles.htm`.

Because this is a desktop application, we can't assume the images will use a standardized palette, so it's important to create an array of standard color transforms so that even non-standard palettes remain useful. The resulting arrays act as an in-memory database that provides lookup values. Listing 4-1 shows the code used to initialize these arrays.

Listing 4-1. Initializing the Palette Transform Arrays

```csharp
// Define the transformation arrays.
private Color[,,]   aProtanopia = new Color[6, 6, 6];
private Color[,,]   aDeuteranopia = new Color[6, 6, 6];
private Color[,,]   aTritanopia = new Color[6, 6, 6];

public frmMain()
{
    // Required for Windows Form Designer support
    InitializeComponent();

    // Fill the color arrays.
    aProtanopia = FillColorArray(aProtanopiaData);
    aDeuteranopia = FillColorArray(aDeuteranopiaData);
    aTritanopia = FillColorArray(aTritanopiaData);
}

private Color[,,] FillColorArray(int[,] InputData)
{
    int         DataCounter = 0;            // Data array counter.
    Color[,,]   Temp = new Color[6,6,6];    // Color array.

    // Loop through the various count value until the Protanopia array
    // is filled.
    for (int RCount = 0; RCount < 6; RCount++)
        for (int GCount = 0; GCount < 6; GCount++)
            for (int BCount = 0; BCount < 6; BCount++)
            {
                // Get the array value.
                Temp[RCount,GCount,BCount] =
                    Color.FromArgb(InputData[DataCounter, 0],
                    InputData[DataCounter, 1],
                    InputData[DataCounter, 2]);

                // Increment the data counter.
                DataCounter++;
            }

    // Return the results.
    return Temp;
}
```

As you can see, the application uses a three-dimensional array for each transform array. The red, green, and blue colors act as indices to the array to select a proper color combination based on the current color. The application constructor calls on the FillColorArray() method to fill each of the arrays with data based on calculations for that type of color blindness.

Notice that the three-dimensional array is based on the Color class. However, when you perform the color transform calculations, you're not working with actual colors—you're working with numeric representations of those colors. The application uses the Color.FromArgb() method to perform the conversion from numeric to color data. Notice that the FillColorArray() method uses three for loops to cycle through the various elements of the three-dimensional array. The numeric data appears within a two-dimensional int array.

Once the code creates the three-dimensional color array to use for palette conversion, it waits for the user to load a file. The file may or may not have a palette associated with it. If the file lacks a palette, the application will assign one to it. In either case, the application saves the application's default palette as CPNormal. It then performs the required conversions for the other three palettes: CPProtanopia, CPDeuteranopia, and CPTritanopia, as shown in Listing 4-2.

Listing 4-2. Manipulating a Palette Using the Transform Arrays

```
// Color variable used to store the current color settings.
ColorPalette    CPNormal;
ColorPalette    CPProtanopia;
ColorPalette    CPDeuteranopia;
ColorPalette    CPTritanopia;

private void CreatePalettes(ColorPalette CP)
{
    // Create each of the color palettes in turn.
    CPProtanopia = CreateModifiedPalette(CP, aProtanopia);
    CPDeuteranopia = CreateModifiedPalette(CP, aDeuteranopia);
    CPTritanopia = CreateModifiedPalette(CP, aTritanopia);
}
```

```
private ColorPalette CreateModifiedPalette(ColorPalette CP, Color[,,] Data)
{
    ColorPalette    Temp;    // Temporary data holder.
    PixelFormat     PF;      // The standard pixel format.
    Bitmap          Sample;  // Holds sample color table.
    Int32           Red;     // Red value index.
    Int32           Blue;    // Blue value index.
    Int32           Green;   // Green value index.
    Double          RConv;   // Red conversion value.
    Double          BConv;   // Blue conversion value.
    Double          GConv;   // Green conversion value.

    // Create a temporary palette.
    // Begin by creating a sample graphic.
    PF = PixelFormat.Format8bppIndexed;
    Sample = new Bitmap(1, 1, PF);

    // Use this generic bitmap for the palette it contains.
    Temp = Sample.Palette;

    // Modify the entries to simulate color blindness.
    for (int Counter = 0; Counter < CP.Entries.Length; Counter++)
    {
        // Obtain the current color values.
        RConv = CP.Entries[Counter].R;
        GConv = CP.Entries[Counter].G;
        BConv = CP.Entries[Counter].B;

        // Define the index value used for looking up the conversion
        // colors.
        Red = Convert.ToInt32(5 - RConv / 51);
        Green = Convert.ToInt32(5 - GConv / 51);
        Blue = Convert.ToInt32(5 - BConv / 51);

        // Obtain the entry from the lookup table and place it in the
        // new palette.
        Temp.Entries[Counter] = Data[Red, Green, Blue];
    }

    // Return the result.
    return Temp;
}
```

Because the palettes are global to the application, the application can experience a number of very weird contamination scenarios. Consequently, you need to develop the palette conversion routines in such a way that contamination is eliminated. The CreatePalettes() method accepts a copy of the normal palette as input, but it doesn't use the CPNormal palette because that would result in contamination. The CP variable contains a copy of the palette created from the image the user selected for input.

The CreateModifiedPalette() method performs the actual task of creating the modified palettes for each of the common forms of color blindness. Notice that this method begins by creating yet another palette—this one based on the standard Windows palette. The reason for creating another palette is to ensure that the input palette is completely separate from the output palette so that the application doesn't experience palette contamination.

The next set of steps is performed in a loop. The application must create a converted color value for each color value in the existing palette. It does this by obtaining the current color values: red, green, and blue from the CP.Entries palette array. Creating an index in the transform array comes next. Performing this step means dividing the conversion color by 51 to create an index. The transform array is in reverse order from white to black, so the index value must reflect this fact by subtracting the color value from 5. Once the application computes an index into the transform array, it can place the resulting color value into the appropriate array entry of the Temp ColorPalette. The loop continues until all of the entries in the palette are converted; then the CreateModifiedPalette() method returns the resulting ColorPalette object.

Loading the Image

Earlier, I mentioned that the application creates the transform array and then waits until the user loads an image. Most of the task of loading the image is the same as for any other application. You create a File Open dialog box, let the user select a file as input, and then begin working with the resulting input value. Listing 4-3 shows the process for loading an image in this application. Notice that the user can filter the images and can choose from a number of image types.

Listing 4-3. Loa)ding an Image

```csharp
private void mnuFileOpen_Click(object sender, System.EventArgs e)
{
    OpenFileDialog   Dlg;         // File Open Dialog
    String           File2Open;    // Selected Filename
    Bitmap           Graphic;      // The opened bitmap.
    PixelFormat      PF;           // The standard pixel format.
    Bitmap           Sample;       // Holds sample color table.

    // Set up the File Open Dialog
    Dlg = new OpenFileDialog();
    Dlg.Filter = "Windows Bitmap (*.bmp)|*.bmp|" +
        "Enhanced Metafile (*.emf)|*.emf|" +
        "Graphics Interchange Format File (*.gif)|*.gif|" +
        "Windows Icon (*.ico)|*.ico|" +
        "Joint Photographic Experts Group (*.jpg;*.jpeg)|*.jpg;*.jpeg|" +
        "Portable Network Graphic (*.png)|*.png|" +
        "Windows Metafile (*.wmf)|*.wmf";
    Dlg.DefaultExt = ".gif";
    Dlg.Title = "Open File Dialog";

    // Display the File Open Dialog and obtain the name of a file and
    // the file information.
    if (Dlg.ShowDialog() == DialogResult.OK)
    {
        File2Open = Dlg.FileName;
    }
    else
    {
        // If the user didn't select anything, return.
        return;
    }

    // Open the document and make a copy.
    Graphic = new Bitmap(File2Open, true);

    // Change the title bar.
    frmMain.ActiveForm.Text =
        "Application Color Blindness Tester - " + File2Open;

    // Draw a graphic normally.
    pbSample.Image = Graphic;
```

```
// Store the color palette used for this image.
if (Graphic.Palette.Entries.Length > 0)
{
    // Use the color palette stored in the image if possible.
    CPNormal = Graphic.Palette;

    // Create the alternate palettes.
    CreatePalettes(Graphic.Palette);
}
else
{
    // Create a sample graphic.
    PF = PixelFormat.Format8bppIndexed;
    Sample = new Bitmap(1, 1, PF);

    // Use this generic bitmap for the palette it contains.
    CPNormal = Sample.Palette;

    // Create the alternate palettes.
    CreatePalettes(Sample.Palette);
}

// Enable the Color Setting menu.
mnuColor.Enabled = true;
CheckThis(mnuColorNormal);
}
```

Once the `mnuFileOpen_Click()` method gets past the act of opening the file for use, it begins to manipulate the file. In this case, the application creates a new bitmap that holds the file pointed at by the File Open dialog box. The code checks the input image for a palette by checking the `Graphic.Palette.Entries.Length` value—a value of 0 indicates that the graphic has no palette attached. If the image does have a palette, the application saves the palette to `CPNormal`. It then calls the `CreatePalettes()` method discussed as part of Listing 4-2 to create the specialized palettes for the color blindness simulation.

If the image doesn't have a palette, the application creates one for it using a standard `Bitmap` object. Note that you must supply a `PixelFormat` object as part of the creation process. The new palette is saved in `CPNormal` and also used for the `CreatePalettes()` method call. As a final step, the method enables the Color Setting menu and checks the Normal color option on it.

Creating Application Output

At this point, you know how the application creates the color transform array and modifies the image palette. Actually, the application maintains four palettes, one for each of the options on the Color Setting menu. Listing 4-4 shows the final part of the process. This listing only shows one of the color selection menu handlers because they all work the same.

Listing 4-4. Modifying the Image Appearance

```
private void CheckThis(MenuItem MenuOption)
{
    // Clear the current checks.
    mnuColorNormal.Checked = false;
    mnuColorProtanopia.Checked = false;
    mnuColorDeuteranopia.Checked = false;
    mnuColorTritanopia.Checked = false;

    // Check the selected menu option.
    MenuOption.Checked = true;
}

private void mnuColorNormal_Click(object sender, System.EventArgs e)
{
    // Check this option on the menu.
    CheckThis(mnuColorNormal);

    // Restore the image.
    pbSample.Image.Palette = CPNormal;
    pbSample.Invalidate();
}
```

The CheckThis() method modifies the appearance of the Color Setting menu. It's important to keep the correct color option checked so that the user knows which color is in use at the time.

The mnuColorNormal_Click() method begins by calling the CheckThis() method to check its option on the menu. The next step is to assign the CPNormal palette to the image and then invalidate the image so that the .NET Framework knows to redraw it. Because all of the work is done beforehand, the process of switching from one color to the next is nearly instantaneous.

Performing a Color Blindness Test

At this point, you're ready to begin working with some graphics. The source code folder contains a simple color bar that you can use for initial testing. It helps you see the range of color changes that occur for various types of color blindness. Figure 4-7 shows the output from this application for Protanopia.

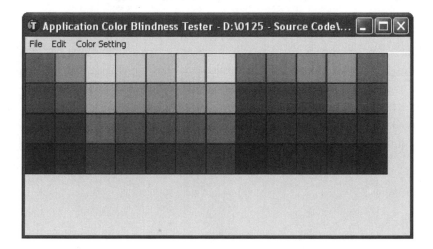

Figure 4-7. It's time to test your applications and Web site for color blindness issues.

Summary

This chapter has demonstrated a fourth accessibility consideration for all applications—it contains the guidelines developers will need to create usable and accessible applications. You've learned about the needs of the user and seen how those needs are reflected in the design of your application. We also discussed application decisions that developer must make.

As mentioned at the beginning of this chapter, every application is unique. It's time for you to begin mapping a strategy for designing or updating your application to meet the Section 508 requirements. The examples throughout the rest of the book show various strategies you can use to meet these requirements, but in the end, you have to make a decision on how your application will comply with the requirements.

You'll also want to test the Color Blindness Simulator. This application demonstrates how your Web site or desktop application will look to someone who has color vision problems. In some cases, you'll be surprised at how some color combinations will make text or other screen elements invisible. It would probably be a good time to test all of your applications for compliance with this particular Section 508 requirement. It's actually the easiest requirement to meet from a programming perspective, yet the hardest requirement for someone with normal vision to accommodate because normal vision prevents the developer from seeing what the person with color blindness sees.

Chapter 5 begins the desktop application portion of the book. At this point, we'll begin looking at various techniques you can use to make applications comply with the Section 508 requirements. The examples in Chapter 5 will demonstrate such features as user interface elements, screen tracking, and use of animation. You'll also learn how to obtain the current screen settings. This task is exceptionally important for all accessible applications because you want to preserve the user environment and ensure your application interacts correctly with it.

Part Two

Writing Accessible Desktop Applications

Desktop Application Essentials

In This Chapter:

What Can You Use to Perform Automated Application Testing?

What Effect Does File Format Have on Application Output?

How Can Your Application Track the Screen Focus?

What Can You Do to Ensure Applications Use Consistent Controls, Status Indicators, and Other Elements?

When Should You Implement Colors in Controls and UI Elements?

How Can You Obtain and Use the Current Display Settings?

What Are the Animation and Animation Alternatives?

How Should You Create a Data Entry Form?

IT'S FINALLY TIME to look at some specifics for the desktop environment. This is the first chapter where we concentrate on the needs of this portion of the Section 508 requirements. Just in case you've forgotten, this chapter begins coverage of the Software Applications and Operating Systems (Section 1194.21) requirements.

One of the problems that developers will face in implementing Section 508 requirements is ensuring that their applications actually follow the rules. It's relatively easy to check many of the requirements for a Web page using automated techniques because they rely on tags that test applications can easily check using a parser. However, checking a desktop application for problems can prove a little more difficult. We discuss some methods for automating testing in the first part of this chapter.

NOTE   We'll discuss Web site automation in the "Using an HTML Checker" section of Chapter 9. The effectiveness of these tools varies. Some experts say that they check as little as 55% (especially when working with the more stringent Web Accessibility Initiative [WAI] criteria) and as much as 80% of the required accessibility functionality. No one says that these tools will check everything and you should assume they don't.

Sometimes desktop applications have hidden problems that you won't know about until you actually begin making them accessible. One of the most common problems is the issue of the file format used for data storage. You might think that this is a simple issue with a simple solution, but this chapter will show you that there are hidden problems that defy simple resolution. In fact, you might find that you have to trade one set of problems for another in order to ensure that your application is accessible.

After we discuss these preliminary issues, the chapter will begin by looking at the user interface—often abbreviated UI or GUI, the latter for graphical UI. We'll begin by looking at the issue of tracking screen focus. This is a Section 508 requirement because the user might not be able to see the current screen focus— you usually have to provide alternatives so that the user can track the screen focus without visual verification. (It's even more important that the assistive technology be able to track the change, so you need to provide programmatic as well as visual indicators.) We'll also discuss requirements for creating controls, status indicators, and other screen elements. The discussion continues with a look at color usage in applications.

The final three examples in the chapter discuss some practical design decisions you'll need to implement. The first example describes how you can obtain and use the current display settings in an application. This technique avoids applications that have small text elements when the user really needs something larger. In addition, it shows how to reorganize a window for better display in high contrast, large text mode. The second example shows how you can avoid using animation in your application. Using animation can help, in some cases, but it can definitely hinder in others. For example, an animation that guides the user in making selections is useful, but an animation that distracts the user is not. We'll discuss both situations as part of the example. Finally, you'll see how to create a simple data entry example that responds to specific accessibility needs.

Using Automated Testing Techniques

All applications require some form of testing to ensure that they meet the original design goals with few, if any, errors. For some developers, the process of debugging the application and making sure that it's technically correct is the end of the testing process. In fact, some users would claim that the developers don't even get that far. Applications that don't meet design goals often cause more problems than they solve. An application must provide a good user interface, easy access to application features, and perform all of the tasks it's designed to do with a minimum of errors (bugs).

 TIP Sometimes you'll need additional resources to test your application or bring it up to standard when a test fails. When this happens, you'll want to visit ABLEDATA, one of the most comprehensive (and oldest) databases of accessibility products and information on the Internet. The National Institute on Disability and Rehabilitation Research (http://www.ed.gov/offices/OSERS/NIDRR/) sponsors this database. You'll find the ABLEDATA database at http://www.abledata.com/.

Unfortunately, time is a problem for everyone. Management (and marketing) constantly pushes developers to write applications in less time because every second spent writing the application costs money. In many cases, the unfortunate result of such rushing is a buggy application with a reduced feature set. Such applications often come with a host of performance and speed issues, use a lot of resources, such as hard disk space and memory, and work slowly for the number of resources they expend. For the user with special needs, inadequate testing can also mean loss of access and inconsistent application operation.

Automated testing techniques help solve some of these issues, yet they keep the developer cost of the testing low. Of course, there are human issues that still require manual testing to ensure that the application meets the goals. Consequently, complete application testing is often a mix of automated and manual testing—the trick is to learn where to draw the line between automated and manual testing to achieve maximum effect at minimal cost. The testing function and its team members are often referred to as QA (for Quality Assurance).

The following sections help you learn where to draw the line. More importantly, they help you understand the impact of automated and manual testing on accessibility requirements for your application. We'll also discuss some third-party tools you should consider using. Finally, we'll discuss how application testing differs from mere technical proficiency and where automated testing actually gets in the way of accessible application development goals.

Understanding the Advantages of Automated Testing

Some developers embrace automated testing with a never ending bear hug, but many others are less enthusiastic. The main problem is loss of control. Using automated testing means that the developer no longer has complete control over the application testing process and that makes some people uncomfortable. In addition, there's a perception that automated testing is somehow less capable than other techniques. There's some truth to these perceptions, but only if you use automated testing as your only tool. It's important to create a balance between automated and manual testing.

Creating a balanced testing methodology means understanding where both types of testing excel. Most developers are well acquainted with the virtues of manual testing and some have mourned the inadequacies of this technique when an application goes out the door with a major bug. Automated testing is also especially useful in some areas. The following list provides an overview of some of the places where automated testing is especially useful.

Consistency: One of the most common problems that many developers experience is creating a consistent test environment. The problems are many, but normally they involve some type of human interaction. Two users might test the application differently, so the output of a test can vary depending on the user who is conducting it. Developers can also interpret the results differently, further compounding the problem. Automated testing removes much of the human interaction from the equation—it tests the software precisely the same way each time the test is run and provides reports that interpret those results using the same criteria each time.

Accessibility: Automated testing can help resolve a number of accessibility problems. For example, you can test to ensure that every control and field includes a keyboard shortcut. The tests can ensure that clicking a menu option, a toolbar button, and using a speed key all result in the same action for a given selection. These tests are required each time the developer makes a change to the application to ensure that nothing in the user interface is broken. However, actually running these tests manually can prove cumbersome because of their repetitive nature. Checking the constants of a user interface is a perfect use of automated testing.

NOTE Automated testing works well in many cases, such as when you are testing keystrokes. However, you'll still need to perform manual testing of requirements such as captioning videos. In some cases, a human is the only testing tool that will work.

Repeatability: Attempting to replicate a set of tests that use human effort is bound to cause problems. The tester might forget to run the tests in a certain order or with specific setups in place. Automated testing provides repeatable results because it always performs the tests in the same order and using the same setups. When the results aren't the same from run-to-run, the developer can normally narrow the cause down to environmental inconsistencies or even to difficult bugs within the application. (For example, a memory error might not appear on every run, but it could follow a discernable pattern that makes it easier for the developer to trace.)

Speed: Testing takes time. If the tests are precisely the same each time, the human operator can get bored or tired, making the process run even longer. Automated testing can provide test results quickly and reduce the time required for each development cycle. In general, the automated test software inputs data at the speed of the computer, rather than at the speed of the user.

Documentation: Humans often forget to document important test events or lose track of the test sequence. In addition, they often document the information inconsistently from run-to-run, which means that humans document each test run differently. Finally, each person running the test tends to document the issues they feel are most important, which means that the documentation each person produces will be unique. Automated testing techniques remove these concerns.

Analysis: Often, automated testing software analyzes the target software. For example, it can point to the loop that takes the most amount of time and can often suggest ways to make the loop run faster. However, the consistent testing and documentation the automated testing software provides also help the developer perform complex analysis.

How does all of this affect accessibility (beside the obvious accessibility bullet)? Software that's tested, documented, and analyzed consistently tends to provide consistent functionality. The quality assurance system tests everything using the same criteria, which means the behavior is predictable. In the end, predictable application behavior makes the software more accessible. If a user can anticipate and rely on certain behaviors, the software is easier to learn and use, making it possible to improve user performance and enhance the user experience.

There's a danger in only relying on automated testing techniques. These techniques should be one tool of many in a developer toolkit packed with testing aids and techniques. Manual testing is also important because automated testing can only check the things that the test series is designed to test. Accessible application testing includes a range of manual and automated tests that include a variety of users with differing machine setups. For example, you can verify that the user interface acts consistently and isn't broken during an update using automated testing. On the other hand, you can't verify that the interface provides the proper prompts unless you use manual testing. Accessibility testing means using a number of techniques to meet application goals.

Some Third-Party Tools That Make Testing Easier

Visual Studio .NET, like versions of Visual Studio before it, will rely heavily on third-party tools to enable the developer to perform certain tasks. As you create more application code and the code becomes more complex, it becomes important to have a good testing tool. Microsoft does provide some rudimentary testing tools with Visual Studio .NET, but, to be honest, most of these tools only ship with the high-end "Enterprise Architect Edition" and don't provide much in the way of automation. Consequently, third-party developers have filled in the gaps by creating automated tools for the developer.

 NOTE   The two demonstration programs (NUnitDemo and ProfilerTest) in this section include specialized code and specific errors to better demonstrate the functionality of the tools. Don't use these applications as examples of how you should write code for an accessible application. Their only purpose is to help you understand the tools in question.

Automated Testing with NUnit

NUnit represents one of the tools that fill the automated testing gap. You can download this tool from http://sourceforge.net/projects/nunit. Figure 5-1 shows a typical view of the NUnit interface (with errors from a test application showing). You'll find this test application in the \Chapter 05\NUnitDemo folder of the source code that you can obtain from the Downloads section of the Apress Web site (http://www.apress.com).

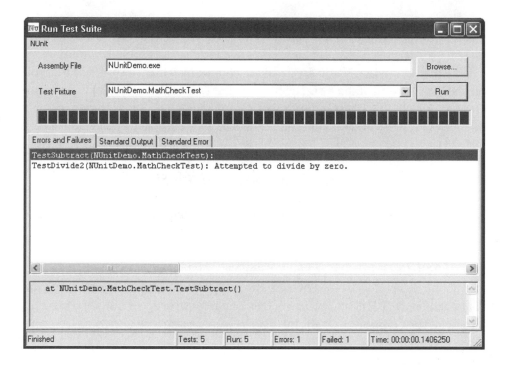

Figure 5-1. NUnit can help you create robust applications with few (if any) errors when released.

NUnit provides two forms of testing application. The GUI version is accessible from the NUnit folder of the Start menu. The GUI version helps you run the application test immediately after adding new code and provides a neater presentation of the logged errors. You'll also find a command line version of the program called NUnitConsole in the \Program Files\NUnit\ folder of your hard drive. The console version lets you place several testing scenarios in a single batch file and perform automated testing on more than one application at a time. You can also schedule testing using the Task Scheduler.

The product works by examining test cases that you create for your application. A test case is essentially a script that compares the result from your code to an anticipated result (what you expected the code to do). The test case can also check the truth-value of a return value. The author, Philip Craig, recommends creating a section of code, and then creating a test case for that code. For example, you'll want to create a minimum of one test case for each method within a class. In this way, you build layers of code and tests that help you locate problems quickly. These additions tell you when a piece of code that previously worked is broken by a new addition to the application.

NUnit helps you perform individual tests based on a single test case or to create a test suite based on multiple test cases. The use of a special function, either `Assert()` or `AssertEquals()`, enables NUnit to check for the required condition when requested. When NUnit sees a failure condition, it logs the event so that you can see it at the end of the test. The point is that you don't have to create test conditions yourself—each test is performed automatically. Of course, the test cases still need to address every failure condition to provide complete application testing.

Profiling Applications Using DevPartner Profiler

Profiling is a part of the automated test process for many developers because it points out areas where the code is less efficient than it could be. Some developers find the profiling support in Visual Studio .NET lacking. Fortunately, DevPartner Profiler from Compuware Corporation enables you to perform a line-by-line analysis of your code. The best news is that this product is fully integrated with the Visual Studio .NET IDE and you can download it for free. You'll find DevPartner Profiler at the Compuware Web site (`http://www.compuware.com/products/numega/dps/profiler/`).

After you install Profiler, you'll see a new DevPartner Profiler entry on the Tools menu of the Visual Studio .NET IDE. Select the Enable DevPartner Profiler option and you'll see a new DevParter Sessions folder added to Solution Explorer. You still need to turn DevPartner Profiler on using the options found in the DevPartner Profiler folder of the Options dialog box shown in Figure 5-2. Once you have the options set the way you want, you can profile your application.

It doesn't matter how you compile your application—you need to start it using the Start Without Debugging option of the Debug menu (or by pressing Ctrl+F5) in order to profile the application. You'll get results that are more accurate if you do create a release build of the application before you run it. After you quit the application, DevPartner Profiler will create an impressive array of statistics about your application. Figure 5-3 shows the statistics collected for the test application found in the \Chapter 05\ProfilerTest folder of the source code that you can obtain from the Downloads section of the Apress Web site (`http://www.apress.com`).

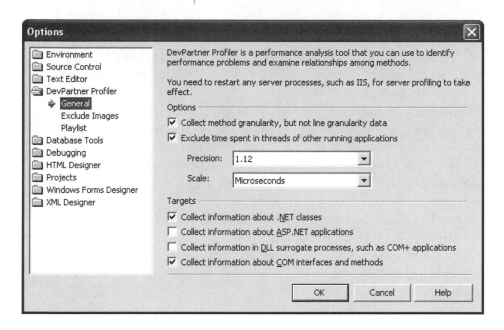

Figure 5-2. Use these options to control how DevPartner Profiler works with your application.

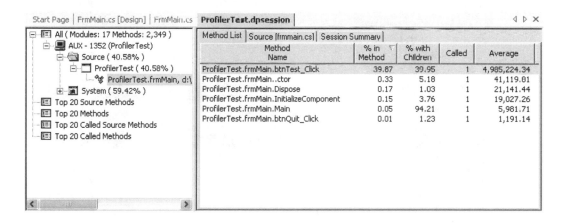

Figure 5-3. DevPartner Profiler will collect an impressive array of statistics about your application.

Application Management with Total .NET XRef

Finding information in a large application can be difficult, to say the least. For example, you might remember that you defined a variable, but finding the definition can prove difficult. FMS provides a series of .NET related tools such as Total .NET XRef (http://www.fmsinc.com/dotnet/default.asp) that make it easier to manage your applications. The Total .NET series includes XRef (cross-references variables and objects in your code), SourceBook (an extensive collection of source code examples), Analyzer (automated error and application speed problem detection), and Renamer (a smart alternative to find and replace). Only the XRef and Analyzer products were available for preview at the time of writing.

The Total .NET XRef tool resides within Visual Studio .NET and displays information about the current application. You use it to determine how a change in your application code will affect the application as a whole. For example, you can quickly learn all of the places where a particular variable appears within the application.

When you start Visual Studio .NET after installing the XRef tool, you'll see a Total .NET XRef window similar to the one shown in Figure 5-4 (this one is already filled in with information—the default is a blank window). To use this product, place the cursor on a variable or object that you want to cross-reference within your code. Click XRef to fill in the dialog box with information. Figure 5-4 shows the result of selecting the txtCurrent object within the Profiler Test application located in the \Chapter 05\ProfilerTest folder of the source code that you can obtain from the Downloads section of the Apress Web site (http://www.apress.com).

Total .NET XRef - txtCurrent : 13 matches found

Match T...	Project	File	Namesp...	Class	Member	Line	Char	Line Pre...
Use	ProfilerTest...	FrmMain.cs	ProfilerTest	frmMain	InitializeCo...	70	9	this.txtCurr...
Use	ProfilerTest...	FrmMain.cs	ProfilerTest	frmMain	InitializeCo...	135	9	this.txtCurr...
Use	ProfilerTest...	FrmMain.cs	ProfilerTest	frmMain	InitializeCo...	136	9	this.txtCurr...
Use	ProfilerTest...	FrmMain.cs	ProfilerTest	frmMain	InitializeCo...	137	9	this.txtCurr...
Use	ProfilerTest...	FrmMain.cs	ProfilerTest	frmMain	InitializeCo...	138	9	this.txtCurr...
Use	ProfilerTest...	FrmMain.cs	ProfilerTest	frmMain	InitializeCo...	139	9	this.txtCurr...
Use	ProfilerTest...	FrmMain.cs	ProfilerTest	frmMain	InitializeCo...	140	9	this.txtCurr...
Use	ProfilerTest...	FrmMain.cs	ProfilerTest	frmMain	InitializeCo...	141	9	this.txtCurr...
Use	ProfilerTest...	FrmMain.cs	ProfilerTest	frmMain	InitializeCo...	142	9	this.txtCurr...
Use	ProfilerTest...	FrmMain.cs	ProfilerTest	frmMain	InitializeCo...	149	26	this.txtCurr...
Use	ProfilerTest...	FrmMain.cs	ProfilerTest	frmMain	btnTest_Cli...	185	5	txtCurrent....
Use	ProfilerTest...	FrmMain.cs	ProfilerTest	frmMain	btnTest_Cli...	186	5	txtCurrent....
Use	ProfilerTest...	FrmMain.cs	ProfilerTest	frmMain	btnTest_Cli...	193	4	txtCurrent....

Figure 5-4. Use Total .NET XRef to build a complete cross-reference library of your application.

I saved the Total .NET Analyzer product for last because it has a unique feature. It performs rule-based analysis of your application. This feature isn't very unusual, but the fact that you have full control over the actions of the rule base is unique. The rule base also contains unique entries that make this product special.

To use this product, you install it as usual and then open your application. You'll see a blank Total .NET Analyzer window. Click Analyze and you'll see the output of the rule-based analysis of your application. Figure 5-5 shows the output from the Profile Test application located in the \Chapter 05\ProfilerTest folder of the source code that you can obtain from the Downloads section of the Apress Web site (http://www.apress.com). Notice the special ControlAccessibileDescription entry highlighted in the figure. This entry says that the application lacks an accessible description that someone with special accessibility devices will require when using your application.

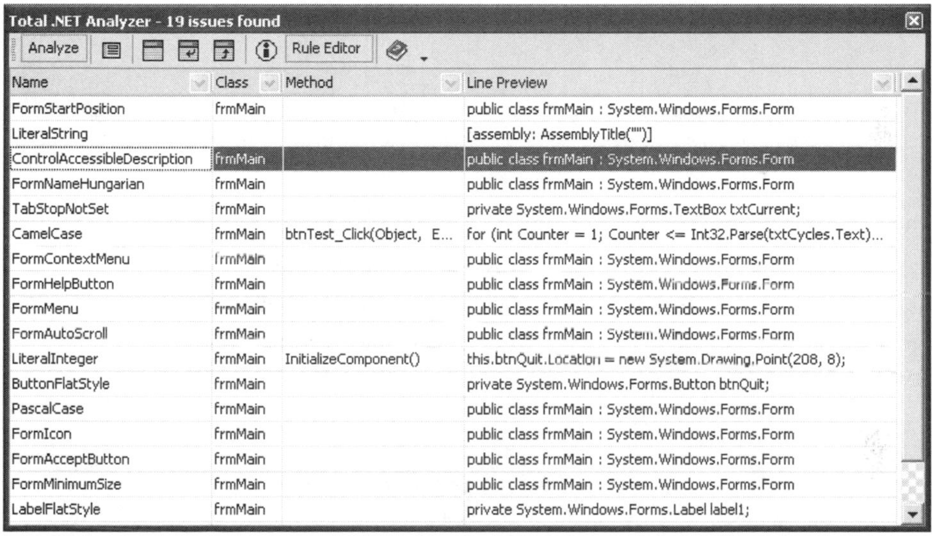

Name	Class	Method	Line Preview
FormStartPosition	frmMain		public class frmMain : System.Windows.Forms.Form
LiteralString			[assembly: AssemblyTitle("")]
ControlAccessibleDescription	frmMain		public class frmMain : System.Windows.Forms.Form
FormNameHungarian	frmMain		public class frmMain : System.Windows.Forms.Form
TabStopNotSet	frmMain		private System.Windows.Forms.TextBox txtCurrent;
CamelCase	frmMain	btnTest_Click(Object, E...	for (int Counter = 1; Counter <= Int32.Parse(txtCycles.Text)...
FormContextMenu	frmMain		public class frmMain : System.Windows.Forms.Form
FormHelpButton	frmMain		public class frmMain : System.Windows.Forms.Form
FormMenu	frmMain		public class frmMain : System.Windows.Forms.Form
FormAutoScroll	frmMain		public class frmMain : System.Windows.Forms.Form
LiteralInteger	frmMain	InitializeComponent()	this.btnQuit.Location = new System.Drawing.Point(208, 8);
ButtonFlatStyle	frmMain		private System.Windows.Forms.Button btnQuit;
PascalCase	frmMain		public class frmMain : System.Windows.Forms.Form
FormIcon	frmMain		public class frmMain : System.Windows.Forms.Form
FormAcceptButton	frmMain		public class frmMain : System.Windows.Forms.Form
FormMinimumSize	frmMain		public class frmMain : System.Windows.Forms.Form
LabelFlatStyle	frmMain		private System.Windows.Forms.Label label1;

Total .NET Analyzer - 19 issues found

Analyze   Rule Editor

Figure 5-5. Use Total .NET Analyzer to check applications for errors as well as speed problems.

Double clicking an entry will take you to that location in the code. Of course, just looking at the error might not tell you how to fix it. That's where the online help comes into play. Highlight the entry you want to know about, and then click the More Information button (the button that displays an I within a blue circle)—you'll see a help window similar to the one shown in Figure 5-6. In general, this combination of features is all you'll need to squash many of the hidden bugs within your application, including omissions of accessibility information.

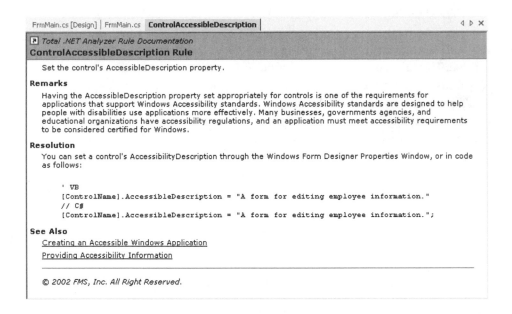

FrmMain.cs [Design] | FrmMain.cs | **ControlAccessibleDescription** ◁ ▷ ✕

🔲 *Total .NET Analyzer Rule Documentation*
ControlAccessibleDescription Rule

Set the control's AccessibleDescription property.

Remarks

Having the AccessibleDescription property set appropriately for controls is one of the requirements for applications that support Windows Accessibility standards. Windows Accessibility standards are designed to help people with disabilities use applications more effectively. Many businesses, governments agencies, and educational organizations have accessibility regulations, and an application must meet accessibility requirements to be considered certified for Windows.

Resolution

You can set a control's AccessibilityDescription through the Windows Form Designer Properties Window, or in code as follows:

```
' VB
[ControlName].AccessibleDescription = "A form for editing employee information."
// C#
[ControlName].AccessibleDescription = "A form for editing employee information.";
```

See Also

Creating an Accessible Windows Application
Providing Accessibility Information

© 2002 FMS, Inc. All Right Reserved.

Figure 5-6. The help provided with Total .NET Analyzer truly helps you create better applications based on the input you receive from the product.

At some point, you'll find that some of the rules conflict with company policy or that you don't normally include some of the application features that the rule base thinks that you should include. When this occurs, click Rule Editor and you'll see a window listing all of the rules the product uses. Simply turn the rules off that you don't need when working with your code.

Working Code Doesn't Necessarily Mean a Working Application

Some developers equate working code with a working application. After all, the code is functional and performs the required task—what else would the user need? However, operational code is the beginning, not the end, of a working application. Some of the tools we discussed earlier in the chapter hinted at the working application solution—a working application is both functional and usable.

The problem for most developers is that the functional part of the equation is easy to quantify. "Functional" generally means that the code performs the task that it's designed to perform without error. At first, the functional goal might seem quite doable, but the vast array of patch files on most users' hard drives say otherwise. The functional goal isn't as easy to attain as it might seem.

If the easily understood goal of functional is so hard to attain, then usable must be nearly impossible. After all, who can even quantify the concept of usability? An application that's usable to someone who spends their days working with computers is unlikely to provide any measure of usability to someone who's never touched a computer. Likewise, an application that's usable to a novice could smother an expert in unwanted help—for many experts, this is sort of the same feeling as drowning in a vat of honey.

Sometimes you can identify a particular audience for your application and create a usability profile based on that audience. Unfortunately, in the real world, this approach seldom works because people are always adapting a technology created for one group to another purpose. They tend to complain if the adaptation doesn't work as expected by saying, "Why didn't the developer think ahead?"

The key to this situation is to create applications that are usable by as many people as possible. This means writing flexible user interfaces that the user can modify as needed. In some cases, such as when the user needs large test, the user interface should modify itself to meet that need. Anticipating user needs is fine, but you also need to consider the unanticipated. Since you can't develop "thinking" applications, helping the user configure every aspect of the user interface for an application is the next best thing.

Getting Good Accessibility Input

By this time, you've come to understand the fine line between using automated and manual testing. Automated testing is helpful for repetitive tasks that you want to perform consistently and document accurately. Manual testing helps in those situations in which a machine can't quantify a result. For example, usability testing is always a manual process because a machine can't tell you how easy it is to use an application. A machine doesn't care if it needs to press Alt three times in rapid succession and then slowly press Ctrl in order to make a magical menu appear on screen—a user does.

We've discussed how you can use automatic testing for many accessibility requirements and obtain completely repeatable results. However, we've also discussed the need for extensive manual testing when it comes to accessibility. Manual testing puts a human back into the picture, which means you'll spend time trying to figure out how to form the various bits of input you receive into a set of changes for an application.

Testing using various unmonitored techniques is a good way to start. You can monitor how many keystrokes the user actually uses to perform a task and compare that value to the number of keystrokes you expected the user to input. Some tests can time the reaction of the user to test the effectiveness of online help or the layout of a dialog box. All of these techniques help monitor application use so that you can obtain quantifiable, easily digested facts about the application.

At some point, you'll need to talk to the users. Sometimes they won't want to talk with you because they feel you won't listen. In some cases, they'll say something you won't want to hear, so you might not listen (or at least digest what they have to say). In a few cases, you'll communicate well with the user and get a wealth of information you couldn't get any other way. Some of the best programming ideas you'll ever implement will come from the user—you'll never figure them out on your own.

NOTE   Obtaining essential user input is another area where you can usually obtain help from outside organizations. Appendix C contains a list of these organizations. Some of the organizations we discussed in Chapter 3 include the American Occupational Therapy Association (AOTA), the American Physical Therapy Association (APTA), and the American Speech-Language-Hearing Association (ASHA).

Consequently, getting good accessibility input means drawing ideas out of the user. It means that you need to listen to them using active listening techniques. For example, you'll generally want to maintain good eye contact and repeat what the user has said in your own words. (If the person you need to work with has special needs that make it difficult or impossible for you to communicate, you might want to seek the help of a third party to enable communication.) In many cases, it means asking the question that all developers dread, "How would you change the interface to make it better?" Asking that question puts the user in the hot seat and often provides them with a good reason to tell you what you need to know.

Understanding the Effects of File Format on Application Output

For most users, the selection of a file format is a matter of convenience. The user will ask questions such as, "How well will the file work with my application?" and "Do I need to convert this file?" However, some file formats work a lot better than others when it comes to storing application data with accessibility in mind. In fact, some vendors have made a commitment to reworking their applications so that the file formats they use provide the maximum accessibility benefit. The following sections explore some of the issues regarding file format in making applications more accessible.

Why Consider the File Format?

Most of this book concentrates on the requirements of the application. The user interacts with the application using the interface elements that you design. In addition, the application interface is the focus of various regulations and laws. Rule makers concentrate their efforts on the interface because the application is the most visible aspect of the accessibility effort. However, you also need to consider the effects of using a given file format on your application and its presentation to the user.

At this point, some of you are probably thinking that I've lost my mind. After all, files are simply data storage. The application renders the content of the file in the way most appropriate for a given situation. Theoretically, any application can choose to display only the content of a file without any of the other information it contains. In most cases, you'd be correct about this assumption.

However, there are a few things to consider that you might not have thought about. One of those issues is the effect of law on your ability to take files apart and display them as you wish. Recent legal wrangling means that you may find your ability to separate content from formatting severely curtailed because a law such as the Digital Millennium Copyright Act (DMCA) protects the file in question. The bottom line for you as a developer is that you might find that you can't do anything but display the content of a file in the form that the vendor originally defined.

 ON THE WEB   The DMCA has become an important law for a number of reasons, many of which companies are testing in the courts. You can learn more about the DMCA at `http://www.loc.gov/copyright/legislation/dmca.pdf`. The ElcomSoft case is one of the most publicized examples of legal wrangling over the inviolability of a file format. The case originally centered on the cracking of the Adobe eBook file format by Dmitry Sklyarov (read the story at `http://www.infoworld.com/articles/hn/xml/01/07/18/010718hndefcon.xml?0719tham` for details). However, the case now centers around the DMCA and how the legal community should interpret it. Read the InfoWorld story at `http://www.infoworld.com/articles/hn/xml/02/08/04/020804hnelcomlaw.xml?0805mnam` for details.

The inability to separate content from formatting means that your application might suddenly experience accessibility problems beyond your control. For example, Figure 5-7 shows a typical PDF displayed in a high contrast, large text font. I chose this particular example because PDF files appear as part of both desktop and Web-based applications on a regular basis. The PDF is an example of one file format that could affect the accessibility of a broad range of application types. If you could separate the content from the formatting, the display would become quite readable, but it's nearly unreadable as currently presented. Imagine that you also have limited mobility and must scroll the image shown in the figure back and forth constantly to read it.

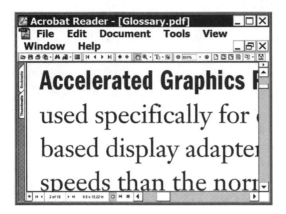

Figure 5-7. Some file formats present significant display challenges.

Considering Potential File Format Problems

It's important to consider all aspects of a file storage format before you use it as part of an application development solution. Obviously, this requires some knowledge of the file format and means that you'll spend time testing it within your application environment. It's easy to see that the wrong choice can be devastating. However, even if you choose the correct file format, using it incorrectly can have unanticipated results. The following list provides an overview of these file format problems.

> **Hidden Formatting Errors:** Sometimes a file format contains hidden problems that you don't know about until you stumble across them. For example, to move to the next section of a PDF using a screen reader, you press Enter. Normally, this feature works fine—the user can move from one topic to the next with relative ease. However, when reading a PDF in two-column format, the user will experience problems. Normally, the user reads the left column on the page and then moves to the right. However, when using a screen reader, the user will hear the left column and then move to the next page—the user will miss the text in the right column completely.

Missing Accessibility Information: Another potential problem certain file formats present is their lack of accessibility information. As an example, imagine that you open a Word DOC file and can't see the illustration that it contains. The Section 508 requirements demand that the developer provide a text description of the illustration. Unfortunately, the Word DOC file format doesn't accommodate such information. Even if the DOC file format did accommodate such information, there's no guarantee that the document originator would include it. Therefore, the problem is two-fold. First, some file formats (not just Word, but other file formats too) don't support accessibility information. Second, there is no way to force the document originator to provide the accessibility information even if the file format does support it.

Compound Document Storage: One of the more interesting problems with some file formats, such as the Word DOC, is the concept of compound document storage. The user can embed a document within a document. Using this technique enables the user to create word-processed documents that look as if they were desktop published. The only problem is that the embedded document might not include any accessibility information and the user might even lack a local application for rendering it. In short, creating a custom application to display the file in a way that provides complete access might mean enduring a loss of content.

Custom File Format Issues: Creating a custom file format (whenever possible) might seem like a safe choice because you have full control over the data storage. However, there are also some problems with this solution. The immediate problem is that only your application can use a custom file format, so it probably doesn't enjoy the broad distribution of something common like a PDF or DOC file. Consequently, there's a chance that the content created by such a file is going to be lost if your application becomes unsupported. This problem can become severe if you work in an environment where data access is a requirement for 5, 10, even 15 years after creation. Because of the need to store long-term data in a reliable format, people are moving completely away from custom file formats.

Application Interaction with the File Format: Another problem with simple or custom file formats is one of design. If you want to make this file accessibility friendly, then you must use compound storage techniques to include the accessibility information. When you do, your application suddenly starts to take on some of the problems of the DOC file format. In addition, you need to ensure that the application user actually provides the required data—a daunting task if the user is an unwilling participant. Part of the application design and implementation process involves ensuring that the data is in the correct format. The need to perform accessible data verification is a new problem for many companies.

The focus of this book is still on the application because that's where you'll do most of your work. However, this section has brought up some interesting points about selecting a file format. If you use a file format that enjoys a wide distribution, you must be willing to overcome the problems inherent in that file format. On the other hand, if you create a custom file format, you must be willing to include the full range of content that an accessibility friendly application will require. This includes providing a way to describe non-text elements and to support applications such as screen readers.

Working with the PDF Format

Adobe has taken steps to make PDFs accessibility friendly starting with Acrobat version 5. You can create documents with tags that help users navigate the PDF using either screen readers or screen enlargers. The tags define the structure of the document, making it easier for an assistive technology application to navigate. Interestingly enough, Microsoft Office versions 2000 and later also have the capability to create tagged PDFs. Other applications, such as Adobe FrameMaker 6, help you create structured PDFs. The structured PDFs are less helpful to assistive technology than tagged PDFs, but they do help. A structured PDF contains data in a specific order, making it easier to read.

Unfortunately, the Internet and local machines already contain so many PDFs that lack accessibility features that you might find complete data conversion a time-consuming project that takes years to accomplish. How can you create an application with accessible data today? Adobe also provides online tools that make document conversion relatively easy for those who need help immediately (it's still better to update the document whenever possible). All you need to do is use one of the options located on the Adobe Web site at `http://www.adobe.com/products/acrobat/access_onlinetools.html`. Figure 5-8 shows an example of the English translation form. Notice the Advanced Form link near the bottom that provides access to additional formatting features. In some cases, you'll need these advanced features to convert a PDF to HTML.

Type the name of the PDF you want to convert, and then click Get This Adobe PDF Document as HTML. Figure 5-9 shows some typical output from the conversion utility. In this case, we're converting the Internal Revenue Service (IRS) form at `http://www.irs.gov/pub/irs-pdf/i1040gi.pdf` that normally appears as a PDF into an HTML format.

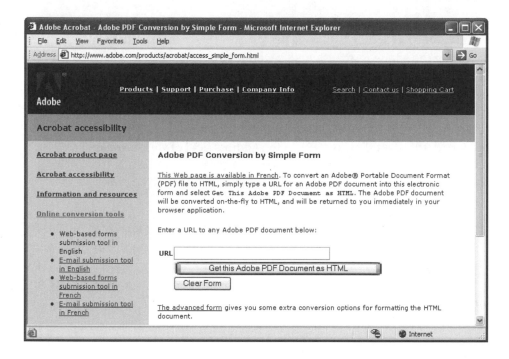

Figure 5-8. Create an HTML form of your PDF document using this handy online utility.

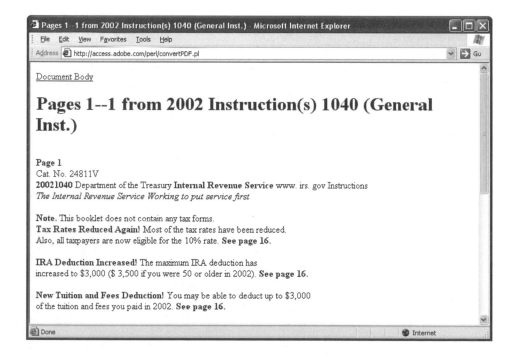

Figure 5-9. Use the output from the utility directly or save it for later inclusion in an application.

The form is nice, but not as useful to a developer as it could be. Developers require some method of displaying the form on screen that doesn't rely on the user accessing the Adobe form. After all, it would be nice to perform the conversion in the background or simply provide a link on your Web site as needed. (This technique can also work for desktop applications that use HTML as a display methodology if the user has an Internet connection.) You can also call the Practical Extraction and Reporting Language (PERL) script directly. For example, you can see the same IRS form using the following URL in the Address field of your browser.

```
http://access.adobe.com/perl/convertPDF.pl?url=http://www.irs.gov/pub/irs-pdf/
i1040gi.pdf
```

This technique works fine for a simple conversion. The features of the advanced form are also available, but require a little more work on the part of the developer. The point is that a company can use PDFs directly for most needs, but they can also use this technique for unique needs. Flexibility is key when working with file formats that might not answer every user requirement.

Working with the DOC Format

The DOC format has been around for a while. Many people have used this format to create information of all sorts. Microsoft uses a compound document structure that enables the data developer to add information, such as captions, to the various data elements. In addition, these documents include a wealth of summary information such as the name of the originator, the company name, and the date the author last modified the document. In fact, the data developer can create custom elements if the summary doesn't include enough descriptive content.

Word also comes with converters that help the developer output the data as an HTML page, formatted text, or even plain text, should the need arise. All of these features are accessible using Dynamic Data Exchange (DDE) or script programming techniques. A developer can create a COM connection to perform the required conversions. You'll also find a full suite of Web components at http://office.microsoft.com/downloads/2002/owc10.aspx that help the developer publish any Microsoft Office data as Web content. From an accessibility perspective, Microsoft has covered all the bases. The biggest problem is getting the data author to add the information needed by someone with special needs.

ON THE WEB   Most of the common document formats also come with support for viewers. These free applications enable someone to view the content of the document, but they don't allow them to create a new document or modify an existing one. In many cases, using a viewer is a perfect solution because it helps you provide data to a party that needs it without the fear that they'll modify the content. You can find a list of plug-ins and viewers for Office products at `http://office.microsoft.com/downloads/` `default.aspx?Product=Word&Version=95|97|98|2000|2002&-` `Type=Converter|Viewer.`

Tracking the Screen Focus

Desktop application developers already have a lot of help available when it comes to tracking the screen focus. However, most developers don't really understand the concept of focus completely, which means that they often miss opportunities to provide output information on the current screen focus. For example, many developers forget to place the cursor at a convenient starting point on forms. Most users want to start typing in the form immediately, but the developer thwarts their efforts by placing the cursor on the Cancel button or in an equally absurd place. Focus problems can also occur when a background application causes a message box to pop up in the foreground. Many users complain that when this happens, they accidentally dismiss a warning or error message because the next key they type after this occurs is right for the foreground application, but wrong for the message box. The screen focus occurs at several levels for the Windows developer:

- Application

- Form or window

- Control or other element

The operating system automatically takes care of the first two levels of screen focus. Whenever the user changes applications or main windows within an application, the operating system records the necessary information. It's still important to provide accessible descriptions for each component, but for the .NET developer, these two levels aren't much of an issue.

The third level of screen focus, the control or other element, does require some attention by the developer. You can set the accessible screen focus options using the accessibility properties in the .NET programming environment. In fact, you'll see an example of how to use this support in the "Using the .NET Accessibility Features Example" section of Chapter 7. The three accessibility properties are AccessibleDescription, AccessibleName, and AccessibleRole as shown in Figure 5-10.

Figure 5-10. Always use the accessibility properties to ensure that your application provides screen focus information.

A fourth property, AccessibleDefaultActionDescription, is accessible from within the application code. The TestAccessibility application, located in the \Chapter 05\TestAccessibility folder of the source code that you can obtain from the Downloads section of the Apress Web site (http://www.apress.com), provides a quick view of how to work with the various properties. For example to set the AccessibleDefaultActionDescription, you'd make an entry in the application constructor as shown here.

```
public frmMain()
{
    // Required for Windows Form Designer support
    InitializeComponent();

    // Set the AccessibleDefaultActionDescription property
    // values for this application.
    btnQuit.AccessibleDefaultActionDescription =
        "Press to quit the application.";
    btnTest.AccessibleDefaultActionDescription =
        "Press to perform the application test function.";
}
```

TIP   The frmMain() method uses standard definitions for the AccessibleDefaultActionDescription value. However, there are times when you want to avoid starting the AccessibleDefaultActionDescription value description with certain words. For example, sometimes you want to avoid the word "Press" or even "This button" when working with a pushbutton because it's hard for someone using a screen reader to grasp the importance of the button. In many cases, you'll need to use a unique formulation of words to ensure the meaning and importance of the button is clear to the end user. This same principle applies to every control on a form—sometimes unique is better, but don't overdo it. Use common terminology when the control in question performs a common task.

Using the accessibility properties is an option when you're using predefined controls, but what happens when you create your own controls? Whenever you create a standard control project using the IDE, the control that the code subclasses will provide the required accessibility support. However, you can easily extend the accessibility support in various ways by creating a control based on the AccessibleObject or Control.ControlAccessibleObject classes.

You can always gain access to focus information within the application as well as outside of it. One of the more useful events for this task is the Enter() event. If you set the Enter() event for all of the controls of interest to the same event handler, you can easily detect which control has the focus and act accordingly. Here's a short example of a technique you can use for tracking the focus internally.

```
private void TestEnter(object sender, System.EventArgs e)
{
    Control  Ctrl; // Control sending information.

    // Show the current accessibility information.
    Ctrl = (Control)sender;
    MessageBox.Show("Name = " + Ctrl.AccessibleName +
                    "\r\nRole = " + Ctrl.AccessibleRole +
                    "\r\nDescription = " + Ctrl.AccessibleDescription +
                    "\r\nDefault Action = " +
                    Ctrl.AccessibleDefaultActionDescription,
                    "Accessibility Information",
                    MessageBoxButtons.OK,
                    MessageBoxIcon.Information);
}
```

You may wonder why the example changes the object, sender, into a Control class object. The Control class is the base class for all controls and provides an easy way to obtain the accessibility information. The application will output a dialog box every time you change the application focus. Figure 5-11 shows a typical example of the output.

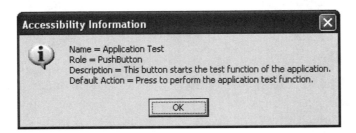

Figure 5-11. Obtaining the accessibility information for this application is relatively easy once you understand how .NET applications change focus.

Using Consistent Controls, Status Indicators, and Other Elements

As part of the research for this book, I talked with many people about accessibility and the common failings of applications. Most users have specific needs and those needs are evident in the elements they find wrong in the typical application. However, one need seems universal and I doubt that it's even unique to accessibility development. The need to provide a consistent interface is nothing new. Schools teach this particular part of the programming picture, yet most application developers seem to ignore the entire concept in production applications.

The need for consistent controls, status indicators, and other user interface element goes well beyond accessibility. Consider the simple task of designing a label. Some developers use long text, while others use short prompts. Some labels are very descriptive—sometimes to the point of abstraction. Other labels hide their meaning so well that no one can figure out what task the associated control performs. In general, use labels that are short, but descriptive. Add to the information the labels provide with balloon help. You do this by adding a ToolTip control to the application form, and then by adding text for each control to the associated ToolTip property. Finally, make sure that your application provides context sensitive help when needed.

TIP   Generally, you can use the same text for the AccessibleDescription and ToolTip properties. One element of consistency is ensuring that everyone obtains the same help information. An AccessibleDescription that's well worded works well for the ToolTip because both user types tend to need the same information.

The TestAccessibilty application, located in the \Chapter 05\TestAccessibility folder of the source code that you can obtain from the Downloads section of the Apress Web site (http://www.apress.com), shows how to use tooltips in an application. We'll also discuss both general and context sensitive help as the book progresses. All of these support issues are important to the user of your application. Figure 5-12 shows a typical tooltip (balloon help) and associated button.

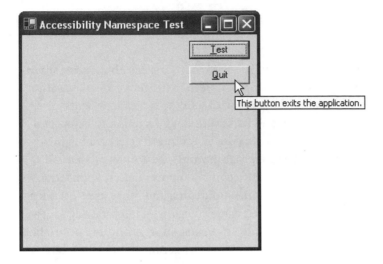

Figure 5-12. Use tooltips with every control to provide a longer description of the short name or description provided on the form.

Status indicators are another accessibility problem. Like other controls, you should always provide a tooltip that explains what information the status indicator provides. For example, you see the number 80 at the bottom of a form. Does that number mean that you've input 80 records? It might mean that you're at the 80th line of the form or just about anything else. Status indicators show a brief overview of important application information, but if the indicator is unreadable, it doesn't actually serve a purpose and you should get rid of it. A good status indicator

- Uses the same format between forms in the same application

- Always provides useful information that the user must know in order to use the application correctly

- Provides good tooltips so that the user can quickly learn the purpose of a particular indicator

Using Serif and Sans Serif Fonts

Normally, the developer doesn't need to think too much about the font used to write the text on a display. However, font usage does become important when you start to create accessible applications. In the "Understanding the Large Text Display" section of Chapter 4, we discussed the need to create applications that work well with large text. For example, in some cases, you need to move display elements around to accommodate the larger text. The bottom line is that the font is larger, so it requires more room.

While I prepared for this chapter, I noticed that several people referenced the type of font used for large text displays, but really didn't provide a reason for the font selection. All of the fonts mentioned are of the sans serif variety. (You can learn about the difference between serif and sans serif fonts at `http://www.redsun.com/type/classification/#sans_serifs`.)

Needless to say, I became interested in finding out why everyone recommended sans serif fonts for large text displays when most sources say that you should use serif fonts for body text because they're easier to read. It turns out that sans serif fonts actually provide a better presentation than serif fonts in large and small sizes. Here is a view of the typical differences between a serif and a sans serif font.

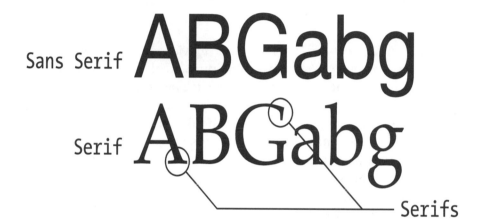

As you can see from the illustration, there are significant differences between the two typefaces. (You can learn about additional typeface terms at `http://www.adobe.com/support/techguides/printpublishing/typography_basics/letterform_anatomy/main.html`.) The important difference is the use of serifs on the serif font. However, you should also notice the treatment of the font shape and font characteristics such as the size of the ascender and descender. Most people who work with type measure the height of a typeface in points. Each point is 1/72nd of an inch.

Everyone seems to agree that 8-point fonts are the smallest you should create using serif fonts—smaller font sizes (such as the 6-point type used for system prompts on most systems) should appear in a sans serif font. The upper limit for serif fonts isn't well defined, so I can't provide you with an exact number. However, given that the serifs tend to break up and provide a poor presentation at around 20-points, you could use that size as a starting point for using sans serif fonts. The issue is one of readability—fonts determine how easy your displays are to read and consequently, the performance of the application.

As more documents get published on the Internet, the issue of fonts is becoming less of an issue for printed matter. The use of Cascading Style Sheets (CSS) makes it possible for people to modify the appearance of a display to meet their particular needs. If the person decides that a serif font doesn't meet with their approval, they can simply change it. To some extent, you could follow this same principle for your desktop applications. Some applications have and do provide settings that the user can change to modify the on-screen font appearance. However, if you choose to add this form of flexibility to your application, be sure you do it with the appearance of the display in mind. Remember, it's still a matter of changing a font, so you need to consider all of the font parameters.

Obtaining and Using the Current Display Settings Example

Generally, you'll find that the .NET Framework provides an ease of use that earlier developers wanted, but never obtained. Unfortunately, there are some situations in which you need to work a little harder to find the information you need. In general, you won't need to worry about the display capabilities of the target machine unless you create complex forms or need to resize graphics to meet special needs. In those situations, the GetDeviceCaps() function is the only way to obtain the information you need. This function helps you obtain information about any device with a device context, which includes the display, printers, and even cameras. Using this function can help you build accessible applications by helping you determine the capabilities of the target devices on the user system.

The GetDeviceCaps() function requires two inputs. The first is a handle to a device context. A *handle* is a pointer to the device context—think of it as a way to grab the device context and see what it contains. A *device context* is the virtual area in memory that represents the device—its capabilities and the data that it's currently using.

The second GetDeviceCaps() function input is an index into the data for that device context. We'll use an enumeration for this example. The enumeration essentially tells the GetDeviceCaps() function which data to retrieve from the device context.

You can only return one value at a time when you use the GetDeviceCaps() function. If you want the vertical and horizontal resolution of the display, then you need to make two calls—one for each value. This function doesn't accept a data structure that returns all of the required values because the values you can request vary by device type.

NOTE Make sure you look through the enumeration values in the source code for this example. You'll be surprised at just how many device parameters you can obtain. In fact, from an accessibility perspective, this one function provides most of what you need to interact with the device. Of course, you'll still need to use other techniques to find all of the information required for other accessibility needs—such as the user's current color choices or the default system font.

Now that you have a better idea of how the GetDeviceCaps() function works, let's look at some code. Listing 5-1 contains the working code for this example. The enumerated values are quite long, so I left them out of the listing. You'll find the complete listing for this example in the \Chapter 05\DevCaps folder of the source code that you can obtain from the Downloads section of the Apress Web site (http://www.apress.com).

Listing 5-1. Using the GetDeviceCaps() Function

```
// The purpose of this function is to retrieve a device context;
// essentially a drawing area for the application.
[DllImport("User32.DLL", CharSet=CharSet.Auto, SetLastError=true )]
public static extern IntPtr GetDC(IntPtr hWnd);

// Use this function to release the device context.
[DllImport("User32.DLL", CharSet=CharSet.Auto, SetLastError=true )]
public static extern Int32 ReleaseDC(IntPtr hWnd, IntPtr hDC);

// This function returns the device capability value specified
// by the requested index value.
[DllImport("GDI32.DLL", CharSet=CharSet.Auto, SetLastError=true )]
public static extern Int32 GetDeviceCaps(IntPtr hdc, Int32 nIndex);

private void btnTest_Click(object sender, System.EventArgs e)
{
    IntPtr        hDC;      // Device context for current window.
    Int32         Result;   // The result of the call.
    StringBuilder Output;   // The output for the method.

    // Obtain a device context for the current application.
    hDC = GetDC(this.Handle);
```

```
// Check for errors.
if (hDC == IntPtr.Zero)
{
   // Display an error message.
   MessageBox.Show("Couldn't obtain device context!",
                   "Application Error",
                   MessageBoxButtons.OK,
                   MessageBoxIcon.Error);

   return;
}

// Obtain the current display capability.
Output = new StringBuilder();
Result = GetDeviceCaps(hDC, (Int32)DevCapParm.DESKTOPHORZRES);
Output.Append("The horizontal resolution: " + Result.ToString());
Result = GetDeviceCaps(hDC, (Int32)DevCapParm.DESKTOPVERTRES);
Output.Append("\r\nThe vertical resolution: " + Result.ToString());
Result = GetDeviceCaps(hDC, (Int32)DevCapParm.BITSPIXEL);
Output.Append("\r\nThe bits/pixel value: " + Result.ToString());

// Display the results.
MessageBox.Show(Output.ToString(),
                "Current Display Capabilities",
                MessageBoxButtons.OK,
                MessageBoxIcon.Information);

// Release the device context when finished.
ReleaseDC(this.Handle, hDC);
}
```

The first piece of code you should notice is the external declaration of the GetDC(), ReleaseDC(), and GetDeviceCaps() functions. Although this book won't provide you with complete instructions on how to use the Win32 API from within the .NET environment, we will look at some specific instances in which you need to access the Win32 API. In this case, the [DllImport] attribute provides information about where to locate the three functions, whether to use the default character set, and whether the application will need the last error information the Win32 API provides. The function declaration tells which managed variable types to use to send information to the GetDC(), ReleaseDC(), and GetDeviceCaps() functions.

The btnTest_Click() method begins by obtaining the device context for the current form using the GetDC() function. It's essential that you obtain the device context for whatever drawing device you query. This might mean creating a managed object of the right type, and using it to obtain the correct device context. In a few cases, you'll need to use additional Win32 API calls to access the device because the .NET Framework doesn't provide the correct support. The this.Handle property will always return a handle to the current application, which, in this case, is the essential input needed for the GetDC() function.

After the code obtains the device context handle, it can begin calling GetDeviceCaps(). The GetDeviceCaps() function always returns a numeric output value that you can convert to something the user will understand or a value your application can use for drawing or other tasks. The application obtains three common values that you can check using the Display Properties dialog box: horizontal resolution, vertical resolution, and the number of bits per pixel. Figure 15-13 shows the output from the application.

Figure 5-13. Use the GetDeviceCaps() *function to return statistics about the user display.*

Some developers will fall into the trap of thinking that the Garbage Collector actually works with unmanaged data—it only works with managed data. Consequently, it's important to remember to release the device context before the application exits or the application will have a memory leak. The last act of the application is to use the ReleaseDC() function discussed in other chapters to release the handle and associated resources obtained using the GetDC() function.

At this point, you know how to obtain information such as the number of colors that the user wants to use. You can use this information to adjust the output of your application so that it looks good and so the user can see all of the elements it contains no matter what color setup the user chooses. In addition, you can resize the windows and make better use of screen real estate. For example, a high-resolution display offers you the opportunity to use slightly larger fonts so that they appear smoother and are easier to read.

Working with Colors and Fonts in Controls and UI Elements Example

Colors and fonts form the two types of expression that many developers use to set their application apart from someone else's application. However, as noted in Chapter 4, issues such as color blindness can make any change in color selection a dubious option at best. In some cases, a color change could make your application nearly invisible to the user. The sections that follow discuss how color affects your application. We also discuss a technique to automate changes to your application based on user interface choices.

Adding Colors to UI Elements

Most users have a color scheme that they like to use. In general, since you're not going to see the color scheme, it's a good idea to use the colors that the user enjoys seeing on screen. The good news is that if you use the Windows system colors for your application elements, the color modifications occur automatically. The user will see the colors they need to see in order to use your application and you won't have to write any code to make the change happen. Figure 5-14 shows the color selections on the System tab for a button ForeColor property. As you can see, it's set for ControlText, one of the standard Windows system colors.

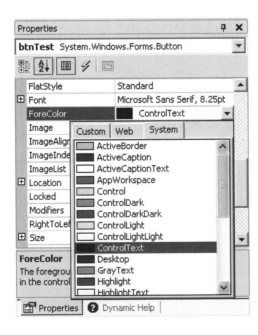

Figure 5-14. Use options on the System tab whenever possible for your applications.

Notice also that you can select other color options. The button color settings might not behave exactly the way the user expects, but at least the user can control them. That's the important issue—every application requires flexibility in the way that the user interface works. The more you can automate this flexibility, the better.

Ensuring the Colors Have Text Equivalents

Sometimes you don't have any choice about which color you use on a user interface element. If this is the case, the color becomes a problem. For instance, consider this scenario. What happens if you tell someone who's color-blind to click the red button? Will they know which button you're referring to? In all likelihood, the user will have to play the odds of finding the right button without color assistance. However, if you add a tooltip that tells the user which button is red, then they can make a good selection. This is where text equivalents come into play. You need to provide a text equivalent for every non-standard color on the display to ensure that everyone can find an interface element that relies on color.

If you require a custom color, the technique of using the system colors that change automatically won't work. You should also provide an Options dialog box that the user can access to change the custom colors of an application. The dialog box should help the user change every custom color individually. Each of the selections should contain descriptive information that helps the user make a smart choice the first time.

Creating the Font Modification Example

We've discussed the problem of the large text display several times. There's no way around this issue—your application must contain code that helps it react properly to the large text display scenario. Normally, you should include this code as a message handler or add it as part of the startup code for the application. The user should also have access to an Options dialog box that helps them make reasonable sizing changes. Listing 5-2 shows the typical resizing code for an application. This code also appears in the \Chapter 05\ColorsAndFonts folder of the source code that you can obtain from the Downloads section of the Apress Web site (http://www.apress.com).

Listing 5-2. Accomodating Font Changes

```csharp
private void btnTest_Click(object sender, System.EventArgs e)
{
   Font  DefFont; // Current font requirement.
   Size  BtnSize; // Current button size.
   Size  DlgSize; // Current dialog size.
   Point TestLoc; // Current Test button location.
   Point QuitLoc; // Current Quit button location.

   // Obtain the default font for our example.
   // Begin by determining the screen state.
   if (SystemInformation.HighContrast)
   {
      DefFont = SystemInformation.MenuFont;
      BtnSize = new Size(135, 42);
      DlgSize = new Size(540, 540);
      TestLoc = new Point(374, 14);
      QuitLoc = new Point(374, 72);
   }
   // Use the default sizes.
   else
   {
      DefFont = this.Font;
      BtnSize = new Size(75, 23);
      DlgSize = new Size(300, 300);
      TestLoc = new Point(208, 8);
      QuitLoc = new Point(208, 40);
   }

   // Modify the display fonts.
   btnTest.Font = DefFont;
   btnQuit.Font = DefFont;

   // Modify the sizes.
   btnTest.Size = BtnSize;
   btnQuit.Size = BtnSize;
   frmMain.ActiveForm.Size = DlgSize;

   // Modify the positions.
   btnTest.Location = TestLoc;
   btnQuit.Location = QuitLoc;
```

```
// Display the information.
MessageBox.Show("Name: " + DefFont.Name +
                "\r\nSize:" + DefFont.SizeInPoints.ToString(),
                "Font Information",
                MessageBoxButtons.OK,
                MessageBoxIcon.Information);
}
```

As you can see, this code detects the `SystemInformation.HighContrast` setting. If the user has enabled the high contrast display, then they're also using large fonts. The application accesses the current font using the `SystemInformation.MenuFont` property. I chose this option because it provides a good font for the user when they are working with data entry or other types of information.

You might find some of the numbers used to resize and relocate the user interface elements mystical. I assure you that I didn't consult my crystal ball. After a lot of experimentation, it turns out that a 1.8:1 ratio works best for resizing and repositioning the screen elements. The numbers found in the listing reflect this ratio. Figure 5-15 shows the results.

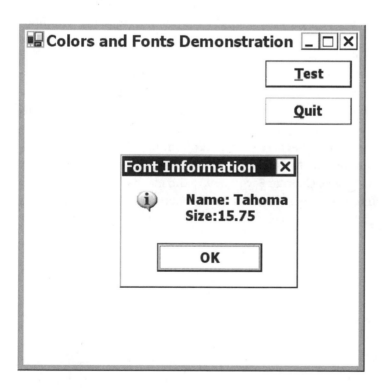

Figure 5-15. Create applications that automatically compensate for changes in the user interface whenever possible.

Summary

This chapter has shown you some of the basics of accessible application design. We've discussed many of the user interface elements, considered various interface criteria, and I've even shown you how to react to some user needs automatically. Even if you stopped at this point in the book and implemented what you know now, you'd find that your applications are a lot more accessible and that your support costs have gone down considerably. All of these techniques apply to every desktop application you'll create.

Of course, the problem is that your applications probably don't follow these guidelines today. One of the first tasks you'll need to perform is deciding how to bring your applications into compliance with the accessibility requirements. After you create a plan, you can begin to implement it. Remember that the government will give smaller companies time to implement these rules, but you still need to make demonstrable progress toward the goal of full compliance. In addition, it's actually in your best interest to comply since these changes will help everyone who uses your application.

Make sure you also consider the discussions of previous chapters as you make your plans. For example, when you decide on how to implement color in your applications, also consider the problems of colorblind users. You might find that someone who's had problems using your application in the past no longer finds the application difficult to use.

We've discussed the inherent lack of accessibility support in Windows on several occasions. However, Windows does provide a wealth of accessibility features, and you should know how to use them. After all, any help you can get in implementing the accessibility requirements is better than no help at all. Chapter 6 is your introduction to Windows accessibility programming. We'll discuss how you can access all of the support that Windows provides and add it to your application. In short, when you complete Chapter 6, you'll have the means to isolate your application from Windows (at least from a user interface perspective) and provide a fuller level of accessibility coverage.

CHAPTER 6

Using Microsoft Active Accessibility

In This Chapter:

Why Should You Care About MSAA?

How Can You Use the AccessibleObject Class to Your Advantage?

What Are the Standard Accessibility Options?

How Can the Standard Accessibility Options Help You as a Developer?

How Can You Access the Keyboard Features?

How Do You Display the Windows Accessibility Feature Status Information?

How Can You Interact with the Sound Features?

How Can You Detect the Display Features?

How Can You Detect the Mouse Settings and Functionality?

WINDOWS COMES WITH support for accessibility built into the system. In fact, this support, when it works, provides many of the features that anyone with special needs would require for a desktop application. The problem is that many developers don't include the required support in their applications, so Windows users don't gain full access to the accessibility features this support could provide. Of course, the other side of the coin is that while Windows does provide good support for accessibility functionality, the topic of accessibility doesn't exactly head the list of developer conference topics. Consequently, the main purpose of this chapter is to make you aware of what accessibility features are available and demonstration how you can use them in your next application.

NOTE Many developers recognize that Windows provides one of the few operating system platforms where it's possible to add a level of accessibility support to an application without a lot of added coding. In this respect, Windows does lead the world in providing the means for those with special needs to help themselves. In fact, Microsoft is helping in other ways. A recent Canadian Nation Institute for the Blind (CNIB) article (http://www.cnib.ca/Thatallmayread/news_release.htm) discusses the contributions that Microsoft has made to the well-being of those with special needs.

The first part of this chapter discusses the Windows Accessibility features from a user perspective. I've talked with over a hundred developers during the writing of this book (and I have over half of the book to write yet). Out of all of those developers, only one had even heard that Windows has Accessibility features and understood how to install and use them. If you already know about the Windows Accessibility features, you can safely skip the first section of the chapter. On the other hand, if you don't know what Windows can provide, this first section will help you understand the features we'll use in the applications in this chapter.

The next several sections discuss each of the Accessibility features in turn. We begin by discussing the keyboard features, then we move on to sound, then the display, and, finally, the mouse. When you finish these sections, you'll see just how complete the Accessibility features are so long as you provide the required support in your application. Of course, the Accessibility features have some support holes that we'll discuss as the chapter progresses. You can plug some of these holes by adding support for special hardware.

The final section of the chapter discusses an essential topic. You need to know when a user has turned on the Accessibility features for a particular machine. More than that, you need to know how the user has configured accessibility support so that your application can work with the Accessibility features, rather than against them. This is especially important for some of the visual and audio features because they require special coding in your application.

What Is Microsoft Active Accessibility (MSAA)?

Microsoft Active Accessibility (MSAA) is a set of COM classes that help you build better accessible applications. These COM classes help you create a bond between the application and the operating system. This bond enables the operating system to perform tasks such as querying the application for additional help information and asking the application to perform specific tasks.

ON THE WEB   You'll find MSAA general information, along with downloads used in this book, on the Microsoft Active Accessibility Web site at `http://msdn.microsoft.com/library/default.asp?url=/nhp/Default.asp?contentid=28000544`. This Web site includes links to a number of helpful articles and other resources. Fortunately, MSAA is built into Windows XP and you can add it to other versions of Windows through service packs (including Windows 98, but not Windows 95). If you need to support Windows 95 users, then be sure to download the MSAA SDK at `http://download.microsoft.com/download/activaxs/SDK/1.3/W95/EN-US/MSAA13SDK.exe`. We'll use a number of MSAA specific tools in this book, so you'll want to download them from `http://www.microsoft.com/downloads/release.asp?ReleaseID=33491`.

However, as with most products, the COM interface is just the tip of the iceberg. You'll find that MSAA also supports registry entries that you can monitor and a few API functions you can use to perform specific tasks. In general, .NET users will find that Microsoft has built the major MSAA functionality into the .NET Framework, but that some ancillary features don't exist yet. Users of earlier Visual Studio product versions will need to work a little harder to gain access to MSAA features.

The reason that the MSAA section appears in this chapter is because it's important for the developer to know a little about the underlying technology before looking at the user interface elements. However, understanding the user interface elements and learning how they work is an important part of working with MSAA—you can't test an MSAA application otherwise. Consequently, we'll discuss the MSAA theory in this chapter before we discuss the user interface.

The sections that follow perform two tasks. First, you'll learn how MSAA works from both an operating system and a development platform perspective. Second, you'll get a quick demonstration of how MSAA works. We'll explorer MSAA programming methods in detail in the "Obtaining and Using Microsoft Active Accessibility" sections of Chapter 7.

Understanding the Technical Details

Working with MSAA requires that you understand a number of technical details. The first is that most of the functionality needed to use MSAA appears in the OLEACC.DLL. It's interesting to open this DLL up using the Depends utility because you can see many of the API calls directly and learn the dependencies of this DLL. Figure 6-1 shows the OLEACC.DLL file opened in Depends (also known as the Dependency Walker as shown in this screenshot). Notice the list of API functions, such as `AccessibleChildren()` in the exports list. Scroll through the list and you'll find essential interface references such as `IID_IAccessible`.

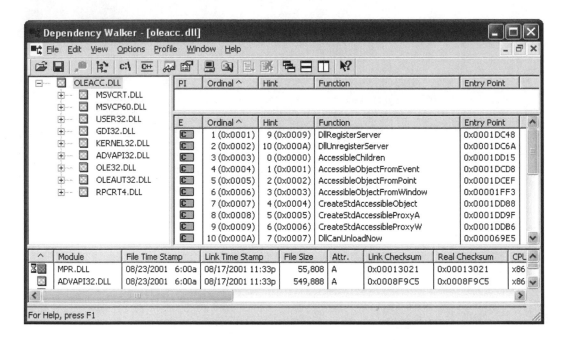

Figure 6-1. The OLEACC.DLL file provides a list of essential API calls, as well as COM functionality.

A second technical detail is that MSAA is a COM object. The interface in question is IAccessible. The .NET Framework wraps the more important parts of the COM functionality found in IAccessible in the AccessibleObject class. The IAccessible interface provides the methods that make it possible to request information about a component or control, such as a description. This interface also provides access to functionality, such as getting the current focus or performing the default action. In short, the IAccessible interface encapsulates most of the programming functionality that a developer needs to interact with the accessibility features of any control.

ON THE WEB You'll find a good summary of the IAccessible functions at http://msdn.microsoft.com/library/en-us/msaa/ msaaccrf_4f51.asp. Note especially the descriptive properties and methods that this interface provides. Another good place to get an overview of the IAccessible interface is at http://msdn.microsoft.com/ library/en-us/msaa/msaaccrf_5q05.asp.

A third technical detail is that MSAA relies to an extent on messaging—the same technique used by a number of other processes in Windows. The OLEACC.DLL uses the WM_GETOBJECT message to retrieve an Active Accessibility server application object. In other words, if you create an MSAA application, you'll need to handle this message in some cases.

A fourth technical detail is the registry entries. You can monitor the registry to obtain the current accessibility settings for Windows. The key your application would need to monitor is HKEY_CURRENT_USER\Control Panel\Accessibility. Figure 6-2 shows the Windows XP registry setup. Older versions of Windows are slightly less robust than Windows XP. For example, Windows 2000 lacks the Blind Access key shown in Figure 6-2. However, you can count on all versions of Windows to support accessibility function keys such as HighContrast, SerialKeys, and MouseKeys. We'll discuss the monitoring process in the "Developing the Windows Accessibility Status Application" section of this chapter.

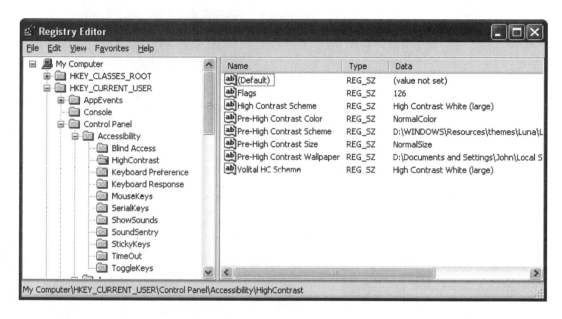

Figure 6-2. Use the registry to determine the status of the various Windows Accessibility options.

The four technical details help you understand what's going on beneath the surface. You'll learn more about the linkage between these technical details and accessibility in general as the chapter progresses. For now, what you need to know is that there's linkage between MSAA and Windows Accessibility. The user interface features the user selects affect messaging, the registry, and the COM interface.

A Quick Demonstration of the AccessibleObject Class

As with many of the other examples we'll discuss in this book, you'll need to add a reference to the Accessibility.DLL that comes with the .NET Framework. When you add this reference, you can view it in the Object Browser. Figure 6-3 shows a typical display of this library. Notice that it contains references to both IAccessible and IAccessibleHandler. In addition, you have access to the majority of the functions found in the OLEACC.DLL file. You also need this reference to gain access to the AccessibleObject class.

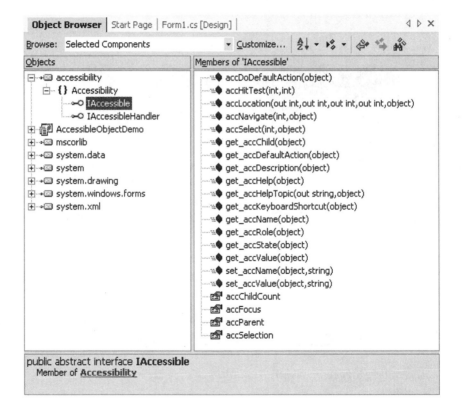

Figure 6-3. The Accessibility.DLL file contains the two interfaces required for the COM portion of an accessible application.

Developers can use the AccessibleObject class in a number of ways. For example, you can use it to create an accessible version of a new component or control. By adding this class to your component or control, and overriding the default actions it provides, you can customize the accessibility information the component or control provides to the user. In many cases, the customization makes it much easier for the user to interact with your application as a whole.

A more common use of the AccessibleObject class is to gain complete access to the accessibility features provided by existing components and controls. For example, you'll need it to gain access to the shortcut key for some types of controls. It also provides a number of handy methods such as DoDefaultAction(), which performs the default action supported by any accessible object. The demonstration application relies on the features of the AccessibleObject class to create a specialized tooltip presentation for the user. Listing 6-1 shows this example. You'll find the complete listing in the \Chapter 06\AccessibleObjectDemo folder of the source code that you can obtain from the Downloads section of the Apress Web site (http://www.apress.com).

Listing 6-1. Specialized ToolTip *Code for Displaying Complete Accesibility Information*

```
public frmMain()
{
   // Required for Windows Form Designer support
   InitializeComponent();

   // Initialize the accessible objects.
   btnQuit.AccessibleDefaultActionDescription =
     "Press to exit the application.";
   btnTest.AccessibleDefaultActionDescription =
      "Press to test the application.";
   txtMessage.AccessibleDefaultActionDescription =
      "Type to change test message.";
}

private void SpecialTip(object sender, System.EventArgs e)
{
   Control          Ctrl;    // The control in question.
   AccessibleObject AO;      // The accessibility information.
   ToolTip          TT;      // Special ToolTip
   StringBuilder    Output;  // ToolTip Output String.

   // Initialize the ToolTip.
   TT = new ToolTip();
   TT.AutoPopDelay = 7000;
   TT.AutomaticDelay = 300;
```

```
// Get the sender information.
Ctrl = (Control)sender;

// Obtain access to the accessibility information.
AO = Ctrl.AccessibilityObject;

// Create the output string.
Output = new StringBuilder();
Output.Append("Name: ");
Output.Append(AO.Name);
Output.Append("\r\nRole: ");
Output.Append(AO.Role);
Output.Append("\r\nDescription: ");
Output.Append(AO.Description);
Output.Append("\r\nDefault Action: ");
if (AO.DefaultAction == null)
    Output.Append("None");
else
    Output.Append(AO.DefaultAction);
Output.Append("\r\nKeyboard Shortcut: ");
if (AO.KeyboardShortcut == null)
    Output.Append("None");
else
    Output.Append(AO.KeyboardShortcut);
Output.Append("\r\nState: ");
Output.Append(AO.State);
Output.Append("\r\nValue: ");
if (AO.Value == null)
    Output.Append("None");
else
    Output.Append(AO.Value);

// Display the information on screen.
TT.SetToolTip(Ctrl, Output.ToString());
TT.Active = true;
}
```

It's important to create a customized AccessibleDefaultActionDescription property value for each component in your application. The reason is simple. The default information simply tells the user to press the spacebar to perform the default action, but it doesn't say what that action is. In some cases, such as a text box, the control doesn't have any type of default action assigned to it. All the user knows is that the text box exists. Telling the user they can type something might seem obvious until you try to use the example without the benefit of seeing it. In fact, you should try this application out by blindfolding yourself and using just the Narrator application described later in the chapter to move from area to area.

The SpecialTip() method has to follow the setup for the MouseHover delegate so that it can act as an event handler. Consequently, it lists the sender as an object, and not a control as you might expect. You need to add this event handler to the MouseHover event of every control on the form, as shown in Figure 6-4.

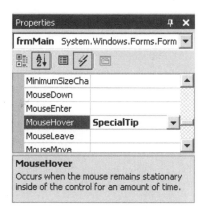

Figure 6-4. Use the MouseHover *event to create linkage between the user action and the* SpecialTip() *event handler.*

The SpecialTip() method code begins by creating the ToolTip object, TT. Notice that TT uses an AutoPopDelay value of 7000 ms and an AutomaticDelay value of 300 ms to ensure proper operation. A few tests will show you that the changes are needed to ensure that the tooltip actually pops up fast enough for someone with mobility difficulties and stays up long enough for someone with cognitive difficulties to read. Interestingly enough, most screen readers will continue saying the text in the tooltip even after it disappears from view provided the user doesn't change focus.

After the code creates the tooltip, it gains access to the sender as a Control object. It uses the Control object's AccessibilityObject property to create the AccessibleObject, AO. Finally, the code uses AO to fill out the entries in a StringBuilder object, Output. At this point, we have a string that contains all of the essential accessibility information provided by the control that activated the SpecialTip() event handler. The final step is to place this information in TT using the SetToolTip() method, and then display the tooltip by setting the Active property to true. Figure 6-5 shows the output of this application.

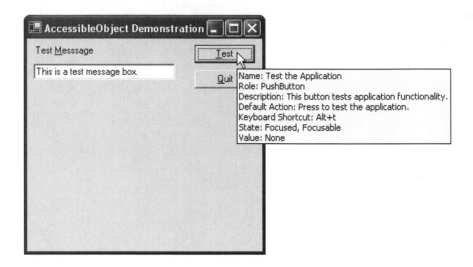

Figure 6-5. The SpecialTip() *event handler outputs tooltips with complete accessibility information.*

The output shown in Figure 6-5 is probably a little too inclusive. However, you could provide a menu option that helps the user customize this information. Some users, especially those who use screen readers, will probably want the keyboard shortcut information as part of the tooltip. Users with cognitive needs might find it helpful to set the tooltip popup and display times individually. Most users will want to see the description—using this technique means you don't have to define that part of the tooltip for every control. Although this example shows what's available, you'll still want to augment the code to provide added flexibility.

An Overview of the Standard Accessibility Options

Windows actually provides a wealth of accessibility features, but many people don't realize they even exist. You can divide the accessibility features into two areas. The first area is utilities that you run as needed. The second are services that you control using the Accessibility applet in the Control Panel. Third party companies probably don't have much to worry about from these utilities, but they do work well enough for many people, including developers of accessible applications.

TIP   You can often find other aids in other Control Panel applets. For example, look in the Keyboard applet and you'll notice options that affect the character repeat delay and the character repeat rate. The Mouse applet contains settings that enable the user to adjust the double click rate and turn on features such as ClickLock. The ClickLock feature is especially interesting because it helps someone drag and drop items without holding the mouse button down. The Mouse applet also provides access to larger pointers and enables the user to switch mouse button functionality. Try using your application with changes to these mouse and keyboard settings in place to see how it reacts. This test can help ensure that time-dependent features work as anticipated.

The following sections provide a user eye view of accessibility in Windows. This material is important because you need to know how the user will view the output of your application. However, the utilities and services described in these sections represent a worst-case scenario for many accessible application users. Third party vendors have developed software and hardware that provide superior performance and usability. In short, if your application works well with this software, it will likely work well with the high-end products that most accessible application users will have installed on their systems.

Utilities

Utilities are applications that the user can run from the Start ➤ Programs ➤ Accessories ➤ Accessibility menu if this feature is installed on the host system. Windows XP installs the feature by default, so most users of that operating system will have this feature at their fingertips by default. Users of older versions of Windows can install Windows Accessibility using the Add/Remove Programs applet in the Control Panel.

ON THE WEB Sometimes a developer will need short-term changes in screen appearance to accommodate environmental conditions (such as the change from daylight to nighttime lighting conditions). NightVision (`http://www.adpartnership.net/NightVision/index.html`) is a free utility that helps the developer make these changes. It helps by modifying the gamma (or brightness) values for the display. The interesting feature of this utility is that you can create your own settings. For example, I found it useful as an aid to seeing the screen as someone with low vision would see it. Using this product can help you make color and brightness choices and keep the display readable even in bright light or low vision conditions.

Several of these utilities actually have interesting uses for developers outside of their use for accessibility development. We'll explore these utilities and their interesting uses in the sections that follow. Make sure you try out each of the utilities as you read about them and then spend time working with them afterward. I've personally found many of the utilities useful as programming aids.

Using the Magnifier

The Magnifier is equivalent to a magnifying lens used for reading. Whenever you start the Magnifier, you'll see a band open at the top of your screen. This band contains a magnified version of the information contained at the mouse cursor. You can change the size of the band by dragging the line separating it from the rest of your display using the mouse, just as you would for the Taskbar.

From a developer perspective, you can use this tool to see how your application reacts to the unexpected. Suddenly cutting off the upper half of the screen is a good way to see what will happen when someone needs that portion of the display for an accessibility need such as a keyboard. The Magnifier also helps you view the fit and finish of your application. For example, when an application displays a logo or other picture element, it's sometimes difficult to determine if the placement on screen is correct.

As previously mentioned, the Magnifier works on the same basis as a lens used for reading. However, this lens is adjustable, making it possible to see the screen at various levels of detail. The default magnifier setting will magnify items by a factor of 2. You can change this setting using the Magnifier Settings dialog box shown in Figure 6-6. This dialog box opens whenever you start the Magnifier.

Figure 6-6. The Magnifier Settings dialog box allows you to control how the Magnifier interacts with your system.

Notice you can change the tracking technique that Magnifier uses to home in on the action. The default setting tells Magnifier to follow any activity on the screen. However, you can clear one or more of these check boxes to reduce the level of activity. When I use the Magnifier to check my application for fit and finish problems, I normally tell it to follow the mouse. On the other hand, when checking the application for usage problems, it's better to have the Magnifier follow the keyboard input. That way you can simply tab between fields on a form as needed.

TIP   As a developer and someone interested in drawing, I often use Magnifier to see how other people create small screen elements such as icons. It's hard to get just the right color combinations without help at times. Viewing someone else's work can mean the difference between trial and error, and getting the drawing right the first time.

You'll also find three check boxes in the Presentation section. The first tells Magnifier to invert the screen colors. This makes it easier to contrast the normal appearance of your display with the magnified version. I also find this an interesting way to check the color settings of my application—it should display well in either mode. You can also start the Magnifier Settings dialog box minimized. Finally, you can clear Show Magnifier to get rid of the band at the top. This is a handy feature if you need more screen real estate for a short time and don't want to disable Magnifier in the interim.

Magnifier does incur a noticeable performance hit on your system, so you'll want to turn it off when you performance tune your application. When you click Exit in the Magnifier Settings dialog box, the Magnifier also stops working and the display returns to normal.

Using the Narrator

The Narrator reads the essential content on screen to you. In addition, whenever it encounters a control, it will provide information about that control. The information provided depends on the developer of the application. In many cases, there's a generic, almost useless bit of text that Narrator will read about the control if the developer provides no other information.

The most obvious use of this utility for the developer is to check the accessibility information provided by the application. Using a screen reader of some type is the only effective means of performing this task. This application acts as a sanity check for both desktop and Web-based applications. A developer can listen to hear if Narrator stumbles on the content. If it doesn't, then no one else is likely to have troubles either.

There are other good uses for screen readers from the developer perspective. I find that it does a relatively good job and use it when I need to "read" documents online. I'll get the document placed on screen, then kick back and let Narrator do the work while I concentrate on the information contained on the Web site.

 ON THE WEB AWS, a screen reader from Freedom Scientific (http://www.freedomscientific.com/), provides a much better environment in which to test your screen reader–capable applications. Not only can you choose from a variety of voices, but you can also select options such as the voice pitch and reading speed with greater accuracy than Narrator can. JAWS also provides Braille support, along with a wealth of other features. You can download a demonstration version of JAWS at http://www.freedomscientific.com/fs_downloads/jaws.asp. The demonstration version provides most of the features of the full product, but you can only use it for about 30 minutes. The Help menu provides an estimate of the time you have left for using the demonstration version.

Sometimes it's also important to use Narrator as a fit and finish tool. For example, closing your eyes and listening to the prompts for an application can help you locate grammar and spelling problems. You can also hear the prompts and determine if they make sense—whether they're consistent and easy to understand. The Narrator dialog box shown in Figure 6-7 contains four options.

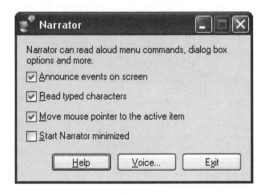

Figure 6-7. Use the Narrator dialog box settings to control how Narrator interacts with your system.

Announce Events On Screen: Tells Narrator to announce when you successfully complete an action such as changing windows. (A window change can also include the appearance of message boxes and other system events that the user didn't cause.)

Read Typed Characters: Tells you which character you typed last, including control characters such as backspace.

Move Mouse To Active Item: Moves the mouse cursor so that you can see which item on screen has the focus.

Start Narrator Minimized: Starts the program with the Narrator dialog box minimized.

The Voice button takes you to the Voice Settings dialog box. This dialog box allows you to choose a new voice for Narrator. The default setting is Microsoft Sam. You can also change the speed, volume, and pitch of the voice. Nothing you do will make the Narrator sound completely human. However, adjusting the pitch and speed does make Narrator friendlier. Adjust the pitch and volume settings to make Narrator easier to understand.

Using the On-Screen Keyboard

The On-Screen Keyboard shown in Figure 6-8 is a replica of the keyboard attached physically to your system. It allows you to type text using a mouse or other pointing device. We initially discussed this accessibility feature in the "Evaluating Your Audience" section of Chapter 4. You'll want to review that section for some of the interesting uses of the On-Screen Keyboard.

Figure 6-8. You can use the On-Screen Keyboard as an alternative means for inputting data.

You can adjust the appearance of the keyboard using the options on the Keyboard menu. For example, you might want to use a 106 key keyboard instead of the 101 key default. You can also choose between a standard and an enhanced keyboard. As mentioned in Chapter 4, many developers find the block layout easier to use because the keys are lined up and easier to access. The staggered layout used by physical keyboards is fine when you need to type, but it can prove cumbersome for mouse or joystick access.

The Settings menu controls how the On-Screen Keyboard interacts with the system. For example, you might want to use a different font for the keys. You can also choose whether the keyboard always remains on top. The Use Click Sound option comes in handy if you're used to a regular keyboard and miss the sound it makes.

The Settings ➤ Typing Mode command displays the Typing Mode dialog box. You'll use the options on this dialog box to control how the user inputs data. You have a choice between clicking, hovering, or using a joystick (or other recognized device). To get a better feel for how frustrating it can be to use an eye gaze system, set the keyboard up for hover mode. You'll find that using a joystick or mouse to select a key, leave it in place for the required time, and then move to the next key is harder than it first appears.

Using the Accessibility Wizard

You'll find the Accessibility Wizard on the Start ➤ Programs ➤ Accessories ➤ Accessibility menu. The main purpose for using this wizard is to set Windows up for an individual's accessibility needs. The user isn't required to use the wizard, but it does make things easier if the user has many changes to make and is not familiar with the actual settings. Once you start the Accessibility Wizard, you'll see a Welcome dialog box and then a series of question dialog boxes like the one shown in Figure 6-9. Just follow the prompts to configure accessibility support to meet a particular need.

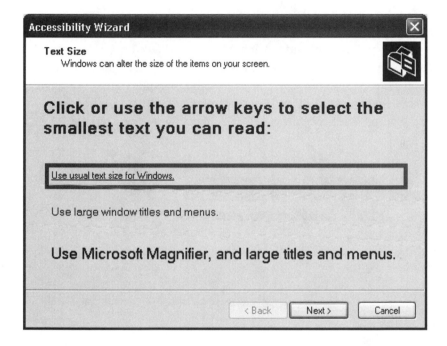

Figure 6-9. Running the Accessiblity Wizard will help a user configure Windows Accessibility support to meet particular needs.

ON THE WEB   If you find that you need additional help with the Accessibility Wizard, you'll find step-by-step instructions for the various setups at http://www.microsoft.com/enable/training/windowsxp/usingwizard.htm. The instructions are targeted at a specific type of setup, so you'll need to decide which of the procedures to follow.

For the developer, the Accessibility Wizard provides a fast means of configuring a test system to meet specific needs. In addition, the Accessibility Wizard shows one technique for providing special needs configuration of your own applications. Although the wizard provided with your application doesn't have to be this complex, the simple question and answer format does make the application a lot easier to configure at the outset. Another product that uses this question and answer format is the JAWS installation program (see the "Using the Narrator" section for details).

Using the Utility Manager

So far, this book has spent a lot of time promoting the advantages of flexible application configuration. The Utility Manager is a special application for managing the Windows Accessibility applications. It controls the Magnifier, On-Screen Keyboard, and Narrator. All three of these applications appear in the field at the top of the dialog box (along with any other Accessibility applications you may install), as shown in Figure 6-10. The Utility Manager demonstrates that you can make an application flexible, yet provide a central configuration point for it.

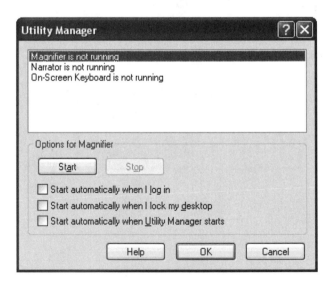

Figure 6-10. Manage your Windows Accessibility applications using the Utility Manager shown here.

As you can see, the Utility Manager displays the status of each of the applications that it manages. To stop an application, highlight it and click Stop. Likewise, click Start to restart the application. Notice that most, but not all of the keys have shortcuts—any management application you create should include shortcuts for all options. In addition, the Utility Manager lacks support for tooltips—something that most users find helpful in determining what action to perform. (Interestingly enough, you can right click an entry or press the Context Menu key, and then select What's This from the context menu to learn more about a particular option.)

You can also set the startup options for each application. The three options will start the program when you log in, lock the system, or start the Utility Manager when they're checked. Again, configuration flexibility is extremely important. Enabling the user to choose when the application will start makes the application itself seem flexible.

From a developer perspective, the Utility Manager provides a quick means of starting and stopping Windows Accessibility applications. Sometimes you need quick access for testing because you might want the feature on during debugging and off while you correct code.

Accessibility Options Applet

The Accessibility Options applet appears in the Control Panel. It helps you configure the Windows Accessibility options individually. Using this applet helps you learn about each option individually and see how the Accessibility Wizard combines them to meet specific special needs. Through observation, you can learn a great deal about how the various accessibility options work under Windows and develop your applications accordingly.

 TIP There's a chance that constantly turning the Windows Accessibility options on and off will cause certain elements of your display, especially the fonts and icons, to become large and stay that way. If this happens, turn off all accessibility features and restart the machine. Open the Themes tab of the Display Properties dialog box and choose the Windows XP theme. Click Apply. The text and icons should appear normal again. Obviously, this fix relies on an unaltered Windows XP theme, so you'll want to ensure that you never make changes to it. Always make any theme changes to another file.

The following sections discuss each of the Windows Accessibility options. Make sure you try each of the options to learn how they work. More importantly, use the options as part of your application testing strategy. The Windows Accessibility options should be part of the manual usability test you perform on every application your organization develops.

Using the StickyKeys Feature

The StickyKeys feature is one of three options on the Keyboard tab of the Accessibility Options dialog box shown in Figure 6-11. It's useful for a variety of purposes. For example, this option forces the Shift, Ctrl, and Alt keys to act as toggle switches. Press one of these keys once and it becomes active; press it a second time and it's turned off. The user can also press the keys sequentially to activate them or press a non-control key to execute the entire key press (such as Ctrl+Alt+A). Afterward, the control keys automatically become inactive. In other words, the toggle feature is only important if the user doesn't want to use that key as part of a key press.

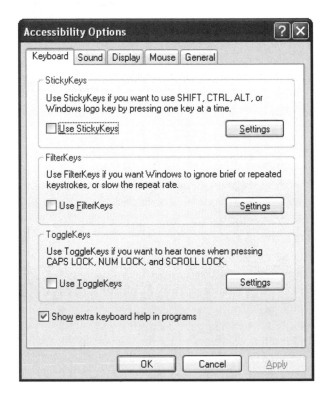

Figure 6-11. Use the keyboard options to modify the functionality of the PC keyboard.

From a developer perspective, there are a number of good uses for the StickyKeys feature. For example, you can use StickyKeys in graphics programs that require you to hold down the Ctrl key to select a group of items. It can be inconvenient to hold down the Ctrl key while you look around for objects to select. The StickyKeys feature alleviates this problem.

At some point, you'll want to configure StickyKeys to meet particular needs. Click the Settings button on the Keyboard tab of the Accessibility Properties dialog box to open the Settings for StickyKeys dialog box shown in Figure 6-12. As you can see, the dialog contains a number of optional settings that enable StickyKeys to react to user input in a variety of ways.

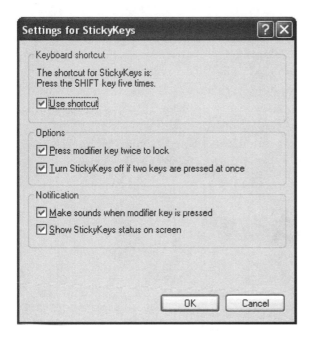

Figure 6-12. Configure the StickKeys options using this dialog box.

There are three groups of settings for StickyKeys. The first group, Keyboard Shortcut, enables you to turn on StickyKeys using the shortcut key. There's no reason to turn this off. It's very unlikely that another application would use the same control key sequence. Actually, it's a little surprising that Microsoft chose such an odd key combination given the reason they provide this feature. We'll discuss an easier technique for turning StickyKeys on and off in the "Developing the Windows Accessibility Status Application" section of the chapter.

The Options group contains two settings. The StickyKeys option usually works like a toggle. Checking the first box tells Windows to wait until you press the same control key twice before making the control key active. The second check box enables two people to use the same keyboard if one needs to use StickyKeys and the other doesn't. Pressing a control key and a non-control key at the same time turns StickyKeys off in multiuser environments where this feature could be disorienting.

The Notification group also contains two settings. The first setting tells Windows to play a different sound for each unique control key it activates. This setting can help prevent you from activating a control key by accident. The second option displays an icon on the Taskbar so that you can control StickyKeys more easily. Select this option to make it easier to turn StickyKeys on and off.

Using the FilterKeys Feature

Many users experience problems typing keys correctly—they sometimes tap the key twice when they really meant to tap it only once. In other cases, the user will press the key too long because they don't have the sense of touch and control. FilterKeys helps eliminate extra keystrokes so you don't get "tthis" instead of "this." It performs this task by setting a minimal time threshold between keystrokes. As with StickyKeys, you can adjust the way FilterKeys works by clicking the associated Settings button. Figure 6-13 shows the Settings for FilterKeys dialog box.

Figure 6-13. Define features such as the timespan between keystrokes using this dialog box.

The first option in this dialog box enables you to turn the shortcut key option on or off. This works just like the same feature in StickyKeys. In fact, you'll find that all of the Windows Accessibility features provide this option, so I'll skip it in future discussions. I also found Microsoft's selection of a shortcut for this feature a bit odd considering how the feature is used.

The Filter Options group provides options to let the user choose between two methods of filtering keystrokes. The first option filters keys that the user presses in rapid succession. This feature would filter the rapid typing of the extra "t" in the previous example. The Settings button displays a dialog box that enables you to select how long an interval must pass between the first and second times you press the same key. It also provides a field in which you can test the setting.

The second option in the Filter Options group filters accidental key presses. At one time or another, everyone presses a key without meaning to. As with the StickyKeys option, the Settings button displays a dialog box in which you select how long you have to press a key before Windows accepts it. This dialog box also lets you change the actual repeat rate or turn the keyboard repeat feature off so that the user must press each key individually.

The Notification group at the bottom of the dialog box should look familiar. The only difference is that FilterKeys beeps when you activate it instead of playing a sound (such as a WAV file). You can also display an indicator on screen to show that FilterKeys is active.

Using the ToggleKeys Feature

How many times have you accidentally hit the Caps Lock key and found yourself typing in all uppercase? I know that when I get busy, it does occasionally happen to me. The ToggleKeys feature emits a tone every time you turn the Caps Lock, Scroll Lock, or Num Lock key on or off. This feature enables you to detect toggle key changes quickly, before you've typed a lot of material using the wrong case.

Using the SoundSentry Feature

The SoundSentry and ShowSounds features both appear on the Sound tab of the Accessibility Options dialog box shown in Figure 6-14. Both features control how Windows XP interacts with sound. The Use SoundSentry option tells Windows XP to display a visual warning when a system sound occurs. The user can choose to flash the active caption bar, flash the active window, or flash the desktop.

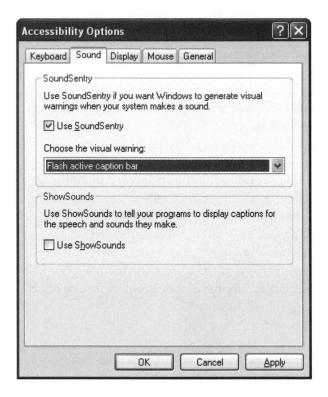

Figure 6-14. The SoundSentry and ShowSounds features determine how Windows reacts to sound events.

Unfortunately, you'll need a copy of the Tweak UI utility to control the number of times the system flashes in response to a sound. We discussed this utility in the "Flashing Text and Other Blinking Issues" section of Chapter 4, so I won't discuss it again.

Using the ShowSounds Feature

The ShowSounds feature tells Windows XP and your applications to display captions for the sounds they make. This includes speech. Instead of actually making the sound, the system requests that the application provide a description of the sound in a balloon help dialog. The only problem is that the application developer needs to intercept the request and act on it. We'll look at an example of the ShowSounds feature in action in the "Using the Sound Features Example" section of the chapter.

NOTE The use of sound presents another situation where the theory of accessibility doesn't quite match the reality. While the SoundSentry and ShowSounds features sound good in theory, the SoundSentry option works more often in practice. Most applications won't display the sounds that they make as text, even if you enable the ShowSounds feature.

Switching to a High Contrast Display

The actual purpose of the high contrast setting is to help those who have poor eyesight see the display better. However, this setting is also useful for the developer to know about. For example, the high contrast screens work well when you're tired. It also works well if you're on a plane using a laptop in bright sunlight. Sometimes a high contrast screen is even the answer for presentations. Figure 6-15 shows the Display tab of the Accessibility Options dialog box.

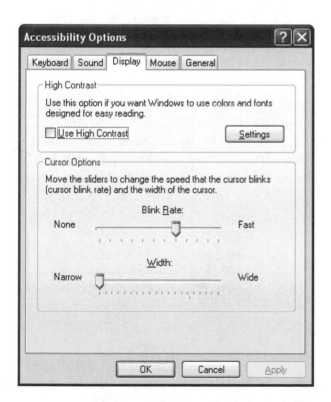

Figure 6-15. Define features such as the cursor blink rate using this dialog box.

To use the high contrast display, check the High Contrast option. The Settings button displays the Settings for High Contrast dialog box that you'll use to adjust the high contrast settings. In general, you don't have to use the large letter setting to gain the benefits of the high contrast display. The settings include those used for normal sized letters as well. In addition, you can choose between a black background (good for nighttime use) or a white background (good for sunny location use).

Controlling Cursor Blink Rate and Width

At the bottom of the Display tab shown in Figure 6-15, you'll find two sliders. The Blink Rate slider controls the rate at which the cursor blinks. The Width slider controls the cursor width. Generally, these settings help someone who has problems with flashing text and other screen elements adjust their display for comfortable use. In addition, using a slower blink rate can help those with cognitive difficulties. (On the other hand, people with attention deficit disorder often need a faster blink rate in order to see the cursor.)

Like many of the other settings, you can use these settings to your advantage as well. For example, many people find that setting the cursor for a slow blink rate aids laptop use in many situations. A wider cursor can also help forms and other situations where finding the cursor might become a problem.

Accessing the MouseKeys Feature

Look at the Mouse tab of the Accessibility Options dialog box and you'll find a single option for turning MouseKeys on or off. MouseKeys enables you to use the arrow keys on the numeric keypad as a mouse. Instead of moving the cursor with the mouse, you can move it with the arrow keys. This doesn't disable your mouse; it merely augments it.

TIP MouseKeys is one of the most useful Windows Accessibility features for designers because it provides very fine control over the mouse. For example, I often use this feature when drawing block diagrams or creating the final version of a dialog box.

Click Settings on this tab to display the Settings for MouseKeys dialog box shown in Figure 6-16. Using the Pointer Speed options, you can optimize the performance of this particular feature. The Top Speed slider helps you to adjust the fastest speed at which you can move the mouse cursor using the arrow keys. The

Acceleration slider determines how quickly the cursor reaches full speed after you press it. Windows doesn't start the cursor at full speed; it brings it there gradually. The combination of these two settings determines how much added control MouseKeys gives you over the cursor. The check box in this group provides another option. You can press the Ctrl key to speed up the mouse cursor and press the Shift key to slow it down.

Figure 6-16. The Settings for MouseKeys dialog box enables you to change how this feature works.

There are two settings at the bottom of the dialog box. The radio buttons control when MouseKeys is active. You must specify whether the Num Lock key should be on or off when you use MouseKeys. The second option determines whether the MouseKeys icon appears on the Taskbar.

Using the Keyboard Features Example

Generally, you don't want to spend a lot of time manipulating the user environment in Windows applications. The reason is simple—if the user wants to change their environment, they have plenty of ways in which to accomplish the task. You do want to monitor the environment at all times, however, to ensure that your application works in a way that's consistent with the current user settings (such as when the user selects a large text display).

There are times when you'll want to provide the user with configuration options—a sort of shortcut to beneficial environmental changes. You don't want the application to modify these settings, but you do want to give the user quick access to them so that they don't have to leave the application environment. In most cases, this is a convenience option that will keep the user happy and make your application easier to use, but it isn't a requirement for accessibility. For example, what happens when you've developed a new graphics application and want to be sure that the user has the ability to use accessibility features as needed? The user can always turn on the StickyKeys feature by pressing the Shift key five times, or they can open the Accessibility Options dialog box. Both of these methods are inconvenient, but they work. However, if you want to make your application truly usable, it's better if you help the user turn StickyKeys on and off as needed directly from your application. Providing a simple menu option doesn't impair the user's ability to control their environment, but it does make the application infinitely easier to use.

The example in this section shows how to create menus that will help the user control the Windows Accessibility environment. You'll want to exercise some discretion in implementing this feature, but it's important to understand that there are times when you might want to do so. For example, I often use the MouseKeys option in my drawing applications because I lack a drawing tablet and must rely on the mouse or the keyboard. Using MouseKeys makes drawing extremely fast and accurate. I wish some graphics designers would include a switch for this option in their application, but so far, none have.

The following sections describe the programming interface. You need to understand the interface because each Windows Accessibility feature has a different control. The .NET Framework doesn't provide a method to manipulate the Windows Accessibility features yet, so I had to build a library named AccesFuncs that relies on Platform Invoke (PInvoke) to perform the task. This second section gets a little technical and you don't have to know how it works in order to use it. Feel free to skip this section if desired. Finally, we'll create an application that uses the AccessFuncs library. I've divided this application into functional areas and provided some tips on how to maximum user choices. You'll need to read all of the sections to get the big picture on how Windows Accessibility works, but you can read just the section you need to implement a specific Windows Accessibility feature in your application.

Understanding the Interface

One of the first problems you'll notice with the .NET Framework is a lack of support for direct Windows Accessibility feature manipulation. You can check the status of the HighContrast, CursorSize, and ShowSounds settings using properties in the SystemInformation class, but that's about it. We've already discussed the HighContrast option as part of the "Creating the Font Modification Example" in Chapter 5. The ShowSounds feature appears in the "Using the Sound Features Example" section of this chapter. The CursorSize feature appears in the "Using the Display Features Example" section of this chapter. We'll also discuss some mouse functionality you need to know about in the "Using the Mouse Features Example" section, but essentially, you can't even access the MouseKeys setting.

Because the .NET Framework doesn't provide the functionality needed, you'll have to use PInvoke to perform the task. Using PInvoke means learning about the Win32 API and understanding how to work with it. Obviously, the first question we need to answer is what Accessibility features Windows provides.

In general, you'll use the GetSystemMetrics() function to get the current on or off status of a standard Windows Accessibility function. You'll use the SystemParamtersInfo() function to enable these functions or to check the current user settings for them. Both of these functions rely on constants to determine which Windows Accessibility feature you want to access. Table 6-1 contains a complete list of the Windows Accessibility features, the access constant you use to access them, and a short description of how the user generally benefits from the Accessibility feature.

Table 6-1. Windows Accessibility Features

Feature	Get Status Constant	Set Status Constant	Description
StickyKeys	SPI_GETSTICKYKEYS	SPI_SETSTICKYKEYS	Makes the Ctrl, Alt, and Shift keys sticky, which means you can press them first and then the associated alphanumeric or function key. This allows users who can only press one key at a time use complex keyboard accelerators.
FilterKeys	SPI_GETFILTERKEYS	SPI_SETFILTERKEYS	Forces Windows to ignore brief or quickly repeated keystrokes. Also slows the repeat rate for the keyboard when a key is held down constantly.

Table 6-1. Windows Accessibility Features (Continued)

Feature	Get Status Constant	Set Status Constant	Description
ToggleKeys	SPI_GETTOGGLEKEYS	SPI_SETTOGGLEKEYS	Sounds a tone whenever the Caps Lock, Num Lock, Scroll Lock keys are pressed. You may need to disable this feature when an application requires extensive use of these keys, but remember to enable it again when you exit the program.
SoundSentry	SPI_GETSOUNDSENTRY	SPI_SETSOUNDSENTRY	Displays a visual warning whenever the system makes a sound. You'll want to disable non-imperative sounds when this option is used.
ShowSounds	SPI_GETSHOWSOUNDS	SPI_SETSHOWSOUNDS	Displays a caption whenever speech or sound occurs. See the "Using SAMI to Improve Your Applications" sidebar for additional details on how closed captioning can help your application.
HighContrast	SPI_GETHIGHCONTRAST	SPI_SETHIGHCONTRAST	This feature uses high contrast colors and large fonts to make reading the screen easier. If your application has formatted displays (like those for database- or dialog-based applications), you may need to adjust the display to make this feature useful.

Table 6-1. Windows Accessibility Features (Continued)

Feature	Get Status Constant	Set Status Constant	Description
MouseKeys	SPI_GETMOUSEKEYS	SPI_SETMOUSEKEYS	Allows the user to use the numeric keypad keys in place of the mouse to move the mouse cursor on screen. This feature shouldn't require changes to most applications. However, you may want to offer this feature when precise mouse placement is required, since using the cursor keys usually produces more accurate results.
SerialKey	SPI_GETSERIALKEYS	SPI_SETSERIALKEYS	Allows alternative access to mouse and keyboard features. In general, you'll never need to directly access this feature in an application (unless the application requires a special input device).

Using SAMI to Improve Your Applications

Closed captioning has moved from your television to the computer. Closed captioning is an alternate form of audio content. It may include descriptions of sounds, symbols, icons, or text to represent the audio content.

The use of closed captioning in applications affects many people. The most obvious users are persons with hearing loss or impairment. It's also useful for people who are learning to read, learning a second language, or in situations where noise is unwelcome, such as libraries or multiuse offices.

Microsoft's Synchronized Accessible Media Interchange (SAMI) improves delivery of closed captioning with multimedia applications by time-synchronizing the captioning file with the media file. This makes it easier to edit or change either file than it is in other applications where the application encodes the accessibility information within the media file.

SAMI can provide closed captioning in more than one language and with different presentation possibilities. The user chooses the appearance of the captions by selecting the color, font, and size of the text. This will increase the ease of reading for children and for people with slight visual impairments, who can select larger screen types. The user also chooses what language the text will appear in, such as American English or Canadian French.

SAMI files use the extension .SMI or .SAMI. The file format specification is free (no licensing fee). You can find the specification, demonstrations, and examples at `http://www.microsoft.com/enable/`, which is Microsoft's Accessibility Web site. The demonstrations require Internet Explorer 4 or above (`http://www.microsoft.com/windows/ie/default.asp`) and Windows Media Player (`http://www.microsoft.com/windows/windowsmedia/download/default.asp`).

SAMI instructions look similar to HTML or XML, but the actual implementation is different. The use of a common programming idiom makes it an easy format to learn. For example, documents begin with a `<SAMI>` tag and end with a `</SAMI>` tag, replacing the `<HTML>` tag in a normal HTML document. (The tags must be uppercase.) Once you have the `<SAMI>` tag in place, a SAMI document looks much the same as its HTML counterpart. It even includes the `<HEAD>` and `<BODY>` tags. You can learn more about SAMI at `http://msdn.microsoft.com/library/en-us/dnacc/html/atg_samiarticle.asp`.

A Quick Description of the AccessFuncs Library

The AccessFuncs library encapsulates all of the code required to work with the Windows Accessibility functions. If you want, you can simply skip this section and use the library as needed in your applications. All you need is a reference to the library and the appropriate using statement in your code. The library has full documentation, so you can read the descriptions in the Object Browser to understand how the library works. In addition, the "Developing the Windows Accessibility Status Application" section describes how to use the library for application development. Of course, you'll eventually want to know how the library works so that you can modify it to meet specific needs.

As previously mentioned, this library contains all of the Win32 API access code you'll need, including data structures. Listing 6-2 provides an overview of the essential functions, enumerations, and data structures. In fact, the listing only contains one sample of each type. The extensive comments are also removed for the sake of clarity. You can see the full listing of this library in the \Chapter 06\ AccessFuncs folder of the source code that you can obtain from the Downloads section of the Apress Web site (`http://www.apress.com`).

Listing 6-2. An Overview of the AccessFuncs Library

```
public enum AccessType : uint
    {
        SPI_GETHIGHCONTRAST  = 0x0042,
        SPI_SETHIGHCONTRAST  = 0x0043,
        SPI_GETSCREENREADER  = 0x0046,
        SPI_SETSCREENREADER  = 0x0047,
        SPI_GETFILTERKEYS    = 0x0032,
        SPI_SETFILTERKEYS    = 0x0033,
        SPI_GETTOGGLEKEYS    = 0x0034,
        SPI_SETTOGGLEKEYS    = 0x0035,
        SPI_GETMOUSEKEYS     = 0x0036,
        SPI_SETMOUSEKEYS     = 0x0037,
        SPI_GETSHOWSOUNDS    = 0x0038,
        SPI_SETSHOWSOUNDS    = 0x0039,
        SPI_GETSTICKYKEYS    = 0x003A,
        SPI_SETSTICKYKEYS    = 0x003B,
        SPI_GETACCESSTIMEOUT = 0x003C,
        SPI_SETACCESSTIMEOUT = 0x003D,
        SPI_GETSERIALKEYS    = 0x003E,
        SPI_SETSERIALKEYS    = 0x003F,
        SPI_GETSOUNDSENTRY    = 0x0040,
        SPI_SETSOUNDSENTRY    = 0x0041
    }


public enum WinIniFlags
    {
        SPIF_NONE            = 0x0000,
        SPIF_UPDATEINIFILE    = 0x0001,
        SPIF_SENDWININICHANGE = 0x0002,
        SPIF_SENDCHANGE       = SPIF_SENDWININICHANGE
    }


public enum HighContrastFlags
    {
        HCF_HIGHCONTRASTON = 0x00000001,
        HCF_AVAILABLE      = 0x00000002,
        HCF_HOTKEYACTIVE   = 0x00000004,
        HCF_CONFIRMHOTKEY  = 0x00000008,
        HCF_HOTKEYSOUND    = 0x00000010,
        HCF_INDICATOR      = 0x00000020,
        HCF_HOTKEYAVAILABLE = 0x00000040
    }
```

```
[StructLayout(LayoutKind.Sequential, Pack=1, CharSet=CharSet.Auto)]
 public struct HIGHCONTRAST
   {
      public UInt32    cbSize;
      public Int32     dwFlags;
      [MarshalAs(UnmanagedType.LPWStr, SizeConst=80)]
      public String    lpszDefaultScheme;
   }

public class Accessible
{
   public Accessible()
   {
   }

   [DllImport("User32.DLL", CharSet=CharSet.Auto, SetLastError=true)]
   public static extern bool SystemParametersInfo(AccessType uiAction,
                                        UInt32 uiParam,
                                        IntPtr pvParam,
                                        WinIniFlags fWinIni);

   public const Int32 SM_SHOWSOUNDS = 70;

   [DllImport("User32.DLL", CharSet=CharSet.Auto, SetLastError=true)]
   public static extern Int32 GetSystemMetrics(Int32 nIndex);
}
```

The actual place to start in this listing is the Accessible class. This class contains two functions. The GetSystemMetrics() function only performs one task—it
obtains the current ShowSounds state. You call it using the SM_SHOWSOUNDS constant.
The GetSystemMetrics() function returns a value indicating whether ShowSounds is
on or off. You can replicate this functionality using the SystemInformation.ShowSounds
property, so generally you should avoid using this function. It's provided in
the interest of completeness and for those times when you want to verify the
ShowSounds status.

The SystemParametersInfo() function isn't replicated anywhere within the .NET
Framework, so you'll find use for this function in your toolkit. Notice that you feed
the function four arguments. The first is one of the members of the AccessType enumeration that appears at the beginning of the listing. Notice that there's a get and set
member for each of the accessibility functions. Consequently, if you want to obtain
the current HighContrast status, you use the SPI_GETHIGHCONTRAST value and if you
want to set the HighContrast feature, you use the SPI_SETHIGHCONTRAST value.

The second and third arguments are related. The uiParam argument contains the size of the data structure passed as the pvParam argument. We'll see how you obtain this information in the "Developing the Windows Accessibility Status Application" section of the chapter. For now, you need to know that the data structure for each accessibility function is different. The HIGHCONTRAST data structure shown in the listing is representative. Every one of the data structures will contain the cbSize and the dwFlags members shown. The cbSize member contains the size of the data structure. The dwFlags member contains a numeric value that you interpret using the bit positions in the associated flag enumeration (HighContrastFlags in this case). Most of the data structures also contain some type of specialized information. For example, the HIGHCONTRAST data structure contains the name of the default high contrast scheme. Notice the technique used to marshal the string from the unmanaged environment. You must tell the Common Language Runtime (CLR) what type of string to create and how large to make it; otherwise, the function call will fail because the Win32 API will lack essential information.

The fourth argument is one of the members of the WinIniFlags enumeration. This value determines how Windows updates the user's profile. In general, you don't want to change the user's profile without the user's permission, so you'll usually set this entry to SPIF_NONE.

When the application makes a call to the SystemParametersInfo() function, the system will return a Boolean value indicating if the call is successful. Notice the SetLastError=true argument in the [DllImport] attribute. This argument tells the CLR to save any error information it receives. If the application detects an error in the function call, it should use the Marshal.GetLastWin32Error() method to retrieve the error number. Never use the Win32 API GetLastError() function to retrieve this information because this function could return unreliable or incorrect results from within the .NET environment.

Developing the Windows Accessibility Status Application

At this point, we have a library that can get and set the various Windows Accessibility feature values. In many cases, you'll never touch the settings, but will need the current setting values so that you can create a truly accessible application. The purpose of this section is to provide a quick overview of how you'd use the AccessFuncs library in an application. Of course, the first task you'll perform is to add a reference to the library to your application.

The sample application uses a standard menu to display the current Windows Accessibility feature status and help the user switch the feature on or off. You could easily add such a menu to your application or make it part of an options dialog. The point is that adding this functionality to your application as needed makes the Windows Accessibility feature easier to use.

Listing 6-3 provides an overview of the code for this example. You'll find a complete listing for this application in the \Chapter 06\AccessSettings folder of the source code that you can obtain from the Downloads section of the Apress Web site (http://www.apress.com).

Listing 6-3. An Overview of the AccesFuncs Library Test Application

```
public frmMain()
{
    Int32            DataSize;    // Size of the data structure.

    // Required for Windows Form Designer support
    InitializeComponent();

    // Initialize the data structures.
    AT = new ACCESSTIMEOUT();      // Access Timeout
    FK = new FILTERKEYS();         // FilterKeys
    HC = new HIGHCONTRAST();       // High Contrast
    MK = new MOUSEKEYS();          // MouseKeys
    SR = false;                    // ScreenReader
    SC = new SERIALKEYS();         // SerialKeys
    SSound = false;                // ShowSounds
    SSentry = new SOUNDSENTRY();   // SoundSentry
    SK = new STICKYKEYS();         // StickyKeys
    TK = new TOGGLEKEYS();         // ToggleKeys

    // Initialize the data structures and Choose menu options. The
    // process includes getting the current option status (which
    // fills out the data structure) and then comparing the flag
    // values to see if the option is on.

    // … Some example code left out here…

    // High Contrast
    DataSize = Marshal.SizeOf(HC);
    HC.cbSize = Convert.ToUInt32(DataSize);
    HC = (HIGHCONTRAST)GetAccessibleOption(
                    HC,
                    DataSize,
                    AccessType.SPI_GETHIGHCONTRAST,
                    WinIniFlags.SPIF_NONE);
    if ((HC.dwFlags & (Int32)HighContrastFlags.HCF_HIGHCONTRASTON) ==
                    (Int32)HighContrastFlags.HCF_HIGHCONTRASTON)
        mnuChooseHighContrast.Checked = true;
```

```
   // Screen Reader
   DataSize = Marshal.SizeOf(SR);
   SR = (bool)GetAccessibleOption(
             SR,
             DataSize,
             AccessType.SPI_GETSCREENREADER,
             WinIniFlags.SPIF_NONE);
   if (SR)
      mnuChooseScreenReader.Checked = true;


   // SerialKeys
   DataSize = Marshal.SizeOf(SC);
   SC.cbSize = Convert.ToUInt32(DataSize);
   SC = (SERIALKEYS)GetAccessibleOption(
                 SC,
                 DataSize,
                 AccessType.SPI_GETSERIALKEYS,
                 WinIniFlags.SPIF_NONE);
   if ((SC.dwFlags & (Int32)SerialKeysFlags.SERKF_SERIALKEYSON) ==
      (Int32)SerialKeysFlags.SERKF_SERIALKEYSON)
      mnuChooseSerialKeys.Checked = true;
   else if (SC.lpszActivePort == null)

      // This is one of the few accessibility options not supported
      // under Windows 2000/XP. Microsoft changed this behavior to
      // ensure that SerialKeys devices would appear as standard
      // input devices to the application.  The lpszActivePort member
      // will always contain a value for operating systems that
      // support the SerialKeys feature.
      mnuChooseSerialKeys.Enabled = false;
// … Some example code left out here…
}


private Object GetAccessibleOption(Object Struct,
                                   Int32 StructSize,
                                   AccessType AccessType,
                                   WinIniFlags IniFlag)
{
   Object   ReturnValue;   // The return data.

   // Allocate enough memory to create an unmanaged version
   // of the data structure.
   IntPtr   DataPtr = Marshal.AllocHGlobal(StructSize);
```

```
    // Point to the managed data stucture using the unmanaged
    // memory pointer.
    Marshal.StructureToPtr(Struct, DataPtr, true);

    // Call the SystemParametersInfo() function using the
    // unmanaged data structure pointer.
    Accessible.SystemParametersInfo(AccessType,
                                    Convert.ToUInt32(StructSize),
                                    DataPtr,
                                    IniFlag);

    // Move the data retrieved from the unmanaged environment to
    // the managed data structure and return this data structure
    // as an object.
    ReturnValue = Marshal.PtrToStructure(DataPtr, Struct.GetType());

    // Deallocate the memory we previously allocated.
    Marshal.FreeHGlobal(DataPtr);

    // Return the data.
    return ReturnValue;
}

private bool SetAccessibleOption(Object Struct,
                                 Int32 StructSize,
                                 AccessType AccessType,
                                 WinIniFlags IniFlag)
{
    bool  ReturnValue;    // The return value of this method.

    // Allocate enough memory to create an unmanaged version
    // of the data structure.
    IntPtr   DataPtr = Marshal.AllocHGlobal(StructSize);

    // Point to the managed data stucture using the unmanaged
    // memory pointer.
    Marshal.StructureToPtr(Struct, DataPtr, true);

    // Return true if the SystemParametersInfo() function call
    // successfully modifies the Windows Accessibility features
    // using the data in the data structure.
```

```
      ReturnValue = Accessible.SystemParametersInfo(
         AccessType,
         Convert.ToUInt32(StructSize),
         DataPtr,
         IniFlag);

      // Deallocate the memory we previously allocated.
      Marshal.FreeHGlobal(DataPtr);

      // Return the data.
      return ReturnValue;
}


private void mnuChooseHighContrast_Click(object sender, System.EventArgs e)
{
      Int32 DataSize;    // Size of the data structure.

      // Set the flag value as needed to toggle the feature on or off.
      if ((HC.dwFlags & (Int32)HighContrastFlags.HCF_HIGHCONTRASTON) ==
                      (Int32)HighContrastFlags.HCF_HIGHCONTRASTON)
         HC.dwFlags = HC.dwFlags ^
             (Int32)HighContrastFlags.HCF_HIGHCONTRASTON;
      else
         HC.dwFlags = HC.dwFlags |
             (Int32)HighContrastFlags.HCF_HIGHCONTRASTON;

      // Call on the library function to set the new FilterKeys status.
      DataSize = Marshal.SizeOf(HC);

      // If the function fails, display an error message.
      if (!SetAccessibleOption(HC,
                               DataSize,
                               AccessType.SPI_SETHIGHCONTRAST,
                               WinIniFlags.SPIF_NONE))
         MessageBox.Show("Could not set the High Contrast option",
                      "Accessibility Option Error",
                      MessageBoxButtons.OK,
                      MessageBoxIcon.Error);

      // If the function succeeds, display a success message and change
      // the menu setting.
      else
         mnuChooseHighContrast.Checked = !mnuChooseHighContrast.Checked;
}
```

The application begins by obtaining the current Windows Accessibility feature status in the constructor. In a production application, you'd probably want to check this status every time the user makes some type of request. In this case, that would mean getting the status every time the user opens the Choose Feature menu. The reason for this constant vigilance is that someone could modify the Windows Accessibility feature settings from outside of your application. Although the listing only shows a few of the feature requests, the complete application requests the status of all Windows Accessibility features.

Obtaining the HighContrast feature status is representative of most of the Windows Accessibility features. The application uses the Marshal.SizeOf() method to obtain the size of the data structure. It uses this information to fill in the cbSize data member and also as input to the GetAccessibleOption() method that we'll discuss later in this section. The GetAccessibleOption() method returns an Object data type since the same method is used for all of the Windows Accessibility feature calls. This means you have to convert the output to the correct data type. The code checks the dwFlags data member for the HCF_HIGHCONTRASTON setting. If this flag bit is set, then the code checks the HighContrast menu entry.

The Screen Reader is one of two Windows Accessibility features that doesn't require a data structure (ShowSounds is the other). The technique used in this case differs from a Windows Accessibility feature that requires a data structure, but the principle is the same. Notice that we still have to obtain the size of the variable and pass it along with the other information to the GetAccessibleOption() method. The output is a bool, so the code can look at this value directly.

The SerialKeys Windows Accessibility feature represents a special case. Older versions of Windows provide access to this feature, so you can read the various settings and provide accommodation for the devices attached using SerialKeys in your code. Newer versions of Windows don't provide this access using the theory that a SerialKeys device shouldn't look any different than any other device attached to the system. In sum, the device shouldn't require any special handling. In some ways, this viewpoint is justified, but it would still be nice to be able to turn the device on or off as needed.

The GetAccessibleOption() method comes next. The first task this method performs is to allocate memory using the Marshal.AllocHGlobal() method. At this point, you might wonder why we have to perform this task. Remember that your .NET application uses managed memory that the Garbage Collector controls. This call is to the unmanaged environment, where we need to use unmanaged memory. The Marshal.AllocHGlobal() method allocates unmanaged memory for this purpose.

The code calls the Accessible.SystemParametersInfo() method next. I described this method in the "A Quick Description of the AccessFuncs Library" section of the chapter. On return from this call, DataPtr (the unmanaged memory) contains the data we need. The code uses the Marshal.PtrToStructure() method to move the data from unmanaged memory into managed memory.

The next step is to free the unmanaged memory because we don't need it anymore. The code uses the `Marshal.FreeHGlobal()` method to perform this task. The `GetAccessibleOption()` method ends by returning the object containing the data to the caller. As mentioned earlier, the caller still needs to convert this generic object into a specific data structure to read the values.

You'll immediately notice that the `SetAccessibleOption()` method is similar, but not precisely the same as the `GetAccessibleOption()` method. The code still allocates and deallocates memory manually. In addition, it still relies on the `Accessible.SystemParametersInfo()` method to set the Windows Accessibility information. Because we're not getting new information, in this case, the code can simply return a `bool` value indicating success or failure.

The `mnuChooseHighContrast_Click()` method is representative of the event handlers for the menu. When a user clicks one of the menu entries, the code has to modify the flag values of the appropriate data structure to turn the feature on or off. The code shows one technique for performing this task. Once the data structure is modified, the code determines the size of the data structure and calls on the `SetAccessibleOption()` method to set the new value. The final step is to check or clear the menu option so that the user can see the current Windows Accessibility option status.

As you go through the code on the disk, you'll notice that some of the event handlers simply display a message, rather than change an option. For example, you can't turn on the screen reader from the application. To perform this task, you must start the associated application. In sum, you can't modify some Windows Accessibility features with this application because it doesn't make sense to do so. However, you can always retrieve the status information, which is a lot more than the .NET Framework allows you to do. Look through the various data structures to determine what types of information are available.

Using the Sound Features Example

Many .NET developers have already run across one problem with sound in this environment—there isn't any support built in for it unless you're using Visual Basic and you're happy with a plain beep. Most developers want something better than a plain beep, which means resorting to PInvoke in .NET. Using the Win32 API `PlaySound()` function enables the developer to play both standard system sounds as well as other media types such as WAV files.

Given the purpose of this book, you might wonder why I'm worried about sound. It turns out that there's also little support for the ShowSounds Windows Accessibility feature in most Windows applications today. In fact, finding an application that supports this feature is difficult at best.

This example starts with the premise that combining these two needs into one component would prove very convenient. The PlaySound control plays a sound and works with ShowSounds at the same time. All you need to do to use it is define a few properties. The sections that follow tell how this control works and demonstrates its use within a simple application.

Creating the PlaySound Control

The PlaySound control performs two tasks. First, it plays a sound. Second, it displays a tooltip if the user turns the ShowSounds feature on. The two tasks are independent of each other. The control can play a sound independently of the ShowSounds feature setting, so it's possible for the control to perform both or either task.

 TIP This control opens some interesting usage possibilities. For example, a developer could set an application up so that it simply displayed sound descriptions for users in office environments. The sound description would still notify the user of an event without disturbing the user's neighbors.

Now that you have some idea of what this control will do, let's look at the code. Listing 6-4 contains a partial listing of the code for this example. You'll find a complete a complete listing in the \Chapter 06\PlaySound folder of the source code that you can obtain from the Downloads section of the Apress Web site (http://www.apress.com).

Listing 6-4. Providing Sound and ShowSounds Functionality with the PlaySound Control

```
public class PlaySound : Component
{
    public PlaySound()
    {
        // Initialize the property values.
        _MakeSound = true;
        _SoundFileName = "";
        _ShowSoundsDescription = "The System Plays a Sound";
        _AutomaticDelay = 300;
        _AutoPopDelay = 7000;
        NoShow = new Timer();
    }
```

```
/// <summary>
/// This event fires when the system displays a
/// ShowSounds message.
/// </summary>
public event EventHandler SoundDisplayed;

/// <summary>
/// This event fires when the system generates a
/// sound.
/// </summary>
public event EventHandler SoundGenerated;

/// <summary>
/// Determines if the system will make a sound.
/// </summary>
public bool MakeSound
{
   get {return _MakeSound;}
   set {_MakeSound = value;}
}

// This property requires a special editor to ensure it works
// as intended.
/// <summary>
/// Contains the name of the file to play.
/// </summary>
[EditorAttribute(typeof(FileNameEditor), typeof(UITypeEditor))]
public string SoundFileName
{
   get
   {
      return _SoundFileName;
   }
   set
   {
      _SoundFileName = value;
   }
}
```

```
/// <summary>
/// Describes the sound to the person using ShowSounds.
/// </summary>
public string ShowSoundsDescription
{
   get {return _ShowSoundsDescription;}
   set
   {
      if (value != null)
         _ShowSoundsDescription = value;
   }
}


/// <summary>
/// Determines the hover delay for the tooltip
/// displaying the sound description. (1 ms minimum)
/// </summary>
public int AutomaticDelay
{
   get {return _AutomaticDelay;}
   set
   {
      if (value >= 1)
         _AutomaticDelay = value;
   }
}


/// <summary>
/// Determines the amount of time the tooltip
/// will appear on screen. (3000 ms minimum)
/// </summary>
public int AutoPopDelay
{
   get {return _AutoPopDelay;}
   set
   {
      if (value >= 3000)
         _AutoPopDelay = value;
   }
}
```

```
/// <summary>
/// Outputs a sound and/or a sound description based
/// upon the current ShowSound Windows Accessiblity setting.
/// </summary>
/// <param name="Parent">The control hosting the sound.</param>
public void GenerateSound(Control Parent)
{
   System.EventArgs  EA;    // Used When Raising an Event.

   // Initialize the EventArgs.
   EA = new EventArgs();

   // Initialize the ToolTip.
   TT = new ToolTip();
   TT.AutomaticDelay = _AutomaticDelay;
   TT.AutoPopDelay = _AutoPopDelay;

   // Intitialze the Timer.
   NoShow.Interval = _AutoPopDelay;
   NoShow.Tick += new EventHandler(this.NoShow_Tick);

   // If the ShowSounds option is selected, display text.
   if (IsShowSoundsSelected())
   {
      // Display the information on screen.
      TT.SetToolTip(Parent, _ShowSoundsDescription);
      TT.Active = true;
      NoShow.Start();

      // Fire the event.
      if (SoundDisplayed != null)
         SoundDisplayed(this, EA);
   }

   if (_MakeSound)
   {
      // Play a sound only when the user requests it.
      WinPlaySound(@_SoundFileName,
         0,
         SND_FILENAME | SND_ASYNC);
```

```
            // Fire the event.
            if (SoundGenerated != null)
                SoundGenerated(this, EA);
        }
    }


    /// <summary>
    /// Obtains the current status of the ShowSounds
    /// Windows Accessibility setting.
    /// </summary>
    /// <returns>True or False depending on setting value</returns>
    public bool IsShowSoundsSelected()
    {
        return SystemInformation.ShowSounds;
    }


    // Define some constants for using the PlaySound() function.
    private const int SND_SYNC = 0x0000;
    private const int SND_ASYNC = 0x0001;
    private const int SND_FILENAME = 0x00020000;


    // Import the Windows PlaySound() function.
    [DllImport("winmm.dll",
        EntryPoint="PlaySound", CharSet=CharSet.Auto, SetLastError=true)]
    private static extern bool WinPlaySound(string pszSound,
                                            int hmod,
                                            int fdwSound);


    private void NoShow_Tick(Object sender, System.EventArgs e)
    {
        // Stop displaying the sound description.
        TT.Active = false;

        // Stop the timer.
        NoShow.Stop();
    }
}
```

As you can see, it's a lot of code (and I cut it down for the purposes of display in the book). The first thing you should notice is that I've based this control on the Component class. The reason for this choice is that the control doesn't include a window of any sort—it's more akin to a timer than to a command button.

The constructor begins by initializing all of the property values for the controls. Notice that we use private variables for the properties. These values are exposed by the properties that appear later in the listing.

The control supports two events. The control fires these events whenever it displays a sound description or generates a sound. Generally, you won't need to handle the events, but sometimes an application needs to know when these events actually occur.

All of the properties come next in the listing. Most of the properties are of the generic get/set variety. Notice that the SoundFileName property includes support for an editor. This editor displays a File Open dialog box that helps the control user locate the sound file on disk. This control only supports external sound files, but you could easily extend it to support embedded resources and system sounds.

I wanted to ensure that the control will always have some type of value to display as a sound description, so the ShowSoundsDescription property looks for a null value. If the value isn't null, it will set the sound description to that value. A production version of this control would probably include additional checks to ensure that the developer provided something that at least looks like a sound description. Of course, there are limits to what the control can check, so someone who really doesn't want to display a usable sound description is certainly free to come up with something less than usable.

The AutomaticDelay and AutoPopDelay properties set timer values for the control, so it's important to ensure that the developer provide realistic values. Both properties look for numeric input that's greater than a baseline value. If the input doesn't meet this requirement, the control uses the current value instead.

The main method for this control is GenerateSound(). This method displays sound descriptions on screen and generates the audible sound as needed. The code begins by creating and initializing the variables used within the control. For example, this is where the ToolTip, TT, is initialized.

The first check the code makes is to verify the state of ShowSounds using the IsShowSoundsSelected() method. The IsShowSoundsSelected() method simply returns the state of the SystemInformation.ShowSounds property. The reason the control uses this technique is to expose this functionality to the developer as well. This makes the SystemInformation.ShowSounds property easier for the developer using the control to access. Otherwise, the GenerateSound() method could have accessed the SystemInformation.ShowSounds property directly.

If ShowSounds is active, the code associates TT with the parent control passed into the GenerateSound() method by the caller. It displays TT so the user can see the description associated with the sound. Unfortunately, TT doesn't go away if you leave it in this state. You have to deactivate it. In this case, we'll use a timer, NoShow, to perform that task. So, the next step the code performs is to start NoShow, which has already been set up with the _AutoPopDelay value. The final step is to fire the SoundDisplayed event so that the application knows the event occurred.

The next task that GenerateSound() performs is to check the _MakeSound value. If the developer chooses to make a sound, the code calls WinPlaySound(), which calls a Win32 API function to generate the audible sound. The final step is to fire the SoundGenerated event.

As you can see from the listing, the WinPlaySound() function is simply a declaration of an imported Win32 API function, PlaySound(). In this case, the declaration requires an EntryPoint argument to ensure that the [DllImport] attribute can locate the proper call. The PlaySound() function accepts three inputs, only two of which we need to provide in this case. The first input is a string that describes the name and location of the sound. In this case, the sound is always a filename. However, you can also specify an internal application resource, the name of a system sound in the registry, or the name of a sound in the WIN.INI file. We don't use the hmod argument in this case, but you must use it when you want to use an application resource as input. Finally, the fdwSound argument contains flags that determine how Windows plays the sound. For example, you can select between asynchronous (where control is returned immediately) and synchronous sound playing.

The NoShow_Tick() event handler is the last essential piece of the control. A single tick is the duration that the developer wants to display the ToolTip, TT. When this single tick occurs, it's time to hide TT until the application wants to play a sound again. This event handler sets TT.Active to false so the ToolTip won't display when the user hovers the mouse of the control associated with the sound. The code then stops the timer so that the control is no longer active and the application can garbage collect it if desired.

Creating the ShowSounds Test Application

The ShowSounds test application is a simple test of the PlaySound control. It includes a few check boxes that enable the developer to test the events and to turn the sound-playing feature on or off. (If you want to turn ShowSounds on of off, use the Accessibility Options applet in the Control Panel.) Listing 6-5 shows the Test button and PlaySound control event handlers. You'll find the complete listing for this example in the \Chapter 06\ShowSounds folder of the source code that you can obtain from the Downloads section of the Apress Web site (http://www.apress.com).

Listing 6-5. The ShowSounds Test Application

```
private void btnTest_Click(object sender, System.EventArgs e)
{
    // Check to see if the user wants to play a sound.
    if (cbSound.Checked)
        MySound.MakeSound = true;
    else
        MySound.MakeSound = false;
```

```
      // Check to see if the user wants the SoundDisplayed event.
      if (cbSoundDisplay.Checked)
         MySound.SoundDisplayed +=
            new EventHandler(playSound1_SoundDisplayed);
      else
         MySound.SoundDisplayed -=
            new EventHandler(playSound1_SoundDisplayed);

      // Check to see if the user wants the SoundGenerated event.
      if (cbSoundGenerate.Checked)
         MySound.SoundGenerated +=
            new EventHandler(playSound1_SoundGenerated);
      else
         MySound.SoundGenerated -=
            new EventHandler(playSound1_SoundGenerated);

      // Perform the sound related task.
      MySound.GenerateSound(btnTest);
   }

private void playSound1_SoundDisplayed(object sender, System.EventArgs e)
{
   // Display a message box.
   MessageBox.Show("Sound Displayed");
}

private void playSound1_SoundGenerated(object sender, System.EventArgs e)
{
   // Display a message box.
   MessageBox.Show("Sound Generated");
}
```

The btnTest_Click() method begins by checking the state of cbSound. If the user checks this control, then the application will play the sound associated with the MySound control. Likewise, the code checks the state of the cbSoundDisplay and cbSoundGenerate controls to determine if they're checked. If so, the code assigns an event handler to the affected events. In this case, the event handlers display a message box. Finally, the method calls MySound.GenerateSound() with the test button as input. Figure 6-17 shows typical output for this application.

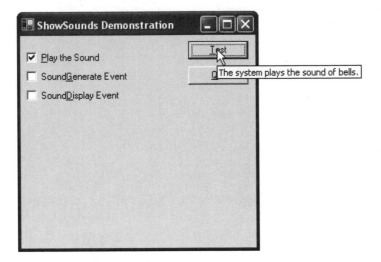

Figure 6-17. The test application helps you see the functionality of the PlaySound control.

Using the Display Features Example

We've already discussed several display-related issues, such as the use of high contrast in the book. However, we haven't discussed one important element—the cursor used to display information on screen. Checking the size of the cursor can help you format the display for easier viewing by those who want to use a large cursor size. Not only that, but checking the cursor size can often provide cues about a user's overall viewing needs. Some users don't use the HighContrast setting, even when they use a large text display to see information on screen. Listing 6-6 shows the simple technique used to determine the current cursor size. You'll find a complete listing for this example in the \Chapter 06\CursorData folder of the source code that you can obtain from the Downloads section of the Apress Web site (http://www.apress.com).

Listing 6-6. A Technique for Obtaining the Cursor Size

```
private void btnGetCursor_Click(object sender, System.EventArgs e)
{
    StringBuilder  CursorData; // Cursor information.

    // Initialize the StringBuilder
    CursorData = new StringBuilder();
```

```
// Get the cursor information.
CursorData.Append("The current cursor size is:\r\n\r\nHeight: ");
CursorData.Append(SystemInformation.CursorSize.Height.ToString());
CursorData.Append("\r\nWidth: ");
CursorData.Append(SystemInformation.CursorSize.Width.ToString());

// Display the information.
MessageBox.Show(CursorData.ToString(),
                "Cursor Data",
                MessageBoxButtons.OK,
                MessageBoxIcon.Information);
}
```

The centerpiece of this code is the SystemInformation.CursorSize property. This property provides the information needed to find the actual height and width of the cursor. In general, you'll find that most standard displays use a 32-pixel×32-pixel cursor size. However, some displays use larger or smaller sizes depending on the needs of the user and the current system configuration. The application generates a message box containing the cursor size information.

 NOTE You'll notice that most of the examples that rely on the SystemInformation class in this chapter don't modify the associated property. In general, the SystemInformation class only allows the developer to view the system setting—not change it. If you want to change a system setting, you'll need to use a Win32 API function such as we used in the "A Quick Description of the AccessFuncs Library" section of the chapter.

Using the Mouse Features Example

One area in which the .NET Framework provides complete information to the developer is the mouse. You still can't modify any of the information without resorting to a Win32 API call, but at least you can determine the mouse status and many of the common features it provides. For example, you can determine how many buttons a mouse has and whether it supports a mouse wheel. Listing 6-7 shows the code for this example. You'll find a complete listing for this example in the \Chapter 06\MouseCheck folder of the source code that you can obtain from the Downloads section of the Apress Web site (http://www.apress.com).

Listing 6-7. Techniques for Determining the Mouse Status and Configuration

```
private void btnTest_Click(object sender, System.EventArgs e)
{
   StringBuilder  MouseData;  // The mouse setup information.

   // Initialize the StringBuilder.
   MouseData = new StringBuilder();

   // Check for the presence of a mouse.
   if (SystemInformation.MousePresent)
   {
      // Begin building the MouseData string.
      MouseData.Append("System includes a mouse with the " +
                     "following characteristics:\r\n");

      // Get the clicking information.
      MouseData.Append("\r\nDouble Click Area (pixels): ");
      MouseData.Append(
         SystemInformation.DoubleClickSize.ToString());
      MouseData.Append("\r\nDouble Click Time (ms): ");
      MouseData.Append(
         SystemInformation.DoubleClickTime.ToString());

      // Get the mouse specific information.
      MouseData.Append("\r\n\r\nNumber of Mouse Buttons: ");
      MouseData.Append(
         SystemInformation.MouseButtons.ToString());
      MouseData.Append("\r\nAre the buttons swapped? ");
      MouseData.Append(
         SystemInformation.MouseButtonsSwapped.ToString());
      MouseData.Append("\r\n\r\nIs a mouse wheel available? ");
      MouseData.Append(
         SystemInformation.MouseWheelPresent.ToString());

      // Display this information only for systems with
      // mouse wheel support.
      if (SystemInformation.MouseWheelPresent)
      {
         MouseData.Append("\r\nMouse wheel scroll lines: ");
         MouseData.Append(
            SystemInformation.MouseWheelScrollLines.ToString());
         MouseData.Append("\r\nNative mouse wheel support? ");
         MouseData.Append(
            SystemInformation.NativeMouseWheelSupport.ToString());
      }
```

```
    // Display the results.
    MessageBox.Show(MouseData.ToString(),
                    "Mouse Access Information",
                    MessageBoxButtons.OK,
                    MessageBoxIcon.Information);
}

// If no mouse is present, display a message and exit.
else
    MessageBox.Show("There is no mouse connected to this system.",
                    "No Mouse Access",
                    MessageBoxButtons.OK,
                    MessageBoxIcon.Exclamation);
}
```

As you can see from the code, all of the mouse statistics appear in the SystemInformation class. Various properties in this class tell you different things about the mouse, such as support for a mouse wheel and the current size of the double click area. Information such as the size of the double click area can cue you about the abilities of the user in some situations. A large DoubleClickSize value could indicate that the user has mobility problems—a large DoubleClickTime value tends to enforce this idea. Figure 6-18 shows the output of this example.

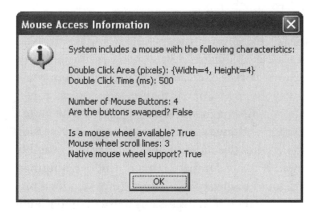

Figure 6-18. Use this test application to learn more about the functionality of the mouse attached to a machine.

Notice that the information in Figure 6-18 is complete, but also generic. For example, the target mouse provides support for four buttons. Although you know the tasks the first two buttons perform, you don't know what the other two do?

Are these buttons available for special use in your application? You won't know unless you ask the user. In short, these properties provide access to some level of automation, but perhaps not the complete automation that many developers would like.

Summary

This chapter has helped you discover the Windows Accessibility features. The main idea behind this chapter is to show that you can provide good accessibility support in an application with only a little extra coding in many cases. The amazing thing is that Microsoft built this support into Windows—the user doesn't have to spend one penny extra to get it. All that they need is for your application to recognize the added support and provide the additional code needed to activate it. Interestingly, the .NET Framework makes this process easier because Microsoft has added some functionality that you would have had to code by hand in the past.

Even so, things aren't perfect with the Windows Accessibility support. So, one of the first things you need to do is determine how far the Accessibility features go in meeting your potential user's needs. In some cases, the Accessibility features provide everything you need; but, in other cases, users will need to buy some special hardware to make the access perfect. The point is that you need to plan for this support during the design phase, ensure it actually works during the testing phase, and then make users aware of the accessibility features and requirements for your application. Otherwise, users might have unrealistic expectations that your application won't satisfy.

It's also time to work with the accessibility features by yourself. Make sure you try your application out using the accessibility features. Sometimes, the best way to learn how the accessibility features work is to do something like try them while blindfolded. Ask yourself how easy your application is to use when you can't see the screen. In this case, not seeing is believing (and learning). You'll also want to try the JAWS demonstration software mentioned in the "Using the Narrator" section of the chapter. This product demonstrates the superior performance and usability of some of the products on the market when compared to the Windows offerings.

Chapter 7 looks at usage cues. Many of the accessibility features Windows provides make application access easier, but they don't necessarily make the application easier to use. Earlier in the book, we had discussed the need for an accessibility friendly application to provide both access and usability. While this chapter concentrated on access, Chapter 7 will help you learn about usability in the world of Windows programming.

Adding Usage Cues to Desktop Applications

In This Chapter:

What Techniques Should You Use to Expose the Screen Focus?

What Is the Difference Between Legal Requirement and Accessibility Need?

How Can You Add Balloon Help to an Application?

Why Should You Prepare Your Tips in Advance?

How Can You Give the User Better Control Over Their Environment?

What Techniques Should You Use to Create Consistent Controls, Status Indicators, and Other Elements?

How Can You Add Context Sensitive Help to an Application?

How Do You Obtain and Install Microsoft Active Accessibility?

What Types of Tools Does Microsoft Active Accessibility Provide?

How Can You Add Microsoft Active Accessibility Functionality to an Application?

What Accessibility Features Does the .NET Framework Provide?

How Can You Add .NET Accessibility Features to an Application?

SO FAR, THE DESKTOP SECTIONS of the book have examined such additions as tooltips and access to the Windows Accessibility features. However, we haven't really discussed the subtle, yet essential, issue of cues. People rely on cues as a subtle means to interpret the meaning behind any contact. For example, body language is a major part of face-to-face communication. When people lack access to essential body language cues, such as during email communication, the communication often fails. Now, consider that most of us learn to communicate long before we learn to use applications and you begin to understand why cues are so important.

This chapter helps you understand how to add cues to your application. Consider again the issue of email communication and the problems it can cause. Email users have devised various emoticons to communicate the missing cues in their communication. The users who communicate best are the ones who've learned to use emoticons successfully—just as people who use body language well communicate best in face to face exchanges. It follows that developers who learn how to add cues to their applications will communicate best with the end user. (You may have already guessed that using emoticons doesn't always guarantee success, but you'll find that most usage cues fail to meet the mark at times, too.)

Fortunately, adding cues isn't difficult. Sometimes all you need to do is ensure that the sequence of fields on a form flows smoothly. However, there are other ways you can add cues to your application. In fact, the .NET environment adds a number of easy ways to add usage cues to your applications that we'll discuss in this chapter. We'll also discuss some special utilities you can download to check the accessibility and usability of your applications from a cue perspective.

Exposing the Screen Focus

You must always expose the focus for your application. We've already discussed some of what this means in the "Tracking the Screen Focus" section of Chapter 5. To provide sufficient focus information, the user environment must track the focus at the Application, Form or Window, and Control or Other Element levels. For some developers, the functionality provided by Windows is enough. Using the standard controls provided by any of the Microsoft development environments ensures that your application will provide the information required by the law.

 ON THE WEB   Although the desktop portion of this book focuses heavily on Windows, it's important to realize that other vendors are making progress in building accessible operating systems too. In fact, we've discussed a few of the Apple contributions already. For example, Sun Microsystems and the GNOME community recently received a Helen Keller Achievement Award in Technology for their work in the GNOME Accessibility architecture. This technology appears as part of the GNOME 2 graphical desktop for UNIX environments. You can learn more about this achievement and the award at `http://www.afb.org/ info_document_view.asp?documentid=1806`, `http://www.sun.com/smi/ Press/sunflash/2002-09/sunflash.20020924.1.html`, and `http:// developer.gnome.org/projects/gap/news.html`.

However, what happens when you develop your own controls and components? Do these controls provide sufficient information to allow assistive technologies to track the screen focus? Questions such as these can keep you awake at night because you're never sure if you addressed all of the user's needs. Because components and controls normally appear in more than one application, and since developers rely on these controls and components to work as advertised, they have to make sure that the component or control is right the first time. Even a small mistake here can cause big problems down the road.

Some developers have the misconception that subclassing the correct existing class is enough to ensure full compliance with accessibility requirements. (The .NET Framework classes tend to support the `IAccessible` interface, which makes implementing accessibility features a lot easier.) This is true to a point, but not if your control falls outside the normal range of functionality that the base class addresses. In some cases, you might have to implement special accessibility requirements using the `AccessibleObject` class (see the "A Quick Demonstration of the AccessibleObject Class" section of Chapter 6 for an overview). In other cases, you can rely on the `ControlAccessibleObject` class to provide the support needed.

Legal Requirement Versus Accessibility Need

Sometimes the source of a screen focus problem isn't apparent, or sometimes the law doesn't provide a precise remedy for the situation. For example, there are instances when it might be helpful to have a button that automatically clicks itself after a specific interval. An exam application could use such a button to signal that time is up for answering a question. Such a button could also provide an automated click when a user doesn't want to bother performing the task manually (such as clearing an informational dialog box). We'll discuss such a button as part of the TimerButton example.

The interesting thing about the TimerButton control is that it conflicts with the requirements in an interesting way. According to requirement 1194.22(p), anytime an application requires a timed response, the developer must provide some way to allow the user to indicate they need more time to respond. Unfortunately, this law supposedly affects only Web controls. However, it's equally necessary for desktop applications to provide this service. That's why the TimerButton control provides the means to give the user more time (if the developer allows it— you might not want to allow extra time for something like an exam).

The TimerButton control points out the dichotomy between legal requirement and user need. Some developers would be inclined to create a TimerButton that lacks any form of user control. Such an addition is a little time consuming to create, requires more extensive testing of the control, and isn't required by the law (the requirements of section 1194.22(p) only affect Web applications). However, logic dictates that if such an accommodation is required for a Web application, it should also apply to desktop applications. In addition, watching users with special needs try to respond to the control in the same 15 seconds that someone with better mobility can perform the task demonstrates that the control doesn't work as anticipated. The need for additional time is easy to understand from this perspective.

Working with the TimerButton Example

Now that we've discussed the functionality of the TimerButton and determined why the user needs this functionality, let's look at the code. Listing 7-1 contains the essential elements of the TimerButton control. (I removed many of the comments and some of the mundane code for space considerations.) You'll notice that it includes properties and methods to affect every part of the control operation and it provides for the accessibility requirements of control focus and user control. The complete listing is in the \Chapter 07\AccControl folder of the source code that you can obtain from the Downloads section of the Apress Web site (http://www.apress.com).

Listing 7-1. An Example of a TimerButton Control

```
public TimerButton()
{
    // Create the countdown display timer. Set it to
    // display once a second.
    CounterTimer = new Timer();
    CounterTimer.Tick +=
        new System.EventHandler(this.CounterTimer_Tick);
    CounterTimer.Interval = 1000;

    // Create the menu item.
    mnuMoreTime = new MenuItem();
    mnuMoreTime.DefaultItem = true;
    mnuMoreTime.Index = 0;
    mnuMoreTime.Text = "&More Time";
    mnuMoreTime.Click +=
        new System.EventHandler(this.mnuMoreTime_Click);

    // Create the context menu and add the menu item.
    mnuTimeSelect = new ContextMenu(new MenuItem[] {mnuMoreTime});

    // Create the tool tip.
    TimeNote = new ToolTip();
    TimeNote.SetToolTip(
        this,
        "This is a timed button. Right click the button and choose " +
        "More Time from the context menu to change the time " +
        "interval.");
```

```
   // Add the features to the control.
   this.ContextMenu = mnuTimeSelect;
   this.Text = "TimerButton";

   // Initialize the property values.
   _CountdownEnabled = true;
   _TimerInterval = 15;
   _AutoClick = false;
   _TimerStarted = false;
   _NoMoreTime = false;
}
#endregion

public Int32 TimerInterval
{
   get { return _TimerInterval; }
   set
   {
      if (value > 0)
         _TimerInterval = value;
   }
}


public Boolean CountdownEnabled
{
   get { return _CountdownEnabled; }
   set { _CountdownEnabled = value; }
}

public Int32 TimerValue
{
   get { return TimeLeft; }
}

public Boolean TimerEnabled
{
   get { return CounterTimer.Enabled; }
}

public Boolean TimerStarted
{
   get { return _TimerStarted; }
}
```

```
public Boolean AutoClick
{
   get { return _AutoClick; }
}

public Boolean NoMoreTimeMenu
{
   get { return _NoMoreTime; }
   set
   {
      // Provide special handling if the developer chooses to
      // turn the menu option off.
      if (value == true)
      {
         // If the control is in design mode, make sure the
         // developer is aware of the effects of this choice.
         if (this.DesignMode)
         {
            // Make sure the developer wants to make the change.
            DialogResult Result = MessageBox.Show(
               "Setting this value to true will prevent " +
               "the user from changing the timeout value. Do " +
               "you want to make this change?",
               "Value Change Warning",
               MessageBoxButtons.YesNo,
               MessageBoxIcon.Warning);

            // If the devveloper does want to make the change set
            // the property to true and turn off support for the
            // event handler.
            if (Result == DialogResult.Yes)
            {
               _NoMoreTime = value;
               this.ContextMenu = null;
            }
         }
         else
         {
            // The control is not in design mode, so make the
            // required changes.
            _NoMoreTime = value;
            this.ContextMenu = null;
         }
      }
```

```
        // If the developer is returning the control to its default
        // value, then make the change.
        else
        {
            _NoMoreTime = value;
            this.ContextMenu = mnuTimeSelect;
        }
    }
}


public void TimerStart(Boolean Start)
{
    if (Start)
    {
        // Reset the AutoClick property.
        _AutoClick = false;

        // Save the old caption for later use.
        _OldCaption = this.Text;

        // Set the time keeper and the timer.
        TimeLeft = _TimerInterval;
        CounterTimer.Start();
        _TimerStarted = true;
    }
    else
    {
        // Stop the timer.
        CounterTimer.Stop();

        // Restore the original caption.
        this.Text = _OldCaption;
        _TimerStarted = false;
    }
}


public void AutoClickReset()
{
    // Reset the AutoClick value.
    _AutoClick = false;
}
```

```csharp
private void CounterTimer_Tick(object sender, System.EventArgs e)
{
   System.EventArgs  EA;    // Used When Raising an Event.

   // Initialize the EventArgs.
   EA = new EventArgs();

   // If the developer enables the count down function, then
   // display the remaining time as the button caption.
   if (_CountdownEnabled)
      this.Text =
         "&Time: " + TimeLeft.ToString();

   // Click the button automatically when time expires.
   if (TimeLeft == 0)
   {
      // Turn the timer off.
      CounterTimer.Stop();

      // Set the result value to reflect an automatic click.
      _AutoClick = true;

      // Fire the event.
      OnClick(EA);
   }
   else
      // Decrement the counter.
      TimeLeft--;
}

private void mnuMoreTime_Click(object sender, System.EventArgs e)
{
   // Stop the timer so the user has time to make a change.
   if (_TimerStarted)
      CounterTimer.Stop();

   // Create an instance of the time change form.
   FrmMoreTime ChangeData = new FrmMoreTime(TimeLeft);

   // Display the form and obtain a result.
   DialogResult MyResult = ChangeData.ShowDialog(this);
```

```
   // If the user clicked OK, change the time value.
   if (MyResult == DialogResult.OK)
      TimeLeft = ChangeData.NewTime;

   // Restart the timer so the button keeps track of the time.
   if (_TimerStarted)
      CounterTimer.Start();
}
```

As you can see, even the condensed listing is a tad on the long side. However, all of the elements in the control are important and you can study it in depth using the test application we'll discuss later.

The constructor is the first method in this control. In this case, the constructor has to create all of the objects used in the control and initialize them. The control uses a timer to determine when it's time to click the button automatically. A context menu and associated menu item enable the user to change the time interval used for the automatic click mechanism. The developer can turn this feature off using the NoMoreTimeMenu property. The constructor also initializes a ToolTip named TimeNote. This ToolTip pops up whenever the user hovers the mouse over the control. (See the "Considering Balloon Help Issues" section for details.) The final task performed by the constructor is to initialize the private variables used to hold the various property values.

An entire assortment of properties appears next in the listing. Some of these properties are of the mundane get/set variety. For example, the TimerInterval property simply checks to make sure the incoming value is at least 1. The timer won't accept values less than that. One potential change for this control is changing that value to something that's more acceptable to a variety of people—15 seconds seems about right, but the time interval should be relatively flexible. Some of the properties, such as TimerEnabled, are read-only. The reason for this limit is that giving access to the timer in this way could cause support problems. You don't want the user of your control turning off the timer without changing the associated internal values. The TimerButton provides other structured methods for modifying this value.

One property requires special attention because it provides special functionality. The NoMoreTimeMenu property should be accessible to the developer, but the developer should also be aware of what changing this property will do to the application as a whole. Turning the context menu off removes one of the important accessibility features of this control. Consequently, the property checks for an incoming true value. If the value is true and the control is in DesignMode, it displays a message telling the developer about the consequences of this change. Every accessibility feature you include in a control you create should include similar protection. Notice that the message doesn't appear if the control is running, rather than in DesignMode. This property is also unique in that it affects two values. The property must reflect any change the developer makes by modifying the _NoMoreTime value. It must also modify the this.ContextMenu property to ensure that the context menu doesn't appear.

The TimerStart() method is next in the list of control features. The developer needs to provide a Start value for this method. An input value of true turns the timer on—a value of false turns it off. Of course, the control performs a number of tasks behind the scenes to make everything happen. The code begins by setting the _AutoClick value to false to ensure that the control properly registers an automatic click event should it occur. One TimerButton feature not mentioned earlier is the fact that the TimerButton will display a "time left" caption should the developer decide to provide one. For this reason, the control must save the exiting caption to the _OldCaption variable. The current code places the _TimerInterval value into the TimeLeft variable. TimeLeft is the countdown variable that holds the current remaining time. The TimerStart() method starts the timer using the Start() method and provides an indication of this status using the _TimerStarted variable. Stopping the timer is less complicated. All the TimerStart() method does is turn the counter off using the Stop() method, restore the previous caption, and set the _TimerStarted variable to false.

The developer might have a need to reset the AutoClick property value before restarting the timer. The AutoClickReset() method performs this simple task. As you can see, all it does is reset the _AutoClick variable to false.

The TimerButton control necessarily relies on a number of event handlers. All of these event handlers are private because the developer need not know they even exist. One of the most important event handlers is the CounterTimer_Tick() method. Every time the counter ticks, Windows calls this event handler. The code begins by checking the status of the CountdownEnabled property. If this property is true, it displays the countdown timer caption. You'll remember that TimeLeft is the countdown timer. If this value is false, then time has elapsed and the control needs to generate an automatic click. To perform this task, the code begins by stopping the timer (so that the code doesn't get into an endless loop or repeat the automatic click event). The code sets the AutoClick property to true because the automatic click event occurred. Finally, the code calls the OnClick() method to generate the actual click. If the time hasn't elapsed, then the only task of the CounterTimer_Tick() method is to decrement the TimeLeft variable.

The mnuMoreTime_Click() method provides the specialized accessibility support for this control. Notice that the code begins by stopping the timer. This step is essential because, otherwise, the timer could elapse long before the user makes a new timer interval choice. This code refers to the FrmMoreTime class. We'll discuss this class in the "Considering User Controls Issues" section of this chapter. All you need to know now is that it contains the form used to allow the user access to the time interval. The code creates an object based on this class and displays the form on screen. If the user clicks OK on this form, then the code uses a property exposed by the `FrmMoreTime` class to change the `TimeLeft` value.

I had considered making the timer interval change affect the control all the time (permanently during the current session) by modifying the `TimerInterval` property. However, performing the task this way would alter the developer's intent for the application. It may be that the user needs additional time for just one of the entries and not all of them—the application should retain the original estimate of the developer when this is the case. Consequently, the developer should provide some other method for making the change permanent such as a registry entry. A registry entry would work best in situations where the user always needs more time to work with the button because the change would continue every session, rather than just in the current session. The dialog technique only affects the control once. After the user makes the change to the timer value, the code restarts the counter and the count will resume at the new `TimeLeft` value.

Considering Balloon Help Issues

Many developers limit their use of balloon help, when they use it at all, to a short description of a control. In fact, most of Windows appears to take this approach, except for those items that appear in the notification area of the Taskbar. For the developer of accessible applications, using balloon help is not an option. The screen reader and other accessibility tools rely on balloon help (in part) to help the user recognize and use the control. Consequently, while it's still important to keep balloon help relatively short, it's also important to make it descriptive enough that someone can actually use the information.

The TimerButton example points out another important balloon help issue. You don't have to relegate this feature to simple control descriptions. In the case of the TimerButton, you'll find that the `TimeNote ToolTip` pops up with instructions on how to use the control's menu. This `ToolTip` pops up in addition to any descriptive information the developer using the control might provide. In many cases, the two tips will overlay each other on the display (especially if the settings conflict), but a screen reader will still pick up both. This means that the user of the application with the TimerButton control will receive a description of how the application uses the control and learn how to change the time interval as well.

There's one other issue to consider here. You won't know how the application user will perceive the balloon help unless you try the application out with some of the accessibility tools mentioned in this book. You won't know whether a screen reader will pick up both balloon help displays from the TimerButton until you actually try the application out with a screen reader. The timing requirements for the two pieces of balloon help won't become apparent until you set the application to provide the balloon help the user needs. In sum, developing applications that include balloon help means using the application output to see how the balloon help really works.

Creating Your Balloon Help in Advance

Many developers make an error by creating inconsistent prompts for their applications. When a user sees the prompts, the inconsistency often confuses the user rather than helps them accomplish a given task. Consistent prompts are an essential element of an accessible application.

One of the best techniques you can use to avoid this problem is to consider the prompt definition as part of the design process. Build a database containing the prompts to make it easy for developers on your team to create consistent use input. Obtain the services of a good writer as part of the process to help build the prompts, ensure that the wording is clear, and check for problems such as grammar and spelling.

Creating the prompts in advance also serves another useful purpose. It forces the developer to think about the functionality of each user interface element. In most cases, the prompts will help the developer refine the user interface and make it more usable. In some cases, creating the prompts in advance could cause a developer to reconsider the user interface element or build it in an entirely different way. In sum, designing a user interface means considering all aspects before committing the design to code.

Considering User Control Issues

The TimerButton control presents some interesting challenges in making it easy for the user to control the time interval. In the "Working with the TimerButton Example" section, we discussed the mnuMoreTime_Click() event handler that the user triggers when they right click the button and select the More Time menu entry. The event handler displays the form based on the FrmMoreTime class shown in Figure 7-1.

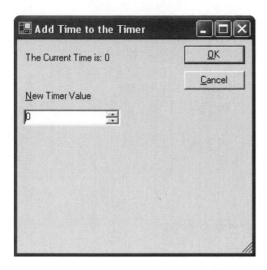

Figure 7-1. The Add Time to the Timer form helps the user adjust the time interval to meet specific needs.

As you can see, the interface for this form is relatively simple. If the user wants to change the time interval, they can do so using the spin button control. This button provides a number of input methods including both the keyboard and mouse. The user can click the up or down arrow to change the value one increment at a time or simply type the new value. Clicking OK makes the change permanent. Listing 7-2 shows the code for this portion of the TimerButton control. The complete listing is in the \Chapter 07\AccControl folder of the source code that you can obtain from the Downloads section of the Apress Web site (http://www.apress.com).

Listing 7-2. The Add Time to the Timer Form Code

```
public FrmMoreTime(Int32 CurrentTime)
{
   // Required for Windows Form Designer support
   InitializeComponent();

   // Initize the current time value.
   lblCurrentTime.Text = "The Current Time is: "
      + CurrentTime.ToString();
```

```
    // Initialize the up/down control value.
    txtNewValue.Value = CurrentTime;
}


// Internal time track variable and associated public property.
private  Int32    _NewTime;

public   Int32    NewTime
{
    get { return _NewTime; }
}

private void btnOK_Click(object sender, System.EventArgs e)
{
    // Save the new value.
    _NewTime = Convert.ToInt32(txtNewValue.Value);

    // Exit the form.
    Close();
}

private void btnCancel_Click(object sender, System.EventArgs e)
{
    // Exit the form.
    Close();
}
```

As you can see, the code begins with the constructor. The constructor includes an input provided by the caller (the control). The CurrentTime argument provides input to the lblCurrentTime.Text property, which affects the time value display, as shown in Figure 7-1. In addition, the code uses the CurrentTime argument to adjust the initial value of the txtNewValue object—the control the user accesses to adjust the time interval.

The form provides access to the final user selection through the NewTime property. Listing 7-2 shows both the private variable and the public property used in this case. The NewTime property is read-only because there isn't any good reason to change it.

The two button event handlers come next. As you can see, clicking Cancel simply closes the form without any change occurring to the NewTime property. The btnOK_Click() event handler modifies the NewTime property before it closes the form so that the caller can inspect this property for a change.

Testing the TimerButton Control

At this point, we have an interesting new control to test. The test program appears in Figure 7-2. Work with the application for a few moments and you'll see the duality of balloon help that the average user will see when both tooltips are present at the same time. However, this application is set up so that the user will see each item individually.

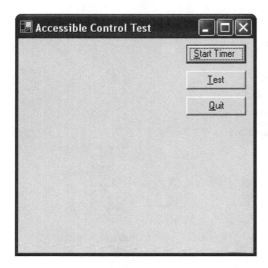

Figure 7-2. The test program helps you test the various feature of the TimerButton control, including the dual balloon help feature.

The code for this example is relatively simple. Listing 7-3 shows the code that we'll use. You'll also find this code in the \Chapter 07\AccControlTest folder of the source code that you can obtain from the Downloads section of the Apress Web site (http://www.apress.com).

Listing 7-3. The TimerButton Test Application Code

```
private void btnStart_Click(object sender, System.EventArgs e)
{
   // Start the TimerButton countdown.
   btnTimer.TimerStart(true);
}
```

```
private void btnTimer_Click(object sender, System.EventArgs e)
{
    // Turn the timer off.
    if (btnTimer.TimerStarted)
        btnTimer.TimerStart(false);

    // Display a message box.
    if (btnTimer.AutoClick)
        MessageBox.Show("The button automatically clicked",
                        "Click Event",
                        MessageBoxButtons.OK,
                        MessageBoxIcon.Information);
    else
        MessageBox.Show("The user clicked the button.",
                        "Click Event",
                        MessageBoxButtons.OK,
                        MessageBoxIcon.Information);

    // Reset the AutoClick property.
    btnTimer.AutoClickReset();
}
```

As you can see, the only task the btnStart_Click() event handler performs is starting the timer using the btnTimer.TimerStart() method. As shown, you must pass a value of true to start the timer.

The btnTimer_Click() event handler performs a number of tasks. It begins by turning the timer off, but only if the timer is actually started (as noted by the btnTimer.TimerStarted property). The event handler checks the btnTimer.AutoClick property value to determine if the user clicked the button or whether the control clicked itself. This value determines which of the two message boxes the application displays. Finally, the code resets the AutoClick property using the btnTimer.AutoClickReset() method. If the code fails to perform this step, then every non-timed user click after the first time out registers as an automatic click.

One of the first tests you'll want to run is checking the automatic timing feature. Figure 7-3 shows typical output. Notice that the button caption has changed to show the user how much time is left.

Figure 7-3. The TimerButton caption can change to show the user the amount of time they have left to click the button.

You'll also want to right click the button and check out the timer interval feature. Figure 7-4 shows the context menu that displays when the user right clicks the button. The user can also use the context menu button on the keyboard to trigger this feature. It's possible that you could add support for a control key combination to the control, but using these standard techniques to make the context menu accessible works better.

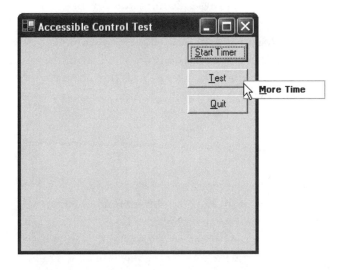

Figure 7-4. Use a right click or the context menu button on the keyboard to access the button's context menu.

Implementing Consistent Controls, Status Indicators, and Other Elements

After bugs and lack of functionality, the programming error that presents the biggest problem for most users is consistency. Consistency starts with the application. If you use property pages to help the user adjust one set of options, you should use them for all options. Likewise, if the application relies on multiple document interface (MDI) in one data display, then it should use MDI in all data displays.

 ON THE WEB   Some people don't realize they have color blindness. You can give yourself a decidedly non-profession test at http:// www.colorsidebyside.com/. This test isn't conclusive, but you might want to get a professional check if you fail to see the colors properly.

Consistency at the application level is a good start, but the developer has to check consistency at the form or window level after that. An application that has a status bar for one form or window should use the same status bar for all forms or windows. In addition, the status bar should always provide the same functionality. If the status bar on one form has a text insert indicator on one form, don't confuse the user by placing an overtype indicator on another form. In addition, the indicator should always appear in the same location.

The issue of control placement comes next. Most users think from top to bottom and left to right. (However, this isn't always a given, so you'll want to set the forms up in the way that the user is used to working.) When you design a form, make sure you take your audience into consideration. Make sure that pressing tab moves the focus from the current control to the next control to its right. If the current control is already to the far right, when the user presses the tab, move the focus to the first control on the next row at the left of the display.

Adding Context Sensitive Help

Many of the applications we've studied so far are simple tests of the Windows Accessibility features or demonstrations of special component functionality. In the real world, applications are usually a lot more complicated, which means that the user is likely to have questions about the operation of individual features. Some developers try to get by with a general help file, some rely on balloon help, and a few enlightened souls actually use both. Unfortunately, most users find this level of support inadequate. They want to know what purpose a particular control or data entry field serves, which means that the developer needs to provide context-sensitive help.

Context sensitive help provides information about a specific application feature. It doesn't confuse the user by telling them about all of the other features on the form. Good context sensitive help is complete—it answers these five essential questions:

- What task does the control or data entry field perform?

- How should the user interact with this control or data entry field?

- Why is this control or data entry field important?

- When should the user interact with the control or data entry field?

- Whom should the user contact when they have trouble using the control or data entry form?

Once the context sensitive help answers the five basic questions, it should also consider answering other questions. For example, it's helpful to provide a list of related topics. The user should also know where to find additional information. In some cases, this means providing vendor information. However, in other cases, the user might need to contact the network administrator or other support personnel for additional information.

NOTE   In some cases, the person accessing the application help system is a caregiver. The caregiver must interpret information for the application user and often helps the user make application-buying decisions. Consequently, the person that sees your product first, in many cases, is a caregiver who might not have a lot of computer experience. Creating help that makes it easy to understand how an application works is essential. In some cases, you'll also want to create the context sensitive help with this caregiver and application user relationship in mind. For example, when you discuss the accessibility features of your application, include information for both the user and the caregiver.

So, how do you add context sensitive help? The process is easy. You begin by adding the HelpProvider control to your application. This control requires a help file of some type as input, usually in the form of an HTML file you create using the HTML Help Workshop provided as part of the Visual Studio .NET package. You'll find the set of example files used for this section in the \Chapter 07\HelpFiles folder of the source code that you can obtain from the Downloads section of the Apress Web site (http://www.apress.com).

The essence of context sensitive help for the .NET environment is the three properties that appear in Figure 7-5. The HelpKeyword, HelpNavigator, and HelpString properties contain the information the user will see when using context sensitive help. As with a ToolTip control, the HelpProvider control adds these entries to every control on the associated form. Note that you'll find the source code and application settings for this example in the \Chapter 07\ContextHelp folder of the source code that you can obtain from the Downloads section of the Apress Web site (http://www.apress.com).

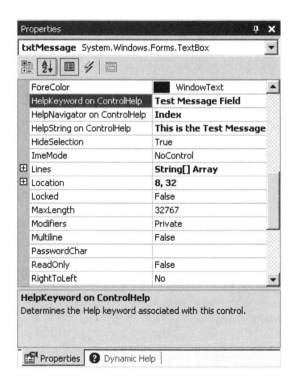

Figure 7-5. Use the HelpKeyword, HelpNavigator, *and* HelpString *properties to control context sensitive help.*

If you want the application to display the help button (?) on the title (caption) bar of the application, you'll need to set the HelpButton property of the form to true. You must also set the MinimizeBox and MaximizeBox properties to false. It isn't clear why the .NET Framework doesn't provide a way to display all three buttons on the title bar, but the choice is clear. The text you place in the HelpString property of each control is triggered when the user clicks the help button (which changes the cursor to a help cursor) and then clicks on the control. Figure 7-6 shows an example of this form of context sensitive help in action.

Figure 7-6. Click on any object with the help cursor to receive help on that item.

Obviously, this form of context sensitive help is only a little better than the balloon help we discussed earlier, but at least the larger text is welcome. If the user really wants extensive help, then highlighting the control or field in question and clicking F1 is the only way to go. This type of help is where the HelpKeyword and HelpNavigator properties come into play. The HelpKeyword property determines what the application will look for in the help file. The HelpNavigator property determines how and where the application looks for the information. In most cases, you'll want to use an Index entry as shown in Figure 7-5 to ensure the application finds the right keyword. Figure 7-7 shows the help file for this application.

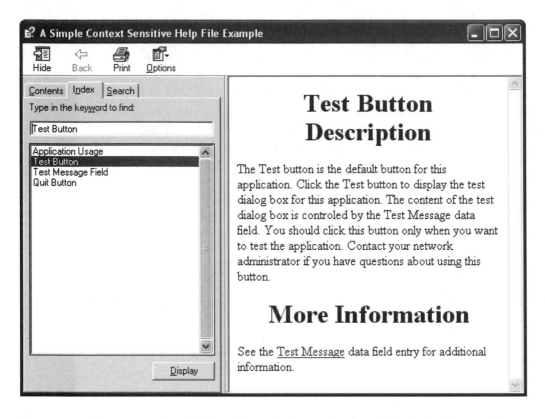

Figure 7-7. Select a control or field and then click F1 to display a help dialog box similar to this one.

Obtaining and Using Microsoft Active Accessibility

Microsoft Active Accessibility (MSAA) is both a Software Development Kit (SDK) and a set of utilities you can use to manage the accessible features of your application. The main Web site for MSAA is http://msdn.microsoft.com/at/. This site has links that you can use to access most of the other MSAA features. When you get to this Web page, you'll notice that it has links for two versions of MSAA. Developers need to use the 1.3 version on Windows 95 only and we won't discuss it in this chapter for that reason.

The COM libraries for MSAA 2.0 come with Windows 98, Windows 2000, and Windows XP. You obtain the MSAA 2.0 libraries for Windows NT 4.0 by installing Service Pack 6. As mentioned in the "Understanding the Technical Details" section of Chapter 6, you'll find most of the MSAA functionality in the OLEACC.DLL file. Some of this functionality appears as part of the .NET Accessibility.DLL file using the IAccessible and IAccessibleHandler interfaces. We'll discuss the details of OLEACC.DLL as one of the first topics in this section.

One library that we haven't mentioned yet is the MSAAText 1.0 Type Library found in the MSAAText.DLL file. MSAA has two levels of services: user interface and text. The text services help you perform tasks such as discovering which document currently has focus. This information is especially important in an environment where the user could have multiple documents opened within the same application. You can learn more about the two document levels at ms-help:// MS.MSDNQTR.2003FEB.1033/msaa/msaaccrf_08md.htm. We'll discuss the implications of using this COM library from within the .NET environment in this section as well. Unfortunately, Microsoft chose not to provide a .NET Framework wrapper for this set of services.

MSAA also provides tools. These tools don't come as part of Visual Studio .NET and you won't find them in the Windows installation. Consequently, you'll need to download them from http://msdn.microsoft.com/downloads/default.asp?URL=/ downloads/sample.asp?url=/msdn-files/027/001/785/msdncompositedoc.xml. These tools only work with MSAA 2.0, so you can't use them on a system equipped with Windows 95 or an older version of Windows NT 4.0.

Looking Closer at OLEACC.DLL

Some developers have made the mistake of thinking that the .NET Framework includes everything that the Win32 API includes. We've already seen several cases in this book where the .NET Framework falls short of the goal. Given the newness of the .NET Framework and the immense size of the Win32 API, it's not too amazing that some features are missing. In fact, some developers think that some omissions are by design because the Win32 API call in question had unfortunate results.

 NOTE   The OLEACC.DLL file won't appear on the list of standard objects that you can import using the Add Reference dialog box. To obtain a reference to this file, you must click Browse and look for the file in the \Windows\System32 folder of your hard drive.

The .NET Framework provides the Accessibility.DLL file that contains the IAccessibility and IAccessibilityHandler interfaces we have discussed at several points in this book. In most cases, you'll never need anything more than these two interfaces to make your application accessible. However, the Accessibility.DLL file is hardly a true replacement for its unmanaged counterpart—the OLEACC.DLL file. Look at the entries in Figure 7-8 and you'll see why.

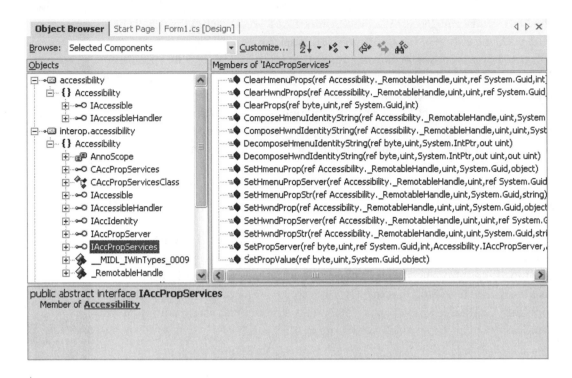

Figure 7-8. Choosing the correct accessibility support file is essential for some types of work.

The upper Accessibility entry is the one provided by the Accessiblity.DLL file. As mentioned, it contains the two essential interfaces that most developers will need. The interop.accessibility entry shows what the OLEACC.DLL file provides. It's not hard to see that this file provides many more interfaces than the .NET alternative. Of all the interfaces provided, the IAccPropServices interface is the most interesting. As you can see, it contains a number of methods that perform interesting tasks with unmanaged applications. In short, you would use this interface when interoperability with an unmanaged component is essential.

In general, you'll want to use the Accessibility.DLL file with your applications to ensure compatibility with future versions of the .NET Framework, lower the probability of import-induced errors, and improve the ease of development. However, it's important to realize that you can obtain additional support when needed using the OLEACC.DLL file. Make sure you use the correct tool for the job.

Understanding the MSAA Text Services

Many of the MSAA features appear as part of the .NET Framework in one form or another. However, one of the entries you'll find on the COM tab of the Add Reference dialog is the MSAAText 1.0 Type Library. Open this library and you'll find a wealth of interesting new functions that you won't find anywhere in the .NET Framework. You'll find the interfaces and classes supported by this type library in Figure 7-9.

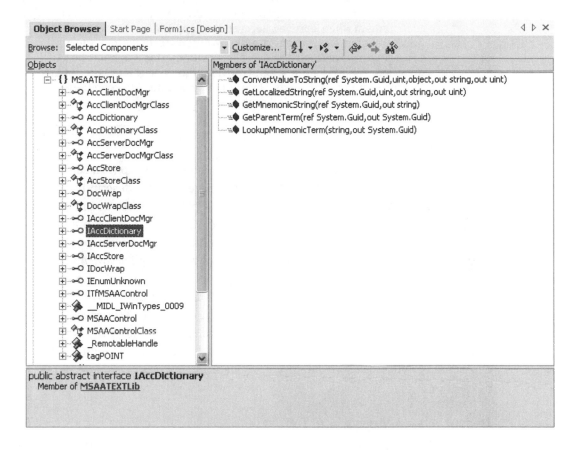

Figure 7-9. Gain access to the MSAA Text Services using the MSAAText 1.0 Type Library.

It turns out that MSAA supports two main interface groups. The first interface group is the user interface services supported by the IAccessibility and IAccessibilityHandler interfaces. The second interface group is the text services that are supported by the IAccClientDocMgr, IAccDictionary, and IAccServerDocMgr interfaces. This second interface group is only important if you create a document-based application such as a word processor or a spreadsheet program. The interface group is also useful if you create a MDI application for a need such as database access.

NOTE You might wonder why you haven't heard much about these interfaces before—even if you spend a lot of time working with COM as a standard part of your work. Unlike many accessibility features, only Windows NT, Windows 2000, and Windows XP currently support the MSAA Text Services. Presumably, the Windows Server 2003 will also support them when it arrives. Because most applications that can actually use these interfaces must also run on Windows 9*x* machines, most developers have decided not to implement them. This is a shame because these accessibility features could provide better document descriptions for those with special needs. Unfortunately, you need to keep these interface limitations in mind as you design your application.

The three interfaces, provided by the second interface group (text services), serve specific purposes. The `IAccDictionary` interface provides descriptive strings about the document that currently has focus. It also provides access to information about the document, such as the document's parent. The `IAccClientDocMgr` interface provides information to the client about the document. For example, you can obtain a list of the documents currently supported by the application or you can learn which document has focus. Finally, the `IAccServerDocMgr` interface provides a server interface for applications that want to expose their documents to other clients.

You'll notice that Figure 7-9 shows other MSAA Text Services interfaces. These interfaces perform ancillary functions such as managing the accessibility store. You won't interact directly with these interfaces unless one of the functions in the three main interfaces requires that you use them.

Using the Accessible Explorer

The Accessible Explorer is one of the first tools you should try when working with MSAA because it provides valuable information about the accessibility of your application. For one thing, you might be surprised when you learn how many hidden elements the typical .NET application contains. We'll use a simple application for this section—the Context Sensitive Help application described in the "Adding Context Sensitive Help" section of the chapter. You'll find the executable for this application in the \Chapter 07\ContextHelp\bin\Debug folder of the source code that you can obtain from the Downloads section of the Apress Web site (http://www.apress.com). Make sure the Context Sensitive Help application is running before you proceed.

Let's begin by opening the Accessible Explorer application. When you first open this tool, you'll see a blank left pane and a form with grayed out fields in the right pane. To populate the window with information, select the Tree ➤ Build New Tree command. Locate the Context Sensitive Help entry in the Choose Window dialog box, and then click Select. Figure 7-10 shows the output for the Context Sensitive Help application. As you can see, the number of actual windows in a .NET application is nothing less than amazing.

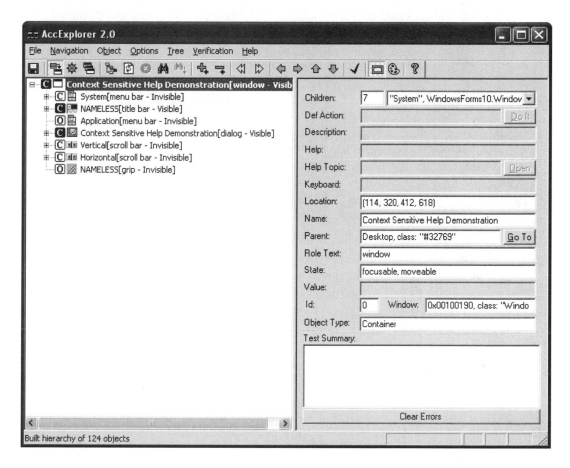

Figure 7-10. Loading a .NET application into the Accessibility Explorer presents a few surprises.

At this point, you're probably saying that this is interesting, but hardly informational. Try selecting a few of the entries and you'll notice that the right pane data changes to match. You can use this information to verify that Windows is actually seeing the accessibility information you have provided in the application. For example, you'll notice that this application doesn't include a system menu. However, if you select the System entry shown in Figure 7-10, you'll notice that the supposedly nonexistent system menu has a keyboard shortcut associated with it. Try this shortcut out when the application has focus and you'll notice that the application that didn't have a system menu suddenly has one. It's interesting to note that .NET dialog applications include scrollbars whether you want them or not. You'll also find that the application has a number of other features that you might not have suspected were there.

 TIP   Every time you select a visible element, the Accessibility Explorer will draw a box around that element on screen. This box helps you ensure that you have selected the correct item when working with a complex application.

I found at least one interesting problem when viewing the Context Sensitive Help application. Open the Context Sensitive Help Demonstration[dialog – Visible] hierarchy and select the Application Test entry. Notice that Windows sees the keyboard shortcut as Alt+M, rather than the Alt+T displayed on screen. If you select the application, you'll notice that pressing Alt+T does indeed trigger the Test button. So, how did this error occur? I gave the lable1 and the txtMessage controls on the form the same Tab Index number of 0. The .NET Framework appears to recognize the error and compensates. Windows, however, sees the error and reports the wrong keyboard shortcut to any software that requests the information. Renumber the controls from 0 through 3, load the window into the Accessibility Explorer again, and you'll notice that the keyboard shortcut is correct. Without this tool, a developer might not find such errors.

You can also run tests with the Accessible Explorer. Select the Context Sensitive Help Demonstration[dialog – Visible] entry, and then select the Verification ➤ Test Selected Object option. Figure 7-11 shows the output of this test. Notice that the application passes most tests, but it fails in a few important places. For example, the get_accDefaultAction test fails because the example doesn't define this value using the AccessibleDefaultActionDescription property described in the "Using the AccessibleDefaultActionDescription Property" section of the chapter.

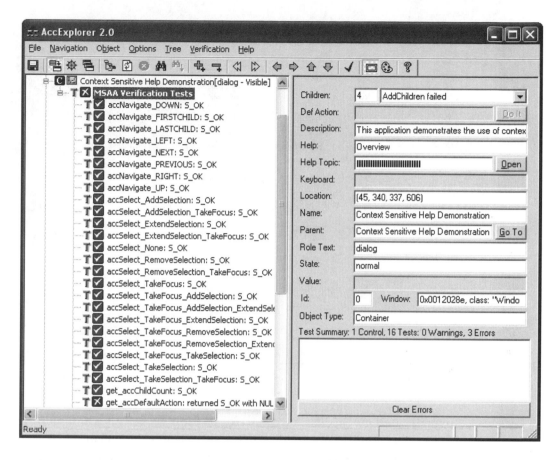

Figure 7-11. Running the accessibility tests shows flaws in your application setup.

Using the Active Accessibility Event Tester

The Active Accessibility Event Tester helps you check your application for proper event handling. Figure 7-12 shows typical output for this application. Notice that all the events listed relate to accessibility requirements—not to standard events such as those that you would access using the Log Messages feature of the Microsoft Spy++ utility. However, Active Accessibility Event Tester and Spy++ do work very much the same. Both utilities provide a standard set of event messages that they handle—you choose the messages that you want to monitor.

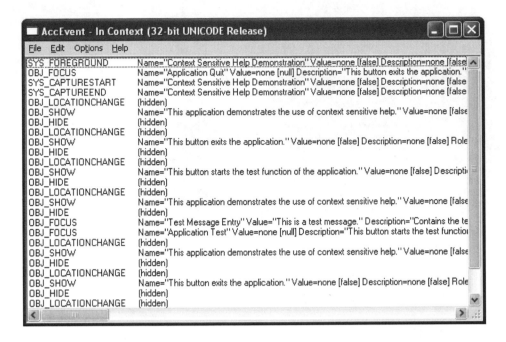

Figure 7-12. Use the Active Accessibility Event Tester to monitor accessibility event handler messages for your application.

To modify the kinds of data that the Active Accessibility Event Tester monitors, open the AccEvent Settings dialog shown in Figure 7-13 using the Options ➤ Settings command. As you can see from the figure, the number of messages you can monitor is impressive and, in many cases, they're different from the ones that you monitor using Spy++.

Notice the hWNDs field near the bottom of the AccEvent Settings dialog. This is the most important field in this dialog box because it enables you to choose the output of just one application for the Active Accessibility Event Tester. The hWND for an application is easily accessible as part of the Spy++ Window Properties dialog output or from the Window field of the Accessible Explorer (see Figure 7-10 for details). If you enter the hWND for the uppermost window of an application and then check the Descendents option, the Active Accessibility Event Tester will output the selected event messages for just that application.

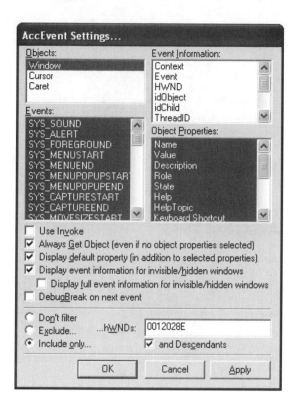

Figure 7-13. Modify the settings in this dialog to control the output of the tester.

Using the Active Accessibility Object Inspector

You know that a developer uses objects to create an application. However, sometimes it's difficult to detect what tasks all of those objects perform in a work environment. The Active Accessibility Object Inspector helps you view the objects from the outside to determine their characteristics. Figure 7-14 shows typical output from this application for the Context Sensitive Help application.

This application helps you wander around the application environment and learn more about it. The various watch buttons determine how the application finds objects to work with. The Active Accessibility Object Inspector can watch the focus, the caret, the mouse, or a tooltip. You can also tell the Active Accessibility Object Inspector to display a number of indicators that indicate the inspection focus, such as a highlighted box around the object. All of these settings affect how the Active Accessibility Object Inspector watches the target application.

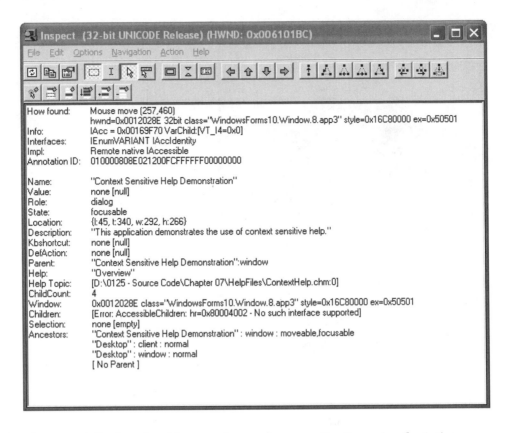

Figure 7-14. Explore the objects used to create an application using the Active Accessibility Object Inspector.

It's easy to move around using the Active Accessibility Object Inspector because you also have access to a number of navigational buttons. For example, you can navigate left or right through the same level of a hierarchy. The buttons also include features for navigating to the parent, child, or sibling of the current object.

The final task the Active Accessibility Object Inspector performs is to check actions that an object can perform. For example, you can request that the object perform its default action or selection action. It's interesting to see what happens when you try to perform certain actions with an object. For example, perform the focus action on a title bar and the application will momentarily highlight the first object that the application would normally select. In short, the actions can tell you a lot about how the application will react to standard input.

Using the .NET Accessibility Features

The best way to make your application friendly is to use a sensible layout, add plenty of help, and use features such as accelerators. These features help a lot; but, in some cases, they aren't enough. That's where the accessibility features come into play. Visual Studio .NET provides the means to add accessibility cues to your applications. For example, these cues could help someone who might not be able to see the application to make more sense out of what they hear about the application.

In addition to filling out the accessibility properties for all of the controls in your application, you can also support some accessibility features directly. For example, one of the accessibility features that many users need is high contrast. This feature is indispensable when working on some laptops because it provides the extra information needed to see the screen in sunlight. While some people use this feature all of the time, others use it at the end of the day to reduce eyestrain.

Your application can detect when the system goes into high contrast mode by monitoring the SystemInformation.HighContrast property. Of course, you'll still need to select high contrast color combinations (with black and white providing the best contrast). The point is that some screens that look great in color, look terrible when put into high contrast mode. If you don't detect this property, the high contrast mode that should help the user might end up causing problems.

The four accessibility cues help user applications learn more about your application. The following sections tell you about each property and tell you how you'd use each to increase the information about your application. Because we've already used these properties in most of the examples in the book, I'll provide a short description of their use. Look at either of the applications in this chapter (and all the previous desktop chapters) for examples of how you can use these properties to meet specific needs.

Using the AccessibleDescription Property

The AccessibleDescription property provides a better description of the use of an application control than might be apparent from the control itself. For example, if you use a picture button, someone with special vision need would require the AccessibleDescription that tells them how to use the button.

Using the AccessibleName Property

This property contains the short name for a control. You'd use it when you need to provide a more descriptive name for the control than space will allow on a form, but when the control doesn't require a complete description. For example, this property might contain a value of OK Button so that someone with a screen reader would know that it's a button with the word OK on it.

Using the AccessibleRole Property

Use this property to define the type of control interface. For example, you can define the role of a button or a button-like control as a PushButton. Visual Studio appears to use the Default setting for all controls, even when it's easy to determine the type of control. All screen readers will use this property, even the reader that comes with the various versions of Windows. Telling the user that they're working with a pushbutton is helpful, especially when the pushbutton had a unique shape or other feature. (Think about the odd buttons on the skin for the Windows Media Player.)

Using the AccessibleDefaultActionDescription Property

The AccessibleDefaultActionDescription property is the only one that you must set using code. This property describes the default action for a control. For example, a pushbutton has a default action of press. However, you might run into situations where a different term is more appropriate. The TimerButton control (see the "Working with the TimerButton Example" section of the chapter) is a perfect example of a situation in which a button requires more explanation than a simple "press" description will provide.

Summary

This chapter has discussed some of the more difficult issues surrounding desktop application usage cues. As you've learned, adding usage cues to an application isn't an exact science. In addition, you'll need to rely on the COM services provided by MSAA to implement many of the required cues. In short, adding usage cues is a little more difficult than adding some of the other elements we've discussed. It's equal parts science and art. Just as people learn to use emoticons and body language for other forms of communication, the developer will need to learn how to use the right kinds of usage cues when creating an application. The lack of these cues will hinder communication with the user.

Chapter 8, "Developing Special Desktop Application Capabilities," contains a wealth of information for adding new technologies to your application. The law doesn't require you to use any of these technologies, so implementing them is a matter of choice. However, sometime in the future you can expect to see requirements for adding voice technology to applications because communicating this way is so natural for many people. Chapter 8 represents a look at this future. You'll want to spend some time learning about the technologies that can enhance your applications today and discover what you might be required to implement tomorrow.

CHAPTER 8

Developing Special Desktop Application Capabilities

In This Chapter:

What Are the Special Desktop Application Capabilities?

What Are the General Assumptions You Can Make About Speech Technologies?

How Can You Improve the Interface Using Microsoft Agent?

How Can You Improve the Interface Using the Microsoft Speech API?

How Can You Improve the Interface Using IBM ViaVoice Technology?

When Can You Use Existing Capabilities in New Ways?

SOMETIMES YOU'LL NEED to use some special functionality in order to meet the Section 508 requirements for a particular application. For example, you might find that many of the users will have trouble using the keyboard or mouse and will require some type of voice input. The fact that users of all types have anxiously awaited the advent of voice input only makes this feature more worthwhile.

The first section of this chapter examines some of the special features you can add to desktop applications. We won't look at actual implementations of many of these special features because they're so specialized. Of course, there's always a tradeoff when you add a new feature to an application, which is why you need to exercise some care when adding a new feature. This section also discusses some of the issues you should consider when adding a special feature—one that makes life easier for someone, but isn't required by any of the Section 508 requirements.

 NOTE   At no time will this chapter discuss the programming required to access special hardware. Each custom device is different, so you'll need to rely on the vendor documentation for help. We'll discuss some of the special hardware so that you know what's available.

After the chapter discusses what you could add, we look at one feature that's commonly available (and free), Microsoft Agent. Yes, there's a certain animosity toward this technology by some people—especially those with well-developed computer skills. However, I've watched the reaction of those with less developed computer skills and can honestly say that Microsoft Agent helps a lot more than it hinders when you need to provide user support in an easy-to-understand form (a Section 508 requirement). The example for this chapter shows how to use Microsoft Agent to maximize its potential without annoying those who don't need it.

The remainder of the chapter discusses the one special addition that you should give increasing priority—voice input. Some developers are approaching voice input with caution and I don't blame them. This technology has progressed slowly over the years and has failed to live up to developer expectations. I'd love to say that voice technology is ready for prime time and that you'll be able to type your next report by speaking to your computer. However, the truth is that voice technology works well for giving commands to the computer and that's about it. Of course, just the ability to speak commands is an improvement. Just about everyone gets tired of moving the mouse around. The examples show you some of what you can do with voice technology today. You might find that a voice interface is just what you need for your next application.

An Overview of Special Desktop Application Capabilities

So far, this book has shown you the many things you can do on the desktop without incurring extra cost. In many cases, we've implemented the accessibility requirements without any additional programming. Whenever you can, you need to maintain this status quo of using what's available naturally on the system. As far as your application is concerned, mouse input is mouse input—the source of the input doesn't matter. An application should never concern itself with the configuration of the hardware or try to understand how the hardware interacts with the system. A joystick, trackball, and mouse can all generate mouse input and the application shouldn't care which device has performed the task.

In fact, if I could say anything about this section of the chapter, it's that it shouldn't really exist. If vendors provided truly compatible devices and drivers that worked perfectly every time, you'd never need to worry about special devices. The system would view these devices as simply another form of a common device. However, reality is that you'll run into some devices that are so unique that they defy easy definition as a standard device. In some cases, you just have to accommodate the device.

Another reason for this chapter is that new technologies appear on the horizon all the time. Just a few years ago, no one imagined that we'd be writing applications for cellular telephones. This is an example of a device that can't act like one of the devices found on the early PC. It has no true keyboard and the display area is extremely limited. In short, a cellular telephone represents a new class of device that developers didn't have to consider until recently. Even so, vendors are working on ways to make the cellular telephone look more like a standard device. As vendors develop these new technologies, other vendors also apply the technology to help those with special needs. Likewise, technology developed for those with special needs is often applied to products used by the general public.

An Overview of Specialty Devices

New devices pop up every day because hardware developers are constantly tinkering with new ideas. A solution to a problem that seemed unsolvable yesterday suddenly becomes solvable today because a new technique, material, or methodology becomes available. In many cases, the hardware developer simply looks at a problem from another angle and sees the solution that was there all along. For example, new technology (the NIST Refreshable Tactile Graphic Display described in the article referenced in the following "On the Web") enables a user to feel graphics on a board containing pins. The pins have a rounded end and the user can feel the relative height of these pins. This same article discusses research on a new Braille wheel (the NIST Rotating-Wheel Based Refreshable Braille Display) that makes it possible to create very small readers that help the user actually read the information faster. While reading this article, you'll notice that both of these devices are still in the research phase, but that's where all new devices start.

 ON THE WEB   You can learn more about the National Institute of Science and Technology (NIST) Refreshable Tactile Graphic Display and NIST Rotating-Wheel Based Refreshable Braille Display at http://www.itl.nist.gov/div895/isis/projects/brailleproject.html. The Web site provides existing pictures of both devices. They may look clunky now, but the production models should be quite small and usable.

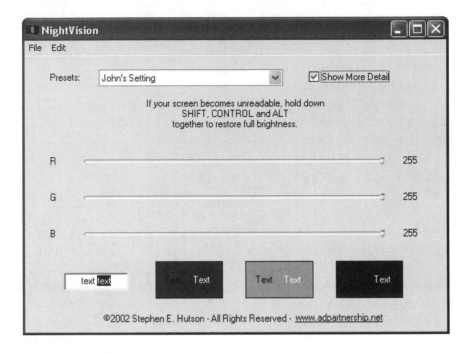

Figure 8-1. Use the NightVision software to adjust the brightness of your display to match the ambient room lighting or your own personal needs.

Normally, you'll want to interact with accessible devices the same way that you do with any other device. However, when you look at these new devices, you have to wonder just how the PC will view them. Will the PC see the NIST Refreshable Tactile Graphic Display as a printer or as a display, or perhaps as something completely different? The problem is interesting because the NIST Refreshable Tactile Graphic Display has an output similar to, but unlike, other output devices. Until standards appear on the scene for such devices (if they ever do), you might find that you need to provide some level of special support for such a device.

The point of this section is that you must try to interact with inputs and outputs in conventional ways unless a vendor leaves you without conventional solutions. When this problem occurs (and it does), your application must provide enough flexibility to work with the device using other alternatives if possible. Sometimes, this means that you must add special support for the device to your application. In other cases, it means that you'll have to wait for the vendor to provide a better interface.

Adding Support for Specialty Devices

Because you can't know in advance what features a special device will have and what type of an interface it will provide, you'll have to wait for a user to ask for device support as part of an application update. The best course of action at this point is to discuss the matter with the vendor. Sometimes a user will have old software for the device and the vendor has already introduced software that provides a more natural interface for the computer. In fact, this is the best assumption to make if the user has just purchased the device because the device can sit on store shelves for months before the user purchases it.

A second option is to create a component that sits in the background and performs the required interpretation for the device and associated device driver. Using this technique has two advantages for the developer.

Quick Upgrade: When the vendor finally does produce a device driver that acts more like a standard device, your application will require minimal modification. All that you need to do is output the information as normal, rather than send it to your specialized component.

Multiple Application Use: Creating a component helps maintain consistency if more than one application requires access to the same device. In addition, you could potentially make money selling the component to other companies that need it to access the same device. In some cases, you might even make a sale to the vendor because vendors often lack the research and development funds to create the component.

The third, and least acceptable, course of action is to add device support directly to the application. This means your application will rely on a specific device configuration, which usually spells trouble for the user and your support staff. It's difficult to update applications once they're at the client site, and you'll find that every little change the vendor makes will require a corresponding change to your application. In sum, this method of providing special device support should be your option of last choice.

A fourth option is to build your own device driver. This option is for the developer who really knows how to work with the operating system. However, it's an option that some developers exercise because they have the expertise to do it. The DVD drive on my system is abandonware—the vendor decided not to support it on Windows XP. Because a developer with the same problem created a device driver, the DVD drive on my system works despite the lack of support by the vendor.

An Overview of Specialty Software

In general, software that's specialized today either becomes part of a standard tomorrow or becomes obsolete. This is good news for the system integrator and developer alike because software makes the computer world go around. Anything that's non-standard tends to create support and logistical nightmares for everyone. However, sometimes a piece of software performs such a special service that the user really can't do without it, yet there's little reason to write a standard for it.

Consider the NightVision software written by Stephen E. Hutson, as shown in Figure 8-1. This software works by modifying the gamma (brightness) value of the display to match environmental lighting. During the day, sunlight streams into a room. Using a higher gamma value makes the display readable. Likewise, during the evening hours, the use of artificial light makes a lower gamma value better for viewing the display. I use this software because the ambient light in my office varies quite a bit.

What I found most interesting about this software is that it actually made it possible to tune a display for someone with color blindness. (See the "Building the Color Blindness Simulator Example" section of Chapter 4 for details on how color blindness affects the user's perception). The user in this example couldn't actually see some elements on the display before tuning it. However, this user needed to share the display with other people, making tuning difficult. Using NightVision enabled me to tune the display for this user by modifying the gamma settings. NightVision can store gamma settings, making it possible to switch between user settings with extreme ease. Software of this sort answers a utilitarian need and often performs multiple tasks well.

 ON THE WEB   You can learn more about the NightVision product at http://www.adpartnership.net/NightVision/index.html. This product comes in both Macintosh and Windows versions, so most people can use it. I was also impressed with the level of support that the vendor provides—the support files include an online history of changes.

When you consider the needs that software can meet, it's easy to get into a gadget mentality. In fact, this issue is so important and so prevalent, that we'll discuss it as a separate topic in the "Avoiding the Gadget Mentality in Application Design" section. The point is that sometimes a utility can mean the difference between using the computer successfully and just getting frustrated. Careful use of specialty software can really make the difference for those with special needs.

Adding Support for Specialty Software

I'm often surprised at how resistant people become to using anything but the software that they've used for years. That's why it's necessary to add support for utilities and other specialty software to some applications. For example, many browsers on the market support the helper application. A *helper application* is a special utility that performs a task such as displaying the source for a Web page when requested or playing a sound. The browser could provide this functionality as a built-in feature, but supporting the user's favorite utility makes more sense.

Another application that relies on support for specialty software is the IDE that most developers use to create applications. In this case, the utility doesn't perform a function that's integral to the IDE, but simply supports the user in some way. Consider the Tools menu on the Visual Studio .NET IDE. This menu doesn't add much in the way of support for Visual Studio .NET, but it does make it easier for the developer to grab tools as needed to develop the application without leaving the IDE.

Sometimes a piece of specialty software acts as a server for an application. For example, you can use products like Word and Excel in this manner. Developers can call on these applications to perform a task in the background and then return a result. The use of specialty software saves the developer time and often creates a superior application for the user as well. Obviously, there are problems with this approach. For one thing, you have to assume the user has the required server software, which isn't always a safe bet. Another problem is that you can't always anticipate how the two pieces of software will work together on different machines. Even so, more than a few applications use this technique to get more functionality with less application development time.

It's important to consider the accessibility aspects of using specialty software. For example, you can't change the user configuration settings to achieve a specific affect—that type of modification goes against the very principles found in the Section 508 rules (among other things).

Any interaction with specialty software must provide the user with a stable and usable interface that doesn't require any special knowledge on the user's part. As with hardware, you must treat input from a piece of software as that type of input—you shouldn't try to program specifically to the software. It's important to treat input from all software of that type the same. Unfortunately, as in the case of browsers, this isn't always possible. Sometimes browsers require different approaches for the same problem.

ON THE WEB   It's possible to avoid development disaster by checking the capabilities of the software in question. For example, you can find a chart of browser capabilities at `http://hotwired.lycos.com/webmonkey/reference/browser_chart/index.html`. Using this chart as a guide helps you create software that will run on every browser targeted by your application equally well.

Using Artificial Intelligence

Many people envision Artificial Intelligence (AI) in the same realm as science fiction. It's true that AI has received a bad image over the years as a technology that promised much, but delivered little. In many ways, AI still hasn't reached the goals originally set for it by those who had a vision of thinking computers. Yes, AI has come a long way, but it still doesn't allow a computer to think—not in the real sense of the word.

However, using AI does make an application more flexible than using standard programming techniques alone. Think about it this way, a standard application can only create yes or no answers. Sometimes a user requires an answer that's neither yes nor no, but simply the right solution (or even one of several right solutions) for the current situation. Deriving the answer often means that the application must factor in environmental conditions and past user choices, as well as consider the goals for application operation.

When is an AI solution something you should consider? One of the most common reasons to use AI is to help a user make a decision. An application can interact with a user, ask questions, and base the course of action on the probability of that action providing the correct output. If the action doesn't meet expectations, the application can continue to interact with the user and try to find a solution that will work. Because the intelligence of any AI is limited, some situations will still require human intervention—the system will run out of potential answers.

Some developers think that AI necessarily equates with a *heuristic-based system*—one that can learn if properly programmed. (Many developers refer to heuristic-based systems as *rule-based systems* because a rule decides which of several potential alternative solutions to a problem the application selects.) You'll hear discussions about neural nets and other arcane approaches that work but require extensive development effort. However, setting up a rule-based system is relatively easy and you can use knowledge gained by technical support to update the system. Such a system calculates the probability of a correct answer based on the content of the database, which can include previous experiences with a particular user. In many cases, all that you really need is some method for dealing with the unexpected based on past experience. Rule-based systems appear as part of many current application components. For example, most grammar checkers in word processors rely on a rule-based system to perform their work.

 ON THE WEB This book can't answer every question you have about artificial intelligence—many developers spend years learning about this area of computer science. You can learn more about rule-based systems in general at the Knowledge Systems Design site (http:// www.knowledgesys.com/technology/technology.html). An interesting use of rule-based technology is the e-Integrated Brokerage System described at http://www.tcs.com/O_products/ibs/products_ibs.htm. You can also learn a lot by reading back issues of *PC AI Magazine* (http://www.pcai.com/). Many of these articles include innovative uses for rule-based technology in applications.

Developers can fall into a number of traps when working with AI. For example, some developers think that AI will solve design issues—things the developer should have considered before AI became part of picture. AI doesn't possess any intuition or creativity. A rule-based system can only derive answers built into it by the experts that designed the rule database. Even a heuristic- or neural net–based system can only learn new information based on the input it receives. No magic exists for making AI into something that can fix human error.

The bottom line is that AI provides a means for adding flexibility to an application that might not serve the user's needs adequately otherwise. It can't replace humans and certainly requires careful monitoring. It may be that AI will eventually approach the goals originally set for it by science fiction authors, but that reality isn't here today.

Searching Doesn't Mean Finding

Companies have invested vast resources in all kinds of technologies that promise to make it easier to find information. Data mining has become a major niche industry because companies have so much information in so many places that no one can keep track of it all. Information that's lost isn't very useful and could become a liability at some point. After all, the company is paying to store information that it can't access. When you create an accessible search engine, it provides full access to the information the application is supposed to handle in a format the user can understand. A usable search engine provides information the user actually needs.

One of the problems with searches is that they often return a wealth of useless information that the requestor never knew existed, while denying the user access to information they need and know exists. Search engine technology has improved over the years, but even the best search engine can't find information if the user doesn't ask the right question. A search engine needs to guide the user into asking the right question. Google (http://www.google.com/advanced_search) does this by creating a search form with plenty of fields with leading questions, as shown in Figure 8-2. If the user still doesn't find the correct information, Google will often ask if the user meant to use a similar word.

An interesting place to look for additional search tips and techniques is the S.L.I. Systems site at http://www.sli-systems.com/tips/search_tips.php. This site concentrates on the requirements for Web site searches, but you'll find that many of these tips also work well for desktop applications. For example, consider how many times you have to go back to the first form of a database application to perform a search. In many cases, detail forms lack the menu or button required to start a search and that situation should never happen. I also found it interesting that this product tends to focus on search usability issues—a search that provides unusable results is worse than not having a search feature at all.

Avoiding the Gadget Mentality in Application Design

Sometimes an application ends up looking like the developer put it together with wire and pieces of anything that happened to be at hand. A simple solution ends up looking like a Rube Goldberg machine counterpart. Even the easy tasks require strange and convoluted maneuvers that would give Houdini nightmares. Yes, the application works, and the developer loves it, but no one else can stand to use it. Such applications are often victims of the gadget mentality. Because of the way the developer designed them, even if these applications follow the accessibility guidelines, they're still not accessible and certainly not usable.

The gadget mentality creeps in when the developer sees something that looks like it might be nice to include in the application but doesn't consider whether it really belongs there. For example, my word processor could easily double as a graphics application. I don't need the graphics capability, but because of the way the developer designed it, I'm stuck with the feature anyway. What purpose does the graphics feature serve? Well, it gets in the way every time I make a change to the system because this little gadget thinks it can do the job better than my dedicated graphics application. In sum, the feature isn't accessible or usable—it's simply in the way.

Developers appear to make all kinds of odd decisions while under the influence of the latest gadget to catch their attention. One data entry application I used recently was missing the spelling checker I really needed to ensure my input was accurate. However, it did have this lovely feature for coloring the input fields so that they would look nice on screen. Actually, I found the colors annoying because they obscured the text. The lesson learned here is that you should add the features your users actually need, but leave out the features they don't want. (If you do add a gadget to your solution, make sure you also provide a way to turn it off.)

Avoiding the gadget mentality often means that a group has to follow a leader to ensure a unity of thought and concept. Applications designed by committee are usually bloated and lack focus. Using them is a nightmare for everyone. An application shouldn't have a learning curve, but most do because the vendor didn't design them with usability and functionality in mind. More likely than not, the committee found itself embroiled in a robust fight and lost sight of the fact that it was creating an application that someone would have to rely on. When designing a complex application, it's best to make sure that every feature can operate separately from every other feature. This strategy makes it possible to create an installation program that at least allows the user to decide they don't want the feature that the committee thought so important.

The bottom line is that you should be able to hand your application to anyone with a minimum of computer knowledge and see them use it with some success. First, an *accessible application* is self-describing and allows interaction using more than one method. Second, a usable application makes the use of any given feature obvious. Third, a *functional application* provides only the features the user needs but does provide a full feature set. The essence of avoiding the gadget mentality is to keep these three issues in mind as you write your code.

Relying On Speech as the Second Input Method

Most developers have heard that speech recognition is going to be the next best thing to appear on the market. We've been hearing that same tune for many years now. I remember the first tinny voice that emanated from my computer when I purchased one of my first sound cards. The fact that the computer could "talk" to me was nothing less that amazing, but I soon realized that the output was more akin to that of a parrot, rather than something that could really understand me. The computer was capable of speech output, but not speech input at this time. Speech output naturally precedes speech input, but it's important not to confuse the two.

 NOTE   This section discusses speech input technology in general—we'll discuss specific speech technologies later in the chapter. It's important to build a base of information before you proceed to products that implement a specific speech input solution.

Herein lies the problem for speech input. The nuances of human speech added to variances in pronunciation and the constantly changing meaning of words makes it nearly impossible to create a computer application that will understand what someone has to say. It's true that vendors such as Microsoft are making progress in this area, but most of the speech input that currently exists works best for command input, not for the actual writing of information.

Does the lack of understanding on the part of the computer relegate speech technology to the back burner of professional development? The fact that you can use speech to communicate with the user is a good starting point because the user can understand the messages presented by the computer. Adding the capability to input a command using a speech interface makes it possible for the user to extend what they can do without typing. A speech interface can help any user get more out of their system, so the functionality has value.

The essential point for developers is determining when input transitions from a command to content. Speech technology provides a good method for inputting commands. Telling the computer, "File Open," would display the Open dialog for most applications. The speech capabilities for most computers could handle this requirement without too much trouble. However, now that you have an Open dialog, what do you do with it? At this point, the input would switch to content—filenames are content because they aren't a static command. The way around this problem is to help the user navigate the hard drive using commands to highlight the desired file, but this can become troublesome and time consuming for the user.

The usefulness of speech as input for any given application depends on a number of factors. Of course, speech will remain a secondary input for the moment, but given time, the technology could mature enough so that it provides equal value to the input currently provided by the keyboard. The following list provides a quick summary of the issues you should consider.

Type of Technology: Speech engines vary a great deal in the capabilities they provide. For example, some speech engines provide great overall reception for a number of users, while other speech engines provide a larger vocabulary for a single user. The speech engine you choose depends on the type of service you expect.

Capabilities of the User: The ability of the user to speak slowly and clearly determines how well the speech engine interprets the input. Speech engines that provide a training mode can help compensate for problems in interpreting the user's speech. In many cases, the training mode can't compensate for users with slurred speech because the user's speech tends to be inconsistent. (If the user speaks consistently, it doesn't matter how difficult it is for an individual to understand it—the computer will still interpret it correctly.)

Capabilities of the Host Device: Speech processing still requires considerable computer resources. Slower machines are less capable of providing good voice output, much less processing voice input. In most cases, a major limiting factor in voice processing is the resources the host machine has to offer.

Complexity of the Application: As application complexity increases, the need for content, rather than command, input increases. The increased need for content means that complex applications are less likely to work well with speech input. For example, surfing the Web is relatively easy using speech input because the user can perform this task naturally using commands alone.

Type of Input: Command input is easier and more reliable to parse than content input. Trying to type a *War and Peace*-type novel would be an exercise in frustration because all of the input is content. Except for saving the document and printing it out, the user would provide all input in the form of content, making speech input almost useless.

TIP You can reduce the complexity of input for some types of database forms by using drop-down lists with predefined answers. The use of input like this for entries such as the state or country makes it possible to enter the information using commands. Developers normally consider the input content, but it becomes command input for the purposes of a speech interface. The use of predefined responses also makes it easier for people with some types of special needs to interact with the form because they can simply select the answer from a list, rather than type it out.

Extensibility of the Grammar and Vocabulary: The grammar and vocabulary that the vendor includes with a speech engine is normally not sufficient to allow anything more than simple command input. A developer has to extend the grammar to determine which words can appear together. In addition, the developer must modify the vocabulary to include terms the vendor doesn't include, especially if the input is laden with jargon (as is most computer input). In general, the more tools the vendor provides to extend the grammar and vocabulary, and the more complete the supplied grammar and vocabulary are, the better the speech engine will work for all types of input.

Using Microsoft Agent on the Desktop Example

Some things in life are a "love it" or "hate it" issue. If you're a novice user who feels intimidated by the computer or someone who just needs a little extra help, Microsoft Agent can be a "love it" feature. On the other hand, if you're an experienced user who feels that any frill is a waste of computing cycles, Microsoft Agent can cause a lot of grief. I'm not here to say that every application requires the use of Microsoft Agent or that this feature is even a good idea. However, more than a few users have told me that they benefited from this particular feature and I have no reason to disbelieve them.

NOTE Some developers *hate* Microsoft Agent and its attendant animations—most power users hate them, too. The trade press has blasted Microsoft Agent in every possible way and in some ways that I considered impossible before I read the articles. Let's just say that you should provide a way to turn this feature off should you add it to an application.

Working with Microsoft Agent can actually add a little fun to a programming project. I find that the animations are interesting from a development perspective because you can use them to add a different kind of help to an application at a very low cost. Of course, you'll want to use this feature with care. Make sure you avoid the gadget mentality when you do use it. Adding Microsoft Agent to an application that could attract a lot of novice users is a good idea—adding it to your latest scientific model of the human brain probably isn't.

With these caveats in mind, let's discuss what you need to do to use Microsoft Agent as part of your next desktop application. The following sections describe a simple application and show how to test it. Once you try this example out, you might want to try Microsoft Agent on some of your low-end applications.

TIP   The example application in this section is basic. It shows you the essentials of working with Microsoft Agent. However, Microsoft Agent is capable of more than the example demonstrates. For example, you can use it to obtain input from the user using both the keyboard and speech. Because the applications you create with Microsoft Agent can quickly become quite complex, it pays to take one step at a time in learning to use it. Work with the animations and speech output first, move on to gestures, and finally begin working with speech input if your application has this need.

Understanding the Importance of Scripting

The one and only good reason to use Microsoft Agent is as an aid to using an application. Consider it another form of help that can guide users in the use of your application. When viewed from this perspective, Microsoft Agent becomes a tool for creating a multimedia presentation of sorts, and that implies scripting. Creating an application that uses Microsoft Agent as a help aid without using scripting usually results in something that most people would rather not view.

NOTE   This book can't teach you the essentials of storyboarding or the techniques used to create a script. If you're a developer who lacks this kind of experience, make sure you find someone to help you create the first few presentations. Otherwise, you'll have an application that gives someone an experience they would rather forget.

Those developers who actually write help files are used to creating the reference-style help that most of us associated with the early days of Windows. This type of help works well for developers, administrators, and power users because they already know the basics of using Windows. However, not everyone is well acquainted with the intricacies of Windows. Performing even simple tasks requires a procedure—essentially a story that helps the user understand what they need to do.

 CAUTION   Using Microsoft Agent incorrectly can result in a help aid that's more distracting than helpful. Keep all of the Section 508 requirements for animation in mind as you create your Microsoft Agent application. Not only does the application require both sound and text output, you need to provide a method for turning the animation off when it isn't wanted or needed as well. The various Microsoft Agent characters have animations associated with them that could cause confusion for some users. Keep motions small and in concert with the task at hand. In sum, exercise care when using this feature to make an application more accessible.

Scripting, the act of creating a storyboard for the Microsoft Agent application, means the developer has to consider all elements of the user's interaction with the application. A procedure of this kind requires as much, if not more, planning than the application itself. The animations, sound, and text have to flow from one step to another in order to provide the help the user needs. In addition, the procedural steps have to be small enough that the application will perform as anticipated. The application should help the user move from one step to another in a logical and easily understood manner.

Writing the Application

Microsoft Agent is a set of COM components that you'll likely have installed on your machine already, especially if you use Windows XP. You'll access Microsoft Agent through the COM tab of the Add Reference dialog box. As you can see in Figure 8-2, Microsoft Agent actually consists of three pieces: Microsoft Agent Control, Microsoft Agent Server, and Microsoft Agent Server Extensions. The example will rely on the Microsoft Agent Control. You can also install this control into the Toolbox. If you install the Microsoft Agent Control in the Toolbox, you'll see an agent icon appear on the form when you add the Microsoft Agent to your project. Unlike managed controls, this unmanaged control doesn't appear on screen when you run the application even though an icon appears in the design window.

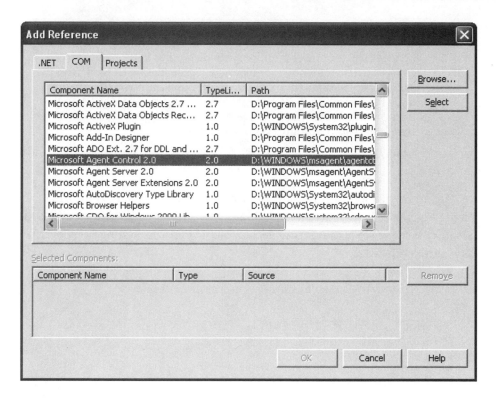

Figure 8-2. Using Microsoft Agent means importing at least one of the three COM components.

 ON THE WEB It pays to keep up with current Microsoft Agent developments if you plan to use this technology in your applications. You'll find the main Microsoft Agent site at http://www.microsoft.com/msagent/. All of the user-related downloads for Microsoft Agent appear at http://www.microsoft.com/products/msagent/downloads.htm. Any developer's tools you need for working with Microsoft Agent are at http://www.microsoft.com/products/msagent/devdownloads.htm.

One of the first tasks you'll perform is selecting a character. When working with Windows XP, Merlin is the best choice because this character is always included in the \WINDOWS\msagent\chars folder. You saw this character immediately after completing the Windows installation. Microsoft Agent also supports three other characters—all of which you can download from the Microsoft Agent Web site.

CAUTION Not all character files are the same. For example, Windows XP users will find three additional character files in the \WINDOWS\ srchasst\chars folder of their machine. These files won't work with the sample application. They'll load, but they don't support the required animation commands. If you decide to use characters other than the ones provided with Microsoft Agent, be sure they provide all the commands and other resources you need.

The example application shows the two tasks that you need to perform to use Microsoft Agent. The first is to load and initialize the character. The second is to develop a scripted set of moves for the character to perform. Listing 8-1 shows how to perform both tasks.

Listing 8-1. A Simple Microsoft Agent Programming Example

```csharp
// Create a speaker object for MS Agent.
AgentObjects.IAgentCtlCharacter  CurrentSpeaker;

 public frmMain()
{
   IEnumerator AniList;    // List of animations.
   String      Voice;      // The current voice.
   String      WinFolder;  // Windows Folder

   // Required for Windows Form Designer support
   InitializeComponent();

   // Obtain the Windows folder location.
   WinFolder =
      Environment.SystemDirectory.Substring(
         0,
         Environment.SystemDirectory.IndexOf("System32"));

   // Try loading a character.
   TestAgent.Characters.Load(
      "Merlin",
      @WinFolder + @"MSAgent\Chars\Merlin.ACS");

   // Make the character the current speaker.
   CurrentSpeaker = TestAgent.Characters["Merlin"];
```

```csharp
   // Get the animation list for this character.
   AniList = TestAgent.Characters["Merlin"].AnimationNames.GetEnumerator();

   // Load the animation list into the CurrentSpeaker command
   // list.
   while (AniList.MoveNext())
   {
      Voice = (String)AniList.Current;
      Voice = Voice.Replace("_", "underscore");
      CurrentSpeaker.Commands.Add((String)AniList.Current,
                                  AniList.Current,
                                  Voice,
                                  true,
                                  false);
   }
}


private void btnTest_Click(object sender, System.EventArgs e)
{
   // Display the speaker.
   CurrentSpeaker.Show(0);

   // Move to the center of the display.
   CurrentSpeaker.MoveTo(
      Convert.ToInt16(SystemInformation.WorkingArea.Width/2),
      Convert.ToInt16(SystemInformation.WorkingArea.Height/2),
      100);

   // Greet the user.
   CurrentSpeaker.Play("Announce");
   CurrentSpeaker.Play("RestPose");
   CurrentSpeaker.Speak("\\map=\"What you hear is not what you " +
                        "see!\"=\"Hello World\"\\", "");
   CurrentSpeaker.Play("Greet");

   // Tell the character to pull rabbit from hat.
   CurrentSpeaker.Play("RestPose");
   CurrentSpeaker.Speak("Want to see me pull a rabbit from my hat?",
                        "");
   CurrentSpeaker.Play("DoMagic1");
   CurrentSpeaker.Play("DoMagic2");
```

```
    // The the character to express surprise that the user doesn't
    // want to see the magic trick.
    CurrentSpeaker.Play("Surprised");
    CurrentSpeaker.Play("Confused");
    CurrentSpeaker.Play("RestPose");
    CurrentSpeaker.Speak("That trick never works!", "");
    CurrentSpeaker.Play("Sad");

    // Goodbye.
    CurrentSpeaker.Play("RestPose");
    CurrentSpeaker.Speak("Goodbye", "");
    CurrentSpeaker.Play("Wave");

    // Hide the character.
    CurrentSpeaker.Hide(0);
}
```

It's important to note that the example doesn't include error-trapping code. You'd normally provide this code to ensure that the application worked as intended. For example, the user might have removed the Merlin.ACS file, in which case, the application wouldn't have any character to load. You'd need to trap this error and determine if any of the characters on the local machine would work.

Let's begin with the class constructor because it performs the loading and initialization tasks required for this application. The first step is to determine the location of the Windows folder. Normally, this is the \Windows folder, but you can't be sure and the user might have Windows installed on something other than the C drive. It's interesting to note that the .NET Framework provides a fast method for locating the System32 folder, but not the Windows folder, so the code has to parse this information using the technique shown.

The next step is loading the character. Note that loading the character in memory doesn't make the character available for use. An application can actually load a number of characters in memory at the same time. Given the proper resources, these characters could interact with each other. Microsoft provides a character editor for Microsoft Agent so that the developer can modify existing characters and create new ones. We won't discuss this topic in detail in this chapter.

At this point, the code has loaded the character into memory, so we can create an individual character. Again, you can create more than one character at a time, but we'll use just one for this example. The code uses the TestAgent.Characters["Merlin"] property to perform this task.

Creating a character doesn't mean that it can do anything. The next step is to load the behaviors that the character can perform. The code begins this task by creating the AniList enumeration. It uses the MoveNext() method to select an individual command (behavior) from the enumeration. Notice how the code uses the `Commands.Add()` method to add each animated behavior to the character.

Now that the code has created a fully developed character, the application is ready for use. Clicking test will start the scripted animation process found in the `btnTest_Click()` event handler. The first step is to display the character using the `Show()` method.

An animation sequence normally includes three essential tasks: moving the character on screen, showing certain animated behaviors (such as blinking or smiling), and causing the character to say words. As you can see, the `MoveTo()`, `Play()`, and `Speak()` methods perform these three tasks.

The character can use the entire Desktop for movement purposes, unless you restrict it in some way. Notice the use of the `SystemInformation.WorkingArea` property to center the character location on screen. This property is important because it lets you know the working area—the area the user hasn't set aside for the Taskbar or other Desktop components. When developing a help sequence of this type, always keep the animated character within the working area to avoid interfering with accessibility aids.

The `Play()` method requires an animation term. You'll find the terms that apply to each Microsoft supplied character in the "Animation Lists for the Characters Available from Microsoft" help topic of the Microsoft Agent documentation. Each animation effect has an associated movement description. You'll also learn if the animation effect supports sound effects and speaking. Finally, you'll learn about the assigned state of the animation effect. Notice that the example application returns to the RestPose animation effect immediately before the character speaks. This animation effect places the character in the Speaking state, which ensures that the character will talk with the voice assigned to it (unless you assign some other voice).

The code also shows one of a number of tricks you can perform with the `Speak()` method. Generally, when you use the `Speak()` method, the balloon displays the same text that the character says. For accessible application purposes, you want to use this technique in most cases. Notice, however, the coded line:

```
"\\map=\"What you hear is not what you see!\"=\"Hello World\"\\"
```

This line tells the animation to output one phrase to the speaker and another to the balloon. You could theoretically use this technique to support multiple languages or perform other tasks. Microsoft Agent supports a number of these speech tags and you can learn about them in the "Microsoft Agent Speech Output Tags" help topic of the Microsoft Agent Help file.

At some point, your animation will complete and you'll want to hide the character. The code uses the `Hide()` method to perform this task.

ON THE WEB   A number of problems can cause the application to display the balloon text but not speak. The Microsoft Agent Web site mentions the most important failure for Windows XP users, the lack of SAPI 4.0 Runtime support. It's also important to install the text-to-speech engine. Even if programs like Narrator work fine, Microsoft Agent can fail to work if you don't have the right text-to-speech engine installed. You can download both of these items at http:// www.microsoft.com/msagent/downloads.htm.

Now that you know how the application works, try it out. Merlin will fly to the middle of the display, say a few things, perform a few tricks, and then disappear. You should see both the sound balloon and hear the sounds produced by the application.

Using Microsoft .NET Speech SDK on the Desktop

Many developers will find the Microsoft Agent technique of working with users childish (although I have seen more than a few adults respond quite favorably to the fun characters). The Microsoft .NET Speech SDK (in beta as I write this) offers speech input and output without using the character system found in Microsoft Agent. You can learn more about this technology at http://msdn.microsoft.com/ downloads/sample.asp?url=/MSDN-FILES/027/002/091/msdncompositedoc.xml.

NOTE   This section concentrates on Microsoft Speech API use for a desktop application. We'll also look at how you can use this technology on the Web (Microsoft's actual focus) in the "Using Microsoft Speech .NET SDK on the Web Example" section of Chapter 12. Make sure you look at both sections to gain a full appreciation of the flexibility of this technology.

The Microsoft .NET Speech SDK is an advanced speech engine that relies on Speech Application Language Tags (SALT) to convey information about the speech. Microsoft actually designed this technology to work with Web applications. The technology enables anyone to send data across the Internet using speech technology, which makes some types of "hands free" applications viable. As with all speech technologies on the market, the Microsoft Speech .NET SDK works best at interpreting commands. However, it does provide a full grammar and you can create specialized grammars for it. This makes the Microsoft Speech .NET SDK more flexible than many other technologies.

In Chapter 12 you'll see a complete example of the Microsoft .NET Speech SDK. It's important to remember that any desktop application can present Web material as if it came from a local source. Consequently, with a little work, you could also use the Microsoft Speech .NET SDK to create a desktop application that includes this modern speech technology.

Using IBM ViaVoice Technology

IBM's ViaVoice Technology has been around for a long time. It appears as part of a number of interesting applications that use speech technology as an application command strategy. For example, the relatively well-known Catz and Dogz programs both rely on ViaVoice to create input commands that control the virtual cat and dog behavior. This technology also runs on a wider range of platforms than the Microsoft alternatives, partially because IBM has gone to great lengths to ensure ViaVoice works well with entertainment products.

 TIP   Sometimes it's easier to see a good use for a technology by seeing how someone else uses it. For example, the IBM ViaVoice technology made a recent appearance in England's post offices. The Text and Sign Support Assistant (TESSA) is a video mannequin (or avatar) that uses sign language to communicate with the hearing impaired. A post office employee speaks into a microphone, the IBM ViaVoice software interprets the input, the underlying computer translates the input into British Sign Language (BSL), and an LCD translates the computer output into motion for Tessa. Tessa signs whatever the postal employee says—making communication possible even if the employee doesn't understand sign language. You can read more about this technology at http://www.wired.com/news/technology/0,1282,51059,00.html. It's worth the time to read because this technique relies on advanced technology that many of us have only seen in scientific magazines— technology that is seldom in real use.

This section of the chapter provides a quick overview of two IBM ViaVoice-related topics. First, we'll discuss a new accessibility product based on ViaVoice technology—the IBM Home Page Reader. This product demonstrates the power of ViaVoice better than most products on the market now. The second section will discuss the requirements for using ViaVoice technology in your next application. The ViaVoice SDK for Windows enables a developer to create applications that rely on this technology.

A Quick Overview of the IBM Home Page Reader

One of the more interesting uses for the IBM ViaVoice technology is the IBM Home Page Reader (`http://www-3.ibm.com/able/hpr.html`). Don't confuse this product with a screen reader. Like screen reader products, this product will help someone with special vision needs make sense out of a Web page. However, unlike screen reading products, Home Page Reader is specific to Web page requirements. This fact means you can't use Home Page Reader as a generic screen reader. Most people refer to products such as Home Page Reader as talking browsers.

Home Page Reader often succeeds where screen readers fail on Web pages because IBM designed it to accommodate the truly awful Web page designs that many developers use. It still doesn't do a perfect job, but Home Page Reader does successfully read a page with frames and tables that are used for display purposes rather than as a means for organizing data. Does this mean that those with special needs should use two products? No. The ultimate goal is still page design that actually meets the needs of those with special requirements. However, Home Page Reader does offer a temporary solution for some problems (it doesn't read complex, poorly designed pages with 100% accuracy, nor can I imagine those with special needs understanding the output when it does describe them accurately).

The reason I mention the IBM Home Page Reader in this section is that it does illustrate how well the ViaVoice Technology works. If you wanted to download and test an application that makes full use of the ViaVoice Technology, this would be the one to try. You can obtain a 30-day trial version of Home Page Reader. I also feel that Home Page Reader demonstrates the absurd levels to which some users would have to go to understand some Web pages at all. Those of us with perfect vision have problems understanding them, too.

Working with IBM ViaVoice Technology

Voice technology is going to become an important part of applications because more people are buying devices that don't readily support full keyboards, such as cellular telephones. Unfortunately, trying to figure out which speech technology to use today is difficult because so many vendors offer this type of product and it appears that each vendor has a different set of support criteria.

The IBM ViaVoice technology does appear in a number of applications, but these products contain just the runtime elements. If you're serious about developing an application using ViaVoice, you'll need to obtain a copy of the full product. In many cases, developers are reluctant to spend their hard-earned cash on a technology that might not pan out for a specific need. Fortunately, you can obtain an evaluation version of the product for development use.

ON THE WEB The ViaVoice information you need doesn't all appear in one location on the Internet. You'll find the main ViaVoice Web site at `http://www-3.ibm.com/software/speech/index.shtml`. The developer resources mentioned in this section of the chapter appear at `http://www-3.ibm.com/software/speech/dev/index.shtml`. It's easy to obtain an evaluation version of the product at `http://www.wizzardsoftware.com/voice/voicetools/download.htm`. Note that you'll need to fill out a form to receive the evaluation copy that states how you'll use the product in development.

To use the ViaVoice technology, you need the ViaVoice TTS Runtime Engine, ViaVoice SDK, and ViaVoice Dictation and C&C Runtime Engine. Downloading these tools is enough to get your started. However, you'll also want to look at the optional offerings at the ViaVoice Developer's Corner. For example, you can currently download a medical and legal vocabulary for use with ViaVoice. This additional vocabulary will certainly come in handy for dealing with the jargon used by these two communities. It's also helpful to look through the Frequently Asked Question (FAQ) sheets provided on this site.

Using Existing Technologies in Alternative Ways

Sometimes, the most accessible application is also the most flexible application. In many situations, a user with a special need can put a feature to another use. This section of the chapter isn't intended to encourage you to provide odd features in your application, just to see what the user will do with them. In general, it's always a good idea to avoid extra features in your application (see the "Avoiding the Gadget Mentality in Application Design" section for details). However, this section does show you a couple of interesting ways to use features that you might not have considered in the past.

The goal of this section is to demonstrate that most users don't have the limitations that developers think they have. One company that I worked with in the past realized this and decided to put the users of their application to the test. They would run contest to see who could come up with the most interesting use for an application feature. It wasn't long before the company had a host of tips for their application—all of which came from the users of that application. I wish more companies would take this approach.

The Word AutoCorrect Options Example

Many of you are familiar with the Word AutoCorrect feature. This Word feature changes an abbreviation into its full counterpart and corrects common word misspellings. For example, when you misspell your as "yuor", the Word AutoCorrect feature sees the error and makes the correction automatically. This feature also changes common symbols into uncommon counterparts. For example, when you type "(c)", Word changes the characters into the copyright symbol ©. In short, the AutoCorrect feature is very helpful.

Some users have modified the use of the AutoCorrect feature from an automatic correction function into an accessibility aid. For example, one of the most common words in use today is "this." Most users have to type four characters to see that word on their screens. However, by careful use of the AutoCorrect feature, a user could simply type "ts" and let the AutoCorrect feature do the rest of the work. Sure, it only reduces the character count by two characters, but when it takes between 20 and 30 seconds to type each character, the time saved at the end of the day can become significant.

Does this use of the AutoCorrect feature make sense for everyone? The problem with AutoCorrect is that it will modify all occurrences of the target letter sequence. If you work in an industry that uses odd letter combinations or jargon, the feature may not work as intended. If you use this technique, it's important to pay careful attention to the letter sequences you select. However, given this caveat, this "accessible" use of an existing technology can help anyone type faster and with fewer errors. In sum, this technique demonstrates yet again that something originally designed for one purpose can become an accessibility aid, which then has the potential to affect everyone—not just those who need it most.

The Scheduled Tasks Example

The Windows Task Scheduler sits in the background and waits for something to do. If you assign it some task, then it will start the task using the criteria that you provide. This is a straightforward service that many administrators use to perform tasks such as performing a backup. Starting a backup is relatively easy once you define the parameters, so letting the computer take care of it makes sense.

TIP Many agencies are cutting funding for caregivers and other forms of support for people with special needs. Developers and others who work with those who have special needs could easily adapt the techniques presented in this book to other uses. A computer system can help people achieve a significant level of independence using techniques such as the ones in this section. Don't look at this book as the end of the quest for accessibility—it's a source book that helps you understand the beginning of the quest.

Like many other tools, the Task Scheduler can perform double duty as an accessibility aid. For example, in this case, a user added tasks that reminded him to take medications and perform other essential tasks during the day. OK, so many people use an appointment schedule for this purpose. However, by creating a simple script, you can create an elegant reminder system that doesn't require use of any additional software. All you need is the VBScript shown here:

```
MsgBox WScript.Arguments(0)
```

This simple script displays a reminder message at the time specified. It's simple and provides everything needed for the task at hand. Sometimes a need is easy to satisfy using simple methods—this is one of those cases.

The Speakonia Text-To-Speech Program Example

Developers are creating a number of new tools that make it easier to read text in a controlled manner. In other words, unlike the Narrator program that comes with Windows, these applications read only the text that you tell them to read. Speakonia (http://www.mywebattack.com/gnomeapp.php?id=105038) is one such tool. It sports a Notepad-type interface where the user can type text. As the user types text, the application reads it aloud. The application also accepts input from a text file or from the Windows clipboard. Using the various means of input this tool provides, a user can read everything from simple text, to a Web page, to email. For the developer, this tool provides a simple method of reading just the information the developer wants to test, rather than constantly hearing everything the computer displays on screen.

One of the most interesting features of this application is that it can output any text it reads to a WAV (wave formatted) file. Many people with special needs find this feature useful because they can create a "talking book" from any text that they can input to the application. Obviously, this feature doesn't affect just those with special needs. Many people use talking books today to hear information they need while performing some other task. In sum, this application addresses a special need that everyone has—the ability to output text in another, more convenient, format.

Addressing Animation and Animation Alternatives

Although this chapter discusses unique ways for the user to interact with the computer and the computer to present information, it's important to realize that these methods are only useful if they convey information that can't appear in other formats. We've discussed the gadget mentality many times in this book. Animation can become a gadget just as easily as any technology. In fact, given that animation is something that many developers are only now beginning to use, the lure of using it when some other method would work fine is intense.

In general, avoid animation when you can use other techniques. Don't use animation when a procedure will work. If you can write a procedure using text alone, then use that technique because text is easily transformed into speech or other types of output. Text with graphics comes next. In some cases, you can't adequately describe a sequence using only text, and graphics provide an easy method to augment the description. However, if you use this technique, you must still provide a text description of the graphic images for those who can't see them.

The animated character or the use of animated sequences can prove distracting to some users. Always make sure you provide an alternative to the animated sequence, even if the alternative won't work as well as the animation. For example, you could provide the same information in a text form as a script or a procedure. Neither option is as aesthetically pleasing as animation, but both avoid the distraction that the animation can provide.

Creating an Accessible Desktop Application Checklist

Sometimes using a checklist is the easiest way to ensure you've addressed all of the requirements for an application. It's time to look at the requirements for a desktop application from a checklist perspective. Table 8-1 contains the Section 508 requirement, the legal requirement, and two columns for making a decision.

Just in case you've forgotten what these rules mean, check out the detailed analysis in Chapter 1. As you design and develop your application, make a choice. Mark the requirement as completed or place a check in the Undue Burden column to indicate that this is a requirement you'll handle later. (Remember from Chapter 1 that you must observe all requirements, but you can postpone some requirements if you can prove that the requirement places an undue burden on your company.)

Table 8-1. Accessible Checklist for Desktop Applications

Section	Legal Requirement	Completed	Undue Burden
SOFTWARE APPLICATIONS AND OPERATING SYSTEMS			
1194.21(a)	When software is designed to run on a system that has a keyboard, product functions shall be executable from a keyboard where the function itself or the result of performing a function can be discerned textually.		
1194.21(b)	Applications shall not disrupt or disable activated features of other products that are identified as accessibility features, where those features are developed and documented according to industry standards. Applications also shall not disrupt or disable activated features of any operating system that are identified as accessibility features where the application programming interface for those accessibility features has been documented by the manufacturer of the operating system and is available to the product developer.		
1194.21(c)	A well-defined on-screen indication of the current focus shall be provided that moves among interactive interface elements as the input focus changes. The focus shall be programmatically exposed so that assistive technology can track focus and focus changes.		
1194.21(d)	Sufficient information about a user interface element including the identity, operation and state of the element shall be available to assistive technology. When an image represents a program element, the infor-mation conveyed by the image must also be available in text.		

Table 8-1. Accessible Checklist for Desktop Applications (Continued)

Section	Legal Requirement	Completed	Undue Burden
1194.21(e)	When bitmap images are used to identify controls, status indicators, or other programmatic elements, the meaning assigned to those images shall be consistent throughout an application's performance.		
1194.21(f)	Textual information shall be provided through operating system functions for displaying text. The minimum information that shall be made available is text content, text input caret location, and text attributes.		
1194.21(g)	Applications shall not override user selected contrast and color selections and other individual display attributes.		
1194.21(h)	When animation is displayed, the information shall be displayable in at least one non-animated presentation mode at the option of the user.		
1194.21(i)	Color coding shall not be used as the only means of conveying information, indicating an action, prompting a response, or distinguishing a visual element.		
1194.21(j)	When a product permits a user to adjust color and contrast settings, a variety of color selections capable of producing a range of contrast levels shall be provided.		
1194.21(k)	Software shall not use flashing or blinking text, objects, or other elements having a flash or blink frequency greater than 2 Hz and lower than 55 Hz.		
1194.21(l)	When electronic forms are used, the form shall allow people using assistive technology to access the information, field elements, and functionality required for completion and submission of the form, including all directions and cues.		

Table 8-1. Accessible Checklist for Desktop Applications (Continued)

Section	Legal Requirement	Completed	Undue Burden
VIDEO OR MULTIMEDIA PRODUCTS			
1194.24(c)	All training and informational video and multimedia productions which support the agency's mission, regardless of format, that contain speech or other audio information necessary for the comprehension of the content, shall be open or closed captioned.		
1194.24(d)	All training and informational video and multimedia productions which support the agency's mission, regardless of format, that contain visual information necessary for the comprehension of the content, shall be audio described.		
1194.24(e)	Display or presentation of alternate text presentation or audio descriptions shall be user-selectable unless permanent.		
DESKTOP AND PORTABLE COMPUTERS			
1194.26(c)	When biometric forms of user identification or control are used, an alternative form of identification or activation, which does not require the user to possess particular biological characteristics, shall also be provided.		
FUNCTIONAL PERFORMANCE CRITERIA			
Subpart C(a)	At least one mode of operation and information retrieval that does not require user vision shall be provided, or support for assistive technology used by people who are blind or visually impaired shall be provided.		
Subpart C(b)	At least one mode of operation and information retrieval that does not require visual acuity greater than 20/70 shall be provided in audio and enlarged print output working together or independently, or support for assistive technology used by people who are visually impaired shall be provided.		

Table 8-1. Accessible Checklist for Desktop Applications (Continued)

Section	Legal Requirement	Completed	Undue Burden
Subpart C(c)	At least one mode of operation and information retrieval that does not require user hearing shall be provided, or support for assistive technology used by people who are deaf or hard of hearing shall be provided.		
Subpart C(d)	Where audio information is important for the use of a product, at least one mode of operation and information retrieval shall be provided in an enhanced auditory fashion, or support for assistive hearing devices shall be provided.		
Subpart C(e)	At least one mode of operation and infor-mation retrieval that does not require user speech shall be provided, or support for assistive technology used by people with disabilities shall be provided.		
Subpart C(f)	At least one mode of operation and information retrieval that does not require fine motor control or simultaneous actions and that is operable with limited reach and strength shall be provided.		
INFORMATION, DOCUMENTATION, AND SUPPORT			
Subpart D(a)	Product support documentation provided to end-users shall be made available in alternate formats upon request, at no additional charge.		
Subpart D(b)	End-users shall have access to a description of the accessibility and compatibility features of products in alternate formats or alternate methods upon request, at no additional charge.		
Subpart D(c)	Support services for products shall accommodate the communication needs of end-users with disabilities.		

Summary

This chapter has helped you understand the requirements for using special hardware or software to enhance an application. We began with a discussion of the special application features that developers normally consider. The chapter then showed you how to create several types of applications using special software. The first application concentrated on Microsoft Agent—a technology that some people love and others hate. The second application showed the current state of Microsoft's voice technology. You learned how to create an application that uses the Microsoft Speech API as a means of input. Finally, we discussed the IBM ViaVoice technology. All three of these technologies can turn a helpful application into something truly useful.

You also learned about the Accessible Desktop Application Checklist in this chapter. A checklist can help ensure that you don't miss any important features when creating an application. Now is a good time to familiarize yourself with the checklist and begin thinking about how to add it to your next project. In some cases, you'll want to customize the checklist so that it reflects the special needs of your organization. For example, if your company doesn't normally add context sensitive help to an application, you might want to break this task into smaller pieces.

Now it's decision time. The Section 508 rules don't require use of any of the technologies in this chapter. If they did, I'm sure that most developers would find it difficult to meet the requirements. In fact, the Section 508 rules specify that you must provide alternatives to some of these technologies. For example, you must provide an alternative to voice input for those users who can't talk. An application must also provide an alternative output method that doesn't rely on sound. In short, these technologies are additions you can make to reduce the user's workload, but you should also provide standard application support. It's up to you to determine if the users of your application have much to gain from technologies such as voice input.

Chapter 9 begins the Web-based application portion of the book. It will show you how to create accessible Web applications that work for everyone without losing any flexibility. Unfortunately, many developers are dragging their feet on Web site updates because they think they'll end up with an ugly text-only Web site. The fact is, Web sites that provide accessibility support don't have to be ugly—they might not provide the same level of pizzazz as some Web sites today, but even that change can net positive effects for users. If you have a Web site you've been waiting to update, check Chapter 9 for the essentials.

Part Three

Writing Accessible Web Applications

Web Site Essentials

In This Chapter:

How Do You Reduce the Effects of Download Time?

When Is It Possible to Use an HTML Checker?

Which HTML Checkers Are Free?

How Can You Avoid Web Site Problems?

How Do You Develop Accessibility Friendly Tables?

How Do You Develop Accessibility Friendly Forms?

What Techniques Should You Use for Keyboard Shortcuts?

What Techniques Should You Use for Alerts and Timers?

How Can You Improve Database Access?

THIS IS THE FIRST CHAPTER where we'll discuss Web-based applications in detail. The first four chapters of the book provided you with a basis for performing updates or creating new applications of any type. The next four chapters discussed desktop application development. In this chapter, we begin looking at the implementation details for Web-based applications.

You could easily divide this chapter into two sections. The first section discusses some of the pitfalls of creating or updating Web-based applications that provide great accessibility support. Many developers are under the impression that every user has a T1 connection (or better) to the Internet. The reality is that most people still rely on a dial-up connection. The special equipment and applications used by people with special needs makes timing even more critical, so creating Web pages with short download times is important. We'll also look at some tools you can use to check the correctness of your Web site. Finally, we'll discuss the common Web site problems and how you can avoid them.

The second portion of the chapter shows several example applications that include accessibility support. We'll begin by looking at tables, forms, and scripts. These three elements are relatively simple to implement, yet they present a number of problems for most developers. The section ends with two examples. The first discusses keyboard shortcuts—an essential element of accessible applications. The second shows how to avoid problems with timers and alerts.

Considering the Effects of Download Time

A developer who begins a Web page design with the idea that everyone has a high-speed connection to the Internet will almost certainly end up disappointing the vast majority of the users that visit the site. Most of the world uses dial-up connections to the Internet. In some cases, the dial-up connection is much slower than the developer would expect. A connection speed of 56 Kbps is somewhat standard in the United States and other developed countries, but you might have visitors who use connections as slow as 14.4 Kbps from other countries. Unfortunately, many people with special needs also have older and slower machines with a 14.4 Kbps or a 28.8 Kbps modem. Imagine downloading several MB of data at such a speed—the user usually gets tired of waiting and leaves long before the page is complete.

 TIP A good rule of thumb for Web page downloads is 20 seconds at 28.8 Kbps. Anything longer and your audience will become impatient. Make sure the download time includes any graphics, special features, and ads. Everything on your Web page should download in the 20-second timeframe.

One of the problems with many Web sites is the non-text elements they contain. Many developers create images for their Web site using standard desktop applications that don't understand the need for compression. Consequently, the images are huge and require excessive download time. You can optimize graphics for download by using products like the GNU Image Manipulation Program (GIMP) (`http://www.gimp.org/`). This product comes in versions for both Windows and Linux. The image will look the same, but it will consume a lot less space—conserving valuable bandwidth.

Another major problem with many Web sites is that the individual pages contain too much information (think about a site that goes on for ten or fifteen printed pages). One of the centerpieces of accessibility is data organization. It's essential to organize your data for easy viewing. As part of the organization process, you can usually divide the information into smaller pieces (a maximum of two or three printed pages)—each of which can appear on a separate page. Think about the home page of your Web site in the same light as a table of contents for a book—the home page should lead the user to additional pieces of information. Of course, every rule has an exception. If you have a relatively small amount of information, it's often more accessible to place the information on a single page. The key is organization, not necessarily the amount of material provided.

ON THE WEB   Do you need an easy way to keep up with accessible programming news for your Web site? The Accessify.com site at http:// www.accessify.com/default.asp may be the answer you've been waiting for. This site provides easy-to-understand information about accessibility requirements using language that's free of legal jargon.

Using an HTML Checker

Trying to meet all of the Section 508 requirements might seem impossible to many developers. After all, you need to conform to all the rules we discussed in Chapter 1, consider the problems in Chapter 2, and get the training discussed in Chapter 3. It's a lot for a Webmaster to do. Fortunately, there's help in the form of an HTML check utility.

Most of the available HTML check utilities are provided by third parties to check an entire Web site. You'll receive a report on the compliance level of all your pages at one time. It's sort of the same as using a compiler to check for errors in your code. The only major difference is that you get a report of Section 508 violations instead of coding errors. Here's a list of some of the tools you can use to evaluate your Web pages.

> **Bobby:** This utility provides a quick check that you can use for any existing Web site. Simply feed the online version of Bobby an URL and you'll receive a report about it. Using the online version is free. The vendor also provides a full version of Bobby that will check an entire Web site without entering the individual pages for a price. Although Bobby does a great job of checking most Section 508, the vendor doesn't guarantee that the product will locate every problem. You can learn more about this product at http:// bobby.watchfire.com/bobby/html/en/index.jsp.

> **Lynx:** This is a text-only browser that comes in versions for the Macintosh and Windows. It helps you check your Web site by displaying it in text only. This check helps you see your Web site as a screen reader will see it— making it possible to detect and correct problems with greater ease. Learn more about this product at http://lynx.browser.org/. You can also use the online version found at http://www.delorie.com/web/lynxview.html.

NIST Webmetrics Tool Suite: This group of tools from the National Institute of Standards and Technology (NIST) helps you test the usability and accessibility of a Web site. For example, the Web Static Analyzer Tool (WebSAT) ensures that your Web page meets specific usability goals. The Web Variable Instrumenter Program (WebVIP) helps track user interaction so that you know how well users are finding Web site features. There are more tools on this Web site (`http://zing.ncsl.nist.gov/webmet/`) and NIST updates them regularly.

Opera: Like Lynx, this browser enables you to see your Web site as a screen reader will see it. However, unlike Lynx, this product also helps you turn certain features on and off as needed for comparison. For example, you can toggle images off so that you can see how `<ALT>` tags will look. Opera is available for a number of platforms including Windows, Macintosh, and Linux. You can learn more about it at `http://www.opera.com/`.

O'Reilly XML.com: This Web site provides an XML syntax checker that also validates XHTML. You can provide the XML input directly or supply an URL containing the XML. This tool runs a test that checks whether the XML is well-formed—it doesn't verify that the XML actually means anything. In most cases, you'll want to use the W3C HTML Validation Service for a final check of your Web page. However, this Web site does perform fast checks of intermediate and test XML. Learn more about this tool at `http://www.xml.com/pub/a/tools/ruwf/check.html`.

W3C HTML Validation Service: This Web site checks the HTML on your Web page for conformance to World Wide Web Consortium (W3C) recommendations and standards. An error on this Web site means that the coding for your Web page is incorrect, even if most browsers will read it, so this tester goes beyond usability and accessibility requirements. Don't get the idea that passing the test on this Web site automatically makes your Web site accessible. Passing on this Web site means that your code is correct. However, making sure you code is correct is a good first step to ensuring that you can add accessibility features. Learn more about this utility at `http://validator.w3.org/`.

Web Design Group HTML Validator: This Web site checks the HTML on your Web page or, as an alternative, on your computer. It also provides an option to validate a single page or the entire site. I also found that this site is a little less picky than the W3C HTML Validation Service about which pages it will check. The site seems to output about the same information, but may not provide complete validation of your Web site. You can learn more about this tool at `http://www.htmlhelp.com/tools/validator/`.

Now that you have a better idea of what tools are available for making your Web site accessibility friendly, let's discuss some specifics of working with an HTML checker. The following sections take you through the process of using a typical utility to update your Web site. We'll discuss several utilities in these sections because most utilities only do the job partially and may not provide an interface that you like. The reason I chose these particular utilities is that they're thorough, free for the asking, and do not depend on a particular platform. We'll examine many other techniques as the book progresses, so consider this your first foray into the world of accessibility updates.

Getting a Free Check

Few things in life are free. I was surprised to find several Web sites that would actually check a given Web site for errors at no cost. In all cases, the vendor who sponsors the free Web site also provides a paid option that includes more functionality than the free product. However, although these free products are a tad less capable, they do help you understand Web site accessibility and that's worth quite a bit to any developer. The knowledge you gain from the tests is essential to understanding how accessibility development should proceed in many ways. Of course, as we discussed in the "Using Automated Testing Techniques" section of Chapter 5, automated testing can only do so much for your application—at some point, you also need to build manual testing skills.

You should consider two levels of errors when creating an accessible Web site. The first level is the code itself. A correctly coded Web site has a better chance of being accessible. The W3C HTML Validation section that follows tells you about this first level of testing and shows you how it works. Make sure you validate your Web site before you test it for accessibility. The second level is verifying the accessibility requirements of Section 508. We'll discuss four Web sites that help you perform this second-level test (Bobby, AskAlice, LIFT, and Wave) in the sections that follow. These four Web sites show examples of automated accessibility testing. Make sure your testing plan also includes manual checks of some type. Always perform at least these two levels of checks before you contemplate a course of action for your Web site.

There's a third level of Web site testing—usability. The LIFT product actually helps you perform this testing on your Web site, but you'll want to add manual testing, in this case, too. A functional Web site isn't necessarily a usable Web site, just as a functional desktop application doesn't necessarily work (see the "Working Code Doesn't Mean a Working Application" section of Chapter 5 for details).

Using High-End Tools

We don't discuss the high-end tools in this section of the chapter because they cost quite a bit and developers normally use them only on the largest Web sites. However, a high-end tool can save you time and effort if you have many Web pages to check. One such product is WebXM from Watchfire (http://www.watchfire.com/products/webxm.asp). You can read some interesting information about this product at (http://www.eweek.com/article2/0,3959,732375,00.asp).

Another series of products that make it much easier to developer accessible Web applications are AccRepair and AccVerify from HiSoftware. These two products have received recent updates that provide better integration and test for all of the latest Web standards. You can learn more about these products at http://www.hisoftware.com/access/Index.html. You can also download trial versions of both these products, making it easy to learn more about the capabilities of a high-end test product.

Using a high-end product has many benefits. For example, one of the free products listed in the sections that follow will help you find at least 55% (but no more than 70%) of the errors on your Web page with complete accuracy. The free products will also suggest ways to look for another small percentage of those errors. A high-end product can help you find around 80% of the errors on a Web page consistently. Nothing out there will help you find all accessibility problems on a Web page with 100% accuracy. This process still requires human intervention and manual testing.

W3C HTML Validation

The first level of Web site checks will ensure that your code is correct. Syntactically correct code doesn't necessarily work, but it does follow all of the specifications provided by the W3C. The reason I emphasize syntactically correct code is that some developers don't check their code for accuracy, while others don't check their code for bugs. You must make sure that your code works and that it's syntactically correct before you perform an accessibility check. To make a syntax check, go to the W3C HTML Validation Service at http://validator.w3.org/. The Web site appears in Figure 9.1. To use this Web site, enter the Web site URL, select any display options, and then click Validate This Page.

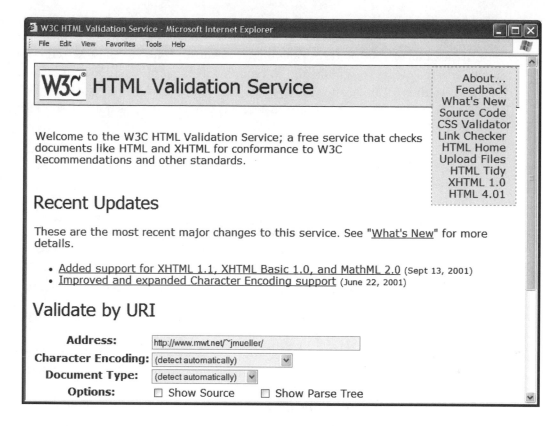

Figure 9-1. Use the W3C HTML Validation Service to ensure the code on your Web page is correct.

NOTE Besides the obvious advantages of validating your code against the specifications, you should also consider some of the less obvious benefits. For example, validating your code first ensures that the accessibility checker you use later has the best chance of finding problems in your code. In addition, some of these accessibility checkers will experience problems (including crashes) if your code is not syntactically correct.

Sometimes the Web page won't validate correctly because it lacks a <!DOCTYPE> tag or character set entry. You can override these problems by selecting a value from the Character Encoding or Document Type fields. However, these selections will skew the results you obtain and you should add the proper tags to your Web page as soon as possible. After you override the selections, try to validate the page again. If it still won't validate, your Web page has serious problems that you should fix immediately.

 NOTE   This book assumes that you already know how to create HTML code. The purpose of this check is to validate your Web site before adding accessibility features. If the code is incorrect, the accessibility features will never work properly. We won't discuss HTML specifics in this book, except as they apply to accessibility requirements.

Validating a page doesn't mean it's error free—it simply means that you've fixed enough problems for the tool to tell you about the remaining errors. Figure 9-2 shows typical output from the W3C HTML Validation Service. This figure concentrates on the errors—you can also view an outline of your Web page, a numbered source listing, and a parse tree of the data.

Notice that the output shown in Figure 9-2 shows the precise location of the error as the parser sees it. The output page also includes a brief message on the error and optionally provides some information on how to fix it. Generally, you'll find that this setup works well for simple errors, but it doesn't provide enough information to fix complex errors. That's where your training in writing HTML will come into play.

Bobby

One of the oldest and most relied-upon methods for checking Web sites for accessibility is Bobby. The fact that Bobby is free only makes it more popular. Bobby will check a single page of a Web site for free and provide a seal of approval should the Web site pass. The Bobby approval relies mainly on the honor system, so you should make sure your Web site actually passes the tests before you use the seal.

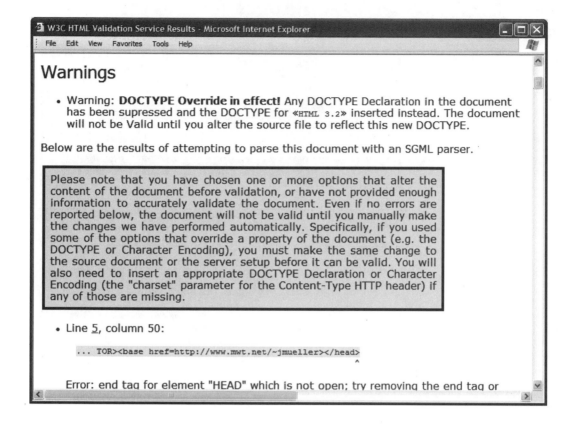

Figure 9-2. The W3C HTML Validation Service provides complete information about the errors on your Web page.

You can check out this valuable resource (shown in Figure 9-3) at http:// bobby.watchfire.com/bobby/html/en/index.jsp. As you can see from Figure 9-3, the Web site performs either Web Content Accessibility Guideline 1.0 or Section 508 checks on a Web site of your choosing. You'll notice almost immediately that the Web Content Accessibility Guideline check is more intense than the Section 508 check, but performing both checks can point out errors on your Web site.

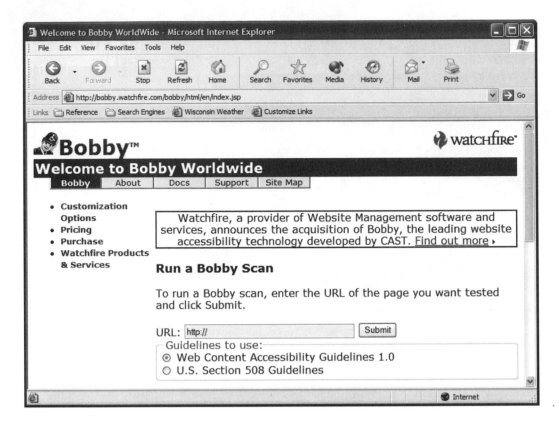

Figure 9-3. Bobby ensures that your Web site meets the vital accessibility requirements.

All you need to do is enter a Web site URL, select the test you want to run, and then click Submit. Bobby retrieves the Web site, checks it for errors, and prints a report for you. I thought that my pure text Web site would pass on the first try, but, as shown in Figure 9-4, my Web site at `http://www.mwt.net/~jmueller/` still had five glitches to fix. (In some cases, a glitch will appear because you need to perform a manual check for the condition and Bobby is simply reminding you to do it.) I've since corrected the problems with my Web site and posted an updated version.

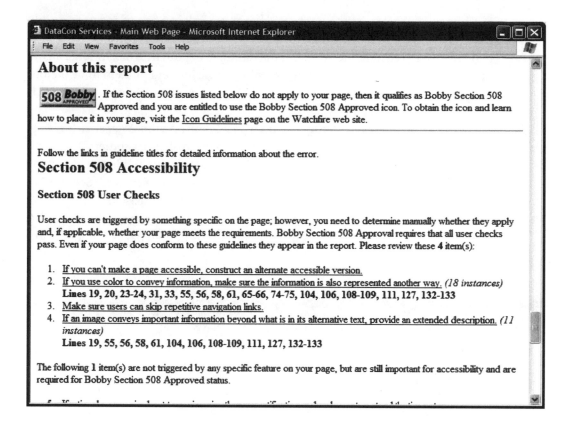

Figure 9-4. Even pure text Web sites can run afoul of Section 508 requirements, as shown in this figure.

Notice that all of these errors are "user checks." A user check error is one that you have to check manually and determine if your site is in compliance. In many cases, Bobby will raise a question that you can answer by saying that your site is in compliance. You can determine the error locations by looking for question marks on the Web page displayed above the report. Every question mark represents an issue that you need to consider, and some locations will contain more than one question mark because they break more than one rule.

Every user check in the report also contains a link you can use to obtain additional information. Generally, the additional information tells you what you need to do in order to correct the error and the rationale behind the rule. In some cases, the help also shows short code snippets with generic implementation information. The point is that you can find out the specifics of the problem using your own Web page as a source of the information.

Many people learn by example. I know that I look on other Web sites for ideas on how to resolve issues with my own Web site and those of my customers. Therefore, Bobby can serve another purpose. Before you use a Web site for ideas, check it for Section 508 compliance. I was a little surprised to find that Microsoft's Section 508 Web site at `http://www.microsoft.com/enable/microsoft/section508.htm` had numerous occurrences of 13 Section 508 errors, two of which are major, as shown in Figure 9-5. In fact, I found that none of the Microsoft Web pages I tried would pass the test.

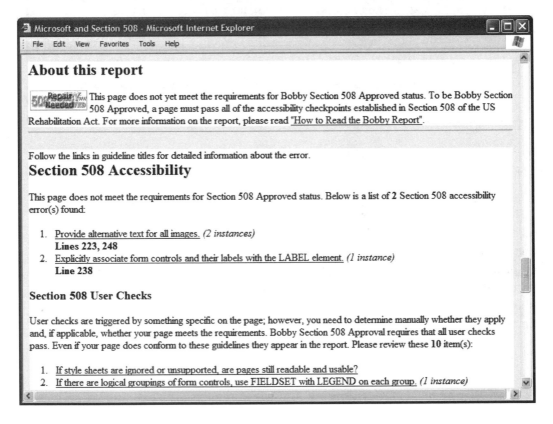

Figure 9-5. Always test Web sites before you trust them as an example of what you should do on your own Web site.

This Web page includes a combination of user checks and Section 508 compliance errors. The errors at the top of the report are issues that the Web site must fix in order to bring the Web site into compliance. As with the user checks, the Web site provides links that give you some general information about the problem so that you can make an informed decision about fixing it. Of course, the remainder of this book provides the detailed examples you'll need to get your Web site up and running quickly.

AskAlice

AskAlice is a Web site checking service that works along the same lines as Bobby. You can find it at `http://askalice.ssbtechnologies.com:8080/askalice/index.html`. Unlike many of the other products and services listed in this book, you must register as a user before you can use AskAlice. The registration process includes the URL that you want to diagnose, which must match the email address you provide.

After you perform the registration process, the Web site will tell you that the report will appear in your email. The email you receive will contain a general rating for your Web site. It also includes an URL that contains the full report for your Web site. The essential information appears in the "Assessment of Your Site" section. A perfect report will look like the one in Figure 9-6.

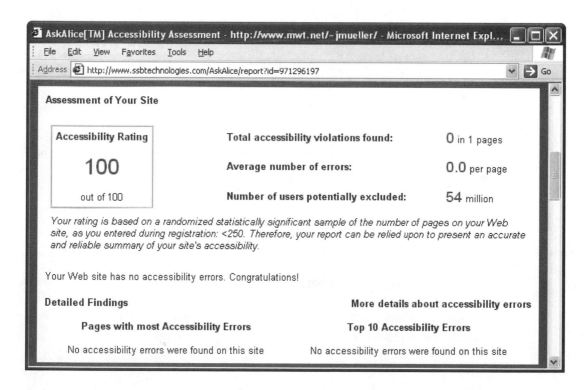

Figure 9-6. The report you receive from AskAlice describes required changes with few false positive errors.

If your Web site does have errors, AskAlice will display them. Overall, AskAlice seems to provide fewer false positive errors than the other automated testers that appear in this section. However, the site doesn't mention the precise testing criteria used, so the value of this testing resource is also somewhat in question. If you're looking for a quick check of a resource and don't need a report immediately, AskAlice does seem to have advantages that other online testers don't provide.

LIFT

LIFT is one of the more versatile products discussed in this section. The online version appears at http://www.usablenet.com. There are also versions for Dream-weaver and FrontPage, so you can receive specific comments using the Web page development product of your choice. This section discusses the free Web site product. Consider this section an introduction to LIFT and not a full review because I'm certain the platform-specific products are more complete than the free Web site offering. This section will help you understand what you can expect from LIFT.

TIP   The LIFT site is filled with free downloads and evaluation products. For example, you'll find a free download for Dreamweaver accessibility extensions on the site. Most of the products also have a Request Demo link you can use to request an evaluation version of the product. Obviously, you'll find the usual marketing information. In this case, the vendor doesn't have to say too much, the awards LIFT has received tend to speak for themselves.

One thing that intrigues me about this product is that the vendor stresses the importance of both functionality and usability. In fact, UsableNet, the maker of LIFT, created a special version of LIFT that incorporates the Nielsen Norman Group's usability advice as part of the product. You can learn more about this concept of usability from the Free Pint article at http://www.freepint.com/issues/141102.htm#feature.

To obtain a report on a specific Web site, you'll need to provide the Web site URL and your email address. The form also asks one question that no one else does—LIFT wants to know what type of Web site the software is testing. I found the question intriguing and was gratified to see that it does make a difference in the output you receive. LIFT tailors the advice it provides to the kind of site and often reflects the vendor's concept of what such a site should provide.

Once you submit the form, the actual analysis takes a few minutes. When the analysis is complete, you'll receive an email message containing the URL of the report. Unlike every other free tester in this chapter, LIFT actually looks at more than one page of your Web site. Figure 9-7 shows a typical report page.

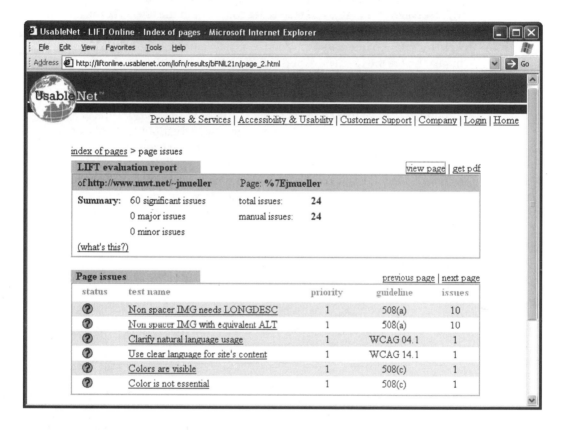

Figure 9-7. LIFT usually provides more than one page worth of analsys and the information is detailed.

Notice the links next to each entry. If you click the link, you'll receive helpful advice about the problem and tips on how to correct it. The link also serves as a means to access details about the entry. The detail information includes the line number of the error and enough information that most developers can find the error. Finally, the details page provides references to the applicable standards. This information helps you make a decision about the necessity of fixing the error and tells how you should go about doing so. Like Bobby, the LIFT checks are intensive, so they produce a number of false positive results that require some level of human interpretation.

Server Load Testing with LoadRunner and LoadTest

Load testing helps the developer simulate conditions where some applications fail because the load on the system is too high. It's important to know that an application or a system will fail before it has thousands of users attached to it asking for services. Generally, you receive feedback about the effects of the load on the system as a whole through performance monitors. The performance monitors record the effects of increased load and help you determine the load that a system can bear before the user will experience speed problems that render your application useless. In short, load testing is essential if you want to create applications that are accessible, perform well, and provide the user with good usability.

LoadRunner from Mercury Interactive (`http://www-svca.mercuryinteractive.com/products/loadrunner/`) enables the developer to place various types of loads on a variety of systems. For example, you could simulate 1,000 network users and 200 Internet users to create a mixed execution environment. Unfortunately, there's no demonstration version of the LoadRunner tool available on the Mercury Interactive Web site at the time of this writing. However, you can find a list of downloadable demonstrations and free tools at `http://www-svca.mercuryinteractive.com/products/downloads.html`.

You can find other load testing demonstration products on the Mercury Interactive site. Mercury Interactive Astra LoadTest (`http://astratryandbuy.mercuryinteractive.com/cgi-bin/portal/trynbuy/index.jsp`) is one of a suite of tools you can use to perform Web site testing. Other tools in the suite include Astra QuickTest (automated Web testing), Astra FastTrack (defect management), and Astra SiteManager (an application management tool). You can download demonstration versions of all four of these tools.

Wave

Wave is yet another online tool that will check your Web site for accessibility problems. This is the newest of the tools that I checked while writing this book. Like Bobby, you can check both WAI and Section 508 compliance. To use Wave, you begin at the main Web site at `http://wave.webaim.org/`. The feature I like about this free checker is that you can type an URL or upload a page from your local hard drive, as shown in Figure 9-8. The Wave checker also provides a method for adding this feature to your Web browser, which is unique among the free checkers tested.

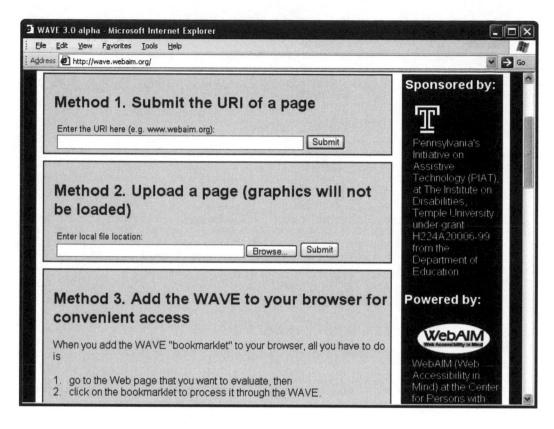

Figure 9-8. Using Wave means that you can submit an URL or upload a file from your local hard drive.

NOTE The latest release of Wave is still in alpha test as of the writing of this book. Some of the screenshots and features mentioned in this section will change by the time you read this. Make sure you visit the Wave Web site and base your evaluation on the actual content provided by this site.

I found the output from this site very appealing visually. This site also found a few problems on my test site that the Bobby check didn't find. Figure 9-9 shows some output from the Wave Web site. Notice that the checker has picked up on the fact that I've used the same <ALT> tag for every one of the Update icon entries. Also, notice that the checker provides analysis of the structural elements, making it easy to find potential problems in this area as well.

Unlike Bobby, the Wave site doesn't provide a report that you can print and use for quick reference. This omission really isn't a problem given the graphical output that the site does provide. However, some developers may find that they prefer the Bobby way of obtaining a Web site report.

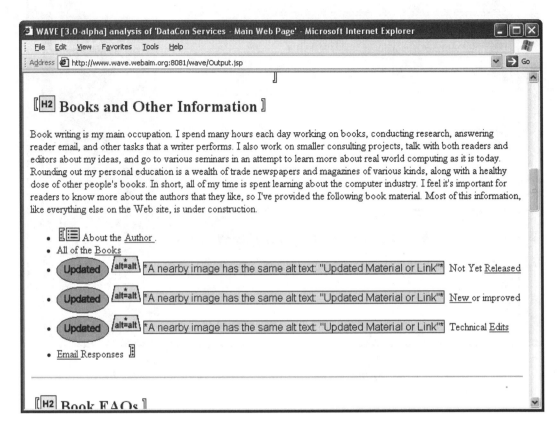

Figure 9-9. Sending your Web page to different checker sites can yeild differing results that will help you refine an accessible update strategy.

Creating an Update Checklist

At some point, you'll have created a complete list of all the errors that the testing programs found on your site. The problem is that you don't know how accurate the testing is or how many other errors lurk in the background, unfound by the testing program. A Webmaster could quickly become overwhelmed with the task at hand because there's so much uncertainty.

NOTE   Updates are never a free ride—there's always a cost. Of course, the biggest issue for most companies today is the effect of any change on a system that has to run 24/7. Adding accessibility support could incur a little downtime and you need to plan for it. Always add downtime planning as one of the items on your checklist.

The divide and conquer technique that has served so many so well all these years also works well in creating your update checklist. The "Creating an Accessible Web Application Checklist" section of this chapter contains a complete list of the requirements for full accessibility. You can keep track of your update progress using this list, but it also comes in handy while you create your update checklist as a point of reference. (Be sure to read the detailed analysis of the legal requirements in Chapter 1 if you find any of the short descriptions confusing.)

Assume for the moment that the testing program has indeed located everything that you need to do (although you know it hasn't). You have a list of errors from the test program; it's time to go through them and see which errors are false hits. For example, most testing programs will hit your site hard with <ALT> and <LONGDESC> tag requirements because the program can't see the graphic. The testing program can't see the graphic, so most vendors assume a worst-case scenario. We'll discuss this topic in depth in the "<ALT> and <LONGDESC> Tags—the Low Tech Solution" section of Chapter 11. For now, all you need to know is that developers normally use the <LONGDESC> tag for complex graphics where an <ALT> tag may not provide enough description. After a thorough check of the legal, accessibility, and usability requirements for an individual check, decide if it's a false hit or not.

You now have a list of updates that the testing program generated and that you've verified as requiring an update. It's time to perform manual testing to verify that the testing program found everything. You should expect your list to grow at least 20% in size if you used a commercial testing program. Otherwise, your list could nearly double depending on the quality of the free testing program you used. Manual testing is critical. Make sure you use testers who are familiar with both the Section 508 requirements and the use of accessible devices. Use the accessible devices during testing.

The list you have is complete, but it is not very usable. It pays to sort the list in some way so that you can take care of all the errors for a particular issue at one time. A good method to use is to group the errors by legal requirement. This technique allows you to address all of the issues for a particular legal requirement at once so that you can check that problem off on the checklist provided in the "Creating an Accessible Web Application Checklist" section.

TIP   Sometimes it's handy to have a troubleshooting guide for times when your development effort doesn't quite go as planned. You'll find such help in Jim Buyens' book, *Troubleshooting Microsoft FrontPage 2002* (Microsoft Press, 2002). Learn more about this book at http://www.microsoft.com/mspress/books/sampchap/5576.asp#SampleChapter.

Don't get the idea that this is a one-time process. Your list actually serves two purposes. First, it does tell you what you need to fix today. Make sure you prioritize the items and get to work immediately. Second, it shows areas where the developers in your particular group are weak. People tend to follow the same practices out of habit. This list will help you learn where to focus training efforts and determine which areas require special testing as you add new pages to the Web site. In short, creating the update checklist correctly helps you obtain better Web site accessibility today and reduce the time required for testing tomorrow.

Avoiding Web Site Problems

The best way to avoid modifying your Web site to address accessibility and usability requirements is to prevent the problem from happening in the first place. It seems that this task would be easy to accomplish, but many developers find it nearly impossible because most Web projects are rushed. In addition, many Web site problems are the result of a failure to plan. In short, a better initial design would prevent the majority of Web site problems because most of them are easy to prevent.

TIP   Most accessibility problems on a Web site occur because the design doesn't consider look and feel issues. Because look and feel issues tend to affect every page on the Web site, failure to plan can mean that the same accessibility problem will appear on every page. Always consider the look and feel issues of your Web site early in the process to ensure that your site won't require a massive rework.

The following sections describe a number of common Web site accessibility and usability problems and tell you how you can prevent them from happening. You'll find that most of these issues are a matter of creating a good Web design at the outset. In some cases, fixing the problem will also require the assistance of other departments in your organization such as marketing (see the "Avoiding Screen Flicker" section). Of course, good Web design has a number of other good effects that developers have already heard about from a number of sources, including ease of maintenance, lower initial cost, and faster development time.

Some Usability Problems Are Hidden

It's easy to get into the mindset that all accessibility and usability problems are part of the user interface or appear as part of a main application feature. In many cases, usability and accessibility problems lurk below the surface—hidden, waiting to strike at the most inconvenient moment. Generally, you'll find that you need to have members of a target group completely test every application feature before you can be sure that the application complies with Section 508 requirements. Of course, some applications are so large that testing every combination of every feature is impossible, which is why we have bug fixes.

Let's look at a real world example. FrontPage, like many other products, presents a few usage problems that cause you to wonder what the vendor was thinking. One such FrontPage problem is the way it adds tables at the beginning of a page. It turns out that once you add the table, you can't add anything before it without some special editing. You can find out more about this particular problem at http://www.pcmag.com/article2/0,4149,382032,00.asp.

This error isn't an issue where Microsoft necessarily dropped the ball—it's one where Microsoft didn't consider a test sequence before product release. More importantly, the issue draws attention to a greater issue of usability and accessibility. Although FrontPage is quite accessible and usable in general, little glitches like this one could send the average user screaming in frustration—not to mention those with special needs.

Because usability and accessibility bugs can remain hidden during even the most aggressive beta test, your company should be prepared to handle them in a timely manner to ensure Section 508 compliance. Handling the bug means providing several methods for reporting errors. It also means creating a fix as soon as possible, and then making the fix available using several methods, including a CD for large updates.

Working with Animations

Animation takes several forms on Web pages, with Macromedia Flash as the most popular form. We've already discussed some of the problems with animations in other areas of the book. You'll definitely want to read the "Addressing Animation and Animation Alternatives" section of Chapter 8 if you haven't done so already. We'll also discuss the captioning requirements for animation in the "Captioning

Movies and Other Video Presentations" section of Chapter 11. Once you decide that you really do need to use animation and have created the animation so that it's accessible, you need to consider how to present the animation on a Web site.

Unlike a desktop application, Web applications have serious bandwidth limitations and animation requires a lot of bandwidth. Although you can say that a specific application required animation to get the point across, you must consider first whether an animated solution is even viable. Developers have tried to solve the problem using solutions like streaming media, but have only been partially successful. For example, RealAudio plays relatively well over a dial-up connection, but the sound quality is definitely not as good as listening to a radio. If your target audience will use mainly dial-up connections, then the use of animation is a real problem.

 NOTE As in many areas of Web design, there are exceptions to the animation rule. A properly designed animated GIF, one in which the developer optimizes every transition, can provide very basic animation at a relatively low bandwidth cost. However, it's important to remember that even a small animated GIF can become a problem if the target user for your Web site is using a low-speed connection.

When working with Web site applications, you should make animation an alternative or optional portion of the presentation. Consider using slide shows (such as those created with Microsoft PowerPoint) as an alternative. Always allow the user to download the animation to play it locally, rather than rely on a high-speed connection from your Web site. The best Web sites are the ones that ask the user what type of connection they're using and set up the animation accordingly. Using this technique, you won't penalize visitors who do have a high-speed connection and those with a dial-up connection can still participate.

Applets and Plug-Ins

Unless you're living in a cave on some far off tropical island devoid of people, you know that crackers have become increasingly flagrant about releasing viruses that affect Web-related activities such as using applets and plug-ins. In addition, the scripts associated with applets and plug-ins often cause problems with screen readers and other accessible products. (We discuss the issue of accessible scripting in Chapter 13.) In fact, many security experts advocate turning off all scripting, plug-in, and applet support to keep the system safe. Consequently, users are wary about installing either applets or plug-ins on their system. Many users have turned all scripting support off in order to avoid the viruses they bring.

NOTE   For the purposes of this book, the term *cracker* will always refer to an individual who's breaking into a system on an unauthorized basis. This includes any form of illegal activity on the system. On the other hand, a *hacker* will refer to someone who performs authorized (legal) low-level system activities, including testing system security. In some cases, you need to employ the services of a good hacker to test the security measures you have in place, or suffer the consequences of a break-in. This book will use the term *hacker* to refer to someone who performs these legal forms of service. The best way to view the difference (at least if you like western movies) is that the hacker wears a white hat and the cracker wears a black hat.

Applets and plug-ins aren't evil and I'm sure the vendors that create them aren't happy about the way crackers exploit these useful tools. The fact remains that you'll reduce the usability of your Web site if it relies on applets and plug-ins for essential services on a public site. You'll notice that I included several important terms in this description. An applet or plug-in used to provide nonessential services that don't affect the content or usability of the Web site are always welcome. In fact, many users recognize the value of adding applets and plug-ins in making a site more accessible.

It's also true that applets and plug-ins provide value to private Web sites—those not in general use by the public. For example, your company could provide a catalog service just to customers. A customer who chooses to use a Web site for private access should have more confidence in the integrity of that site and could add it to a list of trusted sites. Most browsers include separate security settings for the general Internet and trusted sites, as shown in the Internet Options dialog box in Figure 9-10.

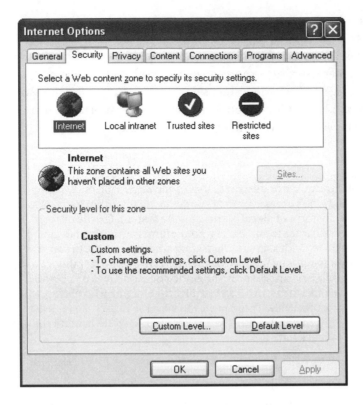

Figure 9-10. The Internet Options dialog box demonstrates the security-level settings many browsers employ today.

To sum it all up, applets and plug-ins are risky additions to public Web sites and you should never rely on them to perform essential tasks. However, it's important to realize that applets and plug-ins are useful for performing optional tasks, especially if that support makes the site more accessible. In general, it's fine to use applets and plug-ins for all tasks on private sites, but only if the people using that site are amenable to adding the site to their list of trusted sites.

Color

We discussed color thoroughly in the "Building the Color Blindness Simulator Example" section of Chapter 4 (as well as other areas in the book). Generally, if a user can't see the color combinations used for a desktop application, they won't see those same colors on a Web site. However, it's important to note that color becomes even more critical on a Web site because many browsers reduce the spectrum from the 256+ colors used on the desktop to the 216-color standard palette used for Web applications.

In general, stick with the high contrast solution of black text on a white background when you can. If you find that you must use color, then try to use the standard color combinations listed at `http://more.btexact.com/people/rigdence/colours/colours1.htm`. This Web site also shows how these colors will appear to someone with color blindness—an important consideration if you want to ensure that someone can see the content your site presents.

Fonts

You might view fonts as one of those no-brainer parts of Web site construction. However, the proper use of fonts can have a big impact on how other people view your Web site. A font that looks fine to you might not appeal to someone else. Aesthetic value aside, the choice of font also determines the readability of your Web site. If you choose a font that's too small or of the wrong type, someone might not be able to read the information on your Web site at all.

Most browsers come with the ability to change the size of the font. For example, all you need to do with Internet Explorer is use one of the options on the View ➤ Text Size menu. Unfortunately, this feature doesn't work when you use a style sheet with your Web site—at least if you code the style sheet using the same techniques that most developers use. When you choose a specific typeface and font size, you're telling the user to read the Web site your way, or no way at all. At first, I thought this was something that only bothered me, but it's attracted the attention of others as you can read in this article: `http://www.useit.com/alertbox/20020819.html`.

 ON THE WEB   Sometimes it's difficult to find just the right character to display on a Web site. For example, you might need to display the copyright symbol (©). One of the better places to find these special symbols is the HTML Character Codes site at `http://home.online.no/~pethesse/charcodes.html`.

Generally, you want to choose a reasonably large font for the default and then use relative sizing to ensure that any changes made by the user will automatically change the rest of the fonts on the page as well. (Make sure you use the header tags wherever possible to ensure that the viewer has maximum flexibility in resizing the fonts.) If you choose to use style sheets, don't force the user to rely on a single fancy style sheet. Provide a separate style sheet for users who want a high contrast, large font presentation. You might also want to include a separate style sheet for those who need to have the page presented in a different way due to color blindness or other visual problems. Always make sure that your Web page will work without the style sheet because a screen reader won't use it.

Fortunately, some browsers are making it easier for the user to determine what they'd like the Web page to look like. For example, click the Accessibility button on the General tab of the Internet Options dialog box for Internet Explorer 4.01 and above and you'll see the Accessibility dialog box shown in Figure 9-11. As you can see, the options on this dialog box make it possible for the user to ignore the fonts and colors selected by the developer, and even use their own style sheet. Unfortunately, only users of the newest and most feature-packed browsers will have access to this functionality.

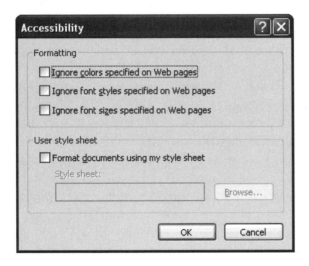

Figure 9-11. Some users will have access to new browser features such as those found on the Accessibility dialog box shown here.

Forms

We've already discussed forms for desktop applications in several areas of the book. In general, forms must provide a way to track the screen focus (see the "Tracking the Screen Focus" section of Chapter 5). A form must also provide the user with assistance in inputting content (see the "Considering Balloon Help Issues" and "Adding Context Sensitive Help" sections of Chapter 7).

As you'll learn in the "Using Keyboard Shortcuts Example" section, the technique for providing shortcut keys and balloon help to a Web application differ from those used for a desktop application. In this case, you'll use the accesskey attribute to provide a shortcut to the field or control. The title attribute provides the balloon help needed for the user. To add context sensitive help, you need to add a "D" type link to each field. The keyboard shortcuts example will show you how to perform this task as well.

PDFs—A Special Type of Form Problem

Making a Web site accessible means creating content that everyone can use, no matter what form that content takes. Many developers associate forms with a type of content that you use to answer questions online and submit immediately. However, many companies make other types of forms available—the most common of which is the PDF form. A PDF form contains content that you download, print, and mail or fax to the company.

The problem with PDFs is that they contain complex text that screen readers find difficult to parse. Consequently, these forms are often difficult for those with special needs to view and understand. Although the user won't add content to a PDF form online, they still must understand the information contained on the form. The user needs to know if they've found the correct form and if the form addresses their needs before they download it.

The Internal Revenue Service (IRS) is one of the companies that use the PDF extensively. Almost any form and accompanying booklet that you need comes in PDF form on the IRS Web site. Unfortunately, like everyone else, the IRS ran into a problem trying to make these forms accessible. Eventually, the IRS found a solution by working with Adobe, and this solution appears in Adobe Reader Version 5.0 and above. You can read more about this solution at http://www.fcw.com/fcw/articles/2002/0624/cov-5081-06-24-02.asp and http://www.washingtonpost.com/wp-dyn/articles/A13536-2002Aug29.html.

As a developer, you can learn three essential lessons from the IRS example. First, all forms must provide accessible content, even PDFs. This requirement means you need to use version 5.0 or above of the Adobe product when creating content for your Web site. Second, sometimes an accessibility solution requires the cooperation of more than one company—the IRS couldn't have solved this problem by itself. In some cases, you'll find that you need a little extra outside help, too. Third, adhering to the accessibility requirements can require time and patience. The IRS has worked on this problem for several years. Your accessibility solution can require time and effort as well—the standards require that you make a continuing effort toward full compliance as company resources permit.

Frames

Unlike many of the other features discussed so far, using frames on your Web site is always wrong. Frames organize data in a way that makes it nearly impossible for many accessibility features to work properly. The fact that each frame in a window requires a separate document also increases the chance that an update in one window won't appear in another. In general, frames are simply a bad idea and you should avoid using them.

 ON THE WEB   Although I personally view frames as one of the worst possible features you can add to a Web page, you can use frames in ways that enhance accessibility. You'll find a full treatment of this topic at `http://www.w3.org/TR/2000/NOTE-WCAG10-HTML-TECHS-20000920/#frames`.

Repetitive Navigation

Many developers neglect the fine art of creating page links when designing their Web pages. It's an art to place the links precisely where the user will need them, and use them in no more than one location on any given page. In many situations, you'll see Web pages that have the same link four or five times on the same page. At first, this would appear to make the page more accessible. However, hearing the page a few times with a screen reader will tell you otherwise. The page reader will continue reading those links no matter how many times the user has heard them. In some cases, leaving the page is better than hearing the same repetitive link one more time.

Legally, you can provide a means to skip repetitive links on the same page. After studying a number of Web sites, you'll learn that no one provides this feature and those that attempt to provide it fail. In sum, forget about providing a method of skipping repetitive single-page links and think about designing your site correctly the first time.

Another type of repetitive link is the type that appears across multiple pages. A developer provides the same set of links across the top or on the left side of the page so that a user can access all parts of the Web site from the current page. You must provide a means of skipping these repetitive links. Otherwise, the user of your site will have to listen to the same links for every page—the ultimate in boring experiences.

Avoiding Screen Flicker

One of the most underrated, yet severe problems that a Web site can have is screen flicker. Screen flicker can occur from a number of sources, and it is one of the few problems that the developer can't control fully. A screen that flickers can cause something as mild as a headache or as severe as death. This problem goes well beyond inconvenient—all countries should make it illegal for any reason.

Avoiding screen flicker is relatively easy from a programming sense because it's something you have to add to the Web site design. There isn't any reason to add timed color adjustments or other pseudo-animation effects to a Web site. The fact that someone is viewing the site means that you've already attracted their attention and making the screen flash does nothing but send them in the other direction.

Animated GIFs and other forms of animation are much harder to consider. The developer inserts the code to display the animated GIF or other animation but doesn't control the content. This is one area where cooperation with other departments in an organization becomes important. The developer needs to contact the art department and ensure that any animated GIFs provide content in a way that's aesthetically pleasing and still conforms to the requirements.

Banner ads present a special problem because someone outside of the local company creates the content. In fact, this is the number one problem with flashing on most Web sites today. The banner ads flash at such a rate that they distract the viewer from seeing the content on the site. The sales staff for your company (the people who contract for the banner ads) should be aware of the problems that flashing banner ads can cause.

Scripts

After reading about the problems with scripts for a while, you'll wonder if they're really worth all the effort. They cause so many problems that some users simply turn the script functionality for their browser off. In general, if you can get by without using a script, do so, because many users won't have them turned on.

You can use scripts successfully when necessary, however, and they can even enhance both the accessibility and usability of your Web site. We'll discuss this use of scripts in detail in Chapter 13. You might be surprised to find that scripts can be a useful ally in making your Web site a better place for users to visit. Once users understand that your site is safe, they may even turn their scripting support back on.

Tables

Developers use several classifications of tables on Web sites. Some tables are extremely helpful and you can't get by without them. Other tables are anachronisms that everyone would be better without.

The most helpful tables organize repetitive data, such as the information returned from a database. Developers can also create tables by hand. In general, make sure that every table has a title. Each column should have a properly marked header and this header should describe the content of the column fully. Avoid creating complex tables—essentially a table within a table. The requirement to develop square tables that contain the same number of columns from top to bottom is easier to understand when heard from a screen reader. Although there are many ways to lay out a table, the two typical formats shown in the "Creating Accessibility Friendly Tables Example" section work best.

Many developers have used tables for a purpose that has nothing to do with data organization. The use of tables to define the presentation of data is still quite common. The table itself is hidden to the viewer, but not to the screen reader. If you must organize the data on a page in a specific way, use a style sheet to do it, not a table. We'll discuss style sheets as part of the "Using CSS Example" section in Chapter 11.

Timed Responses

The first thing you should think about when considering a timed response is if it's necessary. Many Web sites use timed responses for links that could easily work without any timing at all. In some cases, the timing sequence doesn't even work—leaving the user at a screen that says that the Web server will redirect them in a moment. In general, don't use timed responses unless you really need them to provide better service to the user.

In the "Exposing the Screen Focus" section of Chapter 7, we discussed several issues that included the TimerButton control. This control permits the developer to create an automatic click for desktop applications. It's the equivalent of the timed response for Web pages. However, this control emphasized a feature that most Web pages don't include—a feature that enables the user to modify the timing interval to meet their specific needs. You could easily adapt the TimerButton to Web development needs.

If you don't use a control such as the TimerButton to provide access to the timing interval for a Web site response, you must provide some other way to do it. The technique used could be something as easily accessible as a link that takes the user to a page where they can contemplate the issue at their leisure and then provide a non-timed response. Of course, if you can create such a Web site, then the question of whether the Web site needs the timed response comes up again.

Creating an Accessible Web Application Checklist

Sometimes using a checklist is the easiest way to ensure that you've addressed all of the requirements for an application. It's time to look at the requirements for a desktop application from a checklist perspective. Table 9-1 contains the Section 508 requirement, the legal requirement, and two columns for making a decision. Just in case you've forgotten what these rules mean, check out the detailed analysis in Chapter 1. As you design and develop your application, make a choice. Mark the requirement as completed or place a check in the Undue Burden column to indicate that this is a requirement you'll handle later. (Remember from Chapter 1 that you must observe all requirements but can postpone some requirements if you can prove the requirement places an undue burden on your company.)

Table 9-1. Accessible Checklist for Web Applications

Section	Legal Requirement	Completed	Undue Burden
WEB-BASED INTRANET AND INTERNET INFORMATION AND APPLICATIONS			
1194.22(a)	A text equivalent for every non-text element shall be provided (e.g., via "alt", "longdesc", or in element content).		
1194.22(b)	Equivalent alternatives for any multimedia presentation shall be synchronized with the presentation.		
1194.22(c)	Web pages shall be designed so that all information conveyed with color is also available without color, for example from context or markup.		
1194.22(d)	Documents shall be organized so they are readable without requiring an associated style sheet.		
1194.22(e)	Redundant text links shall be provided for each active region of a server-side image map.		
1194.22(f)	Client-side image maps shall be provided instead of server-side image maps except where the regions cannot be defined with an available geometric shape.		
1194.22(g)	Row and column headers shall be identified for data tables.		
1194.22(h)	Markup shall be used to associate data cells and header cells for data tables that have two or more logical levels of row or column headers.		

Table 9-1. Accessible Checklist for Web Applications (Continued)

Section	Legal Requirement	Completed	Undue Burden
1194.22(i)	Frames shall be titled with text that facilitates frame identification and navigation.		
1194.22(j)	Pages shall be designed to avoid causing the screen to flicker with a frequency greater than 2 Hz and lower than 55 Hz.		
1194.22(k)	A text-only page, with equivalent information or functionality, shall be provided to make a web site comply with the provisions of this part, when compliance cannot be accomplished in any other way. The content of the text-only page shall be updated whenever the primary page changes.		
1194.22(l)	When pages utilize scripting languages to display content, or to create interface elements, the information provided by the script shall be identified with functional text that can be read by assistive technology.		
1194.22(m)	When a web page requires that an applet, plug-in or other application be present on the client system to interpret page content, the page must provide a link to a plug-in or applet that complies with §1194.21(a) through (l).		
1194.22(n)	When electronic forms are designed to be completed on-line, the form shall allow people using assistive technology to access the information, field elements, and functionality required for completion and submission of the form, including all directions and cues.		
1194.22(o)	A method shall be provided that permits users to skip repetitive navigation links.		
1194.22(p)	When a timed response is required, the user shall be alerted and given sufficient time to indicate more time is required.		

Table 9-1. Accessible Checklist for Web Applications (Continued)

Section	Legal Requirement	Completed	Undue Burden
VIDEO OR MULTIMEDIA PRODUCTS			
1194.24(c)	All training and informational video and multimedia productions which support the agency's mission, regardless of format, that contain speech or other audio information necessary for the comprehension of the content, shall be open or closed captioned.		
1194.24(d)	All training and informational video and multimedia productions which support the agency's mission, regardless of format, that contain visual information necessary for the comprehension of the content, shall be audio described.		
1194.24(e)	Display or presentation of alternate text presentation or audio descriptions shall be user-selectable unless permanent.		
FUNCTIONAL PERFORMANCE CRITERIA			
Subpart C(a)	At least one mode of operation and information retrieval that does not require user vision shall be provided, or support for assistive technology used by people who are blind or visually impaired shall be provided.		
Subpart C(b)	At least one mode of operation and information retrieval that does not require visual acuity greater than 20/70 shall be provided in audio and enlarged print output working together or independently, or support for assistive technology used by people who are visually impaired shall be provided.		
Subpart C(c)	At least one mode of operation and information retrieval that does not require user hearing shall be provided, or support for assistive technology used by people who are deaf or hard of hearing shall be provided.		
Subpart C(d)	Where audio information is important for the use of a product, at least one mode of operation and information retrieval shall be provided in an enhanced auditory fashion, or support for assistive hearing devices shall be provided.		

Table 9-1. Accessible Checklist for Web Applications (Continued)

Section	Legal Requirement	Completed	Undue Burden
Subpart C(e)	At least one mode of operation and information retrieval that does not require user speech shall be provided, or support for assistive technology used by people with disabilities shall be provided.		
Subpart C(f)	At least one mode of operation and information retrieval that does not require fine motor control or simultaneous actions and that is operable with limited reach and strength shall be provided.		
INFORMATION, DOCUMENTATION, AND SUPPORT			
Subpart D(a)	Product support documentation provided to end-users shall be made available in alternate formats upon request, at no additional charge.		
Subpart D(b)	End-users shall have access to a description of the accessibility and compatibility features of products in alternate formats or alternate methods upon request, at no additional charge.		
Subpart D(c)	Support services for products shall accommodate the communication needs of end-users with disabilities.		

Creating Accessibility Friendly Tables Example

As previously mentioned, accessibility friendly tables store information rather than layouts. However, accessible tables contain a few other elements than just information. This section of the chapter provides a quick overview of the two table types commonly used on Web sites that are easiest to read using a screen reader. Note that Narrator may not be much use when working with this type of content. You'll want to download the JAWS demonstration version (http://www.freedomscientific.com/fs_downloads/jaws.asp) and use it for these examples.

ON THE WEB   If you plan to make your mobile applications accessibility friendly as well, you'll probably need an emulator or two to test your application. Microsoft's eMbedded Visual Tools 3.0 provides three emulators including a Pocket PC, Handheld PC Pro, and a Palm device. You can find this toolkit at `http://msdn.microsoft.com/downloads/` `sample.asp?url=/MSDN-FILES/027/001/963/msdncompositedoc.xml`. If you decide that you want to test a cellular telephone, then the SmartPhone Web site (`http://www.yospace.com/`) offers a five-day trial version of their product that you can use for testing. (Of course, if you like their product, you'll want to buy your own license.) Another good product to try is the Openwave emulator available at `http://` `developer.openwave.com/download/index.html`. This emulator includes several cellular telephone incarnations that can be very helpful for testing.

Figure 9-12 shows the tables we'll discuss in this section. You'll find the code for these tables in the \Chapter 09\Tables folder of the source code that you can obtain from the Downloads section of the Apress Web site (`http://www.apress.com`). The code consists of standard HTML with a few special attributes added to the tags.

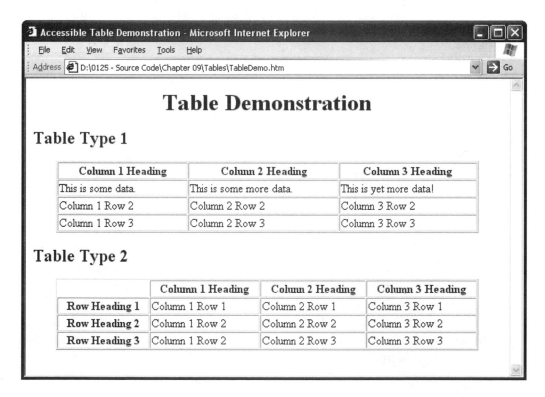

Figure 9-12. An example of the two types of tables commonly used on Web sites

You should notice a few construction details about this table. First, notice that each table has a title. This title describes what the table contains (demonstration information). The column headings rely on the <TH> tag pair, not the <TD> tag pair. If you use the <TD> tag pair for the column headings, the screen reader won't know it's a heading and will read it as data. The same holds true for row headings. If you include a row heading, such as the one shown in Table Type 2, then make sure you use the <TH> tag pair for just the heading (not the data). Data should always appear within the <TD> tag pair.

Each of the headings also produces balloon help containing additional information. The screen real estate for Web applications is often limited, which means that developers use short headings whenever possible. The addition of balloon help makes it possible for the user to receive additional information. To use this feature, add a title attribute to each of the headings. When users hover the mouse over the heading, they'll receive additional information about that heading.

Using Keyboard Shortcuts Example

In the desktop section of the book, you learned just how important keyboard shortcuts can be to the user. Adding these shortcuts was almost too simple for desktop applications. All you needed to do was add a simple entry to the label for a field. Working with shortcuts for Web applications is somewhat similar.

 CAUTION Avoid assuming too much about the capabilities of the browser and other software that the user will employ to access your Web site. For example, some screen readers aren't compatible with the accessKey attribute associated with the on-screen elements. Normally, the user can press Alt, followed by the accessKey value to access a specific screen element. Read more about this problem in the Q306448 Knowledge Base article entitled, "INFO: Some Screen Readers Are Not Fully Compatible with Access Keys." Interestingly enough, this article isn't available online, but it is available in the help file at ms-help:// MS.MSDNQTR.2003FEB.1033/enu_kbie_dev/en-us/ie_dev/Q306448.htm.

Figure 9-13 shows a data entry form. This form isn't functional—I only created it to show some accessibility features. We'll create functional forms later in the book. You can find the code for this example in the \Chapter 09\Forms folder of the source code that you can obtain from the Downloads section of the Apress Web site (http://www.apress.com).

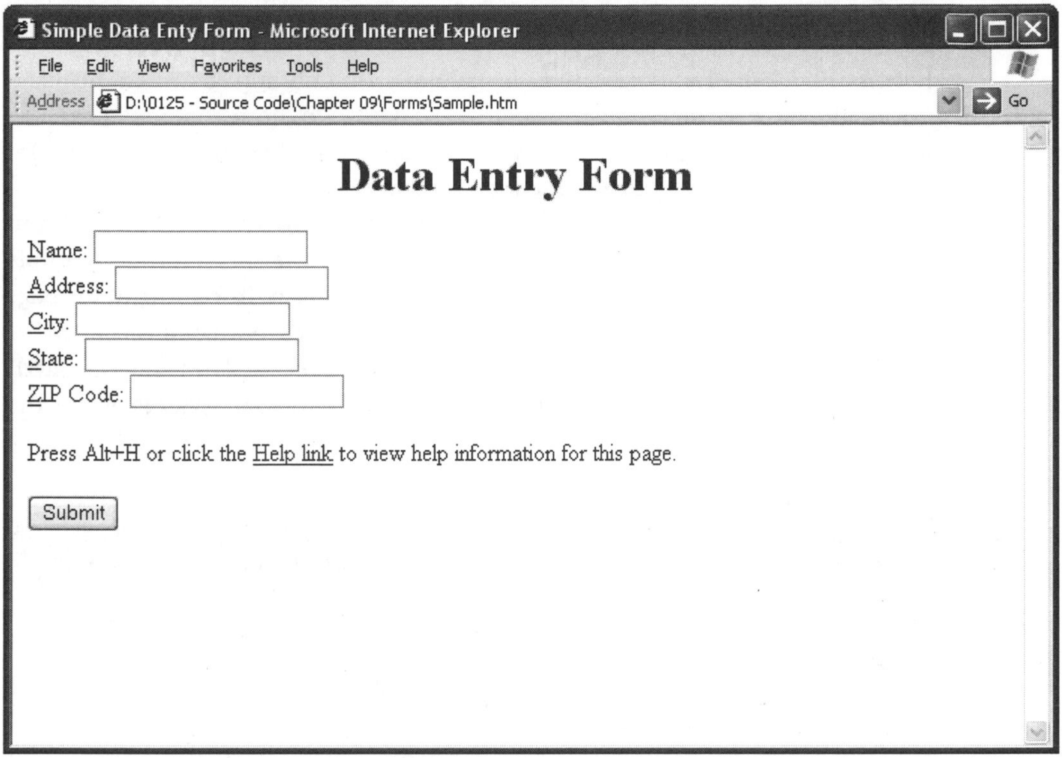

Figure 9-13. Using this simple data entry form will demonstrate the use of both tooltips and keyboard shortcuts.

You should notice a few features about this page. First, each of the labels preceding a field has an underlined letter. This letter doesn't add any functionality as it would for a Windows application. All that the underlining does is provide a visual cue for the viewer. To add the keyboard shortcut, you must include the accesskey attribute as part of the <INPUT> tag for the text box. Consequently, the keyboard shortcut is associated with the actual text box, rather than the label preceding it. (You can also follow the Microsoft conventions where the label is the focus of the shortcut—read about it at http://msdn.microsoft.com/workshop/author/dhtml/reference/properties/accesskey.asp.)

Unfortunately, you have to use the underlined characters carefully. The accesskey attribute accepts a single letter as input. Every shortcut is an Alt key combination. In short, if you have more than 36 fields (letters A through Z and numbers 0 through 9) on a form, then you'll run out of accesskey attribute combinations.

This page also provides balloon help for every field. Like the table example we discussed earlier, you'll use the `title` attribute to create the balloon help. It becomes obvious, in this case, that the balloon help only appears when the user hovers the mouse over the field. Selecting the field with the keyboard doesn't display the balloon help. Fortunately, the screen readers I tested all say the `title` attribute text even if it doesn't appear on screen.

Notice that the bottom of the page in Figure 9-13 shows a help link. All of your data entry forms should include some type of help. Figure 9-14 shows the sample help for this example. The help page also includes a link at the bottom of the page to return to the data entry form. Like the data entry fields, both of these links include a keyboard shortcut that makes them easy to access. The text associated with the link tells the reader what key combination to press in order to access the link quickly.

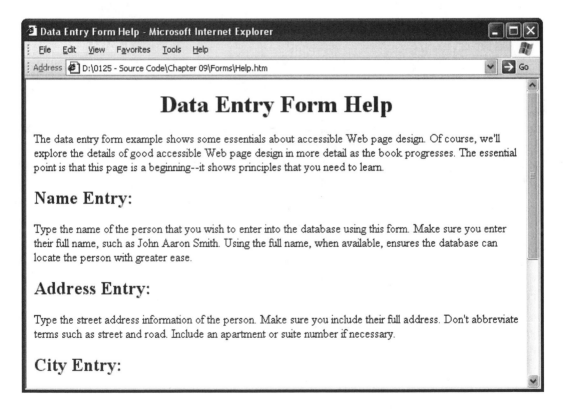

Figure 9-14. Your data entry forms should include some type of help dialog.

Schema Additions for the Database Developer

Many Web sites run off a database today. The developer creates a template page, places the content for the template in a database, and then combines the two when a user makes a request. Using this technique makes it easier to manage large Web sites and reduces the time required to get an update to appear on the Web site. No one has to modify Web pages—all they need to do is modify the database and templates.

Using a database means that you must also consider accessibility concerns as part of the database design. The following sections describe two additions that you'll want to make to any database that contains Web site content. These additions greatly reduce the work required to make your Web site accessible because they work with the templates you've already created.

ALT and LONGDESC Fields

These two fields should appear with the table that manages the images for your Web site. Every graphic on your Web page requires an <ALT> tag to describe the content of that image to someone who can't see it. For example, you might place a small icon on the page that says, "New" on it. The <ALT> tag for the image might say, "This is a new item icon." so that the user will know that the icon simply says "New" on it.

You can't easily describe complex graphics, such as charts, graphs, or drawings, using a sentence or two. Consequently, the various standards committees created the <LONGDESC> tag. This tag points to a Web page that contains a complete description of the complex graphic.

If you keep all of your images in one table, then you'll need to add both fields to that table. In addition, the logic for the template that creates the Web page will need to know that if the LONGDESC field entry is blank, then the image in question is simple and the template should output just the <ALT> tag.

A better choice is to create one table for simple graphics—those that need just the <ALT> tag and a second table for complex graphics—those that need both the <ALT> and the <LONGDESC> tags. Using this technique, you can make your template logic simpler and will also ensure that the database user has to make a conscious decision about the complexity of the image. In general, this method is better because it helps reduce the number of accessibility errors on a Web page.

Script Alternative Text Fields

We've discussed some of the problems with using scripts in this chapter and will continue to discuss them as the book progresses. If you store the scripts for your Web site in a database, then you'll also want to create a script alternative field for the table in question. The script alternative field would contain the text that describes the script. For example, if a script is used to display banner ads, you would include a text description of this function in the script alternative field and display this information if the user doesn't have scripting support enabled.

Summary

This chapter represents your first step into accessibility programming for Web sites. We looked at problem areas you'll need to consider for your own projects and discussed how to solve them. This chapter also contains a number of application programming examples that demonstrate various programming techniques. Together, the elements of this chapter have prepared you to begin creating your own accessibility friendly applications and perform updates of existing Web sites.

So what do you do now? First, you should check your Web pages using one of the tools that we discussed in this chapter. Once you have a report, begin creating a schedule for updating and fixing Web pages with problems. You don't have to fix everything at once, but you should fix as many items as possible.

It's also important to begin narrowing down problems that the reports might not have located for you. For example, does your Web application provide keyboard shortcuts? You also have to ask yourself about the potential problems of hidden timers and alerts that could cause problems for users of your Web site.

Chapter 10 is the next step in the process. You'll learn to create a text-only Web site of your own. The next chapter discusses the viability of using text-only Web sites for many business needs. No, they aren't as glamorous as the Web sites that include a number of gadgets, but they are considerably easier to use. These Web sites concentrate on content and ease-of-use over pizzazz.

Designing Easily Maintained Web Sites

In This Chapter:

Learn Why You Should Avoid the Text-Only Web Site

Learn Why Separate Standard and Accessible Web Page Versions Aren't Equal

Understand Why Universal Design Is So Important

Discover the Benefits of Using an Easily Maintained Setup

Understand When You Should Use an Easily Maintained Setup

Discover How Easy It Is to Use Easily Maintained Design Effectively

Build Your Own Easily Maintained Web Site

MANY OF THE WEB SITES that I visit are so incredibly complex I have to wonder how the person in charge of the site keeps track of the functionality provided. In many cases, it's obvious that the person responsible for maintenance hasn't kept pace with the functionality and the site is in dire need of repair. The purpose of all this glitter is to attract attention—to make the Web site more appealing. The opposite effect actually occurs. A combination of poor maintenance, nonexistent usability, features that don't work on every browser, and information overload often make the site inaccessible even to experts.

This chapter concentrates on the easily maintained Web site. What precisely do I mean by that term? An *easily maintained Web site* uses special features only when they serve a purpose. The same holds true for graphics and other glitter that tend to cause problems for those with special needs. Because an easily maintained Web site is easy to use and understand, it contains fewer failure points and consequently, fewer things that can break. It's easy to maintain using a simple text editor (should that be the only tool the author has).

A special point of this chapter is the need to meet the requirements of section 1194.22(k) of the Section 508 law that reads,

A text-only page, with equivalent information or functionality, shall be provided to make a web site comply with the provisions of this part, when compliance cannot be accomplished in any other way. The content of the text-only page shall be updated whenever the primary page changes.

The essence of this rule is laudable, but reckless, because no one's going to follow it completely. The text-only Web page often becomes a second-class citizen that contains old content and few features that make a Web site unique. This chapter will concentrate on creating a simple Web site that fulfills all of the requirements of the law, allows everyone complete access to the Web site content, and is still easy to maintain. In short, this chapter is about a minimalist approach to Web site design that makes life easy by promoting accessibility for everyone.

Avoiding the Text-Only Web Site

Legally, you can create a text-only version of a Web site and provide that version in place of your "standard" Web site. Several of the places I visited while researching this book use the two-site option—with the second Web site providing a text-only presentation. The problem with this approach is that it doesn't address the essential problem with Web sites that are inaccessible to people with specific needs. Anyone who lived through the 1960s will remember the general problem with the "separate, but equal" approach to providing fair access to resources—it simply doesn't work.

The following sections help you understand why the text-only Web site came into being, what it fails to accomplish, and how you can avoid using it. More importantly, it helps you learn from history so that you don't end up repeating the same mistakes of those who have gone before. It's important to know why these solutions can't meet all the accessibility needs of those who wish to visit your Web site.

History of the Text-Only Option

Many developers are under the impression that the evolution of the Internet was a somewhat orderly progression. Certainly, the abbreviated histories that you find buried on many Web sites would tend to lend credence to such a view. However, the reality is that the Internet has progressed in an almost chaotic fashion, with little rhyme or reason in its evolution.

When developers first began to understand the need for accessible applications for the Web, the Internet had few standards. After all, the Internet, at this point, was mainly used to pass documents between universities. Commercialization of the Internet meant that some content became inaccessible because it was no longer pure text and included a number of new features that made use with screen readers and other accessibility aids nearly impossible.

It was during this time that the first accessibility initiatives began to appear. You have to remember that technologies such as Cascading Style Sheets (CSS) didn't exist at all. Developers originally conceived the HyperText Markup Language (HTML) as an easier-to-use subset of the Standard Generalized Markup Language (SGML), which is a structured markup language separate from presentation. The ability of a developer to create a fully accessible site that also included the functionality that other areas of the company (such as marketing) wanted was somewhat limited. Consequently, some developers and vendors misused tags such as <TABLE> and asked standards committees to add tags such as <FONT>. The misuse of some tags and the addition of others reduced the accessibility of the Web sites. This is the environment where the "text-only" Web page came into being. The requirement recognized the state of the Internet at the time and allowed developers to create two pages—one with, and one without, fancy features.

Today developers do have access to a number of technologies that can make their Web pages accessible without sacrificing the formatting and other features that many users see as needed. You'll learn about a number of techniques for creating accessible Web sites that also have pizzazz as the book progresses. In short, although the various accessibility initiatives still allow the use of a text-only Web page, developers no longer require this alternative to creating an accessible Web page. In fact, as we'll discuss in the "Separate Is Not Equal" section, using this technique is actually counterproductive in many situations.

Separate Is Not Equal

The concept of separate, but equal, has seen many incarnations throughout history. Inevitably, the principle appears shortsighted and unmaintainable at some point, because the concept infers that two implementations of the same concept will receive the same treatment, which is impossible in the best of circumstances. The text-only Web site was doomed from the start for this reason. Users of accessible technology found that the text-only version of pages on most Web sites contained outdated information (when they were maintained at all) and generally lacked features that the "standard" Web page had. The text-only Web site became a second-class Internet citizen.

Even if the developer maintains two versions of a Web page in perfect synchronization and both include the same user-level features, there's another problem to consider. The amount of time and resources spent to keep one Web site updated today are considerable. Many of the Web sites you visit will maintain the same information month after month because there are no resources to perform required updates. Keeping two Web sites running seems impossible given the current economy and yet, this is what the use of a text-only version of every page on your Web site would entail. In short, even if a company has good intentions, economically, a text-only version of your Web page doesn't make sense.

Understanding the Concept of Universal Design

At some point, a company will come the realization that maintaining a single Web site is the only reasonable course of action. However, there's the problem of making the site accessible to consider. In addition, many developers now have to consider access by mobile devices. In short, Web sites require some type of universal design that not only provides desktop users with the information they need, but also addresses accessibility and mobile device needs. The problem seems insurmountable, but you'll find there are a number of solutions.

One alternative that we'll discuss in the "Using the Mobile Device Page as an Example" section of the chapter is to use the mobile device as a basis for your application. It sounds like an unworkable idea, but it really works quite well. By providing alternatives for the Web page configuration based on the type of input device, you'll find that your mobile design is extremely flexible and changes to match the capabilities of the device. In addition, most mobile compatible Web pages are automatically accessible because of the limited capabilities of these devices.

Universal design means creating flexible Web pages that work anywhere with any device. It's a principle that you can use to create accessible Web pages. It's true that the pages will lack some of the usual pizzazz that many developers have fallen in love with over the years. However, you'll find that users complain less because they can always access the information the Web page has to provide. The origins of this concept come from the field of architecture and were advanced in the 1970s by Ron Mace (learn more about the history of universal design at http://www.design.ncsu.edu/cud/center/history/ronmace.htm and http://www.design.ncsu.edu/cud/univ_design/udhistory.htm).

 ON THE WEB   Many companies have become proactive about providing status information about the accessibility of their applications. Of course, getting this information in a format that varies by vendor isn't very helpful, so the vendors have come up with a common format known as Voluntary Product Accessibility Templates (VPATs). For example, you can see the explanation of accessibility conformance and VPAT availability for Siebel at http://www.siebel.com/products/accessibility/products.shtm. The Microsoft form of this information appears at http://www.microsoft.com/usa/government/section508.asp. Estrada Web Technology actually makes their VPAT available for viewing online (http://www.estrada-onstage.com/e/e.asp?durki=683). Learn more about VPATs at http://www.itic.org/policy/access_0106.htm. You can see the actual VPAT format at http://www.itic.org/policy/vpat.html. Learn the U.S. government view of VPATs at http://www.section508.gov/index.cfm?FuseAction=Content&ID=99.

Knowing When an Easily Maintained Setup Is Required

This chapter introduces the concept of the easily maintained Web site. The target site has to be accessible (of course) and run well on any device that tries to access it. We'll use Internet Information Server (IIS) for the example in this chapter, but the same principles apply when using other Web servers. Of course, the essential issue for most developers is learning to see when their company needs this type of site. Not everyone will be happy with the plain appearance of the application in this section.

In general, you wouldn't want to use this type of construction for anything too complex. For example, an e-commerce site relies on pizzazz to a certain extent to attract customers. However, most users won't access such a site using their cellular telephone because it doesn't make sense to do so—at least not today. A business could also restrict mission critical database access to the desktop, which ensures that the user has the resources required to work with the application quickly— using a cellular telephone to input complex data doesn't make sense.

The easily maintained setup does work well for informational or simple input applications. For example, a network administrator might want to know the status of the network. A cellular telephone provides enough capability and screen space to permit scrolling through such information with relative ease. A contact management database is also a good example of a custom application that could work well with the easily maintained approach. Any application where the user is mainly concerned with information retrieval works well.

Using Easily Maintained Design Effectively

The easily maintained Web site eschews some of the gizmos and non-features provided by some Web sites in the interest of speed and efficiency. The point of this Web site design is to create something that a developer can put together quickly, maintain in record time, and yet provides the flexibility and functionality to make it both accessible and usable.

ON THE WEB   You'll find a number of Internet articles that provide insight on ways to use accessible technology to make life easier for everyone. One of the more interesting articles that I've found is, "An Introduction To Accessible Web Design" by Nigel Peck (`http://www.webmasterbase.com/article/952`). Like many other introductory articles, this one discusses the basic reasons for using accessible technologies. However, the author then begins to look at some alternative uses, and that's what makes the article most useful and interesting to someone who's already read quite a bit on the topic. While I'm not sure that using accessible technology is the right thing to do for people who are driving, many of the other suggestions have a lot of merit.

This short description doesn't really do the easily maintained Web site justice. The following sections detail some of the features that make this type of design unique. Of course, the deciding factor is always what you want to achieve. As you read these sections, you'll need to decide whether the easily maintained Web site fits in with the design goals for your project.

The Trouble with Gizmos

We've discussed the gizmo mentality several times in the book. In general, anything that tends to distract the user from the central purpose of your Web application is a gizmo. A gizmo can include everything from scripts and applets, to graphics and fancy audio. In many cases, these additions are added to a Web site to make it seem fancier and to help it attract attention. Unfortunately, the opposite happens in many cases. The user becomes frustrated with the gizmos and looks elsewhere for the information needed.

From a developer perspective, the use of gizmos is time consuming and counterproductive. Using them costs the developer time. Most gizmos, even graphics, cause some type of compatibility problem. For example, just try viewing graphics on a cellular telephone—they're text-only devices. If your Web site relies on gizmos to convey content, then it might be time for a change—look for alternative methods of displaying the information.

ON THE WEB Some Web sites are worse than others are when it comes to gizmo problems. As an example of what not to do, try the TCBY site at http://www.tcby.com/. Make sure you visit with scripting and Macromedia Flash support turned off. What you'll see is a blank page. To get to a page that tells you the site won't work without Macromedia Flash installed (http://www.tcby.com/noflash.htm), the browser you use must run a script. Of course, if your browser doesn't provide script support, you get just a plain, blank page. Try accessing this site with a screen reader and you'll begin to understand how bad things can get. What a waste due to the overuse of gizmos!

Using the Mobile Device Page as an Example

In the world of simply designed Web sites, the mobile device page stands out. Consider the capabilities of a cellular telephone. They have a small screen, no graphics, and a decidedly small command set. Even a Personal Digital Assistant (PDA) has limitations that make many developers cringe—they do support graphics, but many have other limitations such as a black and white display. Some industry leaders say that these small devices will form an important type of computing in the near future and the industry has already felt the impact somewhat. Someday, the main client for your Web application might be a mobile device that someone uses on the way to work.

The restrictions imposed by a cellular telephone force the developer to create Web pages that are succinct, efficient, and flexible. Many developers are creating Web applications that work great with mobile devices. These same applications tend to provide great accessibility support as well. The lack of extraneous functionality that won't work with a mobile device tends to keep the application simple and easily usable with accessible support software such as screen readers. (It's easy to see that technology updates that everyone is using, such as cellular telephones, will also help make the Internet more accessible.)

Another advantage to developing applications with a mobile device in mind is that it forces the developer to keep input to a minimum. Mobile-device users normally don't have a keyboard available. They have to accomplish their tasks using a touch screen or a numeric keypad. Creating an application that works under these conditions will force the developer to consider every input requirement. The same thought processes that go into creating good mobile-device input also help the user with special needs.

A final reason to use the mobile device as an example of a platform that's easy to build and understand is that most language developers now include tools that help you create mobile applications with ease. The proliferation of emulators makes the applications easy to test. Creating a mobile application has become quite easy, and you'll find that it produces favorable results when you check it for problems using the various methods we discussed in Chapter 9.

As an Aid to Those Who Speak Another Language

There are many people in the world who don't speak the language you've used to create your Web site, even if the language of choice is English. Still others don't speak English as a first language—it might be a second language they use as needed to communicate with others. In general, people who fall into these two categories will find accessible technology helpful in their understanding of your Web site. The same features that help those with hearing, visual, and cognitive needs can also make your Web site friendlier on an international level.

For example, the use of both text and graphics on a page helps someone who doesn't speak the language interpret the author's intent. Textual prompts required for those with hearing and visual needs can also act as input to a translator—making it possible for someone to translate the prompts into another language. However, be assured that the translation process isn't error free. Some languages lack words that your language provides and some of the terms in these other languages won't translate well into your language. Consequently, you must overcome a communication hurdle even if your Web site provides textual prompts that another piece of software can translate.

While textual prompts and other features solve some problems, they can create others. That's where the use of cognitive aides comes into play. Consider the need to provide a means to overcome timed-response issues. This particular feature helps someone who's having trouble understanding your site due to differences in language just as much as it helps someone with cognitive needs. Both parties will likely require more time than the average person to complete the entries on the page.

We've discussed a number of other ways in which accessible design will also help someone who speaks another language. For example, we discussed the need to use consistent prompts. In fact, you learned that creating a database of standard Web site prompts is a real plus because it makes the Web site easier for someone with cognitive needs to access. Using consistent prompts also helps someone with language needs. It's easier to translate one set of consistent prompts, than it is to translate every prompt on a Web site individually. Even the difference in one word can cause problems.

Creating an Easily Maintained Web Site Example

Because the idea of creating an easily maintained Web site using a mobile device is so intriguing, that's precisely the model we'll use in this chapter. Of course, the first thought that many developers will have is that creating a mobile device application necessary equates to expensive tools. Contrary to popular opinion, the tools used in this example won't cost you a penny. Instead of the Visual Studio .NET environment used for many of the desktop applications, this example relies on Web Matrix—a free tool you can download at `http://www.asp.net/webmatrix/default.aspx`.

 NOTE The example in this section was freely adapted from my book, *Web Matrix Developer's Guide* (Apress, 2002). This book provides complete coverage of this free tool and shows you how to create complex Web applications in a "no cost" environment (you'll have to pay for download time for the tools). You can learn more about *Web Matrix Developer's Guide* at `http://www.apress.com/book/bookDisplay.html?bID=145`. You can also find the *Web Matrix Developer's Guide* on Amazon at `http://www.amazon.com/exec/obidos/tg/detail/-/1590590929/`.

Once you get Web Matrix downloaded and installed, you're ready to work with the example in this section. Many of you will want to test the application on several different devices to see how the output differs. The first section that follows tells you where to obtain mobile device emulation support and how to install it on your system. The second section contains the instructions for working with the mobile device example.

Installing Mobile Device Emulation Support

One of the problems that developers must solve when working with mobile devices is testing for multiple models. Unlike desktop systems, it's not always easy to determine if an application will provide the correct presentation on a mobile setup. Each mobile device has different capabilities, installed software, and a host of other problem areas for the developer to consider.

The following sections help you install three emulation software options. I chose these options because they provide a broad range of support and you can download evaluation units of all three emulators. Here are the download locations so that you can get your copies of the products before you begin this section. The following sections assume that you've downloaded the software required for the installation.

Microsoft eMbedded Visual Tools: http://www.microsoft.com/mobile/downloads/emvt30.asp

Openwave SDK: http://developer.openwave.com/download/

SmartPhone: http://www.yospace.com/spewe.html

 NOTE You might find that you need other emulators to provide the kind of support needed for your application. The emulators discussed in the following sections provide support for popular devices, but they don't emulate every device on the market today. In general, if you choose an emulator, make sure you test it against the real device so that you know how the emulator compares. Some emulators are less useful than others are because the level of emulation varies.

Microsoft eMbedded Visual Tools

The Microsoft eMbedded Visual Tools package is free and includes eMbedded Visual Basic and eMbedded Visual C++. Newer products have supplanted both of the programming language tools and the emulators supplied as part of the package to some extent. For example, there is a VB.NET version based on .NET Compact Framework (which is *not* free). All you need to do is download the product and unpack it into an installation directory. When you double click the downloaded file, it will suggest an installation directory of Mobile Development Tools. The extraction tool will create two subfolders: Disk1 and Disk2. The Disk1 folder contains the desktop application development tools.

 NOTE Because this book looks only at the accessibility aspects of Web development, we'll install only the emulators. Microsoft eMbedded Visual Tools also includes a full compiler you can use to create embedded applications.

The Disk2 folder contains the three emulators and you can install them individually if desired by using the Setup program found in the individual emulation's product folder. For example, if you want to install just the Pocket PC emulation, you can double click the Setup program in the \Mobile Development Tools\ DISK2\PPC12SDK folder. However, because Web Matrix doesn't provide any means for creating desktop mobile applications, you might find that you want to install the compiler as well. With this in mind, the following steps show how to create a full installation.

1. Double click the Setup application found in the \Mobile Development Tools\DISK1 folder. This Setup program will have the special eMVT icon in lime green letters. You'll see the eMbedded Visual Tools dialog box.

2. Click Next. You'll see the End User License Agreement dialog box.

3. Read the agreement, select the "I Accept The Agreement" option, and then click Next. You'll see the Product Number And User ID dialog box shown in Figure 10-1. The Microsoft Web site provides a User ID that you can enter in this dialog box. You'll also find the User ID in the CDKey.TXT file in the \Mobile Development Tools folder. The current key also appears in the figure.

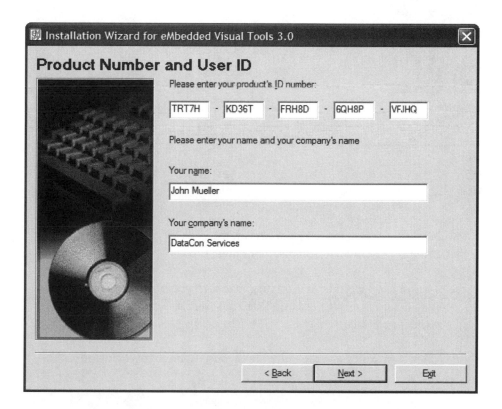

Figure 10-1. Enter the Microsoft-supplied User ID in this dialog box.

4. Type the key code, and then click Next. You'll see the Install eMbedded Visual Tools dialog box shown in Figure 10-2. The only tools that we'll use in this chapter are the three platform SDK options. These options provide you with access to the three device emulators.

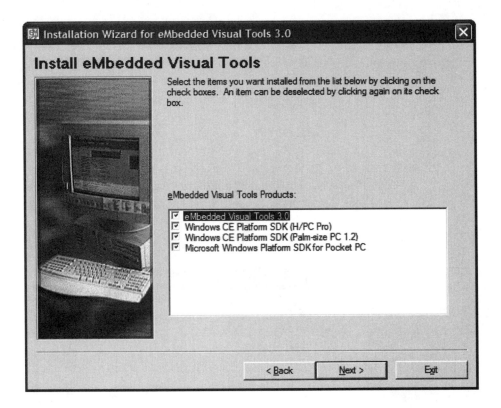

Figure 10-2. Choose the installation options that you want to use from the eMbedded Visual Tools package.

5. Select the three emulator options on the list. Click Next. You'll see a Choose Windows CE Tools Folder dialog box.

6. Type or choose a destination for the tools if you don't want to use the default folder. Click Next. You'll see the Welcome dialog box for the emulator installation.

7. Click Next. You'll see the Software License Agreement dialog box.

8. Read the licensing terms and click Yes if you agree with them. (If you click No, the installation will end.) You'll see a User Information dialog box.

9. Type in your user information, and then click Next. You'll see the Choose Destination Location dialog box.

10. Select an installation location, and then click Next. You'll see the Setup Type dialog box. It pays to choose the Custom option so that you can customize the installation to meet your needs. In addition, the Typical option doesn't always copy all of the features the emulation can provide. If you choose the Custom option, you'll see an additional dialog box like the one shown in Figure 10-3 that contains a list of the features you can install.

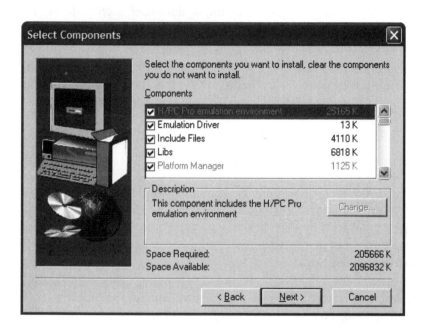

Figure 10-3. Determine which features you want to install when using the Custom setup option.

11. Select the setup options you want to use, and then click Next. You'll see a Select Program Folder dialog box.

12. Choose a location for the program entries in the Start Menu, and then click Next. You'll see a Start Copying Files dialog box.

13. Examine the installation options. Use the Back button to return to previous setup screens if you need to change an option. When you're happy with the setup options, click Next. Setup will begin copying the files to the hard drive. After some time, the installation program will complete and you'll see some installation notes. You can read the notes now or simply minimize the browser window to complete the installation process. After you finish looking at the installation notes, you'll see the Setup Complete dialog box.

14. Click Finish. The next installation procedure will start unless you've installed all of the emulations.

15. Repeat steps 7 through 14 for the Palm-size PC and Pocket PC emulations.

When you finish installing everything, it's important to test each of the emulators to ensure that you received a good installation. If one of the emulators fails to work, you can always uninstall just that emulator using the appropriate entry in the Add/Remove Programs applet. Reinstall the emulator using the Setup program in the appropriate emulator folder in the Setup folder mentioned at the beginning of this section.

Openwave SDK

The Openwave SDK is also a free download, but the Openwave Web site offers plenty of opportunity to purchase paid products as well. The Openwave file you download is an executable, so double clicking it starts the installation process. The following steps assume that you've already started the installation program and can see the Welcome dialog box.

1. Click Next to get past the Welcome dialog box. You'll see the License Agreement dialog box.

2. Read the licensing agreement, and then click Yes if you agree to it. (Clicking No will end the installation process.) You'll see a Screenshots And Image Use Agreement dialog box. Again, you'll need to click Yes to accept the terms of this agreement. After this, you'll see a Safe Country Verification dialog box—yet more legal material. Click Yes if you live in a safe country. At some point, you'll finally get through all of the legal material and arrive at the Choose Destination Location dialog box.

3. Select a destination for your emulator, and then click Next. You'll see a Setup Type dialog box. The Custom option provides the best flexibility for installing this product. If you choose this option and click Next, you'll see a Select Components dialog box similar to the one shown in Figure 10-4. It's important to note that this SDK supports a number of emulators—each of which has different features. You can also obtain different "skins" for the emulators to make them look like specific phones.

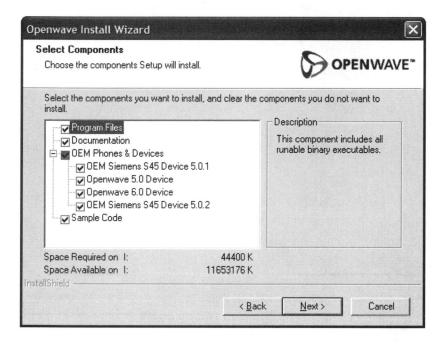

Figure 10-4. Select custom options as needed for your emulator setup.

4. Select a setup type and associated options as needed. Click Next. You'll see a Select Program Folder dialog box.

5. Choose a location for the emulator shortcuts, and then click Next. Setup will begin copying files to the installation folder. At some point, the installation will complete and you'll see the InstallShield Wizard Complete dialog box.

6. Select a restart option, and then click Finish. According to Setup, you must restart your machine to use the product.

Once you get Openwave installed and have restarted your machine, you'll want to test this product out. Unlike some of the other emulators you'll use, this one is actually part of a development IDE. The Openwave SDK 5.1 entry in the Start Menu will open an IDE similar to other IDEs you may have used in the past. However, for this book, the important feature is the emulator that appears in the right pane. To use this feature, you'll need to use the Simulator ➤ Go To Address command, enter a URL in the Go To Address dialog box, and then click OK. Figure 10-5 shows a typical example of the Openwave emulator.

Figure 10-5. Using the Openwave emulator means starting the associated IDE and entering a URL using a menu command.
Image courtesy Openwave Systems Inc.

SmartPhone

The SmartPhone emulator is one of the timed-usage options you can try. After you download the product, you can try it for five days free, at which time your license will expire and the product will cease working. The SmartPhone emulator is in a ZIP that you download and unpack to a temporary folder. The following steps show how to install the product.

1. Double click the setup application that appears in the ZIP file (the actual name varies by SmartPhone version number). You'll see a License Agreement dialog box.

2. Read the license agreement and select Yes if you agree with it. Click Next. You'll see a Choose Install Folder dialog box.

3. Type an installation location and click Install. The setup program will begin installing the files. When the installation is complete, you'll see an Install Complete dialog box.

4. Click Done. The emulator is ready to test.

Now that you have the product installed, you can test it out to see if it works. The first time you start this product you'll see a dialog that requests your licensing details. This dialog box accepts your name, email address, and the key that you were sent in your email. Make sure you use the information from the email because this step is quite picky.

You also have a choice of starting the product in the Development or the Display mode. The Development mode opens an IDE you can use to create applications. This mode also shows multiple forms of the emulation, as shown in Figure 10-6. These aren't the only emulators available. I was surprised by the number of emulation options provided, all of which are available on the Workspace ➤ Add Emulator menu. This product also uses the concept of an emulator group. Figure 10-6 shows the default emulator group. A single test sends the same input to all of the emulators in a group—greatly reducing the time required for testing.

The Display mode opens a single emulator. Use this option when you want to fine-tune the display details of your application. Most of the emulators have a full view and several zoomed views.

Creating a Simple Mobile Page

This might be the first mobile application that many of you have created, even if you've worked with Web sites for some time. Mobile technology is new, somewhat

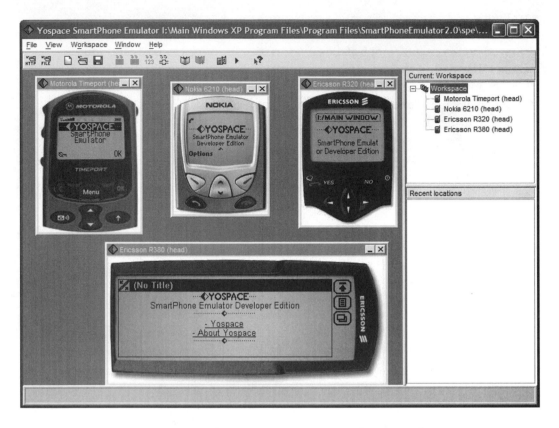

Figure 10-6. Create a complex emulator environment using the SmartPhone Development mode.

difficult due to a number of factors, and represents the latest way to work with data for many people. In a few years, this type of development will seem like old hat. However, today it's new and decidedly different from anything developers have done in the past.

With these factors in mind, the following sections introduce the mobile development in two stages. First, we'll look at the environment that Web Matrix provides. Interestingly, it's very capable of creating robust mobile applications of the caliber that you might normally require Visual Studio .NET to create. Second, we'll discuss a simple project in two steps. The first step is to create the Web page—the second is to create the WEB.CONFIG file that controls the display of the Web page.

Updating Your Server

Your local machine is only one part of the picture for mobile development. Before any of the examples in this chapter will work, you must install Web Matrix on the server. As an alternative, you can move and register the Microsoft.Saturn.Framework and Microsoft.Saturn.Framework.Mobile assemblies in the server's Global Assembly Cache (GAC). These two assemblies provide the support that Web Matrix applications require.

In addition, you must install the Microsoft Mobile Internet Toolkit (MMIT) on the server. You can also install the required System.Web.Mobile assembly in the server's GAC. This assembly provides the MMIT support that the Web Matrix assemblies reference.

If you don't install these assemblies, the application will fail. Fortunately, the error message will tell you about the missing assemblies so that you have a good starting point.

After you install the required support, you might find that the Web server doesn't reply to requests. Restart Internet Information Server (IIS) by right clicking the server entry in the Internet Information Services MMC snap-in and choosing the Restart IIS or the All Tasks ➤ Restart IIS command from the context menu.

An Overview of the Environment

To start the Simple Mobile Page, open Web Matrix and choose the Simple Mobile Page project located in the Mobile Pages folder in the Templates field of the Add New File dialog box. Web Matrix displays the Add New File dialog box when you initially start the application. You can also click the New File button on the toolbar.

You need to provide a location for the project and a project name. The example application uses Simple Page as the project name. In addition, you can specify a class name and a namespace, but these entries are optional in this case. Click OK to create the project.

Once you create the project, you'll see a page that looks like the one shown in Figure 10-7. Notice that this figure shows the specialized features that Web Matrix provides for creating mobile applications.

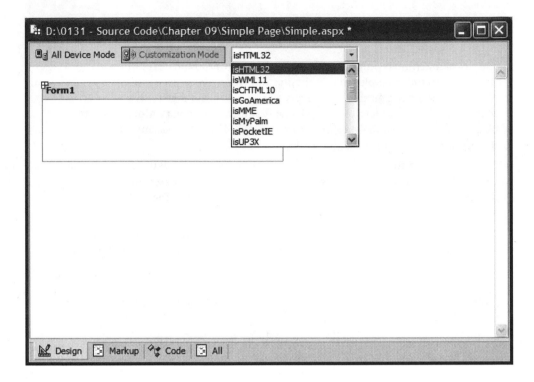

Figure 10-7. Mobile projects include features that other projects we've discussed don't include.

This page includes four tabs—the same number as a standard ASP.NET project provides. However, instead of an HTML tab, you now have a Markup tab. The difference is that mobile device pages don't use strict HTML—they use WML instead because the page has to fit within the confines of a mobile device screen. Mobile devices use the concept of individual screen-sized pages instead of allowing the user to scroll from top to bottom of one long page. (A PDA can often use screen-sized pages or scroll through one long page, making the PDA more flexible than a cellular telephone or a pager.)

The screen-sized page orientation of mobile devices brings us to the form shown on screen. A form outlines a single page of content. You can add multiple forms to one project page. The mobile device will simply inform the user of the additional pages of information in most cases.

Near the top of the page, you'll see two options: All Device Mode and Customization Mode. When you select the All Device Mode, the IDE creates a page that will work on all the devices that MMIT supports. On the other hand, if you select the Customization Mode, the IDE configures itself to match the requirements of the specific device that you select. It's interesting to see the changes in the Properties window as you make configuration choices. Of course, the important changes happen under the covers where you can't see them unless you look at the code.

The customization mode is interesting because it offers options such as supportsCookies and supportsJavaScript. I couldn't find a method for selecting both these options at once—there is one, but it's not apparent.

During my testing, I found that the Customization Mode can also lead to some interesting problems if you don't look at the Markup tag. For example, try this little experiment. Place a Label and a Command control on the form with the isHTML32 option selected. Type **Output** in the Text property of Label1 and **Click Me** in the Text property of Command1. Now, select the isPocketIE Customization Mode option. You'll notice three changes. First, the Command control becomes wider, which is expected since a PDA has a relatively large screen compared to some mobile options. The other two changes are that the text for Command1 and Label1 change back to their original settings. Type **Output** in the Label1 Text property again and **Click Me** in the Command1 Text property a second time. Now, look at the Markup tag and you'll see the code shown in Listing 10-1.

Listing 10-1. Customization Mode Coding Example

```
<mobile:Form id="Form1" runat="server">
    <Mobile:Label id="Label1" runat="server">
        <DeviceSpecific>
            <Choice filter="isPocketIE" text="Output"></Choice>
            <Choice filter="isHTML32" text="Output"></Choice>
        </DeviceSpecific>
Label</Mobile:Label>
    <Mobile:Command id="Command1" runat="server">
        <DeviceSpecific>
            <Choice filter="isPocketIE" text="Click Me"></Choice>
            <Choice filter="isHTML32" text="Click Me"></Choice>
        </DeviceSpecific>
Command</Mobile:Command>
</mobile:Form>
```

Once you look at this code, the method for supporting multiple devices without supporting all of the devices becomes obvious. Notice the use of the filter attribute in this code. The code itself is about the same, but the filter is different. Obviously, this is a simple example. What happens when two machines can't support the same complex setup? That's when you use separate coding for each device. The filter determines which devices use specific controls. Consequently, although the concept of creating mobile pages using the Design window is the same as working with an ASP.NET page, the actual process is different. You need to make different design decisions than when you were working with a desktop machine.

TIP Use the All Device Mode for simple pages where the use of the same controls for all devices is unlikely to cause usage problems. The advantage of using the All Device Mode is that you can design pages quickly and without regard for individual device requirements. Always use the All Device Mode to create your initial design and assign ID values to the controls. Use the Customization Mode for complex pages where each device will require a separate configuration. The advantage of using the Customization Mode is that you can compensate for individual device needs.

The Mobile Controls tab of the Toolbox also differs from the Web Controls tab used for ASP.NET projects, as shown in Figure 10-8. The reason is simple—most mobile devices don't provide the resources to create some of the complex controls used on desktop machines. Even if a mobile device could display the complex control, it probably wouldn't have the local computing resources to make the control functional. Using all server-side resources is out of the question because mobile devices don't provide the data transmission speed of a desktop machine. In short, it's easier to limit the controls to a subset that will work, than it is to create a situation in which you have to pick controls based on platform functionality.

Creating Simple Mobile Solution Example

When developers create a Web page as part of a desktop application, consistent appearance is something that they try to achieve, but let's face the fact that mobile development is different. Just because your friend decides that squinting at the decidedly small text on a cellular telephone is just fine doesn't mean you should live with the same limitation.

Figure 10-8. Web Matrix provides a subset of the controls used for ASP.NET Page projects when working with mobile devices.

For the sake of argument, let's say you'll use the same application to display information on a desktop browser, a PDA, and a cellular telephone. This section shows you how to create a simple mobile example that will work on all three devices. We'll begin by creating the three forms shown in Figure 10-9. (You'll find the complete source for this example in the \Chapter 10\SimplePage folder of the source code that you can obtain from the Downloads section of the Apress Web site (http://www.apress.com)—so you don't even need to design the forms if you don't want to.) Note that some of these controls are only visible to the full browser and some only to the full browser and Pocket PC. You'll see how this ASP.NET controls this functionality in the source code.

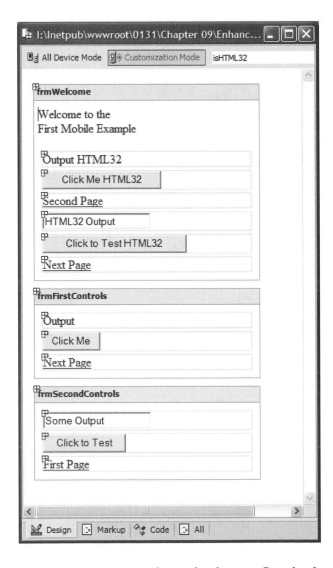

Figure 10-9. Create new forms that better reflect the three target platforms.

Interestingly enough, you can set up the basic elements of this form in Design view, but then you have to switch to Markup view to make some of the adjustments. Listing 10-2 shows the markup for the first page of this example—the first page is the key to making the example work properly.

Listing 10-2. Simple Web Page Markup

```
<Mobile:Form id="frmWelcome" Paginate="True" runat="server">
<p>
    Welcome to the<br />
    First Mobile Example
</p>
<p>
    <Mobile:Label id="lblOutput3" runat="server" Visible="False">
        <DeviceSpecific>
            <Choice filter="isPocketIE"
                    visible="True"
                    text="Pocket PC Output"></Choice>
            <Choice filter="isHTML32"
                    visible="True"
                    text="Output HTML32"></Choice>
        </DeviceSpecific>
    Label</Mobile:Label>
    <Mobile:Command id="btnTest3"
                    onclick="btnTest1_Click"
                    runat="server" Visible="False">
        <DeviceSpecific>
            <Choice filter="isPocketIE"
                    visible="True"
                    text="Click Me"></Choice>
            <Choice filter="isHTML32"
                    visible="True"
                    text="Click Me HTML32"></Choice>
        </DeviceSpecific>
    Command</Mobile:Command>
    <Mobile:Link id="Link1"
                 runat="server"
                 NavigateUrl="#frmSecondControls" Visible="False">
        <DeviceSpecific>
            <Choice filter="isPocketIE" visible="True"></Choice>
            <Choice filter="isHTML32" visible="False"></Choice>
        </DeviceSpecific>
```

```
        Second Page</Mobile:Link>
        <Mobile:TextBox id="txtOutput4" runat="server" Visible="False">
            <DeviceSpecific>
                <Choice filter="isPocketIE"
                        visible="False"
                        text="Some Output"></Choice>
                <Choice filter="isHTML32"
                        visible="True"
                        text="HTML32 Output"></Choice>
            </DeviceSpecific>
        </Mobile:TextBox>
        <Mobile:Command id="btnTest4"
                        onclick="btnTest2_Click"
                        runat="server"
                        visible="False">
            <DeviceSpecific>
                <Choice filter="isPocketIE"
                        visible="False"
                        text="Click to Test"></Choice>
                <Choice filter="isHTML32"
                        visible="True"
                        text="Click to Test HTML32"></Choice>
            </DeviceSpecific>
        Command</Mobile:Command>
        <Mobile:Link id="Link2" runat="server" NavigateUrl="#frmFirstControls">
            <DeviceSpecific>
                <Choice filter="isPocketIE" visible="False"></Choice>
                <Choice filter="isHTML32" visible="False"></Choice>
            </DeviceSpecific>
        Next Page</Mobile:Link>
    </p>
</Mobile:Form>
```

Let's begin with a few generalizations about this code. You'll notice that all of the <Choice filter="isPocketIE"> entries appear before the <Choice filter="isHTML32"> entries. An odd thing happens if you try to reduce the order—your Pocket PC is apt to use the isHTML32 settings instead of the isPocketIE settings. This is the only interaction I ran into during testing, but there may be others that you should consider. If something on screen doesn't look as anticipated, the order of your tags might be the problem.

Look at all of the controls in this example. Except for the introductory text and the final link, all of them have the visible=false property in place. This means that the example assumes that any device not specifically handled by the page can't display the controls on a single page. Using this technique ensures that any browser that visits your site can use it, even if such use is limited to the lowest common denominator.

Of course, if the control is invisible, you have to make it visible in some way. A look at the filter entries shows another series of visible=true or visible=false settings. The controls are displayed or not displayed based on the specific device support required. It can be difficult to keep all of these entries straight, even with the Design view, because you can't see what's happening. Consequently, I normally check the results of changes using the emulators to ensure that what I think is displayed on a particular device is what the user will actually see.

Sometimes you have to duplicate functionality across multiple forms. The only problem is that you can't give two controls the same name. You can use the same handler for more than one control, however. Unless you need to assign different functions to a button with the same function on two different areas of the form, using the same handler makes sense because it's easier to maintain the functional portion of the code. All you really need to do is ensure that each of the affect controls uses the same handler as do the pushbuttons in Listing 10-2. The handler code must include output for every affected output control. Listing 10-3 shows the event handlers for this example.

Listing 10-3. Event Handler Code

```
void btnTest1_Click(Object sender, EventArgs e)
{
    // Only work with the control on the first form.
    lblOutput1.Text = "This is the first control form.";
    lblOutput3.Text = "This is the first output control.";
}


void btnTest2_Click(Object sender, EventArgs e)
{
    // Only work with the control on the second form.
    txtOutput2.Text = "This is the second control form.";
    txtOutput4.Text = "This is the second output control.";
}
```

As you can see from Listing 10-3, the event handlers ensure that each of the output controls receives the information produced by the event. Figures 10-10 through 10-12 show the three output levels from this one ASPX page. As you can see, the browser outputs all of the information, the PDA outputs the information from the first two forms, and the cellular telephone outputs just one form at a time.

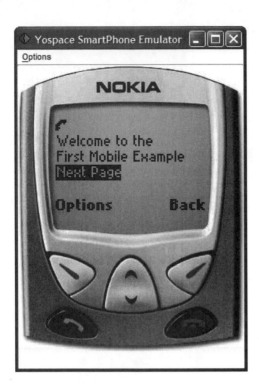

Figure 10-10. Users can view just one form using a cellular telephone.

Figure 10-11. Accessing the site with a PDA allows viewing of two forms.

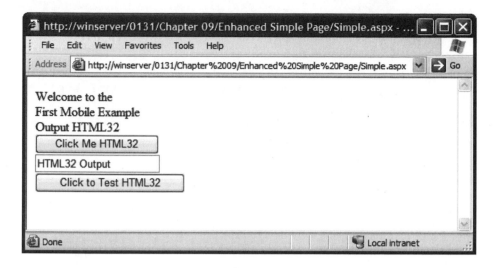

Figure 10-12. Using a browser to access the site allows viewing of all three forms at once.

WEB.CONFIG Considerations for Mobile Applications

ASP.NET applications normally use a WEB.CONFIG file in order to meet certain application requirements. For example, the example WEB.CONFIG file contains an `<customErrors mode="Off"/>` entry to facilitate application debugging.

In some cases, you need to make changes to the WEB.CONFIG file for mobile applications as well. The first of these settings is the standard `<sessionState>` element shown in Listing 10-4.

Listing 10-4. A Typical `<sessionState>` Element

```
<sessionState mode="InProc"
    stateConnectionString="tcpip=127.0.0.1:42424"
    sqlConnectionString="data source=127.0.0.1;trusted_connection=true"
    cookieless="false"
    timeout="20" />
```

Normally, Web Matrix leaves this element commented out. In most cases, you can leave it commented out as well. However, notice the timeout attribute of this element. In some cases, the transmission speed of a mobile device makes this value too small. When this happens, you'll receive an error message.

The `<sessionState>` timeout value of 20 minutes is usually long enough, so you'll also want to check the `<mobileControls>` element. The WEB.CONFIG file doesn't contain this element by default, so you'll have to add it in manually. You can learn all the details about this element in the Mobile Internet Toolkit help file at `ms-help://MS.VSCC/ms.MobileInternetToolkit/mwsdk/html/mwlrfmobileControls.htm` or online at `http://msdn.microsoft.com/library/en-us/mwsdk/html/mwlrfmobileControls.asp`. The attribute you want to change to correct this error is `sessionStateHistorySize`. A typical `<mobileControls>` element appears in Listing 10-5.

Listing 10-5. A Typical `<mobileControls>` *Element*

```
<mobileControls
    allowCustomAttributes="true"
    sessionStateHistorySize="40"
    cookielessDataDictionaryType="">
</mobileControls>
```

You'd include this code as a subelement of the `<system.web>` element—the same location as the `<sessionState>` element. Normally, you won't need to provide the other elements supported by the `<mobileControls>` element unless your application has special needs.

Summary

This chapter has provided you with a unique view of Web site design. Instead of filling the page with gizmos that look great to someone without special needs and a high-speed connection, we've looked at some of the ways you can dress up a plain Web site that's accessible to everyone. In the end, if you don't get visitors to your Web site, then what's the point in creating it? Whom does such a Web site serve? Excluding a large number of people from your Web site seems counter to the open sharing of information that the Internet is supposed to provide. As part of the discussion in this chapter, you've learned that glitter keeps more than just those with special needs out, it also keeps someone with a slow connection or someone with cultural requirements out. Cultural differences can include a variety of needs such as speaking your language as a second language.

Now that you have the knowledge required to create an easily maintained Web site, you should try it out. I'm not saying you should create an entire site based on this idea today—try one or two popular pages and see what your users have to say. Keep statistics of Web site issues so that you can to discover by yourself that these techniques save time and money in support calls. Finally, make sure everyone knows that this is a test site and actively poll them for input. In general, you'll find that people prefer the less glittery, easy-to-understand approach of the easy to maintain Web site.

Chapter 11 builds on some of the concepts found in this chapter, but it also helps you update an existing Web site by adding cues that really help people get the most from your Web site. This chapter is the equivalent of Chapter 7 for Web sites. You'll learn about the techniques you can use to add usage cues, make your Web site flow better, and generally reduce the learning curve for users of your Web site. Making life easy on the user is always an important way to build site traffic and reduce support costs. Obviously, easier to understand is better for those with special needs too.

CHAPTER 11

Adding Usage Cues to Web Applications

In This Chapter:

What Are the Accessibility Tags for Web Sites?

How Do I Use the `<ALT>` and `<LONGDESC>` Tags?

How Do I Add CSS Support to My Application?

What Are the Problems Associated with Image Maps?

When Should I Use Transcripts Online?

What Are the Alternatives to Using Color for Information?

What Are the Requirements for Captioning Movies and Other Video Presentations?

How Do I Use QuickTime?

How Do I Use Macromedia Flash?

How Do I Use RealAudio?

How Do I Use Media Access Generator (MAGpie)?

JUST AS DESKTOP APPLICATIONS benefit from the usage cues, you'll find that users of Web applications enjoy them too. Usage cues help the user understand your application better. A good set of usage cues can help direct the user through the sequence you want them to follow when working with a Web application. In fact, the whole idea of flow is essential for Web applications because users often have to decide how to work with a Web application based exclusively on the cues you provide.

This chapter helps you understand usage cues for Web applications. You'll begin by learning about the standardized accessibility tags you'll need for your application. We then discuss two important tags that can make understanding the Web site easier for most users. This chapter also takes another look at color. In this case, we discuss how you can create effective Web sites that don't rely on any color information. (The issue isn't that using color is a problem—using color alone does affect accessibility—but avoiding color in some situations makes the site easier to maintain.) After learning this new technique, you'll learn about Cascading Style

Sheets (CSS) and see how they can reduce the programming load for the developer while making the Web page easier to use with accessible technology.

At this point, the chapter begins showing you how to use a number of design and implementation technologies. For example, you'll learn how to work with image maps in an accessible manner. You'll also learn video and audio presentation techniques, including those used by QuickTime, Macromedia Flash, RealAudio, and MAGpie. Finally, we'll discus how to use Microsoft Active Accessibility with Web applications.

ON THE WEB In Chapter 1, we discussed the concept of undue burden (see the "Understanding the Concept of Undue Burden" section for details). Credit card purchasers recently received an extension of their Section 508 compliance requirement. This extension is almost certain to affect purchases on the Internet. You can learn more at http:// www.fcw.com/fcw/articles/2002/1230/web-access-01-02-03.asp. It's important to learn about these exemptions as you build your e-commerce Web site because they can help ease the immediate requirements for products sold on a new site or a site update. However, you also need to understand that the exemption will run out eventually, so by planning to meet the full requirements today, you will save your-self considerable time tomorrow.

An Overview of the Accessible Tags

Of course, the first question most developers will ask is what an accessible tag is. For the purposes of this book (and probably for most of your development needs as well) an *accessible tag* is one that helps you create an accessible Web site. In reality, that covers a lot of ground. However, the defining issue isn't necessarily the purpose of the tag, although that does come into play, but how the tag is used.

ON THE WEB It's important to remain updated on the current tags used for accessibility purposes. This requirement means looking at the latest specifications as needed. The World Wide Web Consortium (W3C) maintains these specifications based on the input from its members. You can find the latest HTML Techniques for Web Content Accessibility Guidelines 1.0 specification at http://www.w3.org/TR/WCAG10-HTML-TECHS/.

The following sections discuss the use of accessibility tags and accessibility attributes. You'll learn how these two code elements differ and how to avoid problems when working with them. These sections will also open a new world of interesting tags that you can use for your next development project.

 NOTE   The coding examples supplied in the sections that follow aren't necessarily accessible. I provided the code to demonstrate tag usage in the clearest manner possible. You should use the sample code to understand tag usage, rather than as an example of a method you can use to create an accessible page.

Considering the Use of a Tag

One of the tags that distinctly falls into the method of a use category is the <META> tag. Developers often use specific attributes associated with this tag in a way that makes the Web page difficult to access. For example, many developers want to ensure that the user has fresh content, or they want to simulate push technology with a static Web page. They do this by using the following <META> tag.

```
<META http-equiv="refresh" content="60">
```

Unfortunately, the developer has no idea of how long the viewer will need to read the page. In addition, the constant refresh cycle becomes annoying when using a screen reader because user will often get half way through the page, have it refresh, and have to listen to the page content all over again. There's nothing wrong with using the <META> tag for other uses (such as creating a document summary, adding the author name, or defining an expiration date), but you'll want to avoid using it for this particular purpose.

Another concept that many developers don't understand is how these tags affect accessibility. For example, consider the simple <A> (anchor) tag. If the developer leaves out the accessKey attribute, the user will have to use a mouse or press the tab key multiple times to access the tag with any amount of speed. There's nothing wrong with the <A> tag, but the way the developer uses the tag can make a big difference.

In still other cases, you can use the information located in the specification to determine if an update should remove an existing tag. For example, at one time developers commonly used the <CAPTION> tag exclusively to describe the content of a table. The <CAPTION> tag works fine for sighted users, but it is inadequate for those with special needs who rely on screen readers. Although the <CAPTION> tag modifies the presentation of the table in a positive way, it affects the structure of the table in a negative way and screen readers usually rely on structure to make sense of the table content. The HTML Techniques for Web Content Accessibility Guidelines 1.0 specification recommends that you use the Summary attribute of the <TABLE> tag in addition to the <CAPTION> tag. Using the Summary attribute makes it possible for the screen reader to determine the purpose of the caption information.

Essential Accessibility Tags

Most developers have the tags that they commonly use for development memorized. Even if they use an IDE for development purposes, the IDE doesn't get a chance to pop up a list of acceptable tags before the developer has typed the tag of interest. In some cases, a developer becomes so conversant in the common tags that they can type them as fast as many people talk—the tags become part of the developer's language.

NOTE   Most developers have used the term *tag* to refer to an HTML element placed within angle brackets, such as the <LABEL> tag. With the emergence of the eXtensible Markup Language (XML), some specifications now refer to tags as *elements*. For example, the specification used as a resource for this section of the chapter uses that nomenclature. For the purposes of clarity, the book will always use tag to refer to HTML code and element when working with XHTML, XML, or XML derivatives.

The "browser wars" left the development community with many non-standard tags to work with and various browsers support these tags in different ways. One way to combat this problem is to determine which browsers support standard features and determine in what way they support them. The webmonkey chart at http://hotwired.lycos.com/webmonkey/reference/browser_chart/index.html can help you make this determination. You might also want to review the WebReview chart at http://www.webreview.com/browsers/browsers.shtml.

Unfortunately, this chart is only a start—you still need to know which tags are in the standard used to create the document (as expressed by the <DOCTYPE> tag). You can find a list of standard accessibility tags in the "Index of HTML elements and attributes" section of the HTML Techniques for Web Content Accessibility Guidelines 1.0 specification (http://www.w3.org/TR/WCAG10-HTML-TECHS/). The following list provides an overview of some of the more interesting tags you can use for accessibility purposes. (We'll cover other tags, such as the <NOSCRIPT> and <LABEL> tags, as the chapter progresses.) You'll also find examples of these tags demonstrated in the \Chapter 11\Accessible Tags folder of the source code that you can obtain from the Downloads section of the Apress Web site (http://www.apress.com).

<ABBR> and <ACRONYM>: These two tags help the user understand the meaning of terms on your Web site. An *abbreviation* is a shortened form of a word or term. On the other hand, an *acronym* is general a word or a set of letters derived from a phrase. There's some room for interpretation of the difference between these two words based on whom you talk with. In addition, the <ACRONYM> tag appears to enjoy wider acceptance than the <ABBR> tag. However, the usage for both is consistent: <ACRONYM Title="Women Accepted for Volunteer Emergency Service">WAV</ACRONYM>. Notice the use of the Title attribute as the means to define the acronym or abbreviation.

<ADDRESS>: It's important to provide contact information for your Web site. Otherwise, the user might have a question and not know where to go to find answers. The <ADDRESS> tag encapsulates the contact information for individuals who can provide help with a particular page.

<BUTTON>: You can create pushbuttons on Web pages using a number of techniques. The <BUTTON> tag has the advantage of providing specific properties, events, and attributes that make it easier to create an accessible page. In general, you'll want to use this option to avoid the ambiguity of using the <INPUT> tag.

 NOTE Some tags, such as the <BUTTON>, <DEL>, and <INS> tags, aren't often used on Web sites today. However, given the functionality they provide, it's important to consider using them in your next Web site update. The tags don't necessarily affect high-end screen readers that much, but they can affect low-end screen readers and make your site just a little easier to understand.

<DEL> and <INS>: These two tags are important because they show where an author has deleted or inserted text into the current document compared to a previous version of the document. Always use these two tags in place of the <U> and <STRIKE> tags. The important element to consider is that these tags represent deleted and inserted text, rather than formatted text—the tags serve a specific purpose that you can't duplicate with CSS.

<FIELDSET> and <LEGEND>: The <FIELDSET> and <LEGEND> tags work together to group fields on a form. The <FIELDSET> tag performs the task of grouping the fields. You can actually see a box around the related fields, making it easier to understand which fields are associated with each

other. (According to at least one source, the visible box is an unintended feature added by some browser vendors and the standard doesn't require this feature. In fact, the visible presentation might actually hamper widespread implementation of the <FIELDSET> tag.) The <LEGEND> tag provides identification for the grouped fields. It's helpful to use these tags to make the meaning of controls on a complex form clearer and easier to understand.

<OPTGROUP>: Developers use the <OPTGROUP> tag with the <SELECT> and <OPTION> tags to group like options together. Using this tag makes your application more accessible by making a particular option easier to find. When using the <OPTGROUP> tag, you'll need to include the Label attribute to give the group a name.

<TABLE>: The <TABLE> tag has been around for a long time. However, recent (and continuing) changes to the specifications make it necessary for you to review your table setups. For example, earlier in the "Considering the Use of a Tag" section, we discussed the need to use the Summary attribute in addition to the <CAPTION> tag. You'll also notice that the W3C has deprecated the Align attribute. The best way to format tables today is to use CSS.

Essential Accessibility Attributes

An *attribute* is a code element that modifies a tag. For example, when you add the AccessKey attribute to a <INPUT> tag, the user can use Alt+<AccessKey> to access that entry on the page. We've used this particular attribute in several examples in previous chapters, so you're probably already familiar with it.

The problem with many attributes today is that developers don't know they exist, don't understand how to use them, or don't know which attributes are actually standardized. As with accessibility tags, you can find a list of accessibility attributes in the "Index of HTML elements and attributes" section of the HTML Techniques for Web Content Accessibility Guidelines 1.0 specification (http://www.w3.org/TR/WCAG10-HTML-TECHS/). The following list provides a quick overview of these attributes and tells how they're used.

Abbr: This attribute contains an abbreviated form of the data found in a table cell. A screen reader could use this information to output a short form of a long repetitive table entry.

accessKey: This attribute enables a user to access a screen element, such as a text box or a pushbutton, quickly. You can use this attribute with the <A>, <AREA>, <BUTTON>, <INPUT>, <LABEL>, <LEGEND>, and <TEXTAREA> tags.

Alt: This attribute provides a short description of a graphic element on screen. In many cases, you'll combine it with the LongDesc attribute to ensure that the user receives a complete description of the graphic element.

Axis: This attribute places the cell of a table within a conceptual category. The Axis acts as a single dimension within an *n*-dimensional space. The user can request that the browser organize the data using a particular category as a basis.

Class: This attribute assigns a class name to the element. Browsers often use this feature to select characteristics for the element from a CSS file. More than one element on a Web page can share the same Class attribute value.

Dir: This attribute defines the direction of the text on screen when Unicode doesn't define the direction. The acceptable values include ltr (left-to-right) and rlt (right-to-left).

For: This attribute associates an element with another element. For example, you could use it to associate a label specifically with its associated text box. The value of this attribute must match the ID attribute value of the target element.

Headers: This attribute is associated with the <TD> and <TH> tags. It contains a space-delimited list of cells that form the header for a table. Using this attribute helps users of screen readers because the screen reader will announce that the cells are part of a header. Developers also use this attribute with style sheets.

HREFLang: This attribute defines the language used by a resource pointed at by an HREF attribute. Developers commonly use this attribute with the <LINK> and <A> tags.

ID: This attribute assigns an identifier to the element. Browsers can use this feature to select characteristics for the element from a CSS file. However, the most common use of this attribute is as a means to identify a particular element within a script or other means of page processing.

Label: This attribute assigns a value to the element. The current specification only uses this attribute with the <OPTION> and <OPTGROUP> tags.

Lang: This attribute defines the language used by or associated with a particular element. Developers can use this attribute to help speech and search engines interact more successfully with Web page elements. In addition, this attribute can help the browser provide correct language-specific interaction, such as the use of punctuation.

LongDesc: This attribute provides a reference to a Web page or other resource that contains a long description of a complex graphic element. For example, the developer would use this attribute with a chart or a graph. The referenced page would provide a text description of the content of the chart or graph so that users who rely on screen readers could understand the information conveyed by the graphic image. This attribute often appears with the Alt attribute.

Scope: This attribute often appears in place of the Headers attribute for simple tables. It defines the set of data cells that are associated with a header cell. Acceptable values include row, col, rowgroup, and colgroup. The rowgroup and colgroup values associate the header cell with a group of data cells.

Style: This attribute assigns the inline style for an element. For example, the developer could use it to assign font characteristics to a <LABEL> tag. In general, you'll want to avoid using this attribute and assign style to tags using an external CSS file. Using an external file enables users to substitute the styles they want to use to view a particular page.

Summary: This attribute defines the purpose and content of a table.

TabIndex: This attribute defines the element's position in the tabbing order for a form. It helps the developer control the flow of the page. Defining a tabbing order makes the page easier to use.

Title: This attribute provides ancillary information about the associated element. The ancillary information describes the purpose and content of the element in most cases. In some cases, a developer can also use this attribute to provide basic help information for the element.

UseMap: This attribute associates an image map with the element. The UseMap value must match the value of the Name attribute of the <MAP> tag used to define the image map. Developers can use this attribute with the <IMG>, <INPUT>, and <OBJECT> tags.

Many of the attributes provided by the specification perform special tasks. For example, the Abbr, Axis, Headers, and Scope attributes only appear with the <TD> and <TH> tags used with tables. If you're using a product such as Visual Studio .NET to create your Web applications, the IDE will generally provide you with a list of acceptable attributes for a particular tag. The problem with relying too heavily on the input provided by an IDE is that the IDE will often supply vendor-specific, as well as standardized, attributes. In sum, you need to exercise care to ensure that your Web page uses only standardized attributes to ensure maximum flexibility.

<ALT> and <LONGDESC> Tags: The Low-Tech Solution

I love discussing low-tech solutions to problems that developers commonly face because they usually involve little work, are easy to understand, and best of all, are free. The <ALT> and <LONGDESC> tags (actually attributes, but referred to as tags by many developers) are the free solution to the problem of describing on-screen elements that too many developers miss.

NOTE   The various examples in this chapter were tested for accessibility using Bobby. Although Bobby noted manual checks that I needed to perform after the text, the examples did pass the automated tests.

The <ALT> tag sees the most common use because more developers know about it. An <ALT> tag provides a short description of a Web site element. When the user hovers the mouse over the element or selects the element in some other way (such as using a screen reader), a browser that supports the <ALT> tag will provide descriptive information about the screen element. In many cases, the help is in the form of an audio description or the appearance of balloon help. However, the rendering of the <ALT> tag depends on the browser you use.

ON THE WEB   It's often helpful to have a number of tools to use to test your Web site. Of course, buying these tools can become quite expensive, so getting free or low-cost solutions is always helpful. The Sayz Me text-to-speech reader (http://www.mywebattack.com/gnomeapp.php?id=105755) is one such solution. It provides basic text reading capability that helps you hear what your page will sound like to someone who can't see it. This Web site also lists a number of other free tools that you can download and try. It's often best to try your Web page out with several readers to ensure that it works with a broad range of software.

Some pictures literally are worth a thousand words. The problem with placing all thousand words in an <ALT> tag is that they'd be hard to read and not every user will want to hear them. Imagine waiting for a screen reader to finish saying all this information before moving on to the next element on the Web page. The <LONGDESC> tag provides a link to another page with a complete text description of complex graphics. In general, the description should talk about every element of the graphic. You want to create a word picture that matches the graphic element. Listing 11-1 shows these two tags in use. You'll also find the listing in the \Chapter 11\ALT and LONGDESC folder of the source code that you can obtain from the Downloads section of the Apress Web site (http://www.apress.com).

Listing 11-1. Using the <ALT> *and* <LONGDESC> *Tags on a Web Page*

```
<!DOCTYPE HTML PUBLIC "-//W3C//DTD HTML 4.0 Transitional//EN">
<html>
<head>
<title>Sample of &ltALT&gt and &ltLONGDESC&gt Tags</title>
</head>
<body>
<h1 align=center>Using the &ltALT&gt and &ltLONGDESC&gt Tags</h1>

<p>Simple graphics only require use of the &ltALT&gt tag.</p>
<img align=middle
     alt="A green diamond shape that contains the word New in red."
     src="new.GIF">

<p>Complex graphics require both the &ltALT&gt
   and the &ltLONGDESC&gt tags</p>
<img align=middle
     alt="A picture of John"
     src="JohnPic.JPG"
     height=200
     width=150
     longdesc="JohnDesc.HTM">
<a href="JohnDesc.HTM"
   title="A text description of John's picture.">[D]</a>

</body>
</html>
```

Figure 11-1 shows the output from this example. As you can see, the first image is simple, so it doesn't require the use of the <LONGDESC> tag. However, as you can see from Listing 11-1, we still use the <ALT> tag. Although this first image is simple, notice that describing it still presents problems. Drawing a word picture of any graphic element is going to take time, but it's an essential task. It's important to separate the artistic elements of the graphic from the content it provides. You need to discuss the content of the image, not necessarily the artistic elements.

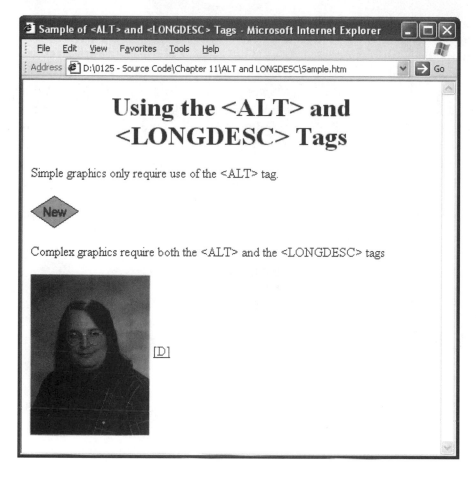

Figure 11-1. Make sure you use the right set of tags to describe graphic elements based on their complexity.

The second image is more complex than the first. In this case, I used my picture, but any complex graphic qualifies as something that you'll want to describe in more detail than an ‹ALT› tag will allow. As you can see from Listing 11-1, the second image uses the ‹LONGDESC› tag in addition to the ‹ALT› tag.

Unfortunately, if you click on the second picture shown in Figure 11-1 when using Internet Explorer, nothing will happen. Even the 6.0 version of Internet Explorer lacks support for the <LONGDESC> tag. This means that you wasted your effort unless you can come up with another solution to the problem. You'll notice that Listing 11-1 contains a strange looking [D] link in it. The [D] link is the W3C solution to the problem and you should always include it with your Web page so that everyone can access the long description for a graphic element. Note that the [D] link was originally proposed by the National Center for Accessible Media (NCAM) (http://ncam.wgbh.org/aboutncam.html) and adopted by the W3C.

The JohnDesc.HTM file that contains the long description for my picture is relatively simple text. You can see this text in the source code folder and by clicking the [D] link shown in Figure 11-1. However, there is one feature in this file that you should know about. To format the text, I included the following tag.

```
<p align=justify style="LEFT: 15%; WIDTH: 70%; POSITION: relative">
```

Normally, you won't format your text using this technique because the viewer may have a style sheet that works better for their particular needs. However, in this case, I chose to include the formatting information. Notice that the tag doesn't include any mention of font size and that all layouts rely on percentages. This tag will work for most users, even those who need to use large text displays, because the formatting is flexible. It's still better to use an external CSS file whenever possible, but you can use this approach for simple formatting on simple pages.

Using CSS Example

We've discussed CSS in quite a few places in the chapter but haven't really looked at it yet. CSS provides the means to describe the layout of a page separately from the content. The separation of format and layout from content is essential if you want to make a page truly accessible. The use of an external CSS file means that someone can substitute their CSS file for your CSS file and obtain an entirely different look for the same content. This new look might help someone with color blindness see the page better or someone who needs a large-text display obtain it without a lot of extra setup. The following sections describe a basic CSS file, show how to apply it to a simple Web page, and demonstrate how to test the completed example.

Creating the CSS File

For the developer, using CSS means creating a separate CSS file. Listing 11-2 shows the CSS file we'll use for this example. You'll also find the listing in the

\Chapter 11\CSS Example folder of the source code that you can obtain from the Downloads section of the Apress Web site (`http://www.apress.com`).

Listing 11-2. A Typical CSS File

```
BODY {
    font-size: 100%;
    color: black;
    background-color: white;
}


H1 {
    font-size: 200%;
    color: black;
    background-color: white;
}


H2 {
    font-size: 150%;
    color: black;
    background-color: white;
}


.highlight {
    font-size: 100%;
    color: red;
    background-color: white;
}


.highlight-i {
    font-size: 100%;
    color: red;
    font-style: italic;
    background-color: white;
}


.underline {
    font-size: 100%;
    color: black;
    text-decoration: underline;
    background-color: white
}
```

As you can see, Listing 11-2 creates the styles we'll use later to format the test page. It contains two types of entries: elements and classes. An *element* provides basic formatting for a tag such as a header <H1>. A *class* typically provides specialized formatting for an element, such as the various highlights used in this example. CSS also supports other types of formatting, such as a format associated with a particular element ID that we won't discuss in this book.

ON THE WEB   The W3C currently has two active CSS specifications that you can use. The first is CSS1 (http://www.w3.org/TR/REC-CSS1), which is the current favorite with developers. The second is the recently released CSS2 (http://www.w3.org/TR/REC-CSS2/), which is currently at the recommendation stage. Most browsers don't fully implement either of these standards. You'll also want to view the Accessible Features of CSS standard at http://www.w3.org/TR/CSS-access. This document helps you understand the accessibility issues surrounding CSS and learn how CSS can improve accessibility for every Web site.

You should notice a few features of this style sheet. The most important feature is that it relies on percentages for the font sizes, rather than precise sizes. Using a percentage means that the user can set the base size for a page and see the remaining elements sized according to the base size. Users with limited vision will appreciate this feature because many Web pages use fonts that are too small for them to see. Likewise, users with great vision will appreciate this setting because they can display more information on screen. It's never a good idea to display fonts in a specific size.

Another feature of this style sheet is that it uses high contrast color combinations. It's important to consider using high contrast settings whenever you can. Using a high contrast display is better because it helps a variety of users get more from your Web site including those with the following needs:

- Overcoming low vision

- Seeing in a sunlit area

- Using alternative input devices such as cellular telephones and PDAs

- Using small font sizes

- Overcoming color blindness

The listing also includes one setting that the standards require. Notice that every setting includes a foreground and a background color setting. The standards require this information to ensure that the display looks as anticipated.

Defining the Web Page Using CSS

Generally, if you know how to create an HTML file, it isn't difficult to add CSS support to it. Of course, the missing component is linkage between the HTML page and the CSS style sheet. The code used throughout this section appears in the \Chapter 11\CSS Example folder of the source code that you can obtain from the Downloads section of the Apress Web site (http://www.apress.com). Figure 11-2 shows the output of the page we'll use for this example.

Figure 11-2. The test page contains a number of interesting features that show how CSS can improve accessibility.

So how do you connect the CSS file to the HTML page? You begin creating the CSS linkage by adding a tag to the heading area of the HTML page, as shown here.

```
<link media="screen" href="MyStyle.css" type="text/css" rel="StyleSheet">
```

This single line of code tells the browser to use the styles found in the MyStyle.CSS file. The style sheet automatically adds styles to the general styles we added to the file such as Body and H1 (see Listing 11-1 for details). However, the page also includes the special .highlight, .highlight-i, and .underline styles. We'll begin by addressing the text that appears in red in the original example, as shown here.

```
<span class="highlight">This text is in <span class="highlight-i">RED</span>
and the word "RED" is in italics.</span>
```

As you can see, adding some nested <SPAN> tags takes care of the formatting. The first <SPAN> tag relies on the .highlight class, while the second relies on the .highlight-i class. The result is the same text that we saw earlier. The difference is that the formatting code appears in the style sheet, rather than the HTML file.

 NOTE Some developers view the <SPAN> tag as a means of circumventing the whole purpose of using CSS in the first place. These developers feel that all formatting should appear as part of a structural element, such as a <LABEL> tag. You should avoid using the <SPAN> tag whenever possible, but it's not necessary (or even possible) to avoid it completely.

Adding underlined text is similar to changing the text color. The following code adds underline style. In this case, we don't need to use a <span> tag since there's a <p> tag handy.

```
<p class="underline">
    This text is underlined.
</p>
```

Using CSS also answers an accessibility need. According to the specification, the W3C has deprecated the <U> tag—you shouldn't use it to mark text any longer.

Of course, this causes a problem in identifying the Alt+<Key> combination the user should use to access a field. The example includes an .underline style that solves the problem, as shown here.

```
<label><span class="underline">O</span>utput Textbox</label>
<input id="txtOutput"
       title="This is the output textbox."
       accesskey="O"
       type="text"
       value="Page Output" />
```

As you can see, the code uses a <LABEL> for the text as normal. Within the <LABEL> the code relies on a <SPAN> tag to underline the appropriate letter. This value matches the accessKey attribute found in the <INPUT> tag that follows. Notice that the <INPUT> tag also includes attributes that define the default value (Value) and provide additional information during a mouse hover (Title).

 TIP The source code for this example has additional functionality you should review. For example, you'll learn how to use the <NOSCRIPT> tag. This example relies on a script to modify the txtOutput value, so the <NOSCRIPT> tag is essential.

That's all you need to do to add the style sheet to the example. It isn't a complex example, but it does demonstrate several important CSS features.

Testing the CSS

Just as it's important to test the code for your HTML page, it's also important to test the CSS you use for standards compliance. In fact, it might be more important to test this functionality because it has such a big impact on the appearance of your Web site as a whole. The W3C Web site includes the functionality required to test your CSS at http://jigsaw.w3.org/css-validator/. In fact, as shown in Figure 11-3, you have four options for testing your CSS.

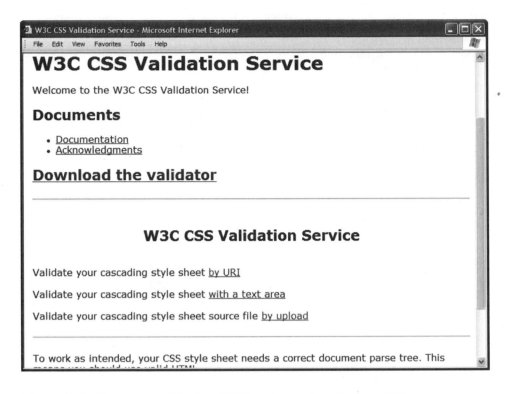

Figure 11-3. Choose any of the four W3C testing options for your CSS.

The option you choose depends on the number of style sheets you have to test, the location of the CSS, and your testing goals. The following list explains the four testing options.

Download The Validator: The W3C wants to make testing as easy as possible. If you have many style sheets to test, it might be easier to download the validator, rather than upload each style sheet for separate validation. The validator works essentially the same no matter where you test, so this option simply allows for local testing in place of using the W3C site directly.

By URI: This is the option to use if you have the CSS coded into the HTML page. Some developers use this technique so that they don't have to maintain separate Web and CSS pages.

With A Text Area: Use this option to perform "what if" analysis of style sheets or when you need to validate a small style sheet. You'll see a text area where you can type style information. The text area also allows text pasting, so you can copy the style sheet information you want to test from an existing document and paste it.

By Upload: In many cases, you'll have a copy of the style sheet you want to test on a local drive. Use this option to upload the style sheet to the W3C Web site and test it. Most developers will use it because it's the easiest. In fact, we'll use this technique in this section.

This section assumes you only have one style sheet to test, so we'll use the upload method. When you select this method, you'll see a form that asks you to supply the name of the file you want to check, as shown in Figure 11-4. This entry holds the location of the file on your hard drive. If you don't want to reveal this information to a non-secure Web site, you can still use the text area method.

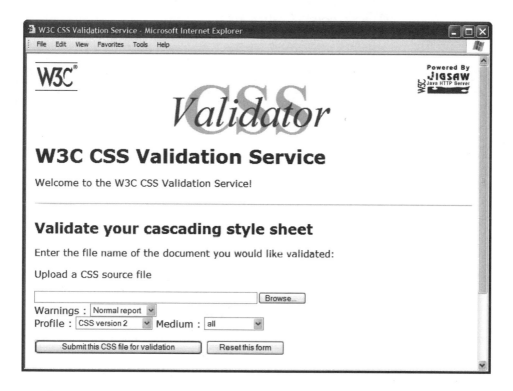

Figure 11-4. Enter the location of the style sheet that you want to check in this form.

Notice that this page contains settings you can use to change the level of the check. It normally pays to set the form to provide you with a complete list of all warnings the style sheet will generate. You'll also want to verify the style sheet against CSS Version 2. The medium is an important setting. If you create a style sheet to answer a particular need, then you should check that medium. For example, you can choose special mediums for handheld devices. Because the style sheet in this example will have to work for all mediums, I set the validator to check all of them. Click Submit This CSS File For Validation and you'll see some output. Figure 11-5 shows the output for the example code shown in Listing 11-1.

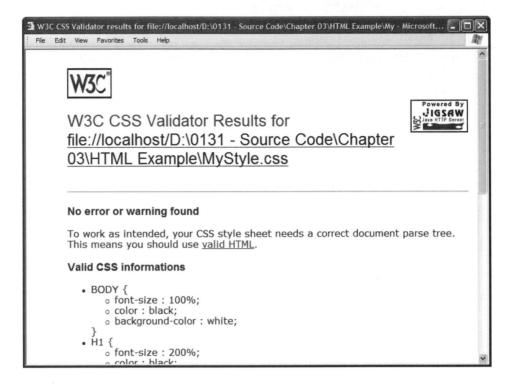

Figure 11-5. Check the output from the validator to learn if you need to make changes to your style sheet.

It's important to realize that creating a CSS file that conforms to the specification is not the same as creating a CSS file that formats the output correctly. This check is an important part of the automated testing processing for your Web application. However, you need to combine it with manual testing as we discussed earlier in the book. Make sure the page looks good and determine whether it works well for users with a variety of needs before you consider the CSS file a success.

Alternatives to Using Color for Information

For many people, color is the highlight of their day. Seeing a colorful display makes life seem better somehow. In fact, there's nothing wrong with using color, and lots of it, on your Web site. The problem comes when the use of color inhibits someone's enjoyment of the content. Consequently, using color for decoration is probably a good idea, but using it to convey information is problematic.

The "Using CSS Example" section describes how you can use CSS to create special effects on your Web page. It should also provide you with some ideas of how to overcome the color problem on your Web site. You can define a style sheet that uses different fonts and font weights to decorate the display without adding any color. For example, you could use a bold font or make the font italic for emphasis. However, you still can't use these features to convey information, as such, because someone with a screen reader won't know that the decoration exists.

In most cases, the best option is to create a plain style sheet for testing—one that lacks any form of color or font decoration. If the Web page still conveys the information you want, then you've provided for the needs of those who use a screen reader. At this point, you can create a colorful display for those who want it and a high contrast display for those with special vision needs. That's one of the benefits of using CSS—everyone can view the information on your Web site using the method that they prefer.

Some developers will use a short sound to indicate an event or special area of the display. In many respects, this technique overcomes the problem of using color to convey information, but it introduces a new problem. Someone with a special hearing need may not hear the sound. In this case, you could overcome the problems of using sound by also adding visual prompts. We discussed this particular issue as part of the "Creating the ShowSounds Test Application" section of Chapter 6. You'd probably need to use a script to display an alert on screen so that the user could see that a system event has occurred.

One of the options that many developers don't use is to exchange description for color. Describing what the color would normally do for the Web site is an option that most people can understand. For example, what if you placed the word, "Stop" in red on your Web site in order to convey danger? Why not simply provide a description of the danger in parenthesis after the word? The prompt might say, "Stop (Going any further will result in loss of data for this session.)" No, the prompt method isn't as short or as visually appealing as the word "Stop" displayed in red, but this technique can help you overcome the problems that color might present. In addition, the user is far more likely to stop if they know that they'll lose data by moving ahead—the prompt method does have the advantage of providing better information to the user.

Working with Image Maps Example

Image maps enable a Web developer to use a color image as a means for navigating to another part of the Web site rather than use standard links or a menu. It's a popular choice with developers because it adds pizzazz to the Web page and looks clever. The problem is that if you can't see the image, it's hard to move the mouse to the right location to use the image map. For that matter, some image maps are so convoluted (think large image with irregularly shaped selection regions), that even a sighted user has problems using them.

A good image map can help make a Web site easier to use. For example, some Web sites use navigational bars to good effect. The navigational bar looks nice and presents the selections in an easy-to-understand format. That's the type of image map we'll discuss in this section—a navigational bar that makes it easy to get from one place on the Web site to another.

Avoiding Server-Side Image Maps

In general, all of the accessibility texts will tell you that server-side images maps are nearly impossible to make accessible. The Web Content Accessibility Guidelines 1.0 specification Section 7.4.3 goes so far as to say you should avoid them unless the image map uses irregularly shaped regions. As previously mentioned, the image maps with irregularly shaped regions often cause more problems than they solve. If you do decide to use a server-side image map, make sure you follow the guidelines in Section 7.4.4 of the specification.

Writing the Code

Working with a navigation bar image isn't difficult. All you need is a graphic containing a series of rectangles with the information needed to navigate from one location to another on the Web site. Listing 11-3 shows the code for the navigation bar used in this example.

Listing 11-3. Client-Side Image Map Code

```
<!DOCTYPE HTML PUBLIC "-//W3C//DTD HTML 4.0 Transitional//EN">
<html>
<head>
<title>Image Map Home Page</title>
</head>
<body>
<h1 align=center>Home Page</h1>
<IMG src="NavBar.gif"
     alt="Select one of the common areas on the site."
     usemap="#map1">
```

```
<MAP name="map1">
    <area shape=rect
          coords="0, 0, 50, 29"
          href="Home.HTM"
          alt="Use this option to go home.">
    <area shape=rect
          coords="51, 0, 100, 29"
          href="Help.HTM"
          alt="Obtain help.">
    <area shape=rect
          coords="101, 0, 200, 29"
          href="About.HTM"
          alt="Learn more about us.">
</MAP>
</body>
</html>
```

If you look through the specification, you'll notice that it recommends other techniques of implementing a project like this one. The problem is that few of the browsers on the market will actually work with those other coding examples. You'll usually get the best results using the technique shown in Listing 11-3.

As you can see, this technique begins by displaying the image on screen using the <IMG> tag, and then creating the image map to support the image using the <MAP> tag. Each of the <AREA> tags defines a different section of the NavBar.GIF graphic. The big issue to remember is that you need to provide an <ALT> tag for each of the areas so that when the user hovers the mouse over that area, they receive help for that option. Adding the <ALT> tags also makes it easier for someone to use a screen reader with the page. Figure 11-6 shows the output from this example.

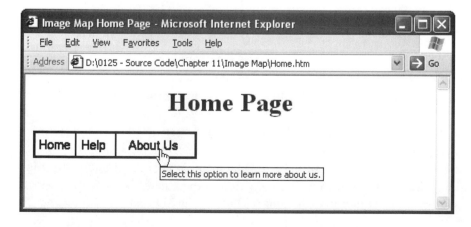

Figure 11-6. Using an image map correctly can make your Web site easier to use.

Captioning Movies and Other Video Presentations

If you decide to add movies or other types of full motion video or streaming audio to your Web site, you'll need to provide captioning for it. The reason is simple. People with special hearing needs can't hear the presentation. To help everyone participate in the presentation, the video or audio must include *captioning*—a text version of the audio presented on screen. If the presentation is a video, you must also provide a descriptive text of the video so that someone with special visual requirements can also enjoy the presentation.

 ON THE WEB   Voice technologies of various sorts have made more than a few appearances. We discussed some voice technologies in Chapter 8, but this discussion focussed on mainstream solutions. Some users have needs that the mainstream solutions don't address, which means that the person creating a solution for these people has to get creative. For example, people who speak Portuguese can find it difficult to locate a program that will meet their needs. One such solution is Motrix (http://intervox.nce.ufrj.br/motrix/). This is a free voice recognition program for those who speak Portuguese. You can read a review of the product at http://www.wired.com/news/technology/0,1282,55539,00.html.

Adding this feature might not be as difficult as you think it will be. Vendors who produce online media products are working on solutions to this problem and many of them have already created solutions that work well. The sections that follow describe a few of the issues you'll want to consider as you create media for your Web site.

Making the Captioning User Selectable

Captioning commonly comes in two forms: open and closed. Open captioning is always on, which might work well in situations where the user always wants the captioning available, but it could prove troublesome for those who don't need the feature. Closed captioning is available at the request of the user. (For a historical overview of one of the initial uses of closed captioning, see the Closed Captioning – Television History site at http://inventors.about.com/library/inventors/blclosedcaptioning.htm. This site also includes a number of links to additional information.) Of course, this means that every time someone needs the feature, they must specifically request it. In general, it's better to use closed captioning and make it very easy for someone to select the feature. Remembering the user's choice through the use of cookies or server-side settings means that the user will only need to make a selection one time for your site—saving everyone a lot of trouble.

NOTE In some cases, you can also check the user's preference for using closed captioning by checking the status of the system flag. However, this would mean having knowledge of the operating system and browser in question.

Captioning with Common Products

As previously mentioned, many of the most popular products on the market today provide the means to create captioned output. In fact, the users of these products have gone to great lengths to ensure that everyone knows how to perform this task. The following list provides a quick overview of the various products and tells where you can learn how to add captioning to them.

QuickTime: The best place to learn about captioning for QuickTime is the WebAIM site at `http://www.webaim.org/howto/captions/quicktime/ quicktime`. These seven pages of instructions provided on this site are extremely clear and easy to follow. You'll also find a wealth of interesting tips and hints on The Captioning Process (`http://www3.cerritos.edu/ vmorgan/captioning/computer_captioning.htm`). Another good place to find tips for captioning your QuickTime presentation (along with good graphics showing the process) is the National Center for Accessible Media (NCAM) site at `http://ncam.wgbh.org/news/webnews16.html`.

Macromedia Flash: Two of the best places to learn about the accessibility features of Macromedia Flash are the Macromedia site at `http:// www.macromedia.com/macromedia/accessibility/features/flash/` and `http://www.trainingcafe.com/macromedia/accessibility/menulist5.asp`. Another good place to find tips for captioning your Macromedia Flash presentation is the National Center for Accessible Media (NCAM) site at `http://ncam.wgbh.org/webaccess/magpie/magpie2_captioner.html`.

RealAudio: The RealPlayer provides captioning capabilities, which is about the only way to tackle this problem. You'll find step-by-step instructions for performing this task at the WebAIM site at `http:// www.webaim.org/howto/captions/real/real`.

Windows Media: Microsoft doesn't make much information available for captioning with the Windows Media Player. However, you can find good step-by-step instructions for performing this task at the WebAIM site at `http://www.webaim.org/howto/captions/windows/windows`.

Media Access Generator (MAGpie): Like many of the other products | discussed in this section of the chapter, WebAIM (`http://www.webaim.org/howto/captions/magpie/`) is the first place you'll want to visit to obtain step-by-step instructions for using MAGpie.

 ON THE WEB   One of the more interesting places to view usage of RealMedia as an accessibility aid is the Assistive Media site at `http://assistivemedia.org/`. Assistive Media makes talking books available to those who need them. Although this Web site is targeted at those with special needs, it's not difficult to see that many other people will use it as well.

Summary

This chapter has taught you a number of usage cue techniques for Web applications. In some cases, you might have already known about the technology, but, hopefully, this chapter has shown you new ways to use the technology in an accessible way. You probably learned about a few new techniques as well. It's important to weigh the various options to see which ones will work best for you. In many cases, using just one of the techniques presented in this chapter can make a big difference in how other people perceive your Web site.

Of course, learning about a technique and knowing how to use it are two different things. You'll want to spend some time looking at your Web applications now to see how you can improve them using the techniques in this chapter. Don't start with a large project; work on something small first, and then build on what you learn from each experience. Make sure you get comments from a number of users as you build updates of your Web site. Try to create a mix of those who have special needs and those who don't so that you can learn from a broader range of users.

Chapter 12 discusses some of the special techniques you can use to enhance a Web site. Many of these techniques involve speech. Because of the wide range of devices in use today, many developers are beginning to take a serious look at speech technology as an alternative to keyboard input. This chapter will help you avoid some of the pitfalls of this technology. It will also help you understand the limitations of speech technology for Web applications. You'll find that many developers think that speech technology will do a lot more for them than it can.

CHAPTER 12

Developing Special Web Application Capabilities

In This Chapter:

- What Are the Potential Web Solutions?
- When Can You Use Java?
- When Can You Use Microsoft Agent?
- When Can You Use the Microsoft Speech API?
- When Can You Use the Speech Application Language Tags (SALT)?
- When Can You Use VoiceXML?
- What Do You Need to Do to Avoid Speech-Only Input Pitfalls?
- How Do You Use Microsoft Agent on the Web?
- How Do You Use SALT?
- How Do You Use Microsoft Speech .NET SDK on the Web?

THE INTERNET HAS BEEN a hot bed of innovative development techniques for quite some time. In some cases, such as HypeText Markup Language (HTML) tags, these techniques are finally starting to mature, but no one actually implements all of the existing standardized tags. In most cases, however, the technology used to provide content on the Internet is evolving every day. The techniques you use today will likely change tomorrow when new standards and specifications arrive on the scene. In short, to provide a consistent and stable environment for their Web sites, many developers take the view that only established technologies need apply for their consideration.

Despite the relatively unstable nature of some Web technologies, it's still worth looking at them when you have special needs to consider. This chapter discusses the latest in special Web technologies, with a focus on speech technologies. You'll learn where these technologies are in their development and what risks you'll take in implementing them on your site. More importantly, you'll discover the accessibility ramifications of using a special technology. In many cases, these new and experimental technologies answer questions that Web users have had for a long time. Using some of these technologies carefully and correctly could actually make your Web site more accessible, not less.

ON THE WEB It's important to note that the speech technology coverage in this chapter only addresses some of the products available at the time of writing. The world of speech application programming has been evolving for many years and will continue to evolve as developer understanding of the speech process improves. In addition, vendors are constantly introducing new products. For example, Sun recently entered the speech market with FreeTTS (`http://freetts.sourceforge.net`), a speech synthesis engine written entirely in the Java programming language. They're also working on a speech recognition engine named Sphinx 4 (`http://cmusphinx.sourceforge.net`)—also written entirely in the Java programming language.

An Overview of the Potential Web Solutions

Conveying information to the user is the result or output of almost any application that you can think of. Everything from the email program you use to communicate with other users to the word processor you use to create your next masterpiece conveys information. The problem with many Web applications is that they don't convey information especially well, or at least not in the right format. To communicate well, the computer and the user have to "speak" the same language in a format they both can use.

Speech technology is a nicety for most desktop applications. The user receives full functionality from the keyboard and the mouse, so speech technology hasn't really caught on as much as it could in this environment. Using a Web application with a cellular telephone is another matter. The lack of a full keyboard and any hint of a mouse can frustrate the user. The addition of speech technology (both voice input and output) in this case represents a logical and necessary step forward.

The following sections will discuss various types of speech technology. Users will rely on some of these products for input, others for output, and some to communicate in both directions. You may want to compare these technologies with the technologies we discussed in Chapter 8. The comparison will reveal some major differences between desktop and Web-based speech solutions.

ON THE WEB The Java products listed in the following sections rely on the Java Virtual Machine (JVM). Windows XP ships without the JVM and some versions of Windows may not include the most compatible version of this product. (The compatibility issues may ease in the future because a judge has ordered Microsoft to ship a compatible version of the JVM with Windows XP—see http://www.eweek.com/article2/ 0,3959,840695,00.asp for details.) In most cases, you'll want to download the current JVM directly from Sun at http://java.sun.com/ getjava/index.html. In addition, to create applications that rely on Java, you'll need the Java 2 Platform Standard Edition (J2SE). J2SE is the replacement for the Java Development Kit (JDK) that most developers have heard about. The best version to get for accessibility needs is the J2SE that's available at http://java.sun.com/j2se/. You may also need the Java Accessibility Utilities found at http://java.sun.com/products/ jfc/accessibility.html.

Java Speech API

The Java Speech API (JSAPI) isn't actually part of the JDK. Sun supports this Application Programming Interface (API) through a specification and third party support. Consequently, if you want to use the JSAPI, you'll need to download one of the third party products available on the Internet. In addition, if you want to ensure that your application will work on the broadest range of systems possible, you'll need to download the specifications guides found at http://java.sun.com/ products/java-media/speech/#fordev. Note that JSAPI is currently undergoing revision through the Java Community Process (JCP)—you can keep apprised of changes at http://www.jcp.org/en/home/index. (You can go directly to the JSAPI efforts at http://www.jcp.org/en/jsr/detail?id=113.) To obtain a complete set of documents, you'll need the following items:

- Java Speech API Specification

- Java Speech API Programmer's Guide

- Java Speech API Grammar Format Specification

- Java Speech API Markup Language Specification

Of these items, only the Java Speech API Specification is a requirement for creating workable applications. The Java Speech API Markup Language Specification is the newest member of the specification list and was still in beta at the time of this writing. You can download the specifications in HTML, PostScript, or PDF format, or view them online if you so desire.

 ON THE WEB   You'll find a wealth of resources for learning to use the Java Speech API online. One of the first places you should look is the Java Speech API Home Page at `http://java.sun.com/products/java-media/speech/`. Another interesting place to look for a good overview of the topic is the alphaWorks site at `http://www.alphaworks.ibm.com/tech/speech`. The IBM site at `http://www-106.ibm.com/developerworks/ibm/library/i-voice/` is also a good place to learn more about this language. One of the more interesting sample applications I found for this technology is VoicePad at `http://www.cloudgarden.com/JSAPI/voice_pad.html`. For example, you can use VoicePad to record text as a WAV or MPEG file. You can find a list of JSAPI implementations at `http://java.sun.com/products/java-media/speech/forDevelopers/jsapifaq.html#implementation`.

Many applications that use the JSAPI rely on IBM ViaVoice technology (see the "Using IBM ViaVoice Technology" section of Chapter 8 for details) as the speech engine. However, you'll also find implementations for the Microsoft Speech API (SAPI) on some Web sites (see `http://www.jpeterson.com/rnd/jepsapi0.2/Readme.html` for details). In fact, those few Web sites that don't have a political axe to grind will show you that JSAPI actually works with a number of speech engines. For example, CloudGarden's JSAPI implementation (`http://www.cloudgarden.com/JSAPI/main.html`) supports the following speech engines:

- IBM ViaVoice (SR & TTS)

- Philips version 2.0 (SR)

- Dragon NaturallySpeaking (SR)

- Lernout and Hauspie (TTS)

- Microsoft SAPI (SR & TTS)

- Infovox (TTS)

- RealSpeak (TTS)

As you can see, the number of successfully tested speech engines is quite large—leaving the choice of which one to use up to you. Note that the acronyms behind each choice stand for Speech Recognition (SR) and Text-To-Speech (TTS). An engine uses SR to convert your speeches to text—it uses TTS to convert text to synthetic speech. The bottom line is that you need the JSAPI packages, a speech engine, and a grammar to use this speech technology.

No matter which speech engine you use, the technique for using the JSAPI is the same. The speech engine accepts input from the user, uses a recognizer to match the incoming words to a grammar, and relies on the `javax.speech.recognition` package to convert the words to text. Likewise, if the application wants to output speech, it uses the `javax.speech.synthesizer` package to create the synthesizer input and the synthesizer to output the audio. The synthesizer relies on the grammar file to produce the audio output in a way that the user will understand.

Java Access Bridge

The Java Access Bridge product helps a developer use the assistive technology found in the Java Accessibility API. Sun implemented the Java Accessibility API as part of the Java Foundation Classes (JFC) Project Swing (`http://java.sun.com/products/jfc/`) user interface components. Consequently, to use this product, you must install support for products such as the JVM and the J2SE.

 ON THE WEB You'll find a wealth of resources for learning to use the Java Access Bridge with Swing online. One of the first places you should look is the Java Access Bridge site at `http://java.sun.com/products/accessbridge/`. One of the more interesting example applications I found is AliceTalker at `http://www.cloudgarden.com/JSAPI/alice_talker1.html`. You might also want to try SwingScroller (`http://www.cloudgarden.com/swingscroller/index2.html`). A compatibility table for this product appears at `http://java.sun.com/products/accessbridge/docs/compatibility.html`. You can find a complete list of Sun-specific accessibility downloads for Java at `http://www.sun.com/access/downloads/`.

At this point, you might ask why Sun called this product an "access bridge." If you want to work with JFC, in most cases, you need to write a Java applet. While this is certainly doable, relying on a Java applet for all your needs is inflexible and limited. The Java Access Bridge provides the means for standard Windows applications, such as a screen reader, to interact with the accessibility portions of the JFC without using an applet. The technology uses two parts: a native Windows DLL and a special Java class. The application communicates its wishes to the native Windows DLL, which translates the information to the Java class. Anyone who's worked with Windows for a long time will realize that the communication is similar to a thunk between the 16-bit and 32-bit environments or the translation that occurs during a PInvoke call in the .NET Framework.

 NOTE For those readers who don't know what a *thunk* is, it's a Microsoft term for moving data between the 16-bit and 32-bit environments. A thunk handles the processor differences between the two environments, including the use of memory locations. Every time a 16-bit function calls a 32-bit function, the operating system must perform a thunk. The same thing happens in the opposite direction. Older versions of Windows actually included a Thunk.DLL file, but this functionality appears as part of the operating system in newer versions.

It helps to have a familiarity with C/C++ if you want to use the Java Access Bridge—at least in the form in which it arrives from Sun. The descriptions of the various API calls appear in the AccessBridgeCalls.H, AccessBridgePackages.H, and AccessBridgeCallbacks.H files. Each of these files corresponds to a particular area of the API as listed here:

- API Calls (http://java.sun.com/products/accessbridge/docs/api.html#API_calls)

- API Data Structures (http://java.sun.com/products/accessbridge/docs/api.html#API_data_structures)

- API Callbacks (http://java.sun.com/products/accessbridge/docs/api.html#API_callbacks)

For the developer, working with the native DLL is very similar to working with other Windows add-ons such as SAPI. You must start the session using the initializeAccessBridge() function and complete it using the shutdownAccessBridge() function. In between these two functions, you can initiate communication, obtain information about the various accessibility elements, and work with the Java objects. In some cases, you'll need to use callbacks to receive information. For example, you'll use callbacks to obtain mouse control information such as a click. Of course, the goal of most of this activity is to locate and retrieve accessibility information using functions such as GetAccessibleTextInfo().

Microsoft Agent

Microsoft Agent is one of the more interesting solutions for speech solutions in Web applications. For one thing, this solution works on both the desktop and on the Web. We discussed the desktop form of the product in the "Using Microsoft Agent on the Desktop Example" section of Chapter 8. In that example, you learned about the essential techniques for creating a Microsoft Agent application.

 ON THE WEB All of the Web links from Chapter 8 also apply to building Web applications. However, some developers have tried to make Web development easier by creating special tools. For example, you'll find an interesting scripting tool called Microsoft Agent Scripting Software (MASS) at http://www.abhisoft.net/mass/. In fact, this product is so good, that we'll discuss it in detail in the "Using Microsoft Agent on the Web Example" section of this chapter. Another good place to look for Microsoft Agent tool software is the EPSScentral site at http://www.pcd-innovations.com/infosite/agents.htm. A good site for obtaining general information and help is BreezeB's DigiWorld at http://breezeb.freeyellow.com/MSAgent.html. If you plan to make a major investment in Microsoft Agent applications, then it pays to look at HelpAgent UCD (http://www.gantekmultimedia.com/helpagen.htm). This product will help you determine information such as whether the user has installed Microsoft Agent, and it will provide access to a number of characters.

People who like Microsoft Agent on the desktop don't necessarily like it on the Web and vice versa. However, one thing remains consistent with this product—people either like it or they don't, there's no middle ground. Either the little characters fill you with delight or they make you cringe as no other Windows feature can. Consequently, you need to consider your audience before you use this option to develop applications with speech.

Desktop applications tend to use the Microsoft supplied characters because these characters usually appear on the user's hard drive and their behavior is well known. More than a few of the Web sites that rely on Microsoft Agent also appear to use custom characters that the user must download. Using a custom character does enhance the appearance of the Web site and does make it unique, but it also increases the download time for the Web application. Because many users still use dial-up connections, it's a good idea to try to use the Merlin character, which tends to appear on every machine that has Microsoft Agent installed. For example, Merlin is the default character for Windows XP.

Whether you use Microsoft Agent on the desktop or as part of a Web application, it requires the same usage procedure. You saw a simple desktop application in Chapter 8—a Web application would require the same functionality. The big difference, as you'll learn in the "Using Microsoft Agent on the Web Example" section of the chapter is that a Web application requires you to use the <OBJECT> tag to create an instance of the agent object. This use of the <OBJECT> tag is Microsoft-specific and may not work with every browser on the market. You'll also need to add an <OBJECT> tag for any voice technology you want to use with Microsoft Agent. In both cases, all you need to provide with the <OBJECT> tag are the ID, ClassID, and CodeBase attributes. You can use these sample <OBJECT> tags in most cases.

```
<Object ID="AgentControl"
  Width=0
  Height=0
  ClassID="CLSID:D45FD31B-5C6E-11D1-9EC1-00C04FD7081F"
  CodeBase="http://activex.microsoft.com/activex/controls/agent2/MSagent.exe">
</Object>
<Object ID="L&HTruVoice"
  Width=0
  Height=0
  ClassID="CLSID:B8F2846E-CE36-11D0-AC83-00C04FD97575"
  CodeBase="http://activex.microsoft.com/activex/controls/agent2/tv_enua.exe">
</Object>
```

Note that you can add an optional version number to the CodeBase attribute. For example, if you want to use version 2.0 of Microsoft Agent, you'd specify the version number as: CodeBase="http://activex.microsoft.com/activex/controls/agent2/MSagent.exe#VERSION=2,0,0,0". The CodeBase attribute ensures that the Web application has the best chance possible to work. If the browser doesn't find the requested objects on the local system, it will offer to download them from the supplied Web site.

The example code also includes the Width and Height attributes. It isn't necessary to include these attributes, but doing so ensures that the user won't see the two objects. In some cases, you'll want to give the objects a size during testing so that you can verify that they appear as anticipated.

Speech Application Language Tags (SALT)

In general, when you want to work with a speech technology, you face the problem of platform dependence. For example, Microsoft Agent and the Microsoft SAPI solutions presented in this chapter rely on the Windows platform. While JSAPI is slightly less platform dependent, some developers will still run into problems with it. For example, Windows XP does ship with the JVM and most platforms don't include other support to use JSAPI. One of the biggest issues that SALT is trying to solve is this issue of platform dependence—it relies on standardized markup languages as a basis for communicating sound information from one machine to another.

 ON THE WEB One of the first places you'll want to visit to learn more about SALT is the SALTForum site at http://www.saltforum.org/. You'll find a good overview of how Microsoft interprets and implements SALT on the Microsoft Speech site at http://www.microsoft.com/speech/evaluation/speechtags/ and Microsoft Developer Network (MSDN) at http://msdn.microsoft.com/library/en-us/getstarted_beta2/html/netspeechtech.asp. The Cover Pages site at http://xml.coverpages.org/salt.html provides news and a number of useful links. Intel's Web site provides an interesting view of the future directions of SALT (http://www.intel.com/home/trends/future/salt.htm).

Another reason for creating SALT is to ensure that there's an open standard that developers can use on a range of devices, including cellular telephones and Personal Digital Assistants (PDAs). The cellular telephone is a speech-oriented device and many PDAs now ship with full voice capability as well. The small devices require speech input capability because the user often lacks access to a keyboard. Because the standard relies on tags, rather than complex scripts, the implementation and interpretation of speech capability can reflect the functionality provided by the device. In short, it doesn't matter if the device has limited memory and a slow CPU; SALT has a good chance of working depending on how the vendor implements support for the tags.

Note that the browser you use with SALT must provide the audio functionality to support speech. Creating a Web page that includes SALT tags doesn't guarantee that the application will work. In fact, most browsers simply ignore any tags they don't understand. Consequently, while you can probably rely on some level of speech support for a device such as a cellular telephone, a browser on a desktop computer doesn't necessarily provide the required support. (Obviously, relying exclusively on speech input isn't the accessible way to develop applications anyway.) In fact, the specification divides browsers into the voice-only type used for small devices such as cellular telephones and the multimodal browsers used with desktop machines.

Most developers will use some type of package to work with SALT. For example, the Microsoft SAPI product relies on SALT for communication—it's a specific implementation of SALT with packaging that makes SALT easier to use. No matter how you use SALT, the tags that SALT uses are a form of eXtensible Markup Language (XML) that will appear within the HTML page. Here's a list of the four upper-level tags.

<PROMPT>: The output tag—the one that enables the application to speak to the user. Applications also use this tag to perform some speech synthesis (output) configuration tasks.

<LISTEN>: The input tag—the one that enables the user to communicate with the application using speech. Applications also use this tag to perform some speech recognition (input) configuration tasks.

<DTMF>: This tag helps an application perform Dual-Tone Multiple Frequency (DTMF) tasks such as dialing the telephone. However, this tag could also provide input normally associated with pressing keys on a telephone. For example, an application could use this tag to select options on a menu based on the menu option number.

<SMEX>: This tag helps an application perform general-purpose communication tasks with the platform using Simple Messaging EXtension (SMEX). For example, the application could use this feature to tell the operating system to log an event.

The capabilities of the host platform determine the potential functionality of a SALT application. The specification divides these platforms into two groups and defines separate modes of operation for each group.

Object Mode: Most desktop and some PDA applications will use this mode. In this mode, the browser and SALT interpreter provide full programmatic access to the various SALT elements. The application can make use of events and scripting to create a fully functional speech environment.

Declarative Mode: Some PDA applications and most cellular telephone applications will use this mode. This mode assumes that events and scripts aren't available. It also assumes that the host device has limited processing capability. An application can still input and output sounds, but the SALT environment limits processing to direct method calls. The application can't perform tasks such as direct manipulation of the Document Object Model (DOM).

As you can see, SALT is an extremely flexible way to work with speech in your application. As a developer, you'll need to choose a particular SALT implementation for your application. This chapter will discuss the Microsoft SAPI implementation, but there are other implementations available. They all use the same elements and element attributes, making SALT portable between platforms as long as you don't use any vendor-specific functionality. (The vendor extensions provided in a particular implementation are normally not standard.)

Microsoft Speech API

The Microsoft Speech API (SAPI) is the latest feature Microsoft has added to the Visual Studio .NET package. Using SAPI can help you create speech-enabled ASP.NET applications quickly and easily. Underlying Microsoft SAPI (or SAPI for short) is SALT, the standard we discussed in the "Speech Application Language Tags (SALT)" section of the chapter. However, SAPI is the Microsoft implementation of SALT and includes many features that aren't part of the SALT specification. You can see a block diagram that shows the relationship between SALT and SAPI at http://www.microsoft.com/speech/evaluation/speechtags/.

ON THE WEB   Microsoft has centralized all of its speech information at http://www.microsoft.com/speech/. However, there are some special places to visit if you want to use SAPI. The first place is the Speech API SDK site at http://www.microsoft.com/speech/techinfo/apioverview/. This site provides an excellent overview of what you can expect from the current SAPI implementation. At the time of writing, Microsoft hadn't released this product. The example found in the "Using Microsoft Speech .NET SDK on the Web Example" section relies on the Beta 2 product found at http://msdn.microsoft.com/library/en-us/getstarted_beta2/html/netspeechtech.asp. Note that this site contains a link where you can order, not download, the SAPI SDK. The site also contains a wealth of information on using SAPI, including usage information.

The SAPI SDK installs as an integrated solution. The controls and projects it adds to Visual Studio .NET appear as a standard part of the installation. Normally, you'll begin by creating an ASP.NET application and adding controls to it as needed to provide voice support for users. We'll look at the implementation details in the "Using Microsoft Speech .NET SDK on the Web Example" section of the chapter.

NOTE   At the time of this writing, SAPI only worked with the .NET Framework 1.0 version—not with the 1.1 version used with Visual Studio .NET 2003. This means you're limited to using Visual Studio .NET 1.0 as a development platform for your SAPI applications. It's very likely that Microsoft will update SAPI to work with Visual Studio .NET 2003 and you may even find this support available now. Make sure you check the SAPI Web site for detailed information.

Developers will also find a number of tools provided with the SAPI SDK. The four main tools include a prompt editor, a grammar editor, a speech control creator, and a special console for debugging speech applications. You'll learn more about these tools when we create the sample application. In general, the tools help you create robust applications with few limitations. For the purposes of the SAPI SDK, a *prompt* represents speech output to the user. On the other hand, a *grammar* represents the words that the user can speak as input and the order in which those words can appear.

The SAPI SDK comes with a number of sample applications of varying complexity. You can find a list of these samples and links for their explanation in the SDK Samples for Speech Controls help topic at `ms-help://MS.NETSpeechSDK.1033/GetStarted/html/SDK_Samples.htm`. Depending on how you install the SAPI SDK, you'll find the actual samples at `http://localhost/speech/samples/selector.aspx` on the installation machine.

You might be wondering if the SAPI SDK works only with Microsoft's vision of SALT. It's possible to create an application that relies exclusively on the SALT tags. However, you give up much of the automation the IDE provides to do it. You'll find the instructions to pursue this route in the help topic at `ms-help://MS.NETSpeechSDK.1033/Authoring/html/AH_SALTMarkupDev.htm`. The text indicates that you'll have to write your code by hand using a simple text editor to follow this route. Using the SALT markup-only solution does mean your application will be compatible with more machines, but it also means that you'll spend a great deal more time writing the application.

One of the problems you'll note when following the SALT markup-only instructions is that there are separate sections for developing and deploying the application. The SAPI component is different from the stand-alone speech component. Consequently, the first deployment options show how to change Globally Unique Identifiers (GUIDs) from the SAPI component to the stand-alone component. Notice that the second deployment option removes any mention of a specific speech component and depends on the browser to locate the right object. Use this option if you want to ensure maximum compatibility for your Web application. Unfortunately, no matter how you look at it, the Web application you create using SAPI will require separate stand-alone testing after you complete it to ensure that the application works as anticipated.

Voice eXtensible Markup Language (VoiceXML)

VoiceXML is another speech API based on XML. The main vendors supporting this standard are AT&T, IBM, Lucent Technologies, and Motorola. As with SALT, VoiceXML relies on a series of elements to perform speech input, output, configuration, and control. The functionality of the two standards is similar, but VoiceXML is actually the older and the more stable of the two.

ON THE WEB   One of the first Web sites you'll want to visit is the VoiceXML Forum at `http://www.voicexml.org/`. You'll definitely want to download the specification from `http://www.w3.org/TR/2001/WD-voicexml20-20011023/`. The VoiceXML Reference site at `http://www.zvon.org/xxl/VoiceXMLReference/Output/` is extremely helpful if you need to learn the meaning of a tag quickly. This reference site also includes short examples that you can use to learn how the tags appear in code. Learn about the IBM VoiceXML offerings on the alphaWorks site at `http://www.alphaworks.ibm.com/tech/voicexml/`. The VoiceXMLCentral site at `http://www.voicexmlcentral.com/` is an essential place to find VoiceXML applications and servers. If you want to experiment with VoiceXML, you can use the Extensible Laboratory of Speech and Dialogue (LSD) VoiceXML Interpreter for Dialog Applications (ELVIRA) interpreter found at `http://gin2.itek.norut.no/elvira/_elvira.php?p=introduction`. The ELVIRA interpreter comes in versions for both the Windows and Linux platforms.

VoiceXML also uses a <PROMPT> element to output information to the user. You'll find a simple version of a program that uses the <PROMPT> element in the \Chapter 12\VXML folder of the source code that you can obtain from the Downloads section of the Apress Web site (`http://www.apress.com`). Here's a simple Hello World application.

```
<?xml version="1.0"?>
    <vxml version="2.0" xmlns="http://www.w3.org/2001/vxml">
        <form id="someName">
            <block>
                <prompt>
                    Hello World
                </prompt>
            </block>
        </form>
    </vxml>
```

As you can see, the example looks a lot like the XML you might have used in the past. The essential tag in this case is the <PROMPT> tag, which tells the interpreter to say, "Hello World." I tried the example out using the ELVIRA interpreter. (You can find additional ELVIRA examples at `http://gin2.itek.norut.no/elvira/_elvira.php?p=examples`.) This is a command line product. You type **ELVIRA HELLO.VXML** at the command prompt to start the application. To hear the output using SAPI, you need to uncomment the following line of code in the ELVIRA.CFG file.

```
output=cz.muni.fi.cons_and_sapi_output
```

Input relies on a <GRAMMAR> element that requires the use of subelements to define the grammar in question. For example, the developer could say that the grammar is based on a rule. The developer could further define the rule as selecting one of three elements using keywords. Here's an example of that type of grammar in action.

```
<field name="MyField"/>
<prompt>Say One, Two, or Three.</prompt>
<grammar mode="voice">
  <rule id="MyRule" scope="public">
    <one-of>
      <item>One</item>
      <item>Two</item>
      <item>Three</item>
    </one-of>
  </rule>
</grammar>
```

In this case, the user would hear a prompt requesting a specific input value. The user could select an item by saying the words: "One," "Two," or "Three." The grammar would ignore any other input, making the input highly selective. When the user says one of the keywords, the interpreter assigns that value to a field named MyField. The specification provides for a number of input types. As in our example, the developer could use a <FIELD> element to define an input field on a form. Likewise, the <MENU> element lets the user choose from one of several menu options.

Like SALT, the client platform must have an interpreter that supports VoiceXML. If this interpreter is missing, the browser ignores the speech tags contained within the HTML. In fact, like SALT, the browser tends to display the text information as simple text on the display. The precise VoiceXML features you obtain will depend on the implementation you use—making the interpreter selection important.

Avoiding the Pitfalls of Speech-Only Input

An unfortunate side effect of many new technologies is that the developer wants to use the technology to the exclusion of everything else. After all, the developer is quite excited about the potential of the new technology and has invested a lot of time in learning about it, so the developer feels that everyone else should be excited too.

Most users are quite wary of new technologies because they make the user feel uncomfortable. The continued existence of the QWERTY keyboard is an example of just how much comfort means to the user. The Dvorak layout is more efficient, produces output faster and with fewer errors, and reduces the incidence of diseases such as carpal tunnel syndrome. (You can see a picture of the Dvorak layout at `http://www.mwbrooks.com/dvorak/layout.html`.) Yet, most users insist that they must continue to use a keyboard designed to slow the typist down. The designers of this archaic keyboard layout intended it to reduce the chance that the typist would press several keys at once on mechanical typewriters.

 ON THE WEB   Sometimes a developer can create a tool out of an application that a user would normally require. For example, the Web Access Gateway (`http://www.cl.cam.ac.uk/~ssb22/access.html`) provides users with better control over the way a Web page displays. However, this tool can also help you learn more about your Web site—especially how any special features you included work with a user setup that isn't designed to support them. For example, you can choose to display the page without graphics or using a large font. The Web Access Gateway also lets you remove color and perform other manipulations such as precise configuration of page options. For example, you can see how your page will react if the user turns off scripts (a real problem when using special features).

We discussed a number of problems with speech technology as a whole in the "Relying On Speech as the Second Input Method" section of Chapter 8. Most of those limitations hold for Web applications as well. However, you need to consider other limitations for Web applications that may not apply as much to desktop applications. The relative merits of speech input often depend on the environment in which the technology is used. Regardless of how excited you are by the use of speech as an input or output technology, you must avoid using it in some situations. Here are some of the most common situations where you should avoid using speech technology as the sole source of input.

- The user is working in a noisy environment.

- Other people will talk with the user during data input.

- An application must present large quantities of text or text that includes a lot of jargon.

- The task requires the user to perform comparisons.

- The sounds produced by the speech technology will disrupt other people in the workplace.

- The user must work with sensitive or personal information.

- The connection to the network isn't completely reliable.

- The user can accomplish the task easier with a keyboard and/or mouse.

Web applications can include a number of devices that you wouldn't normally consider for a desktop application. For example, the user might need to use the speech technology from a cellular telephone. In some cases, the user will also work from a kiosk or using a PDA. The assortment of devices used for Web applications make this environment a better candidate for speech technology because there's often no other good way to accomplish the task at hand. Successful uses of speech technology for Web applications include situations where

- The user lacks access to a keyboard and/or a mouse.

- The user's hands are occupied performing some other task or the user can't touch the device for other reasons (such as a doctor performing surgery).

- The application relies on a complex menu structure.

- Personal applications are used in situations in which the user will respond better if the computing device has a personality.

- The user doesn't know how to type.

- An emergency requires the user's immediate attention.

- The user has special mobility needs that prevent the use of a keyboard and/or mouse.

Given the pluses and minuses of using speech technology as part of a Web application strategy, you need to decide how much emphasis to place on it during application design. An application could rely on speech technology as the primary means of input. However, you need to avoid situations in which speech technology is the only input because this approach presents the same problems the user will encounter using speech on a desktop application. In general, make sure the user can at least configure the application to use both keyboard and mouse if desired.

Using Microsoft Agent on the Web Example

You learned in the "Using Microsoft Agent on the Desktop Example" section of Chapter 8 that creating an application that uses Microsoft Agent isn't difficult, but it does require some interesting coding techniques at times. Wouldn't it be nice if you could leave the typing exercise to someone else and consider only the animation you want to present? That's the premise behind Microsoft Agent Scripting Software (MASS) (http://www.abhisoft.net/mass/). This software makes it easy to create a script that's output as a Web page. Of course, you'll need to download and install it before you can work with the example in this section.

To start a project, you use the File ➤ New Script command. You'll see an Open dialog box that contains a list of the characters loaded on the machine. The application uses the standard \Windows\msagent\chars folder as a starting point, but you can always select a new folder. Once you select a character, click Open and the application will load the character for you. It also adds the Show script entry for the animation, as shown in Figure 12-1. This action displays the character on screen. In short, the actions you perform in MASS appear on screen, so you can see the animation as you build it.

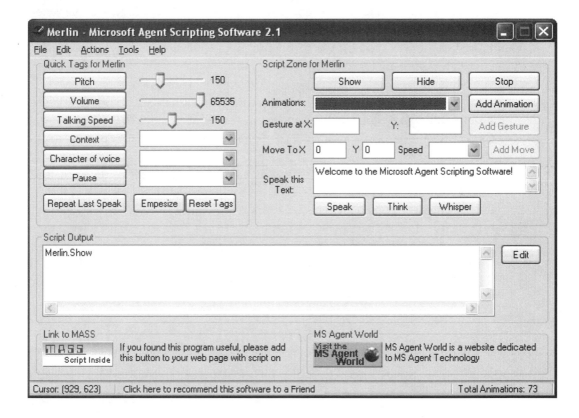

Figure 12-1. When MASS loads the character, it also creates the first animation command for you.

NOTE　The example in this section will replicate the animation demonstrated in Chapter 8. You'll also find the listing in the \Chapter 12\MSAgent folder of the source code that you can obtain from the Downloads section of the Apress Web site (http://www.apress.com).

Creating the animation sequence is easy. Start by selecting the animation you want the character to perform from the Animations list. The Animations list content changes to match the character you've loaded. In fact, you can use the Actions ➤ Show All Animations command to display all of the animations the character can perform so that you can easily see the difference between the DoMagic1 and the DoMagic2 script commands. Consequently, MASS eliminates some of the problems we discussed in Chapter 8 regarding animation usage. You always know precisely which animations you can use with a particular character.

When you select one of the animations from the list, the on-screen character performs that action. Again, this feature helps you see the animation as you create it. (If the character remains idle for a while, the application also performs the correct idle animation.)

Animations usually include sounds. You can tell your character to speak, think, or whisper using the three buttons shown in Figure 12-1. To use this functionality, type what you want the character to speak, think, or whisper, and then click the appropriate button. The application will add the action to the Script Output window.

It's interesting to note that you can map the character speech. However, don't follow the Microsoft instructions precisely. You don't need to include all of the escape characters normally required to make this feature work. The mapped text we used in Chapter 8 becomes `"\Map=""What you hear is not what you see!""=""Hello World""\"` for this example. Fortunately, you don't have to create this code by hand. Use the Actions ➤ Map Text command to change the display, as shown in Figure 12-2. Simply type the text you want to use for each part of the map, click Test It! to check the effect, and then click Add to add it to the script.

```
Merlin - Microsoft Agent Scripting Software 2.1                    [_][□][X]

File   Edit   Actions   Tools   Help
┌─ Map Text ──────────────────────────────────────────────────────────────
│   The map text feature allows character to speak something, but show something else in the word balloon. (Example: URLs,
│                    E-Mail Addresses, Currency Symbols and other language words.)
│
│   Before Text:    [1                                              ]    ┌──────────┐
│                                                                        │   Add    │
│   When this is    [2                                              ]    └──────────┘
│   spoken:
│   Show this text  [3                                              ]    ┌──────────┐
│   in Balloon:                                                          │  Test it!│
│   After Text:     [4                                              ]    └──────────┘
│                                                                        ┌──────────┐
│                                                                        │Script Zone│
│                                                                        └──────────┘
┌─ Script Output ─────────────────────────────────────────────────────────
│  Merlin.Show                                                    [▲]    ┌──────┐
│  Merlin.Play "Announce"                                               │ Edit │
│  Merlin.Play "RestPose"                                               └──────┘
│  Merlin.Speak "\map=" + chr(34) + "What you hear is not what you see!" + chr(34) + "=" + chr(34) + "Hello World"
│  Merlin.Play "Greet"                                           [▼]
│  [◄]                           ....                             [►]

┌─ Link to MASS ──────────────────────────┐  ┌─ MS Agent World ──────────────┐
│  mass          If you found this program useful, please add │  Visit the   MS Agent World is a website dedicated
│  Script Inside this button to your web page with script on │  MS Agent    to MS Agent Technology
│                                         │  World

Cursor: (1081, 346)    Click here to recommend this software to a Friend       Total Animations: 73
```

Figure 12-2. Create text maps using the Map Text feature.

You'll add each action one at a time until the animation sequence is complete. Of course, the last action is to hide the character from view. Figure 12-3 shows part of the completed script for this section. Placing the cursor at the end of a line in the Script Output window enables you to add a new script item at that point. For example, you might want to add a pause or additional speech.

 CAUTION   Using fully escaped text for speech can cause problems with MASS. The product froze twice during testing when I inadvertently used a fully escaped version of the test text. Fortunately, this is the only flaw I experienced and even it's easy to avoid.

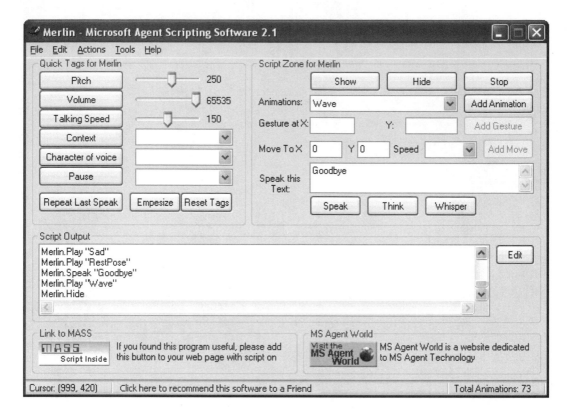

Figure 12-3. The completed script appears in the Script Output window.

Once you complete the script, use the File ➤ Save Script command to save it to disk. The result is an HTML file that contains all of the commands required to run the animation. You'll still need to add other content to the page. MASS doesn't provide the tools require to perform other types of HTML editing, but it does make using Microsoft Agent on a Web page almost too simple.

MASS provides a lot more functionality than we've used in this short example. For example, you can move the character around. The main window shown in Figure 12-1 provides simple movement commands. However, you can create complex movement using the Actions ➤ Move Plus command. Figure 12-4 shows the Move Plus window. As you can see, it provides control over features such as the assumed screen resolution and the precise location of the figure.

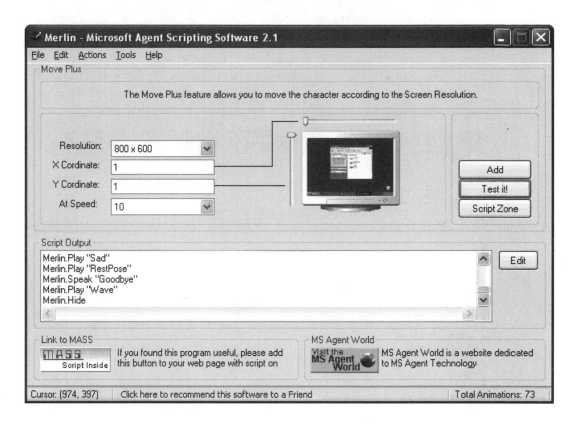

Figure 12-4. Define character movement pricisely using the options in the Move Plus window.

TIP Make sure you try out the other options on the Actions menu. You'll find that you can control options such as the character size and the size of the text balloon. The Actions ➤ Speak Wave option even lets you present the content of a WAV file as output.

You'll also find that MASS provides tools for modifying the character voice and performing other tasks with relative ease. Click the Edit button to see the script that the program has developed for you in the Edit Script window shown in Figure 12-5. You can use this window to fine-tune the script, but the character won't actually perform the new actions. This window also provides the means for you to paste existing script into the editor.

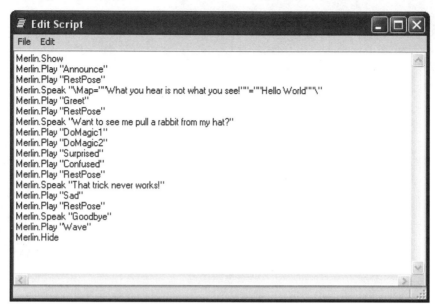

Figure 12-5. Use the Edit Script window to fine-tune your script.

The Tools menu provides access to a number of useful features. At the top of the options list is the Accessibility Options entry. This is the first time I've seen an application that provides this feature. Selecting this option displays the Accessibility Options dialog box so that you can test your animation using various Windows Accessibility options. For example, you can use this feature to see how your character performs using a high contrast display or with features such as StickyKeys turned on.

About the only problem with MASS is that it doesn't use project folders. This means that any output you create for the current session is very hard to reload into the MASS for the next session. The best way around this problem is to open the HTML file in a text editor, copy the script commands, and then paste them into the Edit Script window shown in Figure 12-5. I hope that the author will correct this flaw because in all other ways MASS represents a fine addition to any developer toolbox.

Using Microsoft Speech .NET SDK on the Web Example

The central idea behind adding speech to your application is to make it more accessible to everyone. Using speech adds one more option for the user—input can now occur using the keyboard, mouse, or voice. Output is no longer limited to the display—the user can hear it as well. From an accessibility perspective, this can mean a great deal to the user of your application because the user will have more ways to interact with it.

The following sections will discuss a simple application and introduce you to the SAPI as well. In this case, I chose not to follow the pure SALT route because the benefits of using the automation provided by the IDE are too great to ignore. You'll learn about the controls that Microsoft provides for working with speech applications and the tools you'll need to create application data.

 NOTE The example in this section assumes that you have the SAPI SDK installed (along with all of the required support for Windows). You'll find the development materials in the \Chapter 12\SAPIDemo of the source code that you can obtain from the Downloads section of the Apress Web site (http://www.apress.com). The IIS materials appear in the \Chapter 12\SAPIDemo (Server) folder. Copy this second folder to your IIS \Inetpub\wwwroot folder. Rename the folder SAPIDemo without the "(Server)" portion.

Tuning Your Microphone

It's easy to tell if your speakers aren't set up correctly for using SAPI. All you need to do is listen. If no sound comes out when the computer is supposed to be saying something and you can't get sound any other way, it's almost certain that there's something wrong with your speaker setup (either hardware or software).

Determining if your microphone requires tuning is a little more difficult. You don't know what the computer is hearing. For this reason, make sure you open the Microsoft Internet Explorer Speech Add-in Start Page at \Program Files\Microsoft .NET Speech\Client\SpeechAdd-inStartPage.htm. This page includes a number of tests you should run. It begins with the output test, but as previously stated, it's relatively easy to determine the output status. When you get to the Test Speech Input section of this Web page, click Open Speech Control Panel. You'll see a Speech Properties dialog box similar to the one shown in Figure 12-6.

Figure 12-6. Tune your microphone using the options in the Speech Properties dialog box.

Click Configure Microphone and you'll see a Microphone Wizard dialog. Simply follow the steps this wizard provides to tune your microphone. When you complete the wizard, the volume should work well for your voice. The reason this step is so important is that setting the microphone volume too low means the computer can't hear what you're saying. Conversely, setting the volume too high introduces distortion, which makes it nearly impossible for the computer to understand you.

A Look at the Controls

After you install the SAPI SDK on your system, you'll notice a new set of controls like the ones shown in Figure 12-7. These controls make it easy to add input or output functionality to your application. The Question and Answer (QA) control is the one that you'll use most often for applications of any complexity. In addition, you'll commonly use the QA control to create prompts. However, notice that the control list includes predefined inputs for some needs, such as answering yes and no using the YesNo control.

Figure 12-7. Add speech controls to your application to make it talk or listen.

Some controls provide linkage or other management functionality. For example, the SemanticMap control will route speech input from the various speech controls to the user interface controls on the form. The example uses a combination of QA and a SemanticMap control to provide speech capability.

CAUTION   Some developers assume that placing a control in a certain order on screen necessarily guarantees the order of that control in the HTML. This isn't the case, but normally it's not an issue because the application will eventually draw all of the required controls. However, with a speech application, the order of the controls is important because the browser will receive the controls in the order that they appear in the HTML. Consequently, you might find yourself spending hours trying to figure out why your application asks the last question in a sequence first. When this problem occurs, make sure you check the HTML tab of the designer window to ensure that the tags for the speech control appears in the proper order.

Defining a Grammar

You can save yourself some time if you define the grammar for your application before you attempt to create other speech-oriented portions of the application. The grammar defines the words the user can speak as input and the order in which those words can appear. Developing a grammar requires preplanning because you need to know what each field will require as input, the position of that field in the chain of spoken input, and how you want the application to interpret the input.

Of course, before you can work with a grammar, you need to add one to the application. You can perform this task by right clicking the project entry in Solution Explorer, selecting Add ➤ Add New Item from the context menu, and selecting Grammar File from the list of templates. Click Open to complete the process.

The example application has two fields. The first field asks a simple yes/no question—it asks whether the user want to display the remaining on-screen controls. The answer to this question determines whether the application even asks the second question, so it obviously has to come first. The second field contains a selection of three colors: red, green, and blue.

The easiest way to create a grammar is to begin from the bottom up. That means defining the input for each field. If you want to have precise control over the user input, you'll need to create an input list. Otherwise, you can use any of a number of other input types, including a Wildcard control that allows the user to input anything. Figure 12-8 shows a typical field grammar entry. This figure shows a list with two phrases attached to it. Each phrase requires a definition in the Semantic Tags window. Notice the Yes phrase shown in Figure 12-8 will return a value of Yes to the value property of the calling control. (The value property is associated with JavaScript, not with the C# code behind for the ASP.NET page.)

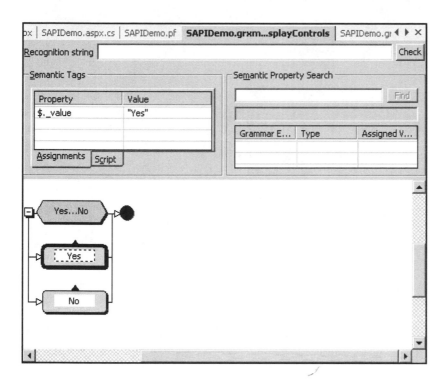

Figure 12-8. Create a grammar rule for each field on the form.

The next level of defining the grammar is to create the relationships between elements. To do this, you'll need to add additional rules to the grammar by right clicking the grammar file in Grammar Explorer and selecting New Rule from the context menu. Figure 12-9 shows a typical relationship grammar. (You see how this process works by looking through the grammar provided with the source code.) This figure shows the first level grouping. It includes both the yes/no question and the color question. A second-level grouping includes just the color selection. I'll explain how this works a little later in this section.

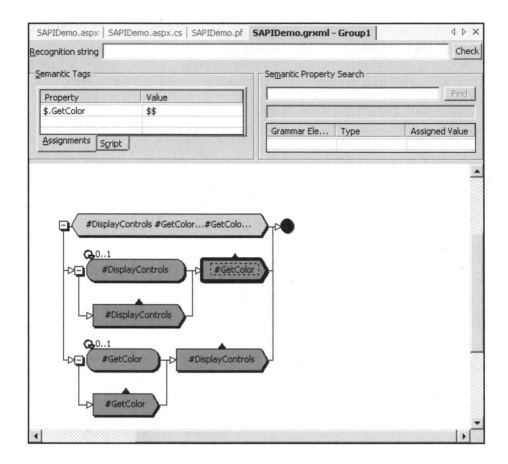

Figure 12-9. Create a grammar rule for each field on the form.

Once you have the various rules in place, you'll need to select a [Root] node. This node is always associated with the grouping for the first field of the form. In this case, it's the grouping (Group1) associated with the yes/no question. You can see how these rules appear in Figure 12-10. To set the [Root] node, right click one of the rules and choose Make Root from the context menu.

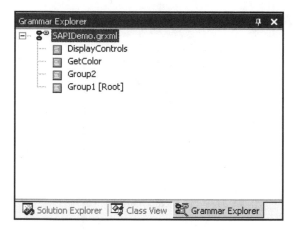

Figure 12-10. Select one of the rules to act as the [Root] node.

Associating the Grammar with Controls

Now that you have some rules in place, it's time to associate the grammar with the controls that will use them. The first task is to create some entries for the SemanticMap control. You'll normally have just one of these controls for an application. The purpose of this control is to create linkage between the user interface control and the associated speech control. Create this linkage by defining a collection of items for the SemItem property. Click the ellipses and you'll see a SemanticItem Collection Editor dialog box. Figure 12-11 shows a typical entry for this collection. The three values you must provide appear in bold in the figure. Most important is the name of the user interface control and the JavaScript (not the object) property you want to modify.

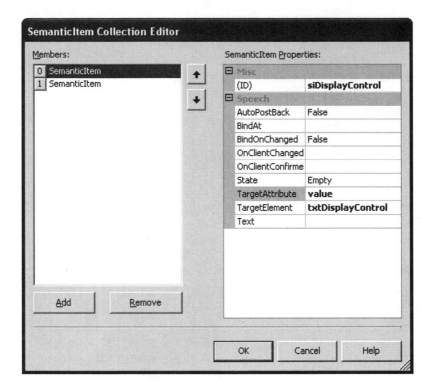

Figure 12-11. Add SemanticItem entries so that you can access the user input control from the speech control.

The second step in associating a grammar with the controls is to create linkage between the SemanticItem and the grammar. Look at the Properties Window for the QA control that you want to work with. Notice the Property Builder link. Click this link and you'll see a dialog box similar to the one shown in Figure 12-12.

As shown in Figure 12-12, you must define three elements to make the linkage between the SemanticItem and the grammar. First, add the grammar to the Speech Grammars list. Notice that the example has the name of the grammar file, followed by a pound sign (#), followed by the name of the grouping we want to use (see Figure 12-9) for this control. Second, select the SemanticItem that this control will access in the Semantic Item column of the Answers tab. Third, type the name of the grammar to associate with the SemanticItem (./DisplayControls in this case).

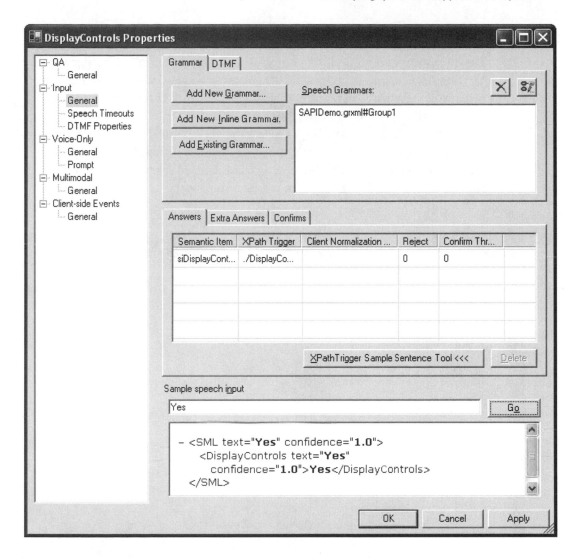

Figure 12-12. Define the relationship between the QA control and the grammar rule.

At this point, you should test the grammar to make sure it works. You can do this by clicking XPathTrigger Sample Sentence Tool. Figure 12-12 shows the resulting dialog box addition. Type each of the words for that control in turn and click Go to check the returned value. For this example, the output should look the same as the output in Figure 12-12 for the inputs provided in the figure. If you're testing something other than the first-level control, you should also try works from those previous controls. The dialog should return an error message. If not, you're probably using the wrong group level for that control.

Defining Prompts

The SAPI supports two kinds of prompts. The first type of prompt is straightforward because the control simply outputs the text you provide. The second type requires more work because SAPI requires that you create a function to define it. However, this second type is a lot more flexible.

To create the first type of input, select the Voice-Only\Prompt option of the Properties dialog box shown in Figure 12-13. Type the prompt you want to hear associated with the speech control. You can define QA controls that have only speech input, speech output, or a combination of both.

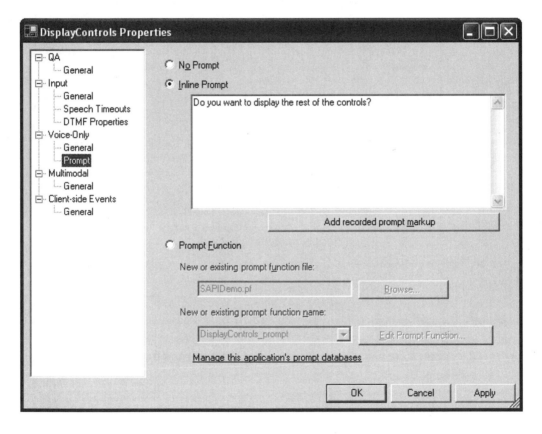

Figure 12-13. Creating a static prompt only requires that you type what you want to hear the speech control say.

Creating a dynamic prompt begins when you add a Prompt Function File to the application using Solution Explorer. The resulting file looks similar to the one shown in Figure 12-14. In this case, I've already added the function required for the Goodbye speech control.

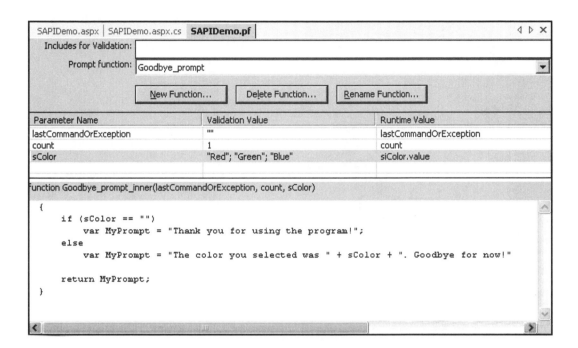

Figure 12-14. Define a dynamic prompt using JavaScript code.

As you can see, creating a dynamic prompt means knowing how to use JavaScript, rather than C# or Visual Basic. You begin by naming the function (as you normally would). Defining input parameters means filling out the grid at the top, as shown in Figure 12-14. You need to provide a SemanticItem name and the property of that object that you want to use as input. The grid also provides a space for valid input values. This function checks the siColor.value property (contained within sColor) for a valid value. If it has none, then the user decided not to display the color input. The function creates one of two messages depending on the user's decisions.

After you create the function, you add the prompt to the control. Figure 12-15 shows the Goodbye Properties dialog box. Notice that you need to provide the name of the Prompt Function File and the name of the function within that file that you want to use.

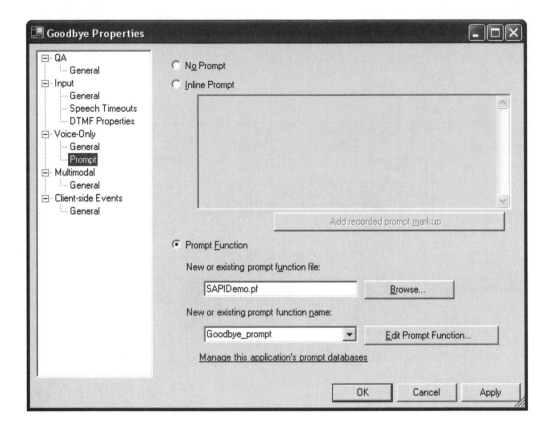

Figure 12-15. Assign the function to a speech control using the Prompt Function File and function names.

At this point, the example is ready to run. Compile it and you'll hear the computer greet you and ask you for the first input. You can tell the computer whether you want to display the remaining controls or not. If you decide to display them, you'll need to select a color. In either case, the computer will say goodbye in a way that depends on the selections you made.

Summary

The chapter has demonstrated several technologies you can add to your Web application to improve the user experience. You've learned that these technologies can also improve the accessibility of your application in some cases, but used incorrectly, they can also cause user problems. Most important, however, is that you've learned the current limitations of these technologies and that they're apt to change in the future.

Even if you decide not to implement one of these technologies in a production application today, it's a good idea to spend time looking at the technology for future use. As users move more into Web applications, you'll find that their expectations will rise. In addition, users no longer encumber themselves with a desktop machine or even a laptop computer if they can use some other solution. Expect users to request improved support for devices such as cellular telephones in the near future. Often, these devices require the use of specialized software, such as the speech-input applications discussed in this chapter.

Chapter 13 will introduce the topic of Web site scripting. Developers use scripting to perform a variety of tasks. In some cases, those tasks are cosmetic in nature, such as formatting the page. However, in other cases, scripts form the backbone of an application. The problem with scripts is that they can cause a great deal of trouble for the user. For example, improperly coded scripts can confuse the screen reader. In addition, listening to the screen reader read your script is hardly the way that anyone wants to spend the day. This chapter helps you understand proper use of scripts and shows techniques for ensuring that your scripts will work as anticipated without hindering the user.

CHAPTER 13

Accessible Scripting Solutions

In This Chapter:

When Should You Use Scripts?

How Can You Create Accessible Web Site Script Enhancements?

Why Should You Include Both Mouse and Keyboard Support?

Why Should You Use JavaScript If Possible?

What Are the Basic Element Events?

How Do You Create Accessibility Friendly Scripts?

How Do You Create a Mouseover Script?

SCRIPTS HAVE BECOME prevalent on the Internet because they help developers perform so many important tasks. For example, a script can calculate the total on an order. A developer can also use a script to check input information for correct values. Some scripts are so useful that the Web page would be difficult to implement without them. Of course, some developers believe that scripts are indispensable because they're so useful and perform so many tasks. However, a developer can *always* find an alternative to using scripts and that's one of the first issues we'll discuss in this chapter.

NOTE   Web applications generally use two types of scripts: client-side and server-side. Server-side scripts never cause accessibility problems because the user never sees them—all the user sees is the script output. Consequently, the most accessible sites rely exclusively on server-side scripting to ensure that the user never sees anything but finalized content. Client-side scripts can cause a wealth of problems—not just accessibility-related problems. This chapter focuses on the issues surrounding the client-side script. Whenever you see the word "script" used alone, assume the text is discussing a client-side script issue. In general, I'll use the phrases "client-side script" and "server-side script" whenever there's a potential for confusion.

Obviously, this chapter will concentrate on the accessibility issues created by client-side scripts (those downloaded for execution on the user's machine). We won't discuss server-side scripting except as necessary to make a point about the client-side issues. (You can find an extensive overview of some of the more popular server-side scripting languages at http://hotwired.lycos.com/webmonkey/99/46/index1a.html.) It's also important to note that client-side scripts cause problems other than those described in this chapter. The most prominent problem is that pages that contain scripts can also contain viruses, which is the reason that many people turn scripting support off on their browser. In sum, a single chapter can't tell you everything about scripting languages—a whole book couldn't accomplish that task. However, you will learn about something not found in many books—the accessibility issues of scripting.

Once you determine that you can use scripts safely and you have created a non-script alternative, you need to decide how to attach the script to the Web page. In most cases, you'll attach the script to an event associated with a particular screen element. Some scripts also run when a particular page event occurs, such as the initial loading process. We'll discuss some of the most common events, and you'll learn how they could affect the accessibility of the page.

The chapter also includes two useful examples that demonstrate accessible use of scripts. The first example demonstrates essential principles for a background calculation script and shows how you can overcome the problem of creating a non-script solution. The second example demonstrates the same principles for a visual script—one that presents a visual change to the user.

Understanding When to Use Scripts

Some people approach every problem as a nail that requires a few hits from a hammer. However, not every problem is a nail and well-equipped developers possess an assortment of tools. A script can perform amazing tasks in the right hands. However, scripts can also become a nuisance if the client (normally the user's browser) doesn't provide this functionality. In short, it's important that you use a script only when necessary and then learn to implement the script in such a way that it also accommodates the needs of those clients that don't provide script support.

This section of the chapter examines several important script issues. The first thing you need to avoid is scripts that don't serve a useful purpose. It's also important to avoid scripts that perform a useful task but perform it in an unnecessarily complex manner. Finally, once you decide that you must use a script, it's important to know how to implement it in the most accessible way possible.

Avoid the Non-Useful Scripts

It's surprising to see the number of non-useful scripts on Web pages today. For example, I recently visited a Web site that used a script to modify the size and appearance of the text on screen. Not only does such a script make the Web page less accessible, but also it isn't useful. If someone can see the page well enough to read the instructions to use the script, then they probably can see the rest of the text as well. In general, developers should avoid adding scripts of this sort to a Web page because the user will want to modify the text size using standard browser controls. In fact, if the developer wants to make the Web page completely flexible, it's better to rely on Cascading Style Sheets (CSS) so that the user can replace the default CSS file with one of their own.

Another type of useless script is the one that redirects users all over the Internet. Some Web sites end up with four or five levels of indirection. The only problem with this approach is that anyone who doesn't have script support ends up stuck on the first page. If a Web site must use scripted redirection, it should also provide a direct link so that the user can simply click on the link, rather than wait for the script. Unfortunately, if you disable script support on your browser, you'll find yourself stuck on some page without any text all too often.

Menus are another kind of Web site scripting problem—one that is becoming more common. Consider the InformeDesign Web site (`http://www.informedesign.umn.edu/`) shown in Figure 13-1. At the time of writing, the Web site presents the pop-up menu shown in the figure using scripts. Notice the number of items on this menu. As long as the user has scripting enabled, they can move freely around the Web site. However, if the user doesn't have scripting enabled, clicking the Main Menu icon doesn't do anything at all—the user is stuck using the few links that don't appear on the Main Menu. This Web site is interesting because it breaks a number of other rules too. For example, as you'll learn in the "Creating a Mouseover Example" section of the chapter, the scripting code only addresses the `onmouseover` attribute and not the `onfocus` attribute. You might want to run this site through Bobby (`http://bobby.watchfire.com/bobby/html/en/index.jsp`) to see where the developer made mistakes and avoid those errors on your own Web site.

Some scripts fall into the "useless" category because they violate the trust the user has in the Web site. Any script that gathers any information without the user's consent falls into this category. Why should the Webmaster feel obliged to gather user information covertly? Experience shows that Web sites with covert information gathering mechanisms use them because the Webmaster is sure the user wouldn't provide the information freely.

Figure 13-1. When you assume that everyone has scripting enabled, some people won't be able navigate your site.

Of course, you'll run into any number of scripts associated with banner ads, the bane of the Internet. Yes, banner ads provide the Web site owner with income, but the price of the Web site owner's wealth is often too high for accessibility purposes. Try turning off scripting support for sites that commonly use popup ads and you'll find that the information is still viewable, but many of the ads will stop working. If you decide that your site must use pop-up ads, try to use ads that don't rely on scripts. In general, you'll learn that removing script support doesn't damage the advertising potential of the pop-up ad and it might even improve coverage to those people who decide to disable scripting on their systems.

We've discussed gizmos before in this book. Scripts come in gizmo form, too. For example, is it necessary to create a cascading hierarchical list of Web site locations with vanishing menus? Isn't it easier to provide the user with a site map that leads them to the location without a multitude of weird visual effects? Unfortunately, as Web sites become more complex, this type of visual garbage becomes more common. If the script actually works (and often it doesn't), finding what you need becomes overly complex and the process is cumbersome.

Does the Page Work Without the Script?

If you have the impression that most Web sites would work just fine without scripts at this point, you're correct. It's important to decide if your Web site really needs to use scripts. You can avoid these common negative issues by not using client-side scripts.

Browser Compatibility: Users are still running into browser compatibility problems and it's doubtful this problem will ever go away because the various browser vendors are determined to differentiate their products by making them incompatible. A developer can improve Web site compatibility by reducing the use of features such a scripts.

Clients Without Scripting Support or Scripting Support Turned Off: If your Web site uses scripts, you take the chance that many of the clients visiting your site won't be able to use specific features. It's better to implement as much functionality as possible using server-side scripts and send the result to the client.

Support: Any time you add complexity to an application, it means that more users are going to become confused and your support costs will increase. The use of scripts will significantly increase support costs due to compatibility, usability, and accessibility problems.

Maintenance: Development is expensive. All you have to do is look at the number of recent changes to the Information Technology (IT) industry to see that companies are serious about cutting development costs. Upkeep of an application is even more expensive because it's a continuous and recurring cost. Companies that want to reduce Web costs need to keep Web sites simple in order to reduce upkeep costs.

As you can see from this list, the cost of working with scripts is high. Consequently, if you can create a Web site that works without using scripts, you'll also reduce or eliminate a number of other problems. In many cases, getting rid of the scripts means that your Web site will lack some of the glitter it once had, but you'll find that most users really didn't like the glitter to begin with. In fact, some Web sites that have reduced their glitter factor have actually found that more users are flocking to their door.

I'm not saying that all client-side scripts are bad and that you should never use scripts in your application. Some scripts have an obvious and useful purpose in life and you need to use them or find an alternative. For example, the client-side script that calculates the total cost of an order can reduce bandwidth requirements and improve application speed with little or no effect on accessibility. However, to meet the requirements of the law, you still have to provide a text-only version of the content. Here again is the quote from section 1194.22(l):

> *When pages utilize scripting languages to display content, or to create interface elements, the information provided by the script shall be identified with functional text that can be read by assistive technology.*

The law essentially says that you have to provide a text version of the information—the content—created by the script. This legal requirement makes server-side scripting a far more attractive alternative than client-side scripting. The assistive technology must be able to read the information and it can't do that if the script won't run due to a lack of functionality on the part of the client.

At this point, some of you are probably considering the merits of creating two versions of your Web site—one with and the other without scripting. We've discussed this issue in the past as part of another problem. See the "Separate Is Not Equal" section of Chapter 10. Creating two Web sites for any purpose usually creates more problems than the typical developer wants to work around. In sum, creating your Web site to display content without using client-side scripts is always the best path to take when you can do it.

Accessible Web Site Script Enhancements

Sometimes it's more efficient to create a Web site using a few client-side scripts than it is to rely exclusively on server-side scripts. It's important to remember that you can always use server-side scripts to manipulate information and Web technologies such as CSS to change the user display. You should also remember that most client-specific options require permission from the user to protect privacy and ensure that the user actually wants the service offered. Even so, a small number of tasks can still rely on client-side scripts because they perform the work more efficiently.

The following sections describe a few of the issues you need to consider when using client-side scripts. These enhancements help you comply with the requirements of the law and still use client-side scripting. Unfortunately, these solutions won't work in every case—at which time, you need to go back to the drawing board and come up with another solution for your Web application needs. Remember that the law requires that you provide scripts that present their information in a form that any accessible technology can use, which usually means text.

Implementing the No Script Support Option

The first addition you must make to any Web page that includes a client-side script is the <NOSCRIPT> tag. You saw a very simple example of the <NOSCRIPT> tag in the "Using CSS Example" section of Chapter 11. You'll find this example in the

\Chapter 11\CSS Example folder of the source code that you can obtain from the Downloads section of the Apress Web site (http://www.apress.com). The purpose of the <NOSCRIPT> tag is to provide output for users who don't have a browser that supports scripting or who have turned scripting off.

TIP   Many trade press magazines have noted that more users are turning scripting support off in their browsers as Web-based viruses become more prevalent. The problems with using scripts today are going to increase as more users follow this trend. At some point, you may find that you have only a few users who allow client-side scripts to run. In sum, it's better to use server-side scripts as part of any new designs you create.

If the client-side script on your Web site performs a simple task that you can easily explain in text, you can provide a description of the task within the <NOSCRIPT> tag. For example, if the client-side script creates a cookie on the user's system that holds user settings between sessions, you can explain this fact in the <NOSCRIPT> tag. The loss of the cookie won't affect the content presented by the Web site—it's a convenience for the user. Consequently, you can remain within the letter and the spirit of the law by explaining this functionality to the user and not storing their setup information in a cookie.

One innovative use of the <NOSCRIPT> tag that we'll explore in the "Creating Accessibility Friendly Scripts Example" section of the chapter involves adding a special link to the text within the <NOSCRIPT> tag. Selecting this link will post the page back to the server. The server can then perform any data calculations using a server-side script. This approach allows you to use a single page for everyone, ensures that you have met the legal requirements for accessibility, and ensures that users who do have scripting support in their browser receive the performance benefits of client-side scripting.

The <NOSCRIPT> tag can't fix many problems that many people have seen on Web sites. For example, it can't fix the malfunctioning banner ad that wants to store user information locally so that it can detect a hit rate for that user. In addition, the <NOSCRIPT> tag won't fix gadgets. Using the <NOSCRIPT> tag won't make animations and special sound effects work because there's no text equivalent for these features.

In general, if you can represent a non-scripting fix for a client-side scripting problem as a combination of standard HTML tags and text, then the <NOSCRIPT> tag will probably work. Nothing else will work. If you provide other forms of content on your Web site, then you'll probably need to use a server-side script to do it.

Include Both Mouse and Keyboard Support

Whenever you create a script that involves some type of selection, make sure you include versions for both the keyboard and the mouse. It's important to consider the requirements for both types of input—you can't assume the user will always access your Web page using a mouse or using a keyboard. You'll learn more about the implementation part of this issue in the "Creating a Mouseover Example" section of the chapter.

Use JavaScript If Possible

Most developers today do use JavaScript as their client-side scripting language because the language has become so deeply entrenched. However, a few developers still use VBScript (http://msdn.microsoft.com/library/en-us/script56/html/vtoriVBScript.asp) on their Web sites and some use derivatives such as JScript (http://msdn.microsoft.com/library/en-us/script56/html/js56jsoriJScript.asp).

 ON THE WEB Many developers are aware that JavaScript is actually ECMAScript now. The name change took place when the European Computer Manufacturers Association (ECMA) (http://www.ecma.ch/) formally accepted JavaScript for consideration as a standard. (ECMA itself received a name change in 1994 to European Association for Standardizing Information and Communication Systems.) However, the JavaScript name became so entrenched when the language first appeared that I chose to use that name throughout the book. You can obtain an overview of just what ECMAScript is at the IBM developer-Works site (http://www-106.ibm.com/developerworks/unicode/library/wa-emca.html?dwzone=unicode). Make sure you check the ECMAScript standard found at http://www.ecma.ch/ecma1/STAND/ECMA-262.HTM. You'll find a helpful (and fully compliant) ECMAScript interpreter named Free ECMAScript Interpreter (FESI) at http://home.worldcom.ch/~jmlugrin/fesi/.

The problem with using an alternative is that you limit the number of browsers that can interpret the script. For example, VBScript is essentially limited to Internet Explorer Version 4.*x* and above. However, you'll find that JScript is even more limited because it only works on older versions of Internet Explorer (VBScript appeared earlier and is therefore more compatible with earlier versions of Internet Explorer).

If you must use a language other than JavaScript for some reason, make sure you check compatibility. You can do this using a simple script called with the OnLoad()

event of the <BODY> tag. You'll find a simple version of a program that uses this technique in the \Chapter 13\BrowserCheck folder of the source code that you can obtain from the Downloads section of the Apress Web site (http://www.apress.com). Here's the essential code.

```
<script language="javascript">
   function CheckVersion()
   {
      // Obtain the name, version, and JavaScript enabled status
      // for the browser.
      Name.value = navigator.appName;
      Version.value = navigator.appVersion;
      Enabled.checked = navigator.javaEnabled();
   }
</script>
```

Figure 13-2 shows typical output from this example. Notice that the version information specifies that this browser is Internet Explorer version 4.0 compatible, but that it's actually Internet Explorer 6.0 running on a Windows NT 5.1 (Windows XP) machine. The code also shows a quick method for determining if the browser has Java enabled.

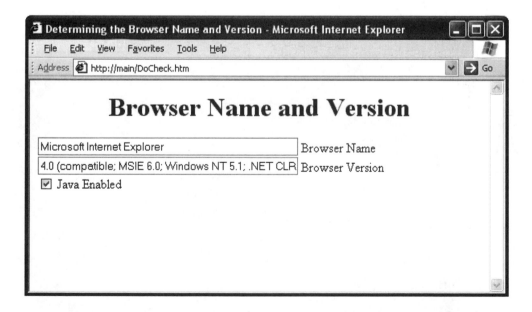

Figure 13-2. Determine the browser capabilities if you plan to use something other than JavaScript for your Web site.

If you run this example on a machine that has JavaScript disabled, the <NOSCRIPT> tag will take over and you'll see an alternate message. The point is that you'll have the information needed to determine the essentials. If the script doesn't work, then you know you need to use a non-script version of the page. Otherwise, the script will tell you if the client can run the code you plan to use for your Web site.

Creating Accessibility Friendly Scripts Example

The example in this section shows a unique use of the <NOSCRIPT> tag. Many developers wrongly assume that this tag is virtually useless. The fact is that this tag is extremely useful and can help you create flexible Web pages that everyone can use. The example in this section is simple from the perspective that it doesn't include error-trapping code. The example performs the simple task of adding two numbers together, but it does so in such a way that the users with scripting support use client-side scripting and those that don't use server-side scripting. Listing 13-1 shows the code for this example. You'll also find this listing in the \Chapter 13\ AccessFriendly folder of the source code that you can obtain from the Downloads section of the Apress Web site (http://www.apress.com).

Listing 13-1. Accessibility Friendly Scripting Code

```
<%@ Language = "JavaScript" %>
<% Response.Buffer = true %>

<!DOCTYPE HTML PUBLIC "-//W3C//DTD HTML 4.0 Transitional//EN">
<html>
   <head>
      <title>Accessible Friendly Script Demonstration</title>
      <script language=javascript>
         function DoAdd()
         {
            var Value1 = parseInt(TheForm.InValue1.value);
            var Value2 = parseInt(TheForm.InValue2.value);
            TheForm.Output.value = Value1 + Value2;
         }
      </script>
   </head>
   <body>
   <form method=get id=TheForm>
      <H1 align="center">Math Demonstration</H1>
      <DIV>
         <INPUT type=text
```

```
          id="InValue1"
          accesskey=1
          title="This is the first input value."
          <%if (Request.QueryString("Input1").Count > 0)
          {
             Response.Write("value=")
             Response.Write(Request.QueryString("Input1")(1))
          }
          else
             Response.Write("value=0")%>
          tabindex=1
          name=Input1>
   <LABEL> Input Value 1</LABEL>
</DIV>
<DIV>
   <INPUT type=text
          id="InValue2"
          accesskey=2
          title="This is the second input value."
          <%if (Request.QueryString("Input2").Count > 0)
          {
             Response.Write("value=")
             Response.Write(Request.QueryString("Input2")(1))
          }
          else
             Response.Write("value=0")%>
          tabindex=2
          name=Input2>
   <LABEL> Input Value 2</LABEL>
</DIV>
<DIV>
   <INPUT type=text
          id="Output"
          accesskey=0
          title="This is the output value."
          <%if ((Request.QueryString("Input1").Count > 0) &&
               (Request.QueryString("Input2").Count > 0))
          {
             var Value1 = parseInt(Request.QueryString("Input1")(1));
             var Value2 = parseInt(Request.QueryString("Input2")(1));
             var Sum = Value1 + Value2;
             Response.Write("value=")
             Response.Write(Sum)
          }
```

```
                  else
                      Response.Write("value=0")%>
                  tabindex=3
                  readonly >
        <LABEL> Output Value</LABEL>
      </DIV>
      <DIV>
        <BUTTON onclick=DoAdd()
                title="Click this button to add the numbers."
                tabindex=4
                id=AddNumbers
                accesskey=A>
           Add
        </BUTTON>
      </DIV>
      <DIV>
        <NOSCRIPT>
           <DIV>
                Your browser doesn't support scripts.
                Use this button instead.
           </DIV>
           <BUTTON type=submit
                   title="Click this button to add the numbers."
                   id=NoScriptAdd
                   accesskey=N
                   tabindex=5>
              No Script Add
           </BUTTON>
        </NOSCRIPT>
      </DIV>
   </form>
   </body>
</html>
```

This example is a simple ASP page. I decided not to delve into ASP.NET for this example. As you can see, the listing begins with the usual declaration of language for ASP. We'll use JavaScript in this case, but you could use VBScript for the server-side script if desired.

Near the top of the listing, you'll see a JavaScript function named DoAdd(). If a user has scripting enabled, clicking the Add pushbutton will call this function. Of course, this only works if the user has scripting enabled. This script is the client-side scripting portion of the Web page.

Each of the inputs includes a server-side script for the value attribute. This script checks for a request string for that input using the Request. QueryString("Input1").Count property. If the user has passed a value to the server, then the server restores that value in the returned page. Otherwise, the server sets the value attribute to 0 using the Response.Write("value=0") method.

The output textbox also has a script associated with it. If the user has passed a request string to the server, then the server uses the values to calculate a sum for the output textbox. Otherwise, the server sets the value attribute for the output textbox to 0 as well. This script is the server-side scripting portion of the Web page.

Notice that the Web page includes two buttons. The first appears as a standalone <BUTTON> tag. Notice that the onclick event is pointed to the DoAdd() method. The second <BUTTON> tag appears within a <NOSCRIPT> tag. This is a submit button and it only appears if the user doesn't have scripting enabled. Using this button, users can still interact with the page, but they have to wait the additional time to perform server-side processing. It's a small price to pay when you consider that the alternative is not being able to interact with the Web page at all. Figure 13-3 shows the output from this example.

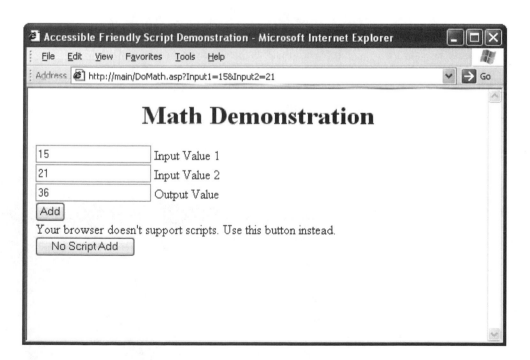

Figure 13-3. This figure shows what the page will look like if the client doesn't provide scripting support.

Creating a Mouseover Example

Developers use mouseover events for a number of purposes on Web pages. In many cases, a mouseover event serves to highlight the affected control or to perform some other display task. Unfortunately, the keyboard doesn't have the same effect on the display. The user moves from control-to-control, never seeing a change in selection. This example shows one technique for combining mouse and keyboard support in a single mouseover-event handler. Listing 13-2 shows the code we'll use for this example. You'll also find this listing in the \Chapter 13\MouseOver folder of the source code that you can obtain from the Downloads section of the Apress Web site (http://www.apress.com).

Listing 13-2. Combined Mouse and Keyboard Focus Handler

```
<!DOCTYPE HTML PUBLIC "-//W3C//DTD HTML 4.0 Transitional//EN">
<html>
   <head>
      <title>MouseOver Demonstration</title>
      <script language=javascript>
         function Emphasize(LabelName)
         {
            // Clear if LabelName doesn't contain anything.
            if (LabelName=="")
            {
               // Change the characteristics as needed.
               Label1.style.border = "";
               Label2.style.border = "";
               Input1.value = "";
               Input2.value = "";
               return;
            }

            // Determine if the first input is selected.
            if (LabelName=="Input1")
            {
               // Change the characteristics as needed.
               Label1.style.border = "black thin solid";
               Label2.style.border = "";
               Input1.value = "Input1 selected";
               Input2.value = "";
            }
```

```
            else
            {
                Label1.style.border = "";
                Label2.style.border = "black thin solid";
                Input1.value = "";
                Input2.value = "Input2 selected";
            }
        }
    </script>
</head>
<body>
    <H1 align="center">Control Selection Example</H1>
    <DIV>
        <INPUT id="Input1"
               type=text
                onmouseover="Emphasize('Input1')"
                onfocus="Emphasize('Input1')"
               title="This textbox doesn't do anything special.">
        <LABEL id="Label1" for="Input1">Input 1</LABEL>
    </DIV>
    <DIV>
        <INPUT id="Input2"
               type=text
                onmouseover="Emphasize('Input2')"
                onfocus="Emphasize('Input2')"
               title="This textbox doesn't do anything special.">
        <LABEL id="Label2" for="Input2">Input 2</LABEL>
    </DIV>
</body>
</html>
```

The scripting code for this example is relatively simple. The `Emphasize()` method receives one variable as input—the name of the currently selected control. If this variable is blank for some reason, the script will clear all of the data selections and return. A value of Label1 will display a border around the Label1 label and place "Input1 selected" into Input1. Likewise, the same changes will occur for Label2 if the user selects it. Figure 13-4 shows a typical selection in this example.

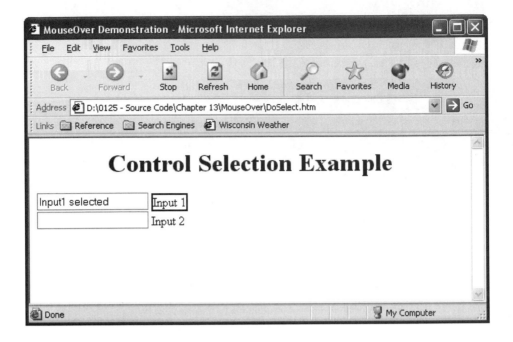

Figure 13-4. Use a combined mouse and keyboard handler to ensure that every user sees focus changes on your Web page.

The method for making this example work with both the mouse and the keyboard is relatively easy to understand. Most developers will add a mouseover event only to the onmouseover attribute. When the user places the mouse over the control, the mouseover event takes place. By also adding this event handler to the onfocus attribute, the user will see the same action occur when they use the keyboard to tab into the control.

Summary

The one piece of information you should take away from this chapter is that client-side scripts are never required. Yes, they can reduce bandwidth requirements and improve performances. Many users will have scripting enabled, so you can use this feature to help the user perform tasks quickly. However, the bottom line is that you need to provide a non-scripting version of your page if the scripts perform some useful task that the user can't simply ignore.

Now that you have a better idea of what the requirements are for an accessible script, you need to look at the scripts currently used for your Web application. Decide if you need these scripts to perform an essential function. If you do, create a non-scripting version of your Web page so that users who don't have scripting enabled can still use the page. You'll also want to check your page with a screen reader to ensure that it truly is accessible. Make sure you also test the page for usability. A page that's accessible, but not usable, isn't going to attract many visitors.

You're at the end of the book! It's my hope that you'll find that accessible development techniques are going to be as important a part of your toolbox as I have found that they are in my explorations. Of course, accessibility is a moving target, so you might come up with questions that I haven't answered. I'd like to hear your ideas about accessibility in general and your programming needs in specific. Be sure to contact me at `JMueller@mwt.net` with your latest accessibility request or idea.

The fun isn't over quite yet. You'll find three appendices at the end of this book. The first provides you with 52 additional ways to improve your accessible development experience. The second appendix provides you with a list of Web sites that you can use as examples for your own programming needs. The third appendix contains a list of helpful organizations that you can contact when you have specific accessibility development needs. These appendices will make your accessible development experience more enjoyable and rewarding. You'll also want to spend time looking through the glossary—it contains all of the unique terms in this book, along with definitions for every acronym.

Part Four
Glossary and Appendixes

Glossary

THIS BOOK INCLUDES a glossary so that you can find terms and acronyms easily. It has several important features of which you need to be aware. First, every acronym in the entire book (except product acronyms) is listed here—even if there's a better-than-even chance you already know what the acronym means. This way, you'll find everything you need to use the book properly.

Second, these definitions are specific to the book. In other words, when you look through this glossary, you're seeing the words defined in the context in which the book uses them. This might or might not always coincide with current industry usage, since the computer industry changes the meaning of words so often.

Finally, the definitions here use a conversational tone in most cases. This means they might sacrifice a bit of puritanical accuracy for the sake of better understanding. The purpose of this glossary is to define the terms in such a way that there's less room for misunderstanding the intent of the book as a whole.

While this glossary is a complete view of the words and acronyms in the book, you'll run into situations when you need to know more. No matter how closely I look at terms throughout the book, there's always a chance I'll miss the one acronym or term that you really need to know. In addition to the technical information found in the book, I've directed your attention to numerous online sources of information throughout the book, and few of the terms the Web site owners use will appear here unless I also chose to use them in the book. Fortunately, many sites on the Internet provide partial or complete glossaries to fill in the gaps:

Acronym Finder: http://www.acronymfinder.com/

Acronym Search: http://www.acronymsearch.com/

The Acronym Database: http://www.ucc.ie/acronyms/

Microsoft Encarta: http://encarta.msn.com/

Webopedia: http://Webopedia.internet.com/

yourDictionary.com (formerly A Web of Online Dictionaries):
http://www.yourdictionary.com/

Because this book addresses accessibility topics, you might also need to locate a Web site that specializes in defining accessibility terms. In some cases, these are the same terms that you've used for years for development computer applications, but they might be applied in a new way. In other cases, the terms are going to be new and unfamiliar. Like any other endeavor, accessible application development means learning some new terms. This list of Web sites provides terms in addition to those found in this book.

> **Cornell Tips for HR Professionals:** `http://www.ilr.cornell.edu/ped/hr_tips/glossary.cfm`
>
> **Curtain University of Technology:** `http://www.curtin.edu.au/corporate/accessibility/glossary.htm`
>
> **Family Center on Technology and Disability (FCTD):** `http://www.fctd.info/resources/glossary.cfm`
>
> **Maryland Cold Fusion Users Group:** `http://www.cfug-md.org/articles/508_glossary.cfm`
>
> **TechDis Accessibility Database:** `http://www.niad.sussex.ac.uk/glossary.cfm`

Let's talk about these Web sites a little more. Web sites normally provide acronyms or glossary entries—not both. An acronym site only tells you what the letters in the acronym stand for; it doesn't provide definitions to explain what the acronym means concerning everyday computer use. The two extremes in this list are Acronym Finder (acronyms only) and Webopedia (full-fledged glossary entries).

The owner of Acronym Finder doesn't update the site as often as some people might like, but it does have the advantage of providing an extremely large list of acronyms from which to choose. At the time of this writing, the Acronym Finder sported 164,000 acronyms.

Most of the Web sites that you'll find for computer terms are free. In some cases, such as Microsoft's Encarta, you have to pay for the support provided. However, these locations are still worth the effort because they ensure that you understand the terms used in the jargon-filled world of computing.

Webopedia has become one of my favorite places to visit because it provides encyclopedic coverage of many computer terms and includes links to other Web sites. I like the fact that if I don't find a word I need, I can submit it to the Webopedia staff for addition to their dictionary, making Webopedia a community-supported dictionary of the highest quality.

One of the interesting features of the yourDictionary.com Web site is that it provides access to more than one dictionary and in more than one language. If English isn't your native tongue, then this is the Web site of choice for you.

Word List

Term	Meaning
A	
Accessibility	A measure of a user's ability to interact with an application. For example, applications should provide both mouse and keyboard access to every control to ensure that the user can reach the control for use. An application should support all devices without providing specialized support for a particular device unless necessary. A Braille input device should receive no special treatment beyond that required for a keyboard.
Active Server Pages (ASP)	A special type of server-side scripting language environment used by Windows servers equipped with Internet Information Server (IIS). This specialized scripting language environment helps the developer create flexible Web applications that include server scripts written in a number of languages such as VBScript, JavaScript, JScript, and PerlScript. The use of variables and other features, such as access to server variables, helps the developer create scripts that can compensate for user and environmental needs as well as security concerns. ASP uses HTML to display content to the user. Recent extensions to ASP in the form of Active Server Pages eXtended (ASPX) provide a broader range of application support functionality, improved debugging, new features such as "code behind," and improved performance.
AI	*See* **Artificial Intelligence**
AOTA	American Occupational Therapy Association
API	*See* **Application Programming Interface**
Applet	A helper or utility application that normally performs a task within a specialized environment such as a browser or as part of an operating system. Java is one of the most commonly used languages for creating applets for browser applications. Another example is the Control Panel applications used to configure Windows. In both cases, the applications perform a limited task within a specialized environment.

Word List (Continued)

Term	Meaning
Application Programming Interface (API)	A method of defining a standard set of function calls and other interface elements. It usually defines the interface between a high-level language and the lower level elements used by a device driver or operating system. The ultimate goal is to provide some type of service to an application that requires access to the operating system or device feature set.
APTA	American Physical Therapy Association
Array	A structure that acts like an in-memory database. An array provides random or sequential access to each element by number (also called a subscript). Arrays normally contain a single dimension. In some cases, arrays provide multidimensional access to data. A multidimensional array has the same number of elements in each subarray in a given dimension. Jagged arrays treat each dimension as a separate subarray, which means that each subarray can contain a different number of elements.
Artificial Intelligence (AI)	A field of computer science focusing on making computers easier to use and making them able to solve useful problems through pseudointelligent behavior. A computer can't possess true creative intelligence, but this functionality is often simulated through the use of heuristics, neural networks, or rule-based systems.
ASHA	American Speech-Language-Hearing Association
ATA	Alliance for Technology Access
B	
BAPI	*See* **Biometrics Application Programming Interface**
Basic Input/Output System (BIOS)	A set of low-level computer interface functions stored in a chip on a computer's motherboard. The BIOS performs basic tasks like booting the computer during startup and performing the Power-On Startup Tests (POST). Disk Operating System (DOS) relies heavily on the BIOS to perform all types of low-level device interface tasks.

Word List (Continued)

Term	Meaning
Baudot	An archaic communication technology that predates many older computer technologies such as Extended Binary Coded Decimal Interchange Code (EBCDIC). The Baudot code relies on a five-bit system to send and receive letters, numbers, and special characters. The system was originally proposed by Emile Baudot in 1870. The system sees use currently in Telecommunication Device for the Deaf (TDD) and Handheld AMateur (HAM) radio sets.
Beta Test	The act or process of ensuring that an application works according to a predefined plan.
Bezel	When used in reference to a display, the outer covering that holds the Cathode Ray Tube (CRT) in place. The bezel is a physical portion of the overall display enclosure. It reduces the display area by some amount in order to hold the CRT in place.
Biometrics	A statistical method of scanning an individual's unique characteristics, normally body parts, to ensure that they are who they say they are. Some of the scanned elements include voiceprints, irises, fingerprints, hands, and facial features. The two most popular elements are irises and fingerprints because they're the two that most people are familiar with. The advantages of using biometrics are obvious—not only can't the user lose their identifying information (at least not very easily), but with proper scanning techniques, the identifying information can't be compromised either.
Biometrics Application Programming Interface (BAPI)	A special set of programming constructs that help developers embed biometric technology into applications. A consortium of vendors including IBM, Compaq, IO Software, Microsoft, Sony, Toshiba, and Novell originated BAPI.
BIOS	*See* **Basic Input/Output System**

Word List (Continued)

Term	Meaning
Bitmap	A file or object containing the binary representation of a graphic image in raster (on-screen display) format. Each pixel on the display image is represented as one entry in the file. The size of the entry depends on the number of colors the image supports. Common sizes include monochrome (1 bit), VGA (4 bits), SVGA (8 bits), and true color (24 bits). The file also contains other information such as the dimensions of the bitmap in pixels. The format information is usually stored in a header that's separate from the bitmap data.
Boolean	A method of determining whether a statement is true or false using rules of logic. Boolean values are often used to help a computer determine whether it needs to take a certain course of action based on current system or application conditions.
Browser	A special application, such as Internet Explorer, Opera, or Netscape, normally used to display data downloaded from the Internet. The most common form of Internet data is the HTML (HyperText Markup Language) page. However, modern browsers can also display various types of graphics and even standard desktop application files, such as Word for Windows documents, directly. The actual capabilities provided by a browser vary widely depending on the software vendor and platform.
BSL	British Sign Language
Bubble Help	A type of context sensitive help that appears on screen for a limited time when the user selects the associated user interface element. The help information appears in a small box not associated with the application window. In most cases, bubble help appears in a specially colored window so that the user can easily differentiate it from other window types. Many developers attach bubble help to a mouse event. When the user hovers the mouse over the selected user interface element, a text box appears for some time interval (usually a few seconds). Some texts call bubble help balloon help.

Word List (Continued)

Term	Meaning
C	
Cascading Style Sheets (CSS)	A method for defining a standard Web page template. This may include headings, standard icons, backgrounds, and other features that would tend to give each page at a particular Web site the same appearance. The reason for using CSS includes speed of creating a Web site (it takes less time if the developer doesn't have to create an overall design for each page) and consistency. Changing the overall appearance of a Web site also becomes as easy as changing the style sheet instead of each page alone. CSS is also a standards supported technology, so it represents an easy method for developers to create Web pages that will work in standards-compliant browsers.
Cathode Ray Tube (CRT)	A specialized tube used to display information. It appears as part of computer systems, televisions, and other devices that display information. The neck of the tube contains electronics that produce and direct an electron beam. This beam strikes phosphors on the front of the tube, causing them to glow. The beam moves from the left to the right of the tube to produce one raster line. When the line is finished, the beam moves down one line to produce the next raster line. The beam continues in this fashion until the entire display area is filled with raster lines of information. The beam then moves to the top left corner of the display and begins the process again. Displays are rated by the number of dots they can display on each raster line and the number of raster lines they can produce.
CITA	Center for Information Technology Accommodation
CLR	*See* **Common Language Runtime**
CNIB	Canadian Nation Institute for the Blind
COM	*See* **Component Object Model**

Word List (Continued)

Term	Meaning
Common Language Runtime (CLR)	The engine used to interpret managed applications within the .NET Framework. All Visual Studio .NET languages that produce managed applications can use the same runtime engine. The major advantages of this approach include extensibility (you can add other languages) and reduced code size (you don't need a separate runtime for each language).
Component Object Model (COM)	A Microsoft specification for a binary-based, object-oriented code and data encapsulation method and transference technique. It's the basis for technologies such as OLE (Object Linking and Embedding) and ActiveX (the replacement name for OLE Custom eXtension or OCX—an object-oriented code library technology). COM is limited to local connections. DCOM (Distributed Component Object Model) is the technology used to allow data transfers and the use of OCXs within the Internet environment. However, difficulties in making DCOM work over the Internet have made the text-based eXtensible Markup Language (XML) technologies such as the Simple Object Access Protocol (SOAP) popular.
Context Sensitive Help	A type of software assistance that depends on environment, selected object, or other condition to determine the precise information to provide. For example, context sensitive help for an application could depend upon the control the user has selected. The help system would provide information about that control, instead of the application as a whole. In most cases, context sensitive help uses the same help file as general help, but it takes the user directly to the most helpful help topic.
Cracker	A hacker (computer expert) who uses their skills for misdeeds on computer systems where they have little or no authorized access. A cracker normally possesses specialty software that allows easier access to the target network. In most cases, crackers require extensive amounts of time to break the security for a system before they can enter it. Some sources call a cracker a black hat hacker.
CRM	*See* **Customer Resource Management**
CRT	*See* **Cathode Ray Tube**

Word List (Continued)

Term	Meaning
CSS	*See* **Cascading Style Sheets**
Customer Resource Management (CRM)	A method of managing all client data, including sales and service. Depending on the company, a CRM system could track everything from buying habits to an individual customer's birthday. CRM affects all kinds of buyers including both individuals and companies.

D

Term	Meaning
DDE	*See* **Dynamic Data Exchange**
Deuteranopia	A color vision deficiency that affects about 1.1% of the male population. The eye cannot detect the color green due to a malfunction of the M cones within the eye. A less severe condition, deuteranomalia, affects another 4.9% of the male population. In this case, the M cones function, but not at the level needed to see green well. Because this deficiency falls between the wavelengths for red and blue, the eye can often partially fill in the missing spectrum using information from the L (red) and the S (blue) cones. The gap filling provided by the eye gives the deuteranopia and deuteranomalia sufferer a limited normal spectrum. However, the affected person will still confuse individual colors.
Digital Millennium Copyright Act (DMCA)	An extension of copyright law signed by President Clinton on October 28th, 1998. This law provides updates to the copyright laws to make them easier to enforce in electronic environments such as the Internet. In addition, the law also includes updates for electronic media such as electronic books and software.
Digital Video Disk (DVD)	A high capacity optical storage media with capacities of 4.7 GB to 17 GB and data transfer rates of 600 KBps to 1.3 GBps. A single DVD can hold the contents of an entire movie or approximate 7.4 CD-ROMs. DVDs come in several formats that allow read-only or read-write access. All DVD drives include a second laser assembly used to read existing CD-ROMs. Some magazines will also use the term digital versatile disk for this storage media.

Word List (Continued)

Term	Meaning
Disk Operating System (DOS)	The underlying software used by many PCs to provide basic system services and to allow the user to run application software. The operating system performs many low-level tasks through the Basic Input/Output System (BIOS). The revision number determines the specifics of the services that DOS offers; check your user manual for details.
DMCA	*See* **Digital Millennium Copyright Act**
DOS	*See* **Disk Operating System**
Dots per Inch (DPI)	A measure of the number of pixels contained within one linear inch of display area. This unit of measure reflects pixel density or resolution for both displayed and printed images of various sorts. The higher the DPI value, the higher the resolution or quality of the image.
DPI	*See* **Dots-Per-Inch**
DRMS	Detroit Resource Management System
DTMF	Dual-Tone Multiple Frequency
DVD	*See* **Digital Video Disk**
Dynamic Data Exchange (DDE)	1. The capability to place data from one application on the Windows clipboard and paste it from the clipboard into another application. A user can cut a graphics image created with a paint program, for example, and paste it into a word processing document. After it's pasted, the data doesn't reflect the changes made to it by the originating application. The source and target applications must provide DDE functionality for this technology to work. They must also support the data formats required for the information exchange. 2. A method of communicating with an application that supports DDE when the application allows requests for data or services. The communication parameters include the application, the topic of the conversation, and a DDE message. In most cases, the DDE message consists of a series of menu or macro sequences that perform the desired task.
E	
EBCDIC	Extended Binary Coded Decimal Interchange Code
ECMA	European Computer Manufacturer's Association

Word List (Continued)

Term	Meaning
Emulator	A specialized application that provides the same features and functionality as a target device. The device on which the emulator runs is normally more capable than the emulated device. For example, emulators commonly enable a developer to test applications designed for use on Personal Digital Assistants (PDAs) using the standard PC.
Event Handler	A special method or function that reacts to specific system or user events such as clicking a button on a form or the loosing focus for a textbox.
eXtensible Hypertext Markup Language (XHTML)	A cross between XML and HTML specifically designed for Internet devices such as Personal Digital Assistants (PDAs) and cellular telephones, but also usable with desktop machine browsers. This language organizes and defines HTML coding in such a way that misinterpretation is more difficult and errors are easier to find. Since this language relies on XML, most developers classify it as an XML application builder. The language relies on several standardized namespaces to provide common data type and interface definitions. XHTML creates modules that are interpreted based on a specific platform's requirements. This means that a single document can serve the needs of many display devices.
eXtensible Markup Language (XML)	1. A method used to store information in an organized manner. The storage technique relies on hierarchical organization and uses special statements called tags to separate each storage element. Each tag defines a data attribute and can contain properties that further define each data element. 2. A standardized Web page design language used to incorporate data structuring within standard HTML documents. For example, you could use XML to display database information using something other than forms or tables. It's actually a lightweight version of Standardized Generalized Markup Language (SGML) and is supported by the SGML community. XML also supports tag extensions that allow various parts of a Web-based application to exchange information. For example, once a user makes a choice within a catalog, that information could be added to an order entry form with a minimum of effort on the part of the developer. Since XML is easy to extend, some developers look at it as more of a base specification for other languages, rather than as a complete language.

Word List (Continued)

Term	Meaning
F	
FAQ	*See* **Frequently Asked Question**
FilterKeys	One of several special features Microsoft provides to help people with special needs use computers better. All newer versions of Windows (starting with Windows NT 4.0) support this feature as part of the Accessibility applet. This feature helps eliminate extra keystrokes so that the user doesn't get "tthis" instead of "this." It performs this task by setting a minimal time threshold that a key must be depressed before the computer accepts it as input.
Flash Rate	A characteristic that determines the time between the on and the off state of a flashing screen element. The flash rate determines the susceptibility of an individual to the effects of flashing screen elements—everything from headaches to seizures and death.
Frequently Asked Question (FAQ)	A document that contains answers to questions that many people ask. FAQs generally reduce support costs by providing answers to commonly asked questions in one place. Vendors use FAQs for many purposes including both hardware and software support.
G	
GAC	*See* **Global Assembly Cache**
GCN	Government Computer News
GIF	*See* **Graphics Interchange Format**

Word List (Continued)

Term	Meaning
Global Assembly Cache (GAC)	A central repository used by the .NET Framework for storing publicly managed components. The GAC contains only components with strong names, ensuring the integrity of the cache. In addition, the GAC can hold multiple versions of the same component, which ensures that applications can access the version of a component that they need, rather than the single version accessible to all applications.
Globally Unique Identifier (GUID)	A 128-bit number used to identify a Component Object Model (COM) object within the Windows registry. The GUID is used to find the object definition and allow applications to create instances of that object. GUIDs can include any kind of object, even non-visual elements. In addition, some types of complex objects are actually aggregates of simple objects. For example, an object that implements a property page will normally have a minimum of two GUIDs: one for the property page and another for the object itself.
Graphical User Interface (GUI)	1. A method used to display information that depends on both hardware capabilities and software instructions. A GUI uses the graphics capability of a display adapter to improve communication between the computer and its user. Using a GUI involves a large investment in both programming and hardware resources. 2. A system of icons and graphic images that replace the character-mode menu system used by many older machines including "green screen" terminals that are connected to mainframes and sometimes to cash registers. The GUI can ride on top of another operating system (such as DOS, Linux, and UNIX) or reside as part of the operating system itself (such as the Macintosh and Windows). Advantages of a GUI are ease-of-use and high-resolution graphics. Disadvantages include cost, higher workstation hardware requirements, and lower performance over a similar system using a character mode interface.

Word List (Continued)

Term	Meaning
Graphics Interchange Format (GIF)	One of two standard file formats used to transfer graphics over the Internet (JPEG is the other). There are several different standards for this file format, the latest of which is the GIF89a standard you'll find used on most Internet sites. CompuServe originally introduced the GIF standard as a method of reducing the time required to download a graphic and the impact of any single-bit errors that might occur. A secondary form of the GIF is the animated GIF; it allows the developer to store several images within one file. Between each image within the file are one or more control blocks that determine block boundaries, the display location of the next image in relation to the display area, and other display features. A browser or other specially designed application will display the graphic images one at a time in the order in which they appear within the file to create animation effects.
GUI	*See* **Graphical User Interface**
GUID	*See* **Globally Unique Identifier**
H	
Hacker	An individual who works with computers at a low level (hardware or software), especially in the area of security. A hacker normally possesses specialty software or other tools that allow easier access to the target hardware or software application or network. The media defines two types of hackers: those that break into systems for ethical purposes and those that do it to damage the system in some way. The proper term for the second group is crackers (*see* **cracker** for details). Some people have started to call the first group "ethical hackers" or "white hat hackers" to prevent confusion. Ethical hackers normally work for security firms that specialize in finding holes in a company's security. However, hackers work in a wide range of computer arenas. For example, a person who writes low-level code (like that found in a device driver) after reverse engineering an existing driver is technically a hacker. The main emphasis of a hacker is to work for the benefit of others in the computer industry.

Word List (Continued)

Term	Meaning
HID	*See* **Human Interface Device**
HTML	*See* **HyperText Markup Language**
Human Interface Device (HID)	A term that references the ergonomic functionality provided by a device or the ability of the device to create a human to computer interface. Generally, a HID provides additional input about the support it provides and could include special functionality. An application must provide special programming to make use of the HID features. General technologies such as DirectX normally treat all devices equally. For example, a mouse is always a mouse when used with DirectX, even if it does include HID features.
HyperText Markup Language (HTML)	1. A scripting and data presentation (markup) language for the Internet that depends on the use of tags (keywords within angle brackets <>) to display formatted information on screen in a non-platform-specific manner. The non-platform-specific nature of this scripting language makes it difficult to perform some basic tasks such as placement of a screen element at a specific location. However, the language does provide for the use of fonts, color, and various other enhancements on screen. There are also tags for displaying graphic images. Scripting tags for using scripting languages such as VBScript and JavaScript are available, although not all browsers support this addition. Another tag addition allows the use of ActiveX controls. 2. One method of displaying text, graphics, and sound on the Internet. HTML provides an ASCII-formatted page of information read by a special application called a browser. Depending on the browser's capabilities, some keywords are translated into graphics elements, sounds, or text with special characteristics, such as color, font, or other attributes. Most browsers discard any keywords they don't understand, allowing browsers of various capabilities to explore the same page without problem. Obviously, there's a loss of capability if a browser doesn't support a specific keyword.
I	
IDE	*See* **Integrated Development Environment**
IIS	*See* **Internet Information Server**

Word List (Continued)

Term	Meaning
Integrated Development Environment (IDE)	A programming language front end that provides all the tools you need to write an application through a single editor. The IDE normally includes support for development language help, access to any tools required to support the language, a compiler, and a debugger. Some IDEs include support for advanced features such as automatic completion of language statements and balloon help showing the syntax for functions and other language elements. Many IDEs also use color or highlighting to emphasize specific language elements or constructs. Older DOS programming language products provided several utilities— one for each of the main programming tasks. Most (if not all) Windows programming languages provide some kind of IDE support.
Internet Information Server (IIS)	Microsoft's full-fledged Web server that normally runs under the Windows Server operating system. IIS includes all the features that you'd normally expect with a Web server: FTP and HTTP along with both mail and news services. Older versions of IIS also support the Gopher protocol; newer versions don't provide this support because most Web sites no longer need it.
IRS	Internal Revenue Service
ITTATC	Information Technology Technical Assistance and Training Center
J	
JCP	Java Community Process
JDK	Java Development Kit
JFC	Java Foundation Classes
Joint Photographic Experts Group File Format (JPEG)	One of two standard graphics file formats used on the Internet (GIF is the other). This is a vector file format normally used to render high-resolution images or pictures. (The current version of the file standard supports 16.7 million colors.) The file extension also appears as .JPG.
JPEG	*See* **Joint Photographic Experts Group File Format**
JSAPI	Java Speech Application Programming Interface

Word List (Continued)

Term	Meaning
M	
Marshal	The act of making data created by one object accessible and acceptable to another object. The process of marshaling usually includes moving the data from one memory space to another memory space. The marshaling process could also include some type of data conversion. The type of data conversion depends upon the requirements of both objects and the data types that they support.
Mathematical Markup Language (MathML)	An XML-based technique for describing math notation. This includes both the structure and the content of the notation. It allows standardized processing of complex equations over the Internet.
MathML	*See* **Mathematical Markup Language**
MDI	*See* **Multiple Document Interface**
Microsoft Active Accessibility (MSAA)	A Software Development Kit (SDK) and a set of utilities a developer can use to manage the accessible features of an application. MSAA relies on COM libraries to perform its work. The utilities include Accessible Explorer, Active Accessibility Event Tester, and Active Accessibility Object Inspector.
Microsoft Management Console (MMC)	A special application that acts as an object container for Windows management objects like Component Services and Computer Management. The management objects are actually special components that provide interfaces that allow the user to access them within MMC to maintain and control the operation of Windows. A developer can create special versions of these objects for application management or other tasks. Using a single application like MMC helps maintain the same user interface across all management applications.
Microsoft Mobile Internet Toolkit (MMIT)	A free add-on toolkit for the .NET development environment that enables a programmer to create applications for alternative computing devices such as cellular telephones and Personal Digital Assistants (PDAs). The tools include special applications, coding examples, projects, and other programming language embellishments. This toolkit addresses the needs of Internet application development for the most part.

Word List (Continued)

Term	Meaning
Microsoft Speech Application Programming Interface (SAPI)	A specialized programming interface based on Speech Application Language Tags (SALT). This API helps the developer create speech-enabled applications for Microsoft Windows.
MMC	*See* **Microsoft Management Console**
MMIT	*See* **Microsoft Mobile Internet Toolkit**
MouseKeys	One of several special features Microsoft provides to help people with special needs use computers better. All newer versions of Windows (starting with Windows NT 4.0) support this feature as part of the Accessibility applet. This feature enables the user to use the arrow keys on the numeric keypad as a mouse. Instead of moving the cursor with the mouse, the user can move it with the arrow keys. This doesn't disable the mouse; it merely augments it.
MSAA	*See* **Microsoft Active Accessibility**
Multiple Document Interface (MDI)	A method for displaying more than one document at a time within a parent window. The interface enables the user to load more than one document at a time within a single application. In most cases, the user can display a single document using the full editing area or display multiple documents using sections of the editing area. Many word processors and spreadsheets use the MDI to help the user create complex document associations and to enable editing between documents.
N	
National Institute of Standards and Technology (NIST)	A government agency that helps businesses develop and apply technology, measurements, and standards. In some cases, NIST also performs independent research and shares the finding with business.
NCAM	National Center for Accessible Media
NINDS	National Institute of Neurological Disorders and Stroke
NIST	*See* **National Institute of Standards and Technology**

Word List (Continued)

Term	Meaning
O	
Object Linking and Embedding (OLE)	The process of packaging a file name or data, server name (generally an application), and any required parameters into an object, and then placing this object into the file created by another application. For example, a user could place a graphic object within a word processing document or spreadsheet. OLE supports both linking (placing a pointer to the source data in permanent storage in the target file) and embedding (placing the actual data into the target file). When you look at the object it appears as if you simply pasted the data from the originating application into the current application, which is similar to Dynamic Data Exchange (DDE). However, the data object created by OLE automatically changes as you change the data in the original object (provided you use the linking portion of the technology). It also contains the intelligence to know which application created the data. Generally, you can start the originating application and automatically load the required data by double clicking on the object.
OLE	*See* **Object Linking and Embedding**
OT	Occupational Therapist
P	
PARC	Palo Alto Research Center
PDA	*See* **Personal Digital Assistant**
PDF	*See* **Portable Document Format**
PERL	*See* **Practical Extraction and Report Language**
Personal Digital Assistant (PDA)	A small handheld device such as a Palm or Pocket PC. These devices are normally used for personal tasks such as taking notes and maintaining an itinerary during business trips. Some PDAs rely on special operating systems and lack any standard application support. However, newer PDAs include some level of standard application support, because vendors are supplying specialized compilers for them. In addition, you'll find common applications included, such as browsers and application office suites that include word processing and spreadsheet support.

Word List (Continued)

Term	Meaning
Plug-In	A descriptive term for special helper applications, such as a sound processing system, normally downloaded as a separate item for container applications, such as browsers. The container application provides an environment in which the plug-in can operate and calls upon the plug-in to perform specialized tasks that the developer of the container application chose not to include.
Portable Document Format (PDF)	A document format originally created by Adobe. This document format initially captured the output of desktop publishing applications. Many other applications, especially graphics applications, now output to the PDF format. Users can view PDF files using the free Acrobat Reader utility.
Practical Extraction and Report Language (PERL)	Originally designed as a report generation language for the Internet, PERL has found other uses as well for more general Internet programming needs. PERL is normally an interpreted scripting language.
Protanopia	A color vision deficiency that affects about 1% of the male population. The eye cannot detect the color red due to a malfunction of the L cones within the eye. A less severe condition, protanomalia, affects another 1% of the male population. In this case, the L cones function, but not at the level needed to see red well.
Q	
QA	Quality Assurance
S	
SALT	*See* **Speech Application Language Tags**
SAMI	*See* **Synchronized Accessible Media Interchange**
SAPI	*See* **Microsoft Speech Application Programming Interface**
SBA	Small Business Administration

Word List (Continued)

Term	Meaning
Schema	A formal method used to describe the structure of a database, storage technology, or data transfer technique such as XML. The schema defines the requirements for constructing the object in question. For example, a schema for a relational database would include information on the structure of tables, fields, and relations within the database.
Screen Reader	A special application designed to read the text from the computer screen. Anyone who needs to know what information the screen contains without actually viewing the text can use a screen reader to listen to the information. Screen readers vary greatly in capability and use. Some screen readers only read information displayed by local applications, while others can read information from any application.
Script	Usually associated with an interpreted macro language used to create simple applications, productivity enhancers, or automated data manipulators. Most operating systems support at least one scripting language. You'll also find scripting capability in many higher-end applications such as Web browsers and word processors. Scripts are normally used to write small utility-type applications rather than large scale applications that require the use of a compiled language. In addition, many script languages are limited in their access of the full set of operating system features.
SDK	*See* **Software Development Kit**
SGML	*See* **Standard Generalized Markup Language**
ShowSounds	One of several special features Microsoft provides to help people with special needs use computers better. All newer versions of Windows (starting with Windows NT 4.0) support this feature as part of the Accessibility applet. This feature tells Windows and your applications to display captions for the sounds they make, which includes speech. Instead of actually making the sound, the system requests that the application provide a description of the sound in a balloon help dialog.

Word List (Continued)

Term	Meaning
Simple Object Access Protocol (SOAP)	A Microsoft-sponsored protocol that provides the means for exchanging data between the Component Object Model (COM) and foreign component technologies like Common Object Request Broker Architecture (CORBA) using the eXtensible Markup Language (XML) as an intermediary. SOAP is often used as the basis for Web services communication. However, a developer could also use SOAP on a Local Area Network (LAN) or in any other environment where machine-to-machine communication is required and the two target machines provide the required infrastructure.
SMEX	Simple Messaging EXtension
SMIL	*See* **Synchronized Multimedia Integration Language**
SOAP	*See* **Simple Object Access Protocol**
Software Development Kit (SDK)	A special add-on to an operating system or an application that describes how to access its internal features. For example, an SDK for Windows would show how to create a File Open dialog box. Programmers use an SDK to learn how to access special Windows components such as the Component Object Model (COM) or the Media Player.
SoundSentry	One of several special features Microsoft provides to help people with special needs use computers better. All newer versions of Windows (starting with Windows NT 4.0) support this feature as part of the Accessibility applet. This option tells Windows to display a visual warning when a system sound occurs. The user can choose to flash the active caption bar, flash the active window, or flash the desktop.
Speech Application Language Tags (SALT)	An XML-based standard used to define techniques used to process and transfer speech using computer systems. One of the biggest issues that SALT is trying to solve is this issue of platform dependence; the specification relies on standardized markup languages as a basis for communicating sound information from one machine to another. Another reason for creating SALT is to ensure that there's an open standard that developers can use on a range of devices, including cellular telephones and Personal Digital Assistants (PDAs).
Speech Recognition (SR)	The process of interpreting spoken input and translating it into text. The text is then used as data or as commands.

Word List (Continued)

Term	Meaning
SR	*See* Speech Recognition
Standard Generalized Markup Language (SGML)	A specification for defining document format originally created for the publishing industry. Most developers consider SGML too complex for standard display purposes. However, both XML and HTML are based on SGML.
StickyKeys	One of several special features Microsoft provides to help people with special needs use computers better. All newer versions of Windows (starting with Windows NT 4.0) support this feature as part of the Accessibility applet. This option forces the Shift, Ctrl, and Alt keys to act as toggle switches. Press one of these keys once and it becomes active; press it a second time and it's turned off. The user can also press the keys sequentially to activate them or press a non-control key to execute the entire key press (such as Ctrl+Alt+A). Afterward, the control keys automatically become inactive.
Synchronized Accessible Media Interchange (SAMI)	A Microsoft technology that improves delivery of closed captioning with multimedia applications by time-synchronizing the captioning file with the media file. This technique makes it easier to edit or change either file than it is in other applications where the application encodes the accessibility information within the media file. SAMI can provide closed captioning in more than one language and with different presentation possibilities. For example, the user can choose the appearance of the captions by selecting the color, font, and size of the text. SAMI files use the extension .SMI or .SAMI. The file format specification is free (no licensing fee). SAMI instructions look similar to HTML or XML.
Synchronized Multimedia Integration Language (SMIL)	A standard developed by the World Wide Web Consortium (W3C) that divides multimedia content into separate files and associated data streams. For example, the video and audio appear in separate files; each audio channel appears as a separate stream within the data file. Using SMIL makes it possible to create captioning files for each language that may need to access the multimedia content. In addition, using separate files often reduces the size of the multimedia download, making it possible to stream complex data even over low-speed connections.

T

Word List (Continued)

Term	Meaning
Tactile Vocoder	A special device that translates sound energy into vibrations that a user can feel. The vendor normally places the apparatus within a belt or other easily wearable garment. The user employs their sense of touch to feel sound emanating around them. In many cases, the user can learn to hear using their sense of touch as an alternative to their sense of hearing.
TAS	Total Access System
TDD	*See* **Telecommunication Device for the Deaf**
Telecommunication Device for the Deaf (TDD)	A specialty device that enables someone to communicate over an audio system (such as a telephone) using non-spoken text. This device normally relies on Baudot code for communication purposes. Many of these devices use newer output techniques such as a Light Emitting Diode (LED) display. Most of these devices rely on a keyboard for input.
Teletypewriter (TTY)	This acronym can also mean teletype or teleprinter. Traditionally, these devices commonly accept information in the form of electrical impulses and output the information as printed or Braille text. The user inputs information using a keyboard. However, modern technology has rendered these traditional meanings obsolete. In general, TTY refers to some type of telephone or other audio communication for those with special hearing needs. See Telecommunication Device for the Deaf (TDD) for comparison purposes.
Text-Based Interface	A user interface that relies on text or text-based graphic characters for display purposes. Most early operating systems relied on a text-based interface because these interfaces use system resources more efficiently than Graphical User Interfaces (GUIs) do. Early GUIs were so poorly implemented, that many users with special needs relied on text-based interfaces to ensure that they would be able to access operating system features.
Text-To-Speech (TTS)	The process of interpreting text data and creating audio output in the form of speech.

Word List (Continued)

Term	Meaning
ToggleKeys	One of several special features Microsoft provides to help people with special needs use computers better. All newer versions of Windows (starting with Windows NT 4.0) support this feature as part of the Accessibility applet. This feature emits a tone every time the user turns the Caps Lock, Scroll Lock, or Num Lock key on or off.
Tritanopia	A color vision deficiency that affects about 0.001% of the male population. The eye cannot detect the color blue due to a malfunction of the S cones within the eye. A less severe condition, tritanomalia, is rarely recorded. In this case, the S cones function, but not at the level needed to see blue well.
TTS	*See* **Text-To-Speech**
TTY	*See* **Teletypewriter**
U	
UI	*See* **User Interface**
Undue Burden	The concept used to determine if an application requires immediate support for a particular accessibility feature. If the accessibility requirement places a severe financial or implementation burden on the individual or company developing the application, the U.S. government will often provide temporary relief from the requirement. However, the developer must show that the application will eventually meet all accessibility requirements.
Uniform Resource Locator (URL)	A text representation of a specific location on the Internet. URLs normally include the protocol (http:// for example), the target location (World Wide Web or www), the domain or server name (mycompany), and a domain type (com for commercial). It can also include a hierarchical location within that Web site. The URL usually specifies a particular file on the Web server, although there are some situations when a Web server will use a default filename. For example, asking the browser to find http://www.mycompany.com, would probably display the DEFAULT.HTM or INDEX.HTM file at that location. The actual default filename depends on the Web server used. In some cases, the default filename is configurable and could be any of a number of files. For example, Internet Information Server (IIS) offers this feature, so the developer can use anything from an HTM, to an ASP, to an XML file as the default.

Word List (Continued)

Term	Meaning
Universal Design	A concept in which every piece of hardware works with every piece of software. In addition, all hardware elements work with each other, as do all of the software elements. The design of the hardware and software is such that no compatibility or usability issues exist. In this environment, it doesn't matter if the actual design of the piece of hardware differs from the standard anticipated by an application, the application will still work with the hardware because the hardware presents the correct interface to the application. In reality, this concept is difficult to implement because vendors try to differentiate their product by adding non-standard features and components.
Universal Serial Bus (USB)	A form of serial bus that allows multiple external devices to share a single port. This technique reduces the number of interrupts and port addresses required to service the needs of devices such as mice and modems.
URL	*See* **Uniform Resource Locator**
Usability	A measure of the user's ability to understand an application's operation, purpose, and contents. Many factors affect usability. For example, the flow of the controls often determines the user's ability to define the use of the control based on the content of the previous controls. The type and length of labels attached to the controls also makes a difference in the usability of the application. The combination of labels and bubble (balloon) help can help the user understand the purpose of the control. Finally, an example entry can help the user understand the desired control content.
Usage Cues	The set of visual, aural, and subliminal communication that helps a user understand the functionality, use, and purpose of application elements. Visual communication can include underlined letters and balloon help. Aural communication can include tones played to signify events such as unsuccessful data entry. Subliminal communication includes the flow of information as the user moves from one screen element to the next.

Word List (Continued)

Term	Meaning
USB	*See* **Universal Serial Bus**
User Interface (UI)	The portion of an application that contains user accessible controls and data manipulation elements. The user interface for a Windows application is commonly comprised of buttons, text boxes, static text, graphics, and other design elements.
User Interface Elements	The controls, text, and other objects used to create the user interface. Some developers would also include the colors and other aesthetic properties of the interface as user interface elements.
V	
Voice eXtensible Markup Language (VoiceXML)	A speech Application Programming Interface (API) based on the eXtensible Markup Language (XML). The main vendors supporting this standard are AT&T, IBM, Lucent Technologies, and Motorola. VoiceXML relies on a series of elements (specially formatted tags) to perform speech input, output, configuration, and control.
VoiceXML	*See* **Voice eXtensible Markup Language**
VPAT	Voluntary Product Accessibility Template
W	
W3C	*See* **World Wide Web Consortium**
WAI	*See* **Web Accessibility Initiative**
WCAG	Web Content Accessibility Guidelines

Word List (Continued)

Term	Meaning
Web Accessibility Initiative (WAI)	An initiative launched by the World Wide Web Consortium (W3C) in 1997 to ensure that everyone has fair and equal access to the Internet, even those with special needs. WAI defines standards that affect the usability of a Web site. The areas of consideration include visual, hearing, physical, and neurological issues. For example, WAI considers the needs of users who might need to use large text to view a Web site or a screen reader to hear the content found on a Web site. Developers will also find that WAI provides for captioning, use of special input devices, and other interface needs. It also considers the effects of strobes and the complexity of the presentation. Some developers are under the misconception that WAI is only for those with special needs. However, WAI helps everyone. For example, even if you have great hearing, you might need captioning to enjoy a presentation in a crowded office where sound would disturb those around you.
WebAIM	Web Accessibility in Mind
Wireless Markup Language (WML)	An XML-based language used to communicate with Wireless Access Protocol (WAP) devices such as cellular telephones or personal digital assistants (PDAs). Most cellular telephones provide support for WML. The pages are served in a manner similar to that used by the Handheld Device Markup Language (HDML).
WML	*See* **Wireless Markup Language**
World Wide Web Consortium (W3C)	A standards organization essentially devoted to Internet security issues, but also involved in other issues such as the special `<OBJECT>` tag required by Microsoft to implement ActiveX technology. The W3C also defines a wealth of other HTML and XML standards. The W3C first appeared on the scene in December 1994, when it endorsed SSL (Secure Sockets Layer). In February 1995, it also endorsed application-level security for the Internet. Its current project is the Digital Signatures Initiative, which W3C presented it in May 1996 in Paris.
X	
XHTML	*See* **eXtensible Hypertext Markup Language**
XML	*See* eXtensible Markup Language

52 Tips for Creating Accessible Applications

EVERYONE LOVES TIPS because they contain essential nuggets of information that make work faster or easier. In some cases, a tip simply provides variable information. This appendix contains 52 tips that you can use to make your accessible application development experience better. In fact, there's one tip to begin each week for a year.

Of course, you aren't the only one who likes tips—I like them too. If you have a tip that you'd like to share with me, contact me at JMueller@mwt.net. Tips that make life a lot easier could appear on my Web site. Let me know if I can give you credit for your contribution when you submit the tip.

1. Always approach the issue of accessibility from the viewpoint of "universal design." The application you create should work equally well with any hardware the user might have attached to the machine.

2. Avoid using scripts whenever possible. Some of the people visiting your Web site won't have scripts enabled, so using a no-script solution is always better than assuming the client will provide support that they don't have.

3. Never confuse performance and speed. The best way to view performance is as a measure of how the application helps someone perform a task, with an emphasis on performing the task well. Performance is a combination of consistency, reliability, accessibility, and usability—speed should rarely enter into the equation.

4. Test your applications as if you had the special need that the application supports. This could mean working blindfolded for a while or using earplugs to ensure that you can't hear the application. It's also important to employ people with special needs as part of your test team.

5. Make sure that accessibility is part of your initial application design. It's easier to design accessible operation into an application than it is to add it later.

6. Use automated testing techniques whenever possible to ensure consistent testing results. However, it's important to remember that automated testing has limitations. You must also test your application using manual testing techniques to ensure accessibility conformance.

7. Remember the needs of the color-blind user when you create your application. In general, make sure to select high contrast color settings. It also helps to test your application using any of the test applications mentioned in this book.

8. Use the Active Accessibility Event Tester utility provided with Microsoft Active Accessibility (MSAA) to monitor the accessibility events generated by your application. Monitoring these events can help you better understand how the system is using the accessibility features of your application.

9. Use the Accessibility Options applet in the Windows Control Panel to adjust specific Windows Accessibility features such as StickyKeys and MouseKeys. Try these features alone and in combination to see how they interact. You may even find some of these features indispensable for your development work.

10. Think about the hardware and the software as a unit. The hardware provides the physical user interface that the software relies upon. When specifying a system, make sure you include hardware and software that are compatible with each other.

11. Consider configuration issues as part of an application design. You want to be sure that your application design is flexible enough to accommodate user needs such as a large text display. Flexibility is your best insurance against application design change requirements of any type—including accessibility needs.

12. Make sure you always define the four essential accessibility properties when working with .NET applications: `AccessibleDescription`, `AccessibleName`, `AccessibleRole`, and `AccessibleDefaultActionDescription`.

13. When creating standard Windows applications, make sure you implement the IAccessible interface so that the operating system can determine the accessibility status.

14. Web applications require that you provide an entry for the `title` attribute to ensure that the user can get complete information for screen elements.

15. Use Windows Accessibility feature status information to help your application provide better support for specific accessibility features. For example, you can use this technique to discover when the user has set the system to use a high contrast display and move application controls as needed for better visibility.

16. Never use tables in Web pages to organize information on screen. The only appropriate use for tables is to convey tabular data to the user.

17. Always add an <ALT> tag to images on your Web site. The <ALT> tag provides essential information that describes simple images to user with special visual needs.

18. Always add usage cues to your desktop applications. In most cases, this means controlling the flow of the application. However, you'll also want to add underlines to speed keys and provide balloon help for each control. Make sure context sensitive helps works as anticipated and the user has contact information.

19. Assume from the outset that you'll run into some changes you can't make to the design of an application due to a lack of information, vendor support, or changing technology. Always be willing to listen to client requests for updates later—make these changes as your level of experience increases and technology catches up with user needs.

20. Always add accessibility support to your application during the design phase, rather than waiting to bolt it on as an afterthought.

21. Using Cascading Style Sheets (CSS) enables you to define formatting for a Web site that a user can easily override with formatting information designed to meet their needs. The rule for an accessible CSS-formatted page is that the page should still make sense even if the CSS file is not available.

22. When creating speech features for a Web application, make sure you use a standardized implementation. One of the most promising standards is the Speech Application Language Tags (SALT). A number of vendors have already implemented this standard as part of their speech solution.

23. No matter what type of accessible development you do, the Windows Accessibility settings and tools can help you get a better feel for the way others will see your application. Make sure you use these tools to gauge the reaction that users with special needs will have when they use your application.

24. When performing an application update, categorize the changes you need to make to ensure accessibility. Perform high priority changes first, and then move on to lower priority items. Using technique ensures that the changes you make will affect the largest number of users possible from the outset.

25. Use JavaScript (ECMAScript) to create your scripts. Most browsers that do provide script support also provide support for the JavaScript language. Avoid using browser-specific extensions to ensure that your script will run on as many browsers as possible.

26. The ultimate error that any developer of accessible applications can commit is to modify the user's environment. Changing the user's environment can cause some accessibility features to stop working and can reduce user access to the system. Even if you have the user's permission to make changes, make those changes with extreme care.

27. Always check the correctness of the HTML on a Web page before you use an accessibility checker to test it. Incorrect HTML will present a number of problems to the accessibility checker and could prevent you from getting accurate results.

28. Whenever you create a selection script for a Web page, such as a mouseover event, make sure the script also works with the keyboard. The user should see the same results using either the keyboard or the mouse. In general, if you add a function call to the onmouseover event, you should also add it to the onfocus event.

29. Never use color alone to indicate content on the Web page. Using color to indicate content can create problems for a number of users with special visual needs. Color means nothing to someone who can't see or has color blindness.

30. Consider adding design support for all Section 508 requirements to your application, even if you won't implement all elements during the first release.

31. Track the user statistics for your application. For example, look at the number of complaints about application content. You can also track how often people actually use an application feature by discretely recording its use in a log. It's also important to create a suggestion box–type application where users can input suggestions anonymously.

32. Always consider file format as one of the essential design features of your application. Custom file formats can store information in a manner that works best with your application, but it isn't very portable and will suffer if you change the format later. When using a standard file format, make sure you can store accessibility information.

33. Ensure that the controls you create include full accessibility support and provide full configuration flexibility. In some cases, this means you'll need to add context menus to the control to ensure that the user can access the configuration features.

34. Always tune your microphone before you test a speech application. If the volume is set too high, the distortion will cause the speech application to fail. Likewise, setting the volume too low can cause the speech application to fail when the computer doesn't receive the full sound.

35. In addition to the <ALT> tag, always add a <LONGDESC> tag to complex images. The <ALT> tag doesn't provide enough information to the user with special visual needs. The <LONGDESC> tag points to a Web page containing additional information that can describe complex elements such as charts, graphs, maps, or even certain types of pictures.

36. Consider the effects of download time on users who have dial-up connections. In general, you should use a 28.8 Kbps connection as the threshold for your application.

37. Always add usage cues to your Web applications. In all cases, you'll want to define the flow of control between screen elements. Always add comprehensive balloon help. While it isn't as easy to add context sensitive help to a Web form, make sure you include a help page and provide good contact information.

38. The Windows Accessibility feature that many developers find hardest to implement is the ShowSounds feature. The reason for this problem is that few Windows applications actually support it, so there are few examples of how the feature should work. Always detect this setting and provide sound descriptions for the user within your application in place of actual sounds when the user selects this setting.

39. One of the most dangerous application additions you can ever make is using flashing displays. A flashing display can cause any number of user problems, including death. At the very least, flashing displays are extremely annoying and cause headaches for most users.

40. Use the accessibility features provided with products such as Windows to perform testing on your application. These features can help you find obvious accessibility implementation errors and reduce the time required to modify the application during beta testing.

41. Although the law allows use of separate text pages for Web sites to accommodate those with special needs, remember that separate is not equal. The use of separate pages usually means that the user with special needs will receive old data and inadequate functionality.

42. Create an update checklist for your accessible application. Make sure you've met all of the requirements for either a desktop or a Web application.

43. Use the Accessible Explorer utility provided with Microsoft Active Accessibility (MSAA) to check your application for accessibility flaws. This tool runs tests on desktop applications to ensure that the interfaces such as IAccessible are fully implemented.

44. Some developers assume the user knows as much about an application as they do. However, this isn't always the case. Assume the user doesn't know about the feature and tell them about it during a training session—body language will often tell you all you need to know about the user's level of knowledge.

45. When you design a user interface, it's important to consider whether the user interface is reliable, consistent, friendly, accessible, and usable. If the user can't understand the interface, then it doesn't matter how well your application performs—the user will never use all of the features you have provided. Communication is the essential element to ensuring that the user interface works as anticipated.

46. Always provide complete help with your application. The help should address the application, the accessibility needs of the user, and the support needs of the caregiver. Never assume anything about the knowledge level of the user.

47. One of the best examples of an easily maintained Web site is the mobile application. In general, a Web application that runs well on a mobile device will present enough flexibility to work well with most assistive technology. However, you still need to test the application to ensure that it meets or exceeds accessibility requirements.

48. No matter which platform you work with, always exercise care when using special functionality such as speech input or output. The use of this technology can greatly extend the platforms on which your applications will run, but the strategy can backfire if you don't implement accessibility features properly.

49. Create your balloon help in advance—during the design phase of an application. In general, this technique ensures that everyone who needs to add balloon help to an application will do so consistently. In addition, defining the balloon help in advance helps ensure that everyone knows about the need to add it to the application.

50. Remember to use the AccessibleObject class in the .NET Framework when you need specialized access to the accessibility features of any object.

51. Use the On Screen Keyboard as a means for testing your application for control placement flexibility. If you can place the On Screen Keyboard in various positions and still use the application, it probably provides enough flexibility to someone with special needs.

52. Working code doesn't necessarily denote a working application. A working application has working code, but it's also accessible and usable; in addition, it performs well and provides an acceptable level of processing speed.

Six Best Web Sites for Accessibility Ideas

SOMETIMES, THE BEST WAY to learn how to perform a task is to look for good examples. This appendix contains some of the best examples of Web site accessibility that you'll find on the Internet today. Although some of these sites still have a few warts, the developer performed more tasks correctly than incorrectly. Use these sites when you need ideas and to determine how to implement some of the ideas presented in the book.

It's interesting to note that I had originally planned to make this appendix larger because I thought that the accessibility sites would be accessible. However, even the U.S. government's Section 508 Web site fails the simple Bobby test as of this writing. I hope that they'll see fit to fix the accessibility problems with their site, considering many people will view them as the authoritative source of information. As mentioned many times in the book, the automated tests are only a starting point. If a site fails the automated tests, they've already failed the manual tests that you should use for your Web site.

 NOTE   Like most Web sites, the Web sites in this appendix will change. The information I've provided is accurate as of the time of writing, but it may change by the time you read this book.

Ability

http://www.ability.org.uk/design.html

The Ability Web site does a lot of things right. For example, you'll find they use <ALT> tags for every image and don't use tables to organize the presentation. This site passed the Bobby test with only a few manual checks needed. You'll find this site best for learning how to work with graphics and links. Figure B-1 shows an example of this Web page.

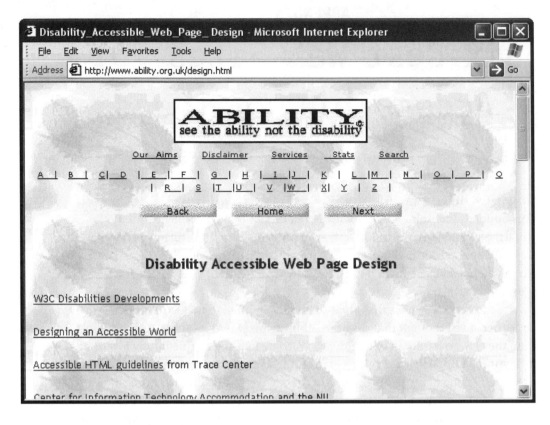

Figure B-1. Use the Ability Web site to learn more about using links and graphics.

You'll find a few problems when working with the Ability Web site. The developer generated the code in some way (likely using a code generator), so it lacks spaces, indentation, and even carriage returns in some cases. The Web site also contains a number of scripts, none of which have <NOSCRIPT> tag alternatives.

Electronic and Information Technology Accessibility Standards

http://www.access-board.gov/sec508/508standards.htm

This is an interesting Web site because it's mainly text. The site manages to avoid some of the most grievous presentation errors, such as using tables to format the page. It also avoids many of the problems other Web sites have with text—you can change the size of the text without any problem. Figure B-2 shows an example of this Web page.

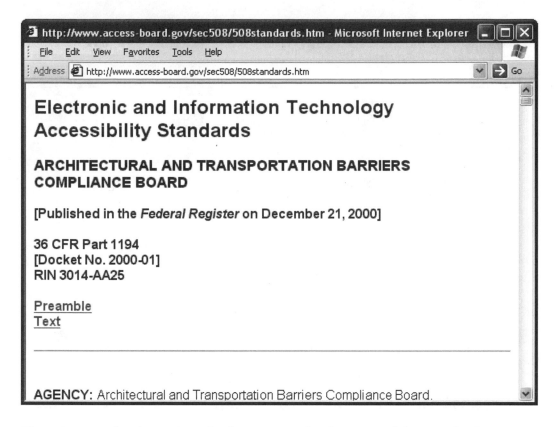

Figure B-2. Use the Electronic and Information Technology Accessibility Standards Web site to learn simple text formatting.

Although this site passes Bobby and it does perform well, the developer could have used CSS to avoid using a few older tags that appear with some consistency. The site avoids defining specific font sizes, but it does embed the font name within the content, which means that users who require large text displays could experience problems. The use of fonts alone could make the site inaccessible to some people. A lack of structure could also cause problems. In sum, this site shows simple text formatting, but you should use CSS for anything more complicated.

World Wide Web Consortium (W3C)

http://www.w3.org/

This site acts as the general guide for your application development. The code for the Web page is a tad hard to read in places, but even Bobby likes this Web site. The W3C site has only a few minor user checks to consider and none of them seems relevant. If you want to see how to make a page work, this is the place to go.

Figure B-3. Consider the W3C site the must-visit place for your Web examples.

The W3C site can help you learn some interesting layout techniques. In fact, if you want to learn how to get around using tables on your site, this code will show you how to do it. You'll also see good use of most tags. It would have been nice to see a few of the more interesting tags in use, but at least this site is a good accessibility citizen.

Epilepsy Action

http://www.epilepsy.org.uk/

It's difficult to find a site that has a properly implemented image map. This Web site provides you with an example that you can use. You'll immediately notice that all of the site features work without scripting and that every option provides the required balloon help. The appearance of balloon help on a page with so many pictures means that the developer used all of the required <ALT> tags. (The site does contain one script, but the purpose of the script is to change the font used for Internet Explorer—an issue that doesn't affect the overall usability of the site.) In addition, the site presents a colorful and cheerful appearance as shown in Figure B-4.

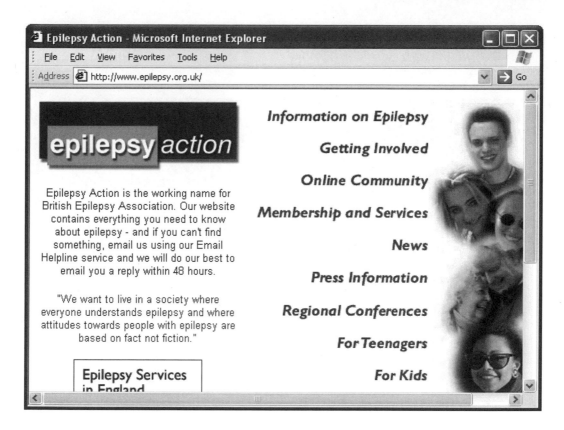

Figure B-4. Use this Web site as an example of how to work with image maps.

You'll notice that this site does use tables to organize the presentation of the data, so you shouldn't use it as an example of how to layout a page. In addition, the site would have benefited from the use of CSS. These points aside, the Epilepsy Action site is a good example in many other ways.

IBMLink

http://www.ibmlink.ibm.com/

More than a few Web sites implement the <NOSCRIPT> tag. However, the IBMLink site was the only one I found in my searches that implements the <NOSCRIPT> tag on a page that can pass even marginal scrutiny in other areas. This site even includes the required <ALT> tag for the single image. However, given the dearth of data on this page (shown in Figure B-5), this example won't show much more than one technique for using the <NOSCRIPT> tag.

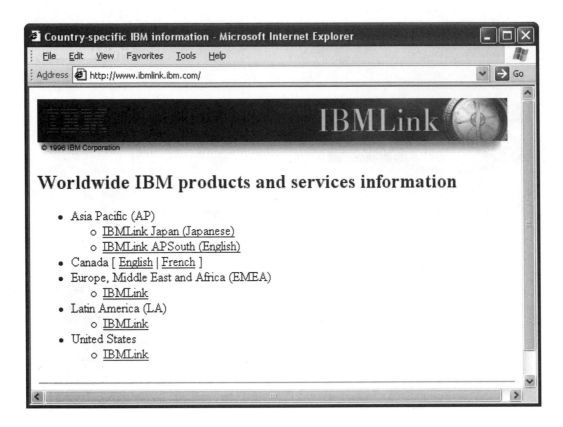

Figure B-5. Check the IBMLink site if you want to see a real world example of the <NOSCRIPT> *tag.*

One of the things you'll notice as you go through the source code for this site is the use of a table for the links. As usual, you'll want to avoid this practice. Use tables only to organize tabular content. If you do use a table, make sure you include all of the required accessibility features with it.

WebAIM

http://www.webaim.org/

Like many of the sites featured in this appendix, the WebAIM site demonstrates some important principles. The most important principle in this case is the use of the <NOSCRIPT> tag. The scripts used on this page present supplementary information, but nothing so important that the lack of script functionality will damage the content. You'll also find that this site organizes a lot of information well, as shown in Figure B-6. It passes the Bobby test, which is unusual for a site of this complexity. The site also includes a special link for reporting accessibility errors.

Figure B-6. The WebAIM site shows good organizational features and use of the <NOSCRIPT> *tag.*

The WebAIM site does follow most of the rules. The most significant problem is the use of tables to organize some, but not all of the data. Some of the art would be easier to see if the site provided an enlarged version. The complex art should have used the <LONGDESC> tag as well.

Helpful Organizations and Agencies

MANY DEVELOPERS CONSIDER the task of creating an accessible Web site difficult, in part, because they lack good information on the topic. Not only that, but they lack the perspective required to create a truly accessible Web site. Even if you understand the basic concept of accessibility, it's often difficult to get the job done due to a lack of resources. That's why it's important to know where you can find help quickly when a deadline looms and you still don't have the required level of support built into your application.

This appendix won't solve every possible problem for you. However, it does contain a list of organizations and agencies that can help. Some of these entries are culled from the book; others didn't fit within the confines of the book for whatever reason, so I've listed them here. Each entry includes the name of the organization or agency, a Web site where you can find addition information, and a short description of how the organization or agency can help.

As complete as this list is, I've probably missed an organization or agency that you know about. New organizations and agencies are created each day to help those with special needs. If the organization or agency that you know about provides a free service that will help application developers, feel free to contact me at JMueller@mwt.net and tell me about it. I'll post updates of this list in my Web site so that everyone can benefit.

 ON THE WEB   You'll also want to review online searchable databases for accessibility information. For example, the Web Accessibility In Mind (WebAIM) site at http://webaim.org/weblinks/ provides a searchable database of accessibility resources. The Section 508 Web site at http://www.section508.gov/ also provides the means to search for both accessible products and resources.

ABELDATA (http://www.abledata.com/Site_2/Default.htm): This organization provides a list of about 18,000 products from approximately 2,000 companies. The resource center will help you locate helpful organizations that can meet specific development requirements for your organization. A reading room area provides lists of books, magazines, pamphlets, and other resources you can use to learn more about assistive technologies. Finally, this organization, like many others, provides a huge list of links you can use to find additional information. Fortunately, this set of links is exceptionally well organized, making information easy to find.

Ability (http://www.ability.org.uk/design.html): This is an interesting Web site because it contains links to a wealth of information you can use to make your application more accessible. In addition, it contains information you'll need when working with other countries. Learning all you can about the requirements other countries have can save a great deal of time if you plan to market an application worldwide.

Ability Hub (http://www.abilityhub.com/): This Web site will help you better understand what equipment is available to meet specific special needs. You could use the content of this Web site to obtain information for a client or to determine what types of equipment your application may have to interact with. Most importantly, this site is about solutions—it discusses issues that users commonly encounter and ways to overcome those issues.

The Access Board (http://www.access-board.gov/): This agency will help you keep up-to-date on the latest government initiatives and requirements. The associated Web site also provides a course you can take to gain a better understanding of accessibility requirements. You can also learn about government-mandated physical accessibility requirements from this Web site.

Alliance for Technology Access (ATA) (http://www.ataccess.org/): This group has a number of goals. However, one of the most important goals is helping both children and adults with special needs obtain the services and training they require. This group sponsors (or at least advertises) a number of conferences each year. You'll find a number of online help resources they produce. Finally, this group can help you locate testers for your application so that you can ensure that it works as intended.

American Council for the Blind (ACB) (http://www.acb.org/): This organization provides a wealth of information about special visual needs. You'll find a list of useful resources, as well as helpful information about issues that affect the blind. In some cases, you'll also find helpful news items that discuss new legislation, helpful technologies, and advances in science.

American Foundation for the Blind (AFB) (http://www.afb.org/): This organization offers news, general information, and a directory of services for a variety of users. For example, you can find out more about the computer training and consulting services offered in this area. The organization also offers access to a community message board. The message board is a good place to ask for help with projects and to learn more about the special needs of this group.

American Occupational Therapy Association (AOTA) (http://www.aota.org/): This Web site can provide exceptional help with current trends in assisting those with special needs. For example, you can learn about the current rules in Medicare and Occupational Safety & Health Administration (OSHA). The site also features a Buyer's Guide that contains a wealth of information about a number of accessibility needs.

American Physical Therapy Association (APTA) (http://www.apta.org/): This Web site can really help the developer learn more about the caregiver perspective of accessibility. You also find a list of helpful publications, products and services, and government agencies. The site also includes a Research link that often provides interesting information about current technology trends.

American Speech-Language-Hearing Association (ASHA) (http://www.asha.org/). This Web site is a gold mine if you want to begin working with speech technology. It provides help with a number of issues that many developers don't understand. For example, you can learn about many types of speech disorders and learn how these issues could affect your application. You'll also find this site helpful in learning the human end of speech technology—a useful subject to know if you want to build the ultimate in speech input for your application.

Americans with Disabilities Act (ADA) (http://www.usdoj.gov/crt/ada/adahom1.htm): This Web page is actually part of the Department of Justice. It provides you with information about all of the current programs that the government sponsors to promote accessibility in all its forms. The links on this page can also point you to other government agencies that you'll want to know about in your quest to meet Section 508 requirements in applications and computer setups.

Assistive Technology Industry Association (ATIA) (http://www.atia.org/): This organization is dedicated to bringing key members of the Information Technology (IT) and Assistive Technology (AT) industries together. It also provides a voice for assistive technology in government. One of the main goals of this organization is to provide training in the form of an annual conference. Visit their Web site for additional information. You'll also find that their site has a comprehensive compatibility guidelines document that is worth reading if great accessibility is your goal.

The Biometric Consortium (http://www.biometrics.org/): This organization can help you create complex security solutions. Accessible applications can't rely on a single body part for identification purposes. As new techniques and standards become available, it may be possible to use a single biometric solution that meets security requirements but is also accessibility friendly.

The Bridge School (http://www.bridgeschool.org/main.html): This Web site is important because it discusses current strategies for using Assistive Technology (AT), and Augmentative and Alternative means of Communication (AAC) applications. Especially helpful are the resources that the site provides because some of them aren't readily available from other resources mentioned in this appendix.

Census Bureau (http://www.census.gov/): This agency can help provide statistical information that will influence development and implementation plans for your application. For example, you could learn how many people in your area have special visual needs versus those with special hearing needs. This information can help you plan a development strategy for meeting the needs of the maximum number of people in the shortest time.

Center for Applied Special Technology (CAST) (http://www.cast.org/): This organization can help developers understand the design techniques that will make their applications truly accessible. The associated Web site even includes a special area for universal design and learning—essentials for creating accessible designs that don't require constant updates and support.

Disability Info (http://www.disabilityinfo.gov/): This Web site contains links to news and government agencies that can help with accessibility needs. It's more of a clearinghouse for information, than an information source in its own right. Even so, you'll want to check this Web site for links and helpful information now found on other government Web sites.

General Services Administration (GSA) (http://www.gsa.gov/Portal/home.jsp?cid=1): This organization helps vendors become involved with selling products to the U.S. government. If you want to know something about U.S. government sales, then this is the organization with which to speak. For example, this is the group that runs the Center for Information Technology Accommodation (CITA) Web site discussed in Chapter 3 as a source of potential Section 508 information.

National Association of the Deaf (NAD) (http://www.nad.org/): This organization provides a centralized resource of information, links, and resources for those who have special hearing needs. The NAD Store contains a catalog of specialty devices that you'll want to know about. You could also use the Members section to ask questions about this special need or to obtain help in testing your application.

National Council on Disability (NCD) (http://www.ncd.gov/): This agency can help you understand how the government is meeting goals for accessibility compliance. For example, you can learn about current compliance levels and how future proposed legislation would ensure that agencies, individuals, and corporations meet accessibility requirements. This agency also reports to the president and congress on the various accessibility compliance issues. The most important asset for the developer is the number of pamphlets and white papers that this agency produces.

National Federation of the Blind (NFD) (http://www.nfb.org/): This organization provides a wealth of information that you'll want to know about when you write applications that help those with special visual needs. In addition, the associated Web site provides information about the latest devices that service the needs of the blind user as well as the latest technology in this area. This particular organization also sponsors a Web testing program where you can submit your application for testing.

National Institute on Disability and Rehabilitation Research (NIDRR) (http://www.ed.gov/offices/OSERS/NIDRR/): You'll find a number of government sources on this Web site, including a full list of government publications. This site also includes accessibility statistics you can use to plan your application. There's a fairly complete contact list of government personnel you can use when you need to ask questions, and there is also a section for obtaining assistance in the form of grants. The NIDRR is also the agency responsible for promoting and maintaining the ABLEDATA database of products.

National Institute of Environmental Help Services (NIEHS) (http://www.niehs.nih.gov/): This agency can help you understand the environmental factors that contribute to various health problems. For example, this is the place to go to find out more about the causes of carpal tunnel syndrome. Developers can often improve the users' health by creating applications that are not only accessible, but are also usable and that monitor for specific conditions. For example, a word processing application that includes a typing time monitor (to ensure that the user doesn't type too long at one time) would be very helpful, but no one has produced such a product yet.

National Institute of Neurological Disorders and Stroke (NINDS) (http://www.ninds.nih.gov/): This organization can help you learn about most health issues that users of your application will face. You can learn about everything from the requirements of someone with back pain to the issues surrounding carpal tunnel syndrome. In fact, you can find a list of many common disorders at http://www.ninds.nih.gov/health_and_medical/disorders/. Not every special need has something to do with the five senses—sometimes you need to provide special access to those with other needs, too.

National Institute for Standards and Technology (NIST) (http://www.itl.nist.gov/): This agency always has interesting projects going on, many of which seek to help those with special needs. In many cases, you can learn about the latest technologies, some of which aren't even on the market yet. Knowing this information can help your organization prepare for future needs and requirements.

National Organization on Disability (NOD) (http://www.nod.org/): This organization provides links for a number of areas not covered by other organizations in this appendix. For example, you'll find a link on how religious organizations are helping those with special needs. You'll also find a number of popular news stores (like those found in the local newspapers) as well as links to current trends in technology. The associated Web site also includes links for general information on various special needs.

National Science Foundation (NSF) (http://www.nsf.gov/): This organization can keep you apprised of current government research projects, including those that could enhance the computing environment for those with special needs. Not only do many of the articles on this Web site make for good reading in their own right, but they can also help you plan for the future of your organization and its development needs.

Self Help for Hard of Hearing People (SHHH) (http://www.shhh.org/): This organization provides helpful information for those with special hearing needs. It includes some general news links, sources of additional information, and even a few surveys. The site also includes links for a bookstore and other resources. The Members Only section can provide useful contacts for the developer who wants help in testing an application to meet special hearing needs.

Web Accessibility in Mind (WebAIM) (http://www.webaim.org/): This organization's site contains so much information that you could probably spend days here and not exhaust all of the resource potential. The simulations (both screen reader and low vision) are exceptionally useful. The captioning tutorial is helpful if you plan to include multimedia content on your Web site. The site also contains links to a number of videos and books that help the developer understand accessibility issues.

World Wide Web Consortium (W3C) (http://www.w3.org/): This organization is the source of many specifications we have discussed in the book (too numerous to mention in this appendix). The associated Web site also provides access to a number of useful resources (see http://www.w3.org/WAI/References/). In sum, if you want to learn the correct way to create a Web application, this is the place to start.

Index

Symbols

& (ampersand), for speed keys, 48
? (help button), displaying on application title
    bar, 257

A

<A> (anchor) tag, accessKey attribute, 383
abbr attribute, 386
<ABBR> tag, 385
abbreviations, 385
abilities, range of, 8
Ability Hub, 81, 508
Ability Web site, 4, 499–500, 508
ABLEDATA, 88, 89, 149, 508
ACB (American Council for the Blind), 508
accelerators. *See* shortcut keys
Access Board, 37, 508
AccessFuncs library, 214–217
    use of, 217–223
accessibility, 465
    as design issue, 115–117
    error levels when testing, 313
    for everyone, 5–7
    getting good input, 159–160
    information lacking in file formats, 163
    properties in .NET programming
        environment, 168
    tips for application creation, 491–497
    vs. usability, 42
Accessibility Forum, 87
accessibility guidelines, side effects, 45
Accessibility Options dialog box, 120, 201–209, 492
    Display tab, 124, 125, 207–208
        cursor settings, 208
    in high contrast mode, 50–52
    Keyboard tab, 52, 121, 203
        FilterKeys, 204–205
        StickyKeys, 202–204
        ToggleKeys, 205
    Mouse tab, 208–209
    Sound tab, 205–206
        ShowSounds, 206–207
        SoundSentry, 205–206
Accessibility Systems Inc., 94
Accessibility Wizard, 199–200
Accessibility.DLL, viewing in Object Browser, 188
accessible application, 283
Accessible class, 216
Accessible Explorer, 262–264, 496
accessible technology, 354
AccessibleDefaultActionDescription property
    (.NET), 168, 270

AccessibleDescription property (.NET), 168,
    171, 269
AccessibleName property (.NET), 168, 270
Accessible.net, 92
AccessibleObject class, 186, 188–192, 497
AccessibleRole property (.NET), 168, 270
Accessify.com web site, 311
accesskey attribute, 386
    for <A> (anchor) tag, 383
    for form field, 334
    for <INPUT> tag, 345, 386
AccRepair (HiSoftware), 314
AccVerify (HiSoftware), 92, 314
<ACRONYM> tag, 385
acronyms, 463
Actions menu (MASS)
    >> Map Text, 424
    >> Move Plus, 426–427
    >> Show All Animations, 424
    >> Speak Wave, 427
activated accessibility features, application
    disruption of, 17
Active Accessibility Event Tester, 265–266, 492
Active Accessibility Object Inspector, 267–268
Active Server Pages (ASP), 465
ADA (Americans with Disabilities Act), 509
Add New File dialog box (Web Matrix), 367
Add Reference dialog box
    .NET tab, 97
    COM tab, 98, 260–261
        to access Microsoft Agent, 288
<ADDRESS> tag, 385
Adobe eBook file format, 161
advocacy groups, for special needs, 129
AFB (American Foundation for the Blind), 509
AI (artificial intelligence), 466
AliceTalker, 411
All Device mode in Web Matrix, 368, 370
Alliance for Technology Access (ATA), 114, 508
AllocHGlobal() method, of Marshal class, 222
alphaWorks site, 410
Alt attribute, 6, 386, 388–392
    accessibility testing and, 327
    for images, 347–348, 493
    Section 508 Standard on, 22
Alt key, as toggle switch, 202
alt.comp.accessibility newsgroup, 90
alternative input devices, 80–82
amber, 65
American Council for the Blind (ACB), 508
American Foundation for the Blind (AFB), 509
American Occupational Therapy Association
    (AOTA), 129, 509
American Physical Therapy Association (APTA),
    129, 466, 509